Karl Marx

Karl Marx

The Divine Tragedy

Robert Orlando

"History repeats itself, first as tragedy, then as farce."

—Karl Marx[1]

TAN Books

Gastonia, North Carolina

Cover image is courtesy of Nexus Media, as is the artwork.

Library of Congress Control Number: 2025947551

ISBN: 978-1-5051-3514-5
Kindle ISBN: 978-1-5051-3769-9
ePUB ISBN: 978-1-5051-3768-2

Published in the United States by
TAN Books
PO Box 269
Gastonia, NC 28053
www.TANBooks.com

Printed in the United States of America

For my mother, Rosalie Orlando, December 13, 1937—January 20, 2025, who taught me how to rise through tragedy.

To Alasdair MacIntyre, January 12, 1929—May 21, 2025, who reminded us that ideologies—whether Marxism, capitalism, or liberalism—cannot be renewed without a return to the stories that once gave us moral clarity.

Contents

Preface

This book began with a fiery riot, an audiobook, and a dream that was transformed into a vision and later distilled into a straightforward question that sparked my desire to delve into the legacy of Karl Marx: Would Dante place Marx in hell? As obscure as that question might seem, it captured the seminal ideas of what I wanted to explore. Dante's Divine Comedy, according to Thomas Carlyle, "a mystic unfathomable song,"[2] provides a moral map of the soul's journey after death and assigns each figure to their proper place based on their destiny and a review of their sins,[3] virtues, and efforts to repent. As I discovered, Marx wrote of Dante: "There is no such thing as a pure bourgeois morality. A proletarian morality must be developed, and we will not be able to develop a moral theory without being prepared to use a mixture of Dantean despair and divine comedy."[4] In this work, the great poet guides us through hell, purgatory, and paradise to encounter figures whose actions and beliefs shaped their destinies. Carlyle saw this geography being experienced like compartments of a great edifice; a great supernatural world-cathedral, piled up there, stern, solemn, awful; Dante's World of Souls! It is, at bottom, the sincerest of all poems; sincerity, here too, we find to be the measure of worth. It came deep out of the author's heart of hearts, and it goes deep, and through long generations, into ours.[5]

And so will Marx—having left behind a legacy that inspired some of the bloodiest revolutions and most murderous regimes the world has ever seen. Should we, as the audience watching his journey, find him guilty? As I pondered this, I realized that this question held the key to unlocking Marx's true impact on the world. What began as a one-year project evolved into five years of research, reflection, and inquiry. The deeper I delved into Marx's writings and legacy, the more I saw parallels between his moral vision and the one Dante offers as mirrored journeys—that is, the former was the inverse of the latter, and vice versa. Just as Dante structured his journey through the realms of heaven, purgatory, and hell, Marx's life can be viewed through these stages. In the early years, Marx's idealism reflects a kind of paradise, a hopeful vision of the world where great change seems possible. The middle years, marked by hardship, exile, and disillusionment, parallel Dante's purgatory, a phase of struggle and penance: his "exile was what liberated him to become the poet, not merely of Florence, not merely of Tuscany, but of Italy as a whole."[6] Marx's final years resemble a descent into hell, marked by isolation, bitterness, and a sense of betrayal by the very movement he once inspired. Each phase reflects not only personal growth or decline but also the manifestation of Marx's ideological evolution as he moves from hope to despair, from faith in humanity's potential to disillusionment.

This realization was further driven home during the summer of 2020, a year that saw not only the COVID-19 pandemic but a series of US race riots that caused billions of dollars in property damage.[7] These were not the class-based revolts that Marx had envisioned but something more chaotic—upper-middle-class riots fueled by a housing crisis, stagnant wages, overseas wars, and a deeper undercurrent of rage, envy, and nihilism. The burning of Minneapolis, the destruction of a police station, and widespread lawlessness were not just about racial inequality but a more primal disorder. The fires of 2020 were decades in the making, much of it kindled by post-Marxist academic thought. Yet, instead of Marx's original focus on class struggle, the movement shifted to identity politics, driven less by justice or reform than by revisionism and revenge. Watching these events, I wondered: What was this firestorm truly about? It was neither a traditional class struggle nor a call, like Martin Luther King's, for America to live up to its ideals. Instead, it seemed to be fueled by resentment—forces that once consumed Marx himself. Despite America's progress in race relations and civil rights, the specter of Karl Marx still lingers more than 150 years later, haunting these demonstrations through new media with a distorted, misguided spirit, even as they confront real or imagined inequities.[8]

Jacques Derrida's 1993 Spectres of Marx speaks of Marx as a ghost haunting the corridors of modern history.[9] Marx's ideas were first presented in popular form in the Manifesto of the Communist Party (more commonly known as the Communist Manifesto), a pamphlet written with Frederick Engels and published in 1848. It begins with the bold statement: "A spectre is haunting Europe—the spectre of communism."[10] This was more an expression of hope than a description of the actual situation as it then was. It was written for the Communist League, a tiny revolutionary group that had just been formed in the ferment leading up to the revolutions of 1848 in Europe.[11] Marx's ideas had transcended their original context, morphing and adapting to new cultures and a new era. What had begun as Marx's materialist critique of capitalism became something far more lethal. No longer confined to economic doctrine, it became a spirit capable of transcultural leaps, infecting new generations.

At its core, Marxism sees the world as a network of power struggles and frames any inequality as the few oppressing the many. That lens is both simple and dangerous. It explains inequality too neatly, unlike the worldviews of the classical thinkers, who acknowledged power dynamics without reducing the struggle between groups to such a narrow and cynical belief. In this book, I explore how Marxism critiques narrow views[12] while increasingly becoming one itself and how its core idealism led so easily to terror. As with Dante's work, that haunting quality, the "spectre," is why Marx's work keeps resurfacing in our "civil discourse of the polis"[13] and in the eternal question of what constitutes a good city,[14] as "the most philosophical of art forms"[15] and "a balance between mystery and meaning"[16]—not as a fixed doctrine but as a state of mind or possession that keeps resurfacing.

As I explored this possession, the question that had initially sparked my journey returned: Would Dante place Marx in hell? After witnessing the destruction and chaos sparked by Marx's ideas and after seeing the millions of lives lost under regimes inspired by his teachings, the answer seemed clear. Marx rejected the transcendent, forging a path that, despite its utopian promise, led only to chaos and despair. Yet ironically, his vision retained the very structure of what he opposed: a grand narrative predicting the inevitable course of history, one that could not be altered by human will. This secular eschatology—framed as scientific determinism—mirrored the religious anticipation of redemption found in Christian tradition. Postmodern thinkers, wary of such universalist claims, would later recoil from Marxism's totalizing ambitions, rejecting its faith in historical necessity even as they adopted its suspicion of tradition and power.[17]

Like the figures in Dante's *Inferno*, he dismissed divine order in favor of an earthly vision shaped by hidden desires and undisclosed motives. He saw in Dante's work the struggle of the individual against the system, echoing the class struggle that he had worked on so much.[18] His vision of revolution, meant to liberate humanity, instead eerily mirrors the infernal descent that Dante describes. Marx saw himself as a modern Prometheus, unbound by faith and tradition, crafting a secular hell devoid of transcendence, human aspiration, or grace. While Dante acknowledged human flaws and offered an allegorical path to redemption, Marx externalized all blame, reducing the individual to a function of the collective. Whereas Dante's journey moves toward light and transformation, Marx's vision remains trapped in the shadows—not in endless darkness, but in anticipation of a utopia that would emerge only through perpetual struggle and historical upheaval. His eschatology replaced divine grace with material redemption, but the cost was unrelenting conflict and a future always deferred. Dante spirals into hell to confront the consequences of this willful blindness: "Consider well the seed that gave you birth: you were not made to live your lives as brutes, but to be followers of worth and knowledge,"[19] and in *Karl Marx: The Divine Tragedy*, we too will descend into the depths of Marx's life, philosophy, and legacy to confront the spirit of destruction that has caused so much suffering in the modern world. So, would Dante place Marx in hell? After five years of research and reflection, my answer lies in the pages below. Marx's spirit, as with the spirits of the damned in Dante's *Inferno*, is one of blind idealism and rebellion, though it stands in contradiction to his lifelong desire for wealth and status.

This book is not just about Marx's ideas; it is also about the spiritual forces that drove them. As his friend and mentor Moses Hess (1812–1875) would caution him: while his passion for revolution is inspiring, he should not lose sight of the spiritual elements that drive humanity.[20] Just as Dante's *Divine Comedy* explores the consequences of sin and redemption, this book will examine the consequences of Marx's writings and actions and the world he left behind. This is not just a book about the past but a subtle infusion of the spirit of caution needed for we pilgrims to chart a new course toward redemption and to avoid a life defined by tragedy.[21]

Introduction: The Tragic Descent

"Dante's Hell is an apt metaphor for the worker's alienation under capitalism."[22]

—Karl Marx

This biography, unlike many others, does not focus primarily on Karl Marx's economic or philosophical ideas but instead explores his role as a prophetic figure, albeit one who used Christian theological ideas for a materialist philosophy. His life and works in part can be understood and read as an attempt to dismantle and reconstruct Christian history into a secular apocalypse. Taking this approach, the book presents Marx's journey through a Dante-like framework of descent, as in an eschatological medieval vision,[23] each chapter exploring key events, pivotal works, and significant figures who influenced Marx's transformation from a youthful idealist to the architect of a vision that culminated in some of the horrors of the twentieth century. It integrates his life experiences with the wider world to expose the roots of Marx's secularized prophetic voice, and it offers a carefully structured narrative that weaves together his life story and his ideology.

After years of exploration, I have sifted through and engaged with a broad spectrum of thinkers and interpretations—from academic readings, which largely dismiss or overlook the man and his life, as well as hagiographic readings that depict Marx as a nineteenth-century visionary and those that brand him as a pure villain to more nuanced assessments—academic, theological, and popular—that acknowledge the contributions of and contradictions in his life. What has emerged from this process is the realization that any true engagement with Marx must transcend the binary "for or against" approach that has long characterized debates about his legacy. Instead of reducing Marx to either a hero or a villain, I have chosen to examine the deeper formation of his ideas—rooted in his personal wounds, his early religious and philosophical influences, and the literary canon he absorbed, from Greek tragedy[24] to the Old and New Testaments. But depth is not moral exoneration. To understand Marx is not to excuse him. The same richness of thought that gave rise to his revolutionary vision also produced one of the most destructive ideologies of the modern world. His intellectual gifts were real, but so too was the disordered moral compass that made him blind to the costs of his utopia.

These religious and philosophical texts that he absorbed all shaped his views and together function as a mirror for Marx's self-narrative. And so their examination will help us further understand this self-proclaimed poet and prophet. In the words of Paul Ricoeur: "The narrative constructs the identity of the character, what can be called his or her narrative identity, in constructing that of the story told."[25] In other words, identity is not static but is shaped through the retelling of one's life—through the stories one adopts, crafts, and believes in. Hans-Georg Gadamer said: "Long before we understand ourselves through the process of self-examination, we understand ourselves in a self-evident way in the family, society, and state in which we live."[26] He suggests that self-interpretation is always entangled with the broader cultural, political, and literary influences that precede conscious reflection. What might surprise a contemporary reader is how steeped Marx was in Romantic and Gothic literature. If so, how, through the mirror of these literary sources, did Marx see himself? How did he go about defining his goals? Did he fail or succeed? Here, the mirror serves as the tragic form that provides one not just with a narrative lens but with a critical tool for interpretation "to hold as 'twere the mirror up to nature: to show virtue her own feature, scorn her own image, and the very age and body of the time his form and pressure."[27] As Aristotle framed it, tragedy (or the tragic plot) reveals the inevitable tension between human aspiration and limitation, between fate and agency.[28] It dramatizes the contradictions that define individuals—not as static ideologues but as flawed figures shaped by their struggles.[29]

For Marx, whose own life was marked by a relentless pursuit of a revolutionary ideal at great personal cost, the tragic mode becomes an indispensable structure through which to understand his journey. His aspirations mirrored those of tragic heroes: figures who saw beyond their time who sought to reshape the world and yet who remained ensnared in the very forces they sought to master. Through tragedy, we do not merely recount events; we illuminate the deeper struggle of self-identity—how one enters history, falters or prevails, and ultimately leaves a legacy within its narrative. I have used Dante's structures, metaphors, and allegories from the *Divine Comedy*[30] to trace the arc of Marx's life.

I use them to test his actions against the Christian themes of sin and virtue found in Dante's world. If we imagine Marx as the main character in a classic play, would he have considered his life a success, one full of virtue? How would his self-narrative shape his legacy? These questions guide my analysis as I position myself against the various tracks of thought I have encountered in scholarly literature. My approach is to employ Dante's *Divine Comedy*, in particular as the narrative form of *katabasis*—the descent into hell—as a metaphor for understanding Marx's intellectual and personal journey,[31] and it, of course, "does not depend on the reader's belief that the poet is recounting a literal voyage that he personally took."[32]

Tragedy as Biography

"Karl Marx was another who was acutely conscious of the relation between tragedy and transition."[33] A biography in tragic form can use an individual's life as a means to explore larger philosophical, political, or moral conflicts. Indeed, many biographers of Marx often cast him solely as a symbol of either the triumph of socialist thought or the embodiment of its darkest failures. This kind of biography, shadowed by its "pale cast of thought,"[34] often becomes more of a single-minded argument than an exploration, as the biographer imposes a narrow lens onto the subject to force the subject's life to fit a preconceived ideological framework. This method, while simplistically informative and useful as an argument for one's ideology, can also limit our understanding of the individual as a complex, multifaceted "tragic" being who, like all human beings, is shaped by both internal and external forces. In contrast, biography can also be an intimate, personal narrative that delves deeply into the emotions, relationships, and interior life of its subject, sometimes revealing the "juicy" details, but not in a way that is reliant on shock. This approach often focuses on the lesser-known letters, diary entries, and personal interactions that shaped the individual's lesser-known or never-revealed world.

As for figures like Dante, Shakespeare's Hamlet, or Goethe's Faust, for Marx personal relationships were fraught with conflict and tragedy. There can be no doubt that a biographical approach can yield tremendous insight. Yet even this intimate lens risks reducing the individual to a mere psychological profile. While Marx's personal life was at times filled with very dark and near-macabre moments of neglect and the outright dismissal, if not abuse, of others, to focus narrowly on his worst moments would be to miss the broader ideological currents that he influenced and was influenced by.[35] However, a biography's narrative, like a tragedy, can also serve as a metaphor or plot for the subject's core values and the purpose of his actions.[36] In the case of this book, Dante clearly targets Beatrice as the symbol of divine love; using that same lens, we can ask the same of Jenny Marx. This approach enables readers to reconsider Marx's contributions not just as political ideology but as part of a larger narrative that mirrors the trials and pitfalls of human ambition. With this approach, the life of the subject is not merely a sequencing of events or even of a matter of internal psychology, but it is a mapping of a character's journey—one in which his actions can be seen in the context of larger material, spiritual, or existential concerns.

Marx's journey was influenced by his personal mentors and intellectual guides, each contributing values and perspectives that helped shape his radical thought. These figures begin primarily with his father and his father-in-law and then stretch across time from pre-Socratic philosophers such as Democritus and Epicurus to modern philosophers such as Hegel, Bauer, and Feuerbach. The same can be said for Rousseau and Voltaire, Smith and Riccardo, and Fourier and Saint Simon, who all left their mark on Marx's thinking, even though he diverged from their views. These intellectual ancestors, along with the great biblical prophets, form the backdrop against which Marx's ideas formed, going from the ancient spiritual or religious past to his day. They helped him form his moral quest, which was to establish a human-made utopia, an inverted eschaton, much different from the apocalyptic futures of old.[37] But what for me seems most overlooked is also how profoundly influenced Marx was by the great poet in Dante and the great tragedians in Shakespeare[38] and Goethe.[39] Marx's fascination with the classical poets underscores the enduring relevance of biography as a lens for exploring the hero's journey and the human condition. Dante opens his *magnum opus* by framing his spiritual journey as one that begins "in the middle of the journey of our life,"[40] to emphasize the intertwined nature of individual and collective experience.

Similarly, characters like Hamlet[41] or Faust embody the internal struggles of alienation, ambition, and identity—themes that Marx would later reinterpret within the framework of religious oppression and class struggle. Goethe, in the preface to his autobiographical reflections in *Poetry and Truth*, wrote: "For this seems to be the main object of Biography, to exhibit the man in relation to the features of his time; and to show to what extent they have opposed or favoured his progress; what view of mankind and the world he has formed from them, and how far he himself, if an artist, poet, or author, may externally reflect them." The poet's ability to universalize the specific is what Marx, in his own way, sought to emulate.[42] Goethe's reflections, Dante's allegories, and Shakespeare's tragedies all informed Marx's belief that the story of humanity could be retold not through divine grace but through material revolution. Their works serve as a foundation for exploring how the biography of a man—whether Dante spiraling into hell, Hamlet paralyzed by revenge, or Marx consumed by alienation—can illuminate larger truths about society and history.

In my telling, Marx is not Dante the pilgrim and is not a mere observer but a tragic figure akin to Virgil: a guide through the inferno of modernity whose own descent becomes the map for others.[43] Guided through his *katabasis*, readers are encouraged to see him not just as an economic theorist but as a man on a journey of descent—a journey that leads him into the depths of human struggle, with others, himself, and his dreams and ultimately with his faith. In this biography, I aim to reconsider Marx's contributions—framing them not merely as political ideology but as part of a tragic narrative that portrays a human quest in the light of redemption.[44]

The Power of *Katabasis*

In the realm of modern theory, few figures can command the admiration and condemnation that Karl Marx does. To understand his complex legacy, one must embark on a *katabasis*[45]—a descent into the depths of his readings in literature, history, economics, politics, and religion, and see his ideas as repercussions thereof, which will help them see why Marx chose Dante's *Inferno* to shape the contours of his own journey in *Das Kapital*. Scholar William Clare Roberts writes: "Marx's *Capital* was ingeniously modeled on Dante's *Inferno*, and how Marx, playing the role of Virgil[46] for the proletariat, introduced partisans of workers' emancipation to the secret depths of the modern 'social Hell.'"[47] The juxtaposition of Marx's theories with Dante's moral landscape offers rich insights into the nature of social justice, power dynamics, and the quest for redemption in contemporary society. The intersection of Marx's vision with Dante's moral framework reveals the complexities of human nature, power, and redemption. We must consider whether Marx—like the figures condemned in Dante's *Inferno*—embodies the consequences of rejecting the transcendent in favor of a materialist ethos, one that ultimately gave rise to ideologies devoid of hope, reconciliation, and the dignity of the human soul.

In Ancient Greek literature, which Marx knew well,[48] the term *katabasis* is often used to describe journeys into the Underworld.[49] Perhaps the most famous example of this is Odysseus's descent into Hades in Homer's *Odyssey*. In Roman literature, Virgil's *Aeneid* recounts a similar journey, as Aeneas descends into the underworld to meet his father and learn the destiny of Rome.[50] Virgil, drawing heavily from Homer's work, frames the *katabasis* as both a literal descent and a metaphor[51] for the hero's grappling with the weight of his mission and the inevitable suffering that it entails.[52] In Platonic thought, the journey into the depths of a cave in the *Allegory of the Cave* is a form of intellectual *katabasis*, where the descent into ignorance or illusion is followed by an ascent into the light of truth.[53] In the words of literary critic Terry Eagleton: "If the audience can see itself in an estranging light, one which has the power to unsettle its conventional self-understanding, it can also struggle to assimilate this dangerous knowledge and come to terms with it."[54] Christianity later absorbed this idea into the *Harrowing of Hell*, where Christ descends into the underworld after His crucifixion to free the souls of the righteous, symbolizing the ultimate act of redemption through descent.[55]

In Dante's *Divine Comedy*, which is partly an autobiography, the poet himself undergoes a spiritual *katabasis*, beginning with his descent into the afterlife. Guided by Virgil, Dante is taken on a journey that is an allegory for the human soul's descent into sin, as well as the suffering that results from separation from God. Dante, expressing doubt about his worthiness to undertake his journey through the afterlife, reflects on predecessors who have made similar journeys: "I am not Aeneas, I am not Paul."[56] Hell is a place of eternal torment, but it is also a mirror for the consequences of human choices—each circle of hell reflects a level of moral degradation. The concept of *katabasis* has evolved over time, transforming from a metaphorical journey into the underworld to a much broader cultural and existential theme, often representing a decline into chaos, suffering, or loss, followed by renewal or redemption.[57] Dante's *Divine Comedy* represents perhaps the most sophisticated literary use of *katabasis*, where the journey mirrors the soul's progression through sin, repentance, and redemption. Dante's *katabasis* is both personal and universal, as he descends not just into the realm of hell (*Inferno*) but into a moral universe where each sin is reflected in its "rings," a descent into a moral and metaphysical abyss. It is also a journey through human suffering and the consequences of moral choices. As Marx plummets further, will his journey culminate in something like the ultimate treachery in the ninth circle, where Satan himself is trapped, unable to ascend?

In the twentieth century, the concept of *katabasis* has moved beyond myth and literature into the lived experience of societies.[58] Post-Holocaust literature often grapples with the moral void left by the annihilation of millions. Elie Wiesel's *Night* (1960) and Primo Levi's *If This Is a Man* (1959) both capture this descent into the abyss, where faith, humanity, and hope are stripped away in the face of unimaginable suffering. To quote Eagleton once more: "There are also those for whom tragedy cannot survive the Holocaust, or the pervasive loss of meaning of late modernity or the depthless, decentred subjectivity of postmodernism. . . . [For] Theodor Adorno, the poet after Auschwitz is struck as dumb as his philosophical colleague."[59] The Cold War in general and the Cuban Missile Crisis in particular show how close the world came to nuclear annihilation, how close it came to a full-scale descent, or *katabasis*, into utter destruction. In today's context, the wars in Ukraine, the Middle East, and potentially China, and the ongoing potential for nuclear conflict signal a continued descent into chaos. In this modern context, the need for works of inspiration, allegory,[60] and moral reflection has never been greater, as humanity faces its own potential *katabasis* on a global scale. The descent into hell—whether literal or metaphorical—remains a potent symbol for understanding the human condition, and in our own time, it serves as a warning of the consequences of unchecked ambition, violence, and moral failure without the benefit of ancient wisdom.

This book, following that descent, takes us through three distinct stages of Karl Marx's life, each corresponding to one of Dante's realms, but in reverse order: (1)"Heaven (*Paradiso*)—The Academic's Paradise (1818–1842)"—this section explores Marx's early years, marked by the hope of revolutionary change and the belief that human progress was inevitable; it covers Marx's academic and early political writings, where he envisioned a utopian society free from the shackles of capitalism; (2) "Purgatory (*Purgatorio*): The Revolutionary's Purgatory (1842–1864)"—Marx's revolutionary dreams are tested by the failures of the European revolutions of 1848 and the harsh realities of life in exile. His family life disintegrates, and his once-grand vision becomes clouded by personal loss and political setbacks; (3) "Hell (*Inferno*): The Author's Hell (1864–1883)"—as Marx's vision fades and health deteriorates so does his faith in the revolution.

Each of these stages is marked by distinct "rings" modeled after Dante's circles of hell. As we will witness, Marx's descent into bitterness, isolation, and failure is not just a political narrative, it is a spiritual and moral one. His rejection of divine order and his refusal to recognize the complexities of human nature ultimately led to his personal *katabasis*—a journey into hell. By measuring Marx against his own ideals, and hidden "pacts"[61] with himself or others, we can see the ways in which he succeeded, but we can also see the ways in which he failed. And in doing so, we can view his life and work through the lens of tragedy for a richer understanding of a man's *hubris* ("arrogance"), his *aretē* ("excellence"), and, as is the core of the human condition, his *hamartia* ("tragic flaw").[62]

The Divine Tragedy

Marx and Friedrich Engels considered Dante a Renaissance hero, a genius poet and thinker who was able to inspire the soul with an inflexible warrior's spirit. It is said that Marx had learned by heart every line of the *Divina Commedia*. The introduction to *Das Kapital* testifies to his deep intellectual debt to Dante, as Engels called Dante a person of "unequalled classic perfection" and a "colossal figure."[63] Marx's intellectual journey is one of wild but bold idealism turned into tragic disillusionment—a *divine tragedy*. Engels, like many Marxist thinkers who followed him, interpreted tragedy primarily through the lens of material power and its structures—family, property, and the state—reducing it to a reflection of political and economic systems. While this reductionism has a point and is illuminating, it flattens the profound, multidimensional essence of tragedy by ignoring its existential and transcendent dimensions. Yet tragedy, as it has been explored by figures like Miguel de Unamuno (1864–1936), in *The Tragic Sense*, and others outside the materialist tradition, points to a deeper, more universal form of power: the power of human frailty, moral conflict, and the divine mystery of existence. De Unamuno explains: "Tragedy, by its very nature, speaks not to the outward conditions of life, but to the inward strife that defines us as human. It reveals the tension between what we aspire to and the inevitable limitations of our existence—the moral and existential constraints that we, in our ambition, cannot escape."[64]

Tragedy reveals the paradox of human strength and weakness, the way our greatest virtues often carry the seeds of our undoing, regardless of wealth. It exposes the eternal tension between human ambition and the inexorable forces—be they divine, natural, or psychological—that limit and define us. By focusing solely on the material dynamics of power, did Marx miss what tragedy has to teach us about the human condition? The actual solution to the moral conflict he identifies lies not in a redistribution of power but in a reconciliation of opposing principles—revenge and law, chaos and order—within a cosmic framework. Aeschylus's Prometheus does not give us a mere political commentary; he gives us a vision of humanity struggling to live under the shadow of divine justice[65] as did the privileged Faust turning to power and Hamlet to revenge, both of whom were consumed by excesses.[66] This richer, layered understanding of tragedy[67] is vital to comprehending the life and thought of Marx. His life was, in many ways, a tragedy of the classical kind. His grand ambitions for human salvation were undercut by his personal flaws and the unintended consequences of his actions. He was a man who sought to reshape the world, yet in doing so, he became a figure of immense isolation and alienation.

Unamuno's concept of the tragic sense of life provides a crucial counterpoint here.[68] For Unamuno, tragedy is not about power relations but the eternal conflict between our longing for immortality and the reality of death.[69] It is about the human quest for meaning in a universe that offers none. This "tragic sense" is the ultimate form of power—it is what drives our creativity, our faith, and our relentless struggle against despair. This sense, ignored by Engels and other Marxists, is key to understanding not only the limitations of Marxist interpretations of tragedy but also the deeper narrative of Marx's own life.[70]

Marx envisioned a world liberated from class oppression, with "no chains,"[71] but his failures seem more of a cautionary tale about the dangers of unchecked ambition and revolutionary zeal. Dante alludes to the Apostle Paul's heavenly experience: "If I was merely that part of me which Thou createdst last, Thou know'st, who raised me with Thy light."[72] This passage draws a parallel between Dante's visionary journey and the Apostle Paul's rapture into paradise to suggest a shared experience of divine revelation.[73] Marx's journey is one of great disillusionment, isolation, and blind hubris, which is the outcome of our own awaited apocalypse. We do not have any final remorse or confessions regarding the outcomes of his life, but we know Marx rejected divine grace in this world and instead placed his faith purely in human agency and the mechanisms of revolution, though, as economist Ludwig von Mises said, "for the Marxist, history is predetermined, and human will is irrelevant—echoing the fatalism found in many religious doctrines of the past,"[74] in addition to the ideas of philosopher Baruch Spinoza (1632–1677), known as "the hidden patron saint of the materialist outlook."[75] One of Spinoza's "fantasies" was that "we could act other than we do"; he was, in Eagleton's words, "a full-blooded determinist for whom freedom is the *apatheia* or serenity of mind which springs from knowing that things could not be different. To be truly free is to grasp the necessity."[76]

Ultimately, I hope my biography raises important questions about Marx's legacy as seen through his own vision: Was he a tragic figure—a man whose idealism was consumed by his own rebellion against the world as it was? Was his work a profound critique of power and exploitation,[77] or did it reflect deeper personal struggles with alienation and destruction? At times, Marx appears as a pitiful Falstaff, who is consumed by his own ego and excesses; at others, he is Iago, plotting the downfall of a world he despises. In the end, is he a tragic Hamlet, trapped in internal conflict, an idealist torn between action and thought, and ultimately undone by his inability to reconcile the two?[78] Or is he a Luciferian being, as his early poems reflect in spirit, the one that signed the Faustian pact with Mephistopheles? My aim is to present Marx in his own words as a profoundly complex figure whose legacy continues to shape the world. I believe Marx must be taken seriously—not because he was right, but because his wrong ideas continue to affect us, often in ways more destructive than we admit. To reduce him to a caricature is to risk misunderstanding the enduring danger of his legacy. As Marxist economist Richard Wolff puts it: "We must all acknowledge that words like Marx and Marxism, socialism, communism, and all that have been scare words for many people for many years. In the U.S., even before the Cold War erupted, capitalism's defenders and admirers often demonized capitalism's critics as dangerous, disloyal, foreign, and/or anti-American, anti-Christian, and so on. Since 1945, Americans were widely taught, encouraged or pressed to view socialism, communism, Marxism, the USSR, etc. with fear, anxiety, and hatred. Therefore, most Americans paid little or no attention to the work of Karl Marx."[79]

While his ideas can and do lead to totalitarian conclusions in practice, to reduce Marx to a one-dimensional villain ignores the broader investigation of his ideology linked to totalitarianism, which, I hope to show, offers an alternative to Christianity.[80] Would one blame Nietzsche for the Nazi atrocities or Aquinas for the abuses of the Inquisition? Perhaps not entirely—but Marx differs in kind, not just in consequence. Unlike those thinkers, he explicitly called for revolutionary violence, believing the utopia he envisioned could only be achieved through the force of the state. Regardless of source or intent, however, ideas shape the future—and it is this enduring impact I aim to explore in this work.[81] "Marxism has become a secular religion," according to Von Mises, complete with dogmas, heresies, and an unquestionable belief in historical destiny."[82] Schumpeter, characterizing Marx as prophet, states. "The religious quality of Marxism also explains a characteristic attitude of orthodox Marxist toward opponents. To him, as to any believer in a Faith. Opponent is not merely in error but in sin."[83]

Whether we like it or not, "we live in the age of Marx. Hundreds of millions of people, nearly half the world, are ruled by governments which claim to be practicing Marx's teachings and following the path he set for them, and his ideas still grip modern media, politics, academia, and, more recently, the technocratic business class."[84] His deeply flawed life, teachings, and untamed legacy remain influential because the spirit of his message touches the deepest issues of power, alienation, and inequality and has "taken the place of religious faith for many, with its own sacred texts, prophets, and promises of an earthly paradise through revolution."[85] Discussions of Marxist thought—on social justice, economic reform, and institutional critique—often underestimate the intellectual depth of his work, treating him as merely a relic of failed ideology.[86] Alasdair MacIntyre writes: "Notice that this Christian critique of capitalism relied and relies in key part, even if only in part, upon concepts and theses drawn from Marxist theory. Just as Marxism learned certain truths from Christianity, so Christianity in turn needed and needs to learn certain truths from Marxism. But what does this mean for practice in general and for political practice in particular?"[87] Marx remains influential precisely because his ideas still resonate in political and cultural discourse, sometimes dangerously so. To engage him seriously is not to endorse him but to understand the enduring risks posed by his revolutionary prescriptions.

Master Timeline

Pre-Birth Events (Before 1818)

1215: The Magna Carta is signed in England, limiting the powers of the king and establishing certain legal rights.

1492: Christopher Columbus discovers the Americas, marking the beginning of European exploration and colonization.

1776: The American Revolution begins, leading to the declaration of independence from British rule.

1789: The French Revolution starts, fundamentally altering the political landscape of Europe and promoting ideas of liberty, equality, and fraternity.

1791–1804: The Haitian Revolution takes place, leading to Haiti becoming the first independent Black-led republic in the world.

1798: Friedrich Engels is born on November 28 in Barmen, Prussia.

1811: Jenny von Westphalen is born on February 12 in Germany.

1815: The Congress of Vienna redraws the map of Europe after the Napoleonic Wars, attempting to restore balance and prevent future conflicts.

Karl Marx's Life Events (1818–1883)

1818: Karl Marx is born on May 5 in Trier, Prussia (now Germany).

1836: Marx begins his studies at the University of Bonn and later transfers to the University of Berlin. He reconnects with Jenny von Westphalen, and they become engaged.

1843: Marx and Jenny marry on June 19 and move to Paris, where Karl begins to engage with radical politics and philosophy, meeting various thinkers.

1844: Marx writes *Economic and Philosophic Manuscripts*, exploring themes of alienation and labor. He meets Friedrich Engels in Paris, sparking a lifelong friendship and collaboration.

1845: Marx meets Wilhelm Weitling and other influential socialist thinkers, further shaping his political ideology.

1848: *The Communist Manifesto*, co-authored with Engels, is published in February, calling for the proletariat to rise against the bourgeoisie. The year also sees widespread revolutions across Europe.

1851: Marx begins writing for the *New York Tribune*, establishing connections with American intellectuals.

1852: Marx publishes *The Eighteenth Brumaire of Louis Bonaparte*, analyzing the rise of Louis Napoleon and the class struggle in France.

1857: Marx meets with socialist figures who would be initial members in the International Workingmen's Association (First International).

1864: The First International is founded, with Marx as a key figure in its formation.

1867: The first volume of *Das Kapital* is published, laying the foundation for Marxist economics. Marx continues his collaboration with Engels.

1871: The *Paris Commune* occurs, a radical socialist government that briefly ruled Paris. Marx corresponds with leaders and sees it as a model for the dictatorship of the proletariat.

1881: Marx's daughter Eleanor marries the socialist Edward Aveling.

1881: Marx's wife, Jenny, dies on December 2.

1883: Karl Marx dies on March 14 in London, England.

Post-Death Events (After 1883)

1884: Friedrich Engels publishes *Origin of the Family, Private Property and the State*, expanding on Marx's theories.

1885: The second volume of *Das Kapital*, edited by Engels, is published.

1891: The third volume of *Das Kapital*, also edited by Engels, comes out.

1898: Friedrich Engels dies on August 5 in London.

1898: Eleanor Marx dies by suicide on March 31.

1917: The Russian Revolution leads to the formation of the Bolshevik Party, influenced by Marxist ideology, which seizes power and establishes the Soviet Union.

1922: The Soviet Union is officially established, becoming the first state to implement Marxist-Leninist principles.

1933: Adolf Hitler rises to power in Germany, leading to the persecution of communists and the eventual outbreak of World War II.

1949: The People's Republic of China is established under the leadership of the Communist Party, which follows Marxist principles.

1968: Widespread protests and revolutions occur worldwide, influenced by Marxist thought and anti-establishment sentiments.

1989: The fall of the Berlin Wall symbolizes the collapse of communist regimes in Eastern Europe and the decline of Marxist influence in global politics.

2008: The global financial crisis prompts renewed interest in Marxist critiques of capitalism.

Cast of Characters

Aeneas (Mythological, Trojan War Era)

The Trojan hero from Virgil's *Aeneid*, Aeneas represents endurance, exile, and destiny. Marx referenced Aeneas to illustrate historical inevitability and the role of great individuals in shaping history.

Aeschylus (c. 525–456 BC)

Greek tragedian whose works, particularly *The Oresteia*, influenced Marx's understanding of fate, justice, and historical necessity. Aeschylus's depiction of the clash between old and new orders aligns with Marx's dialectical view of history.

Alighieri, Dante (1265–1321)

Italian poet of the *Divine Comedy*, which serves as the structural metaphor for Marx's ideological descent. Marx referenced Dante's *Inferno* when discussing capitalism's corrupting nature.

Apostle John (c. AD 6–100)

One of Jesus's closest disciples and the (disputed) author of *Revelation*, whose apocalyptic vision of transformation mirrors Marx's eschatological view of historical progress.

Apostle Paul (c. AD 5–67)

Christian theologian and author of the Pauline Epistles. Paul's call for radical transformation and the formation of a new spiritual community contrast with Marx's collectivist materialist vision.

Aquinas, Thomas (1225–1274)

Catholic theologian whose *Summa Theologica* provided a moral and philosophical framework opposed to Marx's materialism. Aquinas's concept of natural law clashed with Marx's dialectical materialism.

Aristotle (384–322 BC)

Greek philosopher whose political theories on class and governance indirectly influenced Marx's critique of private property and economic structures.

Aveling, Edward (1849–1898)

English socialist and partner of Eleanor Marx. His financial irresponsibility and infidelity contributed to Eleanor's eventual suicide, yet another of the personal tragedies of the Marx family.

Bakunin, Mikhail (1814–1876)

Russian anarchist and one of Marx's most famous ideological rivals. He rejected Marx's view of the state, believing in immediate revolutionary abolition rather than transitional dictatorship.

Bauer, Bruno (1809–1882)

German philosopher and early mentor to Marx, particularly in his critique of religion. However, Marx later rejected Bauer's perspectives as too abstract and idealistic.

Bebel, August (1840–1913)

German socialist and co-founder of the Social Democratic Party of Germany (SPD). He worked closely with Engels and helped spread Marxist thought in Germany.

Bernstein, Eduard (1850–1932)

German socialist who challenged Marxist orthodoxy by advocating for gradual reform over revolution, causing a major split in the socialist movement.

Blanc, Louis (1811–1882)

French socialist who proposed cooperative workshops as a state solution to unemployment. Marx criticized his ideas as utopian.

Blanqui, Louis Auguste (1805–1881)

French socialist revolutionary whose theories of insurrection and elite-led coups influenced Marx's ideas on proletarian dictatorship.

Boethius, Anicius Manlius Severinus (c. 480–524)

Roman philosopher whose reflections on fate in *The Consolation of Philosophy* contrast with Marx's deterministic materialist view of history.

Bonaparte, Napoleon I (1769–1821)

French general and emperor. Marx analyzed his rule in *The Eighteenth Brumaire of Louis Bonaparte*, seeing it as an example of class struggle and bourgeois betrayal of revolution.

Bonaparte, Napoleon III (1808–1873)

Nephew of Napoleon I and ruler of France. Marx viewed his reign as reactionary and a betrayal of revolutionary ideals.

Caesar, Julius (100–44 BC)

Roman dictator whom Marx referenced in discussions of historical power struggles and class revolutions.

Carlyle, Thomas (1795–1881)

Scottish historian who critiqued industrial capitalism but rejected socialism. Marx admired Carlyle's attack on economic exploitation but rejected his paternalistic views.

Cohen, Hermann (1842–1918)

German-Jewish philosopher who integrated Kantian ethics with socialist thought, influencing later Marxist interpretations.

Coleridge, Samuel Taylor (1772–1834)

Romantic poet whose explorations of transcendence contrast sharply with Marx's materialist worldview.

Comte, Auguste (1798–1857)

Founder of positivism, which sought to apply scientific principles to society. Marx respected Comte's empirical approach but criticized his failure to acknowledge class struggle.

Democritus (c. 460–370 BC)

Greek philosopher and materialist whose theories influenced Marx's doctoral thesis on Epicureanism.

Demuth, Helene (1820–1890)

Marx's longtime housekeeper and the mother of his illegitimate child, exposing contradictions in Marx's views on class and gender.

Dostoevsky, Fyodor (1821–1881)

Russian novelist who explored themes of nihilism, morality, and revolution. His critique of utopian socialism stood in opposition to Marxist determinism.

Engels, Friedrich (1820–1895)

Marx's closest collaborator and financial supporter. Co-author of *The Communist Manifesto* and posthumous editor of *Das Kapital.*

Fourier, Charles (1772–1837)

French utopian socialist who envisioned cooperative societies. Marx rejected Fourier's model as idealistic and detached from class struggle.

Garibaldi, Giuseppe (1807–1882)

Italian nationalist and revolutionary who admired Marx's ideas but criticized his lack of tactical clarity.

Goethe, Johann Wolfgang von (1749–1832)

German poet whose *Faust* deeply influenced Marx's vision of human ambition and historical progress.

Greeley, Horace (1811–1872)

Editor of *The New York Tribune*, which published Marx's articles on world affairs, connecting him to American intellectual circles.

Grimm, Jacob (1785–1863) and Wilhelm (1786–1859)

German philologists and folklorists who collected and studied folk tales. Marx saw folk traditions as a reflection of class struggle and historical materialism in cultural narratives.

Hegel, Georg Wilhelm Friedrich (1770–1831)

German idealist philosopher whose dialectical method profoundly influenced Marx. Marx inverted Hegel's dialectics from an idealist to a materialist foundation, shaping historical materialism.

Heine, Heinrich (1797–1856)

German poet and Marx's friend, known for his satirical critiques of German politics and religion. Heine's wit and revolutionary spirit resonated with Marx's early writings.

Hobbes, Thomas (1588–1679)

English political philosopher who advocated for absolute sovereignty (i.e., government power). Marx critiqued Hobbes's social contract theory but recognized his insights into class struggle and power dynamics.

Hugo, Victor (1802–1885)

French novelist and political thinker whose works, particularly *Les Misérables*, depicted class struggle and poverty. Marx appreciated Hugo's social critique but rejected his liberal humanitarianism.

Jefferson, Thomas (1743–1826)

American Founding Father and author of the Declaration of Independence. Marx acknowledged Jefferson's revolutionary spirit but critiqued the limits of bourgeois democracy.

Jesus of Nazareth (c. 4 BC–AD 30)

Founder of Christianity. Marx viewed Jesus's teachings on social justice and communal living as an early form of radical socialism but rejected their spiritual foundation.

Kant, Immanuel (1724–1804)

German philosopher whose moral philosophy influenced Marx's early humanist thought before he moved toward materialism.

Kautsky, Karl (1854–1938)

German Marxist theorist and leading figure in the Second International. Initially a staunch advocate of Marxism, he later clashed with Lenin over revolutionary strategy.

Lenin, Vladimir (1870–1924)

Russian revolutionary who adapted Marx's theories into the framework of a vanguard-led proletarian state. Lenin's interpretation led to the establishment of Soviet communism.

Lessing, Gotthold Ephraim (1729–1781)

German writer and Enlightenment thinker. His philosophical dramas and theological critiques influenced Marx's early intellectual development.

Liebknecht, Wilhelm (1826–1900)

German socialist and close associate of Marx and Engels. He played a crucial role in spreading Marxist ideology in Germany.

Lucretius (c. 99–55 BC)

Roman poet and philosopher whose *De Rerum Natura* introduced the materialist philosophy that influenced Marx's early studies on Epicureanism.

Luther, Martin (1483–1546)

Leader of the Protestant Reformation. Marx admired Luther's radical break from the Catholic Church but critiqued his accommodation to political authority.

Luxemburg, Rosa (1871–1919)

Marxist theorist and revolutionary who criticized Leninist authoritarianism while advocating for proletarian democracy.

Machiavelli, Niccolò (1469–1527)

Italian political theorist whose *The Prince* explored power dynamics and statecraft. Marx analyzed Machiavelli's theories in the context of class struggle.

Malthus, Thomas (1766–1834)

English economist known for his theory of population growth outpacing resources. Marx dismissed Malthus as a reactionary defender of capitalist scarcity.

Mao Zedong (1893–1976)

Chinese communist leader who adapted Marxism for peasant-based revolution.

Marx, Edgar (1847–1855)

Karl Marx's son, who died young from illness, reflecting the family's struggles with poverty.

Marx, Eleanor (1855–1898)

Daughter of Karl Marx and prominent socialist activist. She championed women's rights and trade unions but faced personal tragedies, which led to suicide.

Marx, Franziska (1851–1852)

Another child of Marx who died in infancy, showing the personal cost of his revolutionary lifestyle.

Marx, Heinrich Guido (1849–1850)

Died in infancy, another tragic loss for the Marx family.

Marx, Jenny (1814–1881)

Wife of Karl Marx and devoted supporter of his work, enduring financial hardship and political exile.

Marx, Jenny Caroline (1844–1883)

Eldest daughter of Karl Marx, known as "Jennychen," a devoted supporter of his work and active in socialist circles.

Marx, Laura (1845–1911)

Daughter of Karl Marx who married socialist Paul Lafargue and was active in political movements.

Milton, John (1608–1674)

English poet whose *Paradise Lost* influenced Marx's vision of rebellion, struggle, and historical necessity.

Nietzsche, Friedrich (1844–1900)

Philosopher who critiqued morality and religion in ways that overlapped with Marx's rejection of bourgeois society.

Owen, Robert (1771–1858)

Welsh industrialist and utopian socialist whose cooperative communities Marx dismissed as naïve.

Paine, Thomas (1737–1809)

American revolutionary and political theorist. Marx admired Paine's radical egalitarianism but critiqued his faith in democratic institutions.

Plato (c. 427–347 BC)

Ancient Greek philosopher whose *Republic* inspired discussions on ideal states, though Marx rejected his metaphysical framework.

Proudhon, Pierre-Joseph (1809–1865)

French anarchist who famously declared "Property is theft." Marx engaged in fierce debates with him over state power and the nature of capitalism.

Rousseau, Jean-Jacques (1712–1778)

French Enlightenment philosopher who theorized about the social contract. Marx recognized Rousseau's critique of inequality but rejected his focus on the moral regeneration of individuals.

Saint-Simon, Henri de (1760–1825)

French socialist whose vision of industrial governance influenced early socialist movements and who envisioned a technocratic elite governing society. Marx critiqued his vision as insufficiently revolutionary.

Schopenhauer, Arthur (1788–1860)

German philosopher known for his pessimistic worldview. Marx dismissed Schopenhauer's focus on will as too abstract and unscientific.

Shakespeare, William (1564–1616)

English playwright whose works Marx quoted frequently, particularly in *Das Kapital.* Marx saw Shakespeare as a keen observer of social class and power.

Shelley, Percy Bysshe (1792–1822)

Romantic poet and radical thinker whose revolutionary ideals aligned with early socialist thought.

Smith, Adam (1723–1790)

Scottish economist and author of *The Wealth of Nations*. Marx critiqued Smith's classical economics while acknowledging his insights into labor value.

Spinoza, Baruch (1632–1677)

Dutch philosopher whose materialist and determinist views had an early influence on Marx's thinking.

Stalin, Joseph (1878–1953)

Soviet dictator who claimed to follow Marx's ideas but implemented a brutal and repressive state, contradicting Marx's vision of proletarian self-emancipation.

Strauss, David Friedrich (1808–1874)

German theologian whose historical-critical approach to Jesus influenced Marx's critique of religion.

Tocqueville, Alexis de (1805–1859)

French political thinker who analyzed democracy and class struggle. Marx respected Tocqueville's observations but critiqued his liberal perspective.

Turgot, Anne Robert Jacques (1727–1781)

French economist and early advocate of laissez-faire policies, which Marx opposed as tools of bourgeois exploitation.

Trotsky, Leon (1879–1940)

Marxist revolutionary and theorist of "permanent revolution," who was assassinated by Stalin.

Ugolino (Dante's Inferno)

Historical figure punished in *Inferno*. Marx referenced Dante's depiction of suffering to critique capitalism.

Voltaire (1694–1778)

French Enlightenment philosopher and critic of religious dogma. Marx appreciated Voltaire's wit but dismissed his belief in gradual reform.

Weitling, Wilhelm (1808–1871)

German tailor and early communist who influenced Marx's early activism before they parted ways ideologically.

Zola, Émile (1840–1902)

French novelist whose works, particularly *Germinal*, depicted class struggle in a way that paralleled Marx's historical materialism.

Prologue: The Tragic Figure

"Then I will wander godlike and victorious through the ruins of the world. And giving my words an active force, I will feel equal to the Creator."[88]

From the depths of hell to the slow climb of purgatory, Karl Marx found much to invoke in Dante's *Inferno*—the burning indignation of the oppressed, the torments of the damned, the judgment cast upon the old order. But what of heaven (*Paradiso*)? In all his writings, the celestial realm remains unspoken—absent, unworthy of even a passing reference. What does it mean to build a new world without ever looking "to the stars,"[89] especially when Marx's beginnings embodied the best of what this world has to offer?

The early nineteenth century was a time of profound transformation.[90] The Napoleonic Wars had reshaped Europe, leaving behind a fractured yet invigorated continent. In 1818, the Congress of Vienna was still a fresh memory, as the Great Powers sought to redraw borders and restore order. Yet beneath this veneer of stability, the Industrial Revolution was underway, with steam engines roaring through England and factories rising across Europe. Ludwig van Beethoven was composing his late string quartets, breaking musical conventions, while poets like Lord Byron and Percy Shelley were capturing the restless spirit of the age. The world Marx would inherit was one of burgeoning industry, revolutionary ideas, and a restless humanity yearning for meaning in an age of upheaval. As Marx stood at the precipice of his life's journey, he was not in hell (*Inferno*) but in paradise (*Paradiso*), an inversion of the incipit of Dante's journey in the *Divine Comedy*. What follows is Marx's own path "within a forest dark,"[91] where the very goals that seemed to promise salvation wound up, step by step, leading to personal and societal ruin. To map out this descent, we may begin not at the beginning but late in Karl Marx's life, with the aging revolutionary standing at a worktable in his cramped London flat in 1867 about to complete *Das Kapital*, a book delayed more than fifteen years due to his chronic neglect.[92]

The room is laden with the stench of tobacco from Marx's chain-smoking,[93] and though he suffered from bronchitis, his addiction intensified over the years. Just feet away lies the darkened room where the body of his eight-year-old child Edgar once tragically rested, unburied, because Marx could not afford a proper funeral.[94] His life, at this point, is a profound paradox. On the surface, he is the world's visionary who claimed to understand the great movement of history and revolution, but in private, his existence was plagued by poverty, failure, and dependency.[95] On May 24, 1850, the Earl of Westmoreland, the British Ambassador in Berlin, received a translated report from a perceptive Prussian police spy surveilling Marx's life in Cologne. The description paints a vivid portrait of his disordered domestic habits during his time in Germany:

> [Marx] leads the existence of a Bohemian intellectual. Washing, grooming, and changing his linen are things he does rarely, and he is often drunk. Though he is frequently idle for days on end, he will work day and night with tireless endurance when he has much work to do. He has no fixed time for going to sleep or waking up. He often stays up all night and then lies down fully clothed on the sofa at midday and sleeps till evening, untroubled by the whole world coming and going through their room [there were only two altogether]. . . . There is not one clean and solid piece of furniture.

Later, during his years in London exile, reports from visitors and acquaintances would echo this same image—suggesting that the chaos of Marx's personal life transcended national boundaries.

Though he developed a deep love for chess[96] along with his wine[97] and cigars, and gained inheritance, Marx's habits became more regular and more temperate. He no longer worked through the night and slept during the morning. His old bohemian ways were abandoned, as he became more affluent. He lived quietly, according to a fixed schedule, rarely going out, working hard at his correspondence and his books during the morning and afternoon, and he received visitors over a bottle of port in the evening. Except for the regular Tuesday evening meetings on Greek Street—one of the few remaining fixtures in his social and intellectual life—Marx rarely ventured into Central London. The days of pub-crawling through Soho and Bloomsbury, which had marked his earlier years in exile during the late 1840s and early 1850s, were far behind him. By the 1860s and 1870s, he no longer frequented the German clubs or participated in their debates. He had become a creature of habit, a solid and respectable citizen, who read *The Times* over breakfast and spent the rest of the day in very much the same way as any other man of scholarly tastes and independent means.[98]

Those tables heaped with British Blue Books[99] and ancient newspapers, those bulging shelves, those mounting towers of books on the floor, those volumes scattered on the window ledge and the mantelpiece suggest a mind that had never completely escaped from the convulsions of adolescence. He treated books as he treated people, abusing them unmercifully, never demonstrating the least sign of repentance. "They are my slaves," he said, "and they must serve my will."[100] He had no affection for them; they were foreign territory to be raided and conquered as he pleased, and referred to them as slaves. Marx's youthful radicalism was far gone. His revolutionary ideas had yet to come to fruition, and the consequences of his life's work remained largely theoretical. Yet even in this squalid setting,

Marx's ambition remained ironically clear—he desired to be more than a mere revolutionary and to live out the life of an English gentleman, a member not merely their critic.

Sunday picnics and readings of Dante and Shakespeare in the park may have been what Marx once envisioned for his life, but by his early sixties, envy and resentment still lingered.[101] The incendiary rhetoric, the "white-hot phrases"[102] he once hurled against the economic system he despised had grown muted, dulled by years of exile, illness, and disappointment. The air lingered with a contradiction; while Marx's powerful words promised emancipation for the working class, a future where exploitation would be eradicated, he seemed to have lived in a way that betrayed those ideals. He cried out for the labor of others but, other than as a journalist, never held a job[103] and lived off the financial support of his collaborator, Friedrich Engels, friends, and family inheritance.[104] His body seemed to deteriorate along with his wavering ideals: the boils that tormented him, including those on his genitals, were caused, in part, by his refusal to bathe. Biographer David McLellan writes that "the appalling odors, the red sores, the swelling and the pus were all revealed when the bandages were removed, and there seemed to be no way of keeping them under control."[105]

Even *Das Kapital*, the monumental work he was finishing, was only the first book of several planned volumes, the others still unfinished or to be completed by Engels, a familiar role for his lifelong friend and supporter. Marx simply could not commit to the labor of completing them: "As Marx gazed at the mounting manuscript of *Das Kapital*, he felt that he was at the mercy of a monster which was slowly destroying him."[106] The irony is that the man who railed against the exploitation of labor never fully engaged in it himself nor paid those who assisted him. In Marx's mind, workers'[107] productive activity becomes activity under the domination, coercion, and yoke of another man—the capitalist employer.

Peter Singer notes that, according to Marx, "this other human being becomes an alien, hostile being. Instead of humans relating to each other cooperatively, they relate competitively. Love and trust are replaced by bargaining and exchange. Human beings cease to recognize in each other a common human nature; instead, they see others as instruments of production for furthering their own egoistic interests. They are alienated from their common humanity."[108] And this observation brings us to the heart of the matter. Marx, much like the souls of Dante's *Divine Comedy*, lived in isolation—not just from the world but from his imagined self, a self-proclaimed Promethean figure, a liberator of the working class: "The reality, however, was far more troubling. His life reflected a deep inner conflict. In reflection, he betrayed not only his family but refused to see that his own life, as isolated genius, was an example of the very alienation he so vehemently decried.[109]

Marx's deepest betrayal could be imagined as that exercised by Count Ugolino[110] in Dante's *Inferno.* Ugolino, imprisoned and driven to cannibalize his own children, becomes an eternal emblem of betrayal, to consume those he was meant to protect. Likewise, Marx's doctrine, though revolutionary, devoured the ideals of solidarity and communal care that it sought to promote. The early revolutionary doctrine encapsulated in *The Communist Manifesto* (1848) called for the proletariat to rise up against the bourgeoisie. In their boldest work, Marx and Engels envisioned a world transformed by the proletariat's collective will; yet the very nature of this uprising—a call for violent overthrow—seemed to betray the underlying humanist ideals that they purported to champion. As McLellan writes: "The Communist Manifesto was a bold proclamation that crystallized Marx's evolving political thought."[111] Marx, in rejecting the systems of the past, stated that history itself burdens the present. He claimed that "all that exists deserves to perish," echoing Mephistopheles in Goethe's *Faust.*[112] Marx called for a radical upheaval, with the end justifying the means, to use Machiavellian terms, no matter the cost.

Count Ugolino's *Inferno* story is one of treachery, not just against his political allies, but against his own children, whom his neglect in part condemned to a life of squalor and starvation.

Was Marx destined to a fate like Ugolino's? Despite his claims of championing the working class, he spent his life seeking comfort, recognition, and status within the very capitalist structures he so despised,[113] and he scorned the bourgeoisie but aspired to a life with maidservants and housekeepers, whom he would fail to pay.[114] In his 1867 preface to *Das Kapital*, Marx described his work as an exploration of the "laws of motion"[115] of capitalism, suggesting that he was mapping the stages of economic oppression much as Dante had charted the punishments of sin.[116] Our comparison to Dante goes beyond mere influence on the literary structure of this text, because for Marx, the economic world was one where class oppression mirrored the torments of hell and revolution represented a potential path to redemption—a materialist purgatory[117] and then an eventual salvation through class struggle, a new eschaton.[118]

With a slight tremor in his hands, Marx reflects upon the *magnum opus*, the sum total of the analytical rigor and revolutionary fervor that had consumed his years and perhaps his soul. For decades, he envisioned it as a weapon against the forces of oppression: a text so powerful it could turn the world on its head. But now, it feels like a heavy, immovable weight pressing down on him. Marx's face is a battlefield of grim determination and quiet despair, a face that tells of long nights and sacrifices that he never fully understood. Marx's revolutionary ideas, which had once burned bright, now flicker like the last embers of a dying fire. Standing at the worktable in his cramped London flat, he is trapped not by the four walls but in the paradox of his own making: he championed the working class while failing his own family and rallied against exploitation while relying on the financial support of the wealthy Engels. In this fleeting moment, the ideals that had once lifted him above common concerns now appear tainted, as if poisoned by his tiring ambition. His dreams of a workers' paradise feel hollow, drained of their promise by the decades of exile, relentless poverty, and a "gnawing"[119] resentment he cannot escape. It is here, at his darkest moment, that we begin our journey—and we begin it with a riddle: Had Dante known of Marx, where would he have placed him?

As in Dante's *Divine Comedy*, Marx's life takes us through rings of escalating suffering and alienation, with a subsequent descent (*katabasis*) that is not of divine making but rather the result of failed human effort. For a moment, in London, the aging Marx can imagine his youth, glimpses of a world filled with promise, one shaped by ideals of progress and enlightenment. With these youthful glimpses, amid the vineyards of Moselle, inspired by the philosophical currents of Georg W. F. Hegel and Ludwig Feuerbach, the wit of Voltaire, and the vision of the poets like Goethe, Marx dreamed of salvation from ignorance and suffering—a world remade, where humanity could transcend its basest instincts.

Born on May 5, 1818, in Trier, Prussia, he entered a family that would shape his destiny in ways that were both profound and tragic. Karl was one of nine children born to Heinrich and Henrietta Marx. His eldest brother died in infancy, making Karl the eldest surviving son. Of his siblings, four succumbed to tuberculosis—Eduard at age eleven, Hermann and Karolina at twenty-three, and Henrietta at thirty-six. In the end, Karl was the only male offspring of his parents to live into middle age. Trier, nestled in the Prussian Rhineland, was a city on edge—a land of shifting power and revolutionary murmurs.

The forces that shaped his early years would ignite the fire of his radical thought, propelling him into a lifelong battle against what he saw as the injustices of the world. As David McLellan observes: "As a student, Marx exhibited a deep idealism and an early passion for justice, traits that would define his later revolutionary thought,"[120] which was derived in part from Kant, who was "believed to have had a greater influence than any other philosopher of modern times."[121]

The German city impressed upon him a sense of cultural tradition—rooted in centuries of philosophy, art, and religious life—while also exposing him to the harsh realities of economic stagnation and political underdevelopment, conditions that seemed ripe for revolutionary change.

The Marx family, thoroughly Jewish in origin, had converted to Lutheranism out of social and legal necessity, yet they lived in a region dominated by Catholic tradition. This layered religious identity—Jewish by heritage, Protestant by pragmatism, and surrounded by Catholic culture—created a fractured sense of belonging. Marx, shaped by this early tension, would never fully regard religious structures as anything but tools of repression and hypocrisy. His notorious anti-Catholicism reflected not just political hostility but a deeper resentment toward the institution that, in his view, symbolized a suffocating synthesis of tradition, hierarchy, and illusion—everything his revolutionary vision sought to overturn.[122] Arnold Ruge (1802–1880), a friend, German philosopher, and political writer, formulated: "Prussia as a state is still Catholic; absolute monarchy is politically completely the same as what Catholicism is religiously."[123] Despite their limitations, Marx's family was relatively affluent for the time. It may seem paradoxical that Karl Marx, whom so many working-class movements would claim as their master and infallible guide to revolution, should have come from a comfortable middle-class home. It is even more remarkable given that he did not himself epitomize his own doctrine that men are conditioned by their socioeconomic circumstances. His father, Heinrich, a lawyer, was supportive of his intellectual pursuits, though he would later become concerned about his son's radicalism. Marx's early education in Trier set the stage for his later study of law, philosophy, and history at the University of Bonn and later the University of Berlin, institutions where he was exposed to the works of Hegel, whose dialectical methods would profoundly influence Marx's development of historical materialism: "The young Marx displayed an early brilliance, particularly in his fascination with classical literature."[124] But even in these early years, shadows lurked in his soul,[125] hints of defiance, dark inspiration, and ideological rigidity that would shape his life.

In 1836, Marx met Jenny von Westphalen, and their engagement would count as a significant turning point in Marx's life. Jenny was from a higher social class and was well-educated, a companion who would share his intellectual pursuits and become an important influence on his early work: "Karl and Jenny's partnership was not just romantic but also intellectual, forming the foundation of his revolutionary ideas."[126] Their marriage in 1843 cemented their partnership, and Jenny's support would be invaluable in the difficult years ahead. The relationship between Marx and Jenny would remain a source of stability in the midst of the intellectual turmoil and political struggles that Marx faced.

In 1843, Marx moved to Paris, where he became deeply involved in the intellectual and political upheavals of the time. He was drawn to revolutionary ideas with the fervor of a man possessed. Robert Tucker writes: "The early Marx was a humanist and revolutionary moralist, animated by deep ethical passion and a belief in human self-realization."[127] But the allure of rebellion blinded him to the darker truths it concealed. In Paris, he met Friedrich Engels, who would become his closest collaborator and financial supporter, and Marx began to engage more deeply with the works of Hegel and Feuerbach, synthesizing them into a new theory of history and economics. Marx's early writings during this period focused on alienation, the idea that, under capitalism,[128] workers were separated from the products of their labor, leading to a loss of agency and human potential.[129] Marx began developing the core ideas of his critique of capitalism and its inherent inequality. His vision of change, like Dante's false lights in heaven, is captivating but ultimately deceptive, blurring the lines of idealism and fanaticism.

In 1848, the *Communist Manifesto*, co-authored with Engels, was published, offering a call for revolution. It was the first time Marx's theories found a global platform.[130] But Marx's optimism in 1848 was overshadowed by the brutal suppression of the revolutions that had erupted in Europe, and this would solidify his belief that revolution would be a long and difficult struggle.

Marx's engagement with the working-class movements in France, Germany, and London continued in the years that followed. By the time he penned *The German Ideology*[131] with Engels, Marx had reached the peak of his utopian vision. Yet, beneath this summit, seeds of disillusionment began to take root, and the heavy burden of a revolutionary life began to weigh on him. The failed revolutions of 1848 in France, Germany, Italy, and the Austrian Empire[132] marked the first major fracture in Marx's dream. His hopes for a world aflame with change collapsed under the weight of history's indifference. In 1849, he was exiled to London, where he would remain for the rest of his life.[133] Isaiah Berlin adds that "Marx's exile in London marked the beginning of his most productive intellectual period."[134] But there, he watched his family slip further into poverty, to slowly chisel away at the idealism that once fortified his purpose. Though free, Marx's restricted status became his prison as his revolutionary dreams faded and the light ahead grew dim. London was a bustling center of industrial capitalism, which would become the backdrop for his study of economic systems.

The move to London coincided with his increasingly alienated position in the intellectual and political world, though he began writing for the *New York Tribune*, a major outlet for Marx's international ideas, where he commented on the American Civil War, all the while seeing his personal circumstances become increasingly dire. In spite of this, the year 1867 marked the publication of the first volume of *Das Kapital*, Marx's *magnum opus*. This first volume laid out the foundations of Marxist economics, to detail how capitalism's inherent contradictions would ultimately lead to its collapse. The publication brought Marx academic acclaim, but it did little to solve the practical problems he faced. His relationship with his parents had nearly ended, Jenny and his children suffered from poor health, and the alienation Marx had spent his life analyzing seemed to seep deeper into his own life experience. Marx spends the following years trapped in cycles of labor that yield little fruit. His incompletion underscores the relentless, nearly impossible ambition behind his work, a haunting symbol of his unfulfilled vision. His further work on *Das Kapital* became a torturous process, an eternal toil akin to Dante's infernal circles, where each effort to break free only led him deeper into despair. His health deteriorated, his ambitions eroded, and his family suffered, all while he remained bound to the manuscript that was once his purpose but now felt like a curse.

By the end of his journey, Marx was a man consumed by his own ambition, even to the point of turning against the friends and allies who had once stood beside him. Like the souls crossing over the River Styx, his anger trapped him in a prison of his own making. He lashed out at comrades, disowned his allies, and clung to the vestiges of his revolutionary fervor, which became tainted with bitterness and betrayal, as he saw the collapse of his dreams for a united movement. It left him paralyzed, like Dante's traitors frozen in the ice. In his dank apartment, his spirit was drained, and his ideals were left in ruins; his soul was trapped in a cryogenic prison, a bitter, forsaken room haunted by regret.

As we track his descent, each chapter, each struggle, each ring reveals a new layer of his decline—a path where dreams of revolution dissipate, where ideals are suffocated by personal failings, and where a man who set out to change the world finds himself consumed by its unexpected demons.[135] As one author of his literary influences observed: "Marx's life seems less a political journey and more a descent into the great theme of tragedy."[136] As Terry Eagleton adds: "Tragedy cannot tolerate a utilitarian ethics or an egalitarian politics. As an aristocrat among art-forms, it serves among other things as a memory trace of a more spiritually exalted social order at the heart of a distastefully prosaic epoch. It represents a residue of transcendence in an age of materialism."[137]

Perhaps Marx recalls a line from Goethe's *Prometheus* as he stared beyond the dim room, his gaze reaching back into his past: "Wer half mir wider der Titanen Übermut? Wer rettete vom Tode mich, von Sklaverei?" ("Who helped me against the arrogance of the Titans? Who saved me from death, from slavery?") He may also have thought about a line from St. Paul, which translates to "When I was a child, I spake as a child, I understood as a child, I thought as a child: but when I became a man, I put away childish things."[138] But had he actually put away his former pursuits—here, in his cramped space, surrounded by the debris of his life's work? As he stood on the edge of his journey's end, he bore the weight of the question as to whether that bright-eyed child ever became his father's son. Marx, as he surveyed his manuscript, was a man searching for the words to not only explain history but the dialectic alive within himself, the competing ideals he held with the souls he left behind[139]—his father, whose funeral he had missed;[140] his mother, whom he mistreated after she had cut off funding for his misguided enterprises;[141] Jenny, his beloved wife, who had suffered long and at times unnecessarily by his side; and the children he had lost to illness, perhaps caused by his neglect. Was this all a hell of Marx's own making, alienation not *from* society but *by* his own misspent time, talents, and a vision unfulfilled? As we begin this journey through the life and legacy of Karl Marx, we enter a tale woven from the fabric of ambition, ideology, and ultimately, a tragic misreading of the human condition. Much like Goethe's *Faust*, Marx's revolutionary vision was born out of a desire to reshape the world, to fulfill a promise of salvation that would not only transform the political landscape but the very nature of human existence. Marx's revolution to overthrow capitalism mirrors Faust's yearning for the unattainable. But just as Faust's ambition blinded him to the true cost of his desires so, too, did Marx's blind ambition obscure the destructive consequences of his radical ideology. The lesson that runs through *Faust*—the moral price of blind ambition—is one that Marx, in his passionate pursuit of justice, failed to fully comprehend. Goethe's *Faust* is not merely a tale of intellectual dissatisfaction; it is a cautionary tale of one man's attempt to tear open the very fabric of society without fully appreciating or considering the disastrous consequences. This paradox, where the desire for change becomes the same force that perpetuates suffering, is the tragedy of Marx's legacy.

In his quest for a just society, Marx made his Faustian bargain—a vision that sought to tear down the existing order but never fully account for the deeper human costs of such an upheaval. He famously declared: "The philosophers have only interpreted the world in various ways; the point, however, is to change it."[142] Yet, like Faust, Marx's relentless pursuit of a grand ideological vision blinded him to the spiritual and human toll that his theories would take. His ideas, meant to free the oppressed, would, in their real-world applications, lead to authoritarian regimes, violence, and the very alienation that Marx sought to eliminate. This irony—the clash between idealism and reality, between vision and consequence—is what makes Marx's legacy so deeply tragic.

As we explore Marx's life and work, it is essential to recognize that his revolution was not merely political; it was, in many ways, intellectual and spiritual as well. Marx sought to reshape society and human nature itself. In *The German Ideology* (1846), Marx asserts that "men can be distinguished from animals by consciousness, by religion, or anything else you like. They themselves begin to distinguish themselves from animals as soon as they begin to produce their means of subsistence."[143] But in doing so, he sacrificed a crucial part of the human spirit—the moral and ethical considerations that temper ambition and ground ideals in reality. His story, like that of Hamlet, is a reminder of the dangers of an unchecked desire for knowledge and, ultimately, revenge.[144] Marx's ambition to remake the world, to give the proletariat the tools to reshape their own society, and to settle for being a cog in the machinery was noble in intent and self-serving in purpose. Friedrich Engels, in *The Condition of the Working Class in England*, provides vivid accounts of the dire circumstances faced by workers, including pregnant women. He notes that many factory operatives, due to economic necessity and fear of job loss, continued to work up until the moment of childbirth. This often resulted in women giving birth at the factory or on their way home without medical assistance.[145] Engels writes:

> That factory operatives undergo more difficult confinement than other women is testified to by several midwives and accoucheurs, and also that they are more liable to miscarriage. Moreover, they suffer from the general enfeeblement common to all operatives, and, when pregnant, continue to work in the factory up to the hour of delivery, because otherwise they lose their wages and are made to fear that they may be replaced if they stop away too soon.[146]

With London's newly erected belching smokestacks and the factory floors littered with human bodies, someone needed to propose a remedy. G. K. Chesterton underscores that "Marx's critique of capitalism, while flawed, underscores the moral failures of a system that treats labor as a mere commodity."[147] Marx understood the injustices and felt called to combat them,[148] but in pursuing his mission, he ignored the deeper lesson of the *Divine Comedy* that the road to hell is often paved with good intentions and that a moral vision unchecked by any rooted morality—one that understands human nature and values human dignity—can lead to unimaginable horror.

As we will see, Marx's rebellion was not just against capitalism; it was also against the aristocracy he so envied, society as a whole, and, most importantly, himself.[149] His blindness to this aspect of his character—the aristocratic envy driving his revolutionary zeal—was his tragic flaw. Marx's life and his writings from the *Communist Manifesto* through *Das Kapital* become emblematic of a grander metaphor as Marx attempted to redraft the *Divine Comedy* through a new moral allegory of economic theory.[150] Marx's London flat in our allegorical tale serves as his final resting place confined by contradiction and alienation, and a refusal to face the truth about the natural order and its consequences.[151] For a man who betrayed others but was, in the end, his own greatest betrayer, what kinds of blindness emerge in the fractures of such extreme characters? To understand Marx, we must see him not only as a revolutionary thinker but as a deeply flawed human being, a sinner—one who "misses the mark,"[152] whose ideas and life unfolded within the structure of a tragedy. As author George Steiner of *The Death of Tragedy* remarks: "Because of that fall or 'dis-grace,' in the emphatic and etymological sense, the human condition is tragic. It is ontologically tragic, which is to say in its essence. Fallen man is made an unwelcome guest of life or, at best, a threatened stranger on this hostile or indifferent earth."[153]

The power of the tragic lies not in its political implications but in its ability to illuminate the full scope of human existence—its ambitions, contradictions, and inevitable failures. The reader is invited to journey through Marx's life with this lens, understanding that the true power lies not in power structures but in the eternal struggle to reconcile what we are with what we *ought* to be.[154]

Enter below, and let us embark together now on our journey as cautious witnesses to the divine tragedy of Karl Marx.

BOOK ONE

Academic in Paradise

(1818–1842)

"In the same way as the return of the Messiah, in Christian theology, will put an end to history and establish a new heaven and a new earth, so the establishment of communism would put an end to human history."[155]

—*Karl Marx*

RING 1

The Scholar's Eden

(1818–1835)

"All that exists deserves to perish."[156]

—Goethe, Faust, *Part One*

Karl Marx stood on the cusp of history to survey a world teetering between the crumbling shadow of feudalism and the bright, uncharted horizon of industrial modernity. The air was thick with promise, the potential of a new dawn pressing against the weight of old certainties. In the heights of this "Eden" of possibilities, he glimpsed the fractures of civilization, a world at once poised for renewal and yet suffocating in the vestiges of its past. Here, in his academic years, at the apex of his intellect, Marx felt the pull of a larger fate—much like Dante before him—caught between the height of paradise and the depths of his own questions about the human condition. With the world sprawled out before him, he was about to embark on an intellectual journey through the hellish contradictions of society, each step a descent into the labyrinth of exploitation and alienation. It was in this "dark wood" of his own making, where questions outnumbered answers, that Marx would begin his life's work—not as a mere observer of history but as a prophet[157] for a new world, searching for the truth buried deep beneath the surface of a world in chaos.[158]

In Germany, the cultural Romanticism of Johann Wolfgang von Goethe and Friedrich Schiller began to give way to a more pragmatic philosophy embodied by Hegel's dialectics. European capitals were buzzing with cultural and intellectual ferment. Moses Mendelssohn conducted the rediscovered works of Johann Sebastian Bach, and Frédéric Chopin's piano nocturnes filled the salons of Paris. The many themes of the republic in the French Revolution remained in tension with the Prussian state as, "more than ever," given the enmity created by the Napoleonic Wars, "the French were seen as occupiers, and a German national consciousness became widespread."[159] Karl Marx's life from birth until his entrance into college burst with the promise and intellectual curiosity of youth. He was born into an extraordinary "world spirit"[160] or *Geist*[161]—one brimming with privilege, intellectual vigor, and revolutionary potential. His early life and education were filled with the sparks among the dried leaves of a changing world caused primarily by the Napoleonic Wars: "With that conquest the lessons of the 1789 French Revolution and the Napoleonic Code were enshrined in the region, including equality before the law, individual rights, religious tolerance, the abolition of serfdom, and standardized taxation."[162] Marx's early education was imbued with the Enlightenment ideals of reason and progress, but this paradise of knowledge masked a profound discontent. Young Karl veered toward philosophy, drawn to the soaring ideas of Immanuel Kant[163] and Jean-Jacques Rousseau. His writing revealed flashes of pregnant language and poetic brilliance, echoing the lyrical persuasion of Goethe and Shakespeare.[164] Yet, even in these moments of inspiration, there was a growing sense that Marx's core ideas were assembling fragments of other thinkers to construct something grander. Beneath these declarations lay the first notes of a darker melody—a yearning to tear down the existing order, an unspoken disdain for the very traditions that nurtured his intellect. The July Revolution in France had deposed Charles X (1757–1836), the last reigning Bourbon king of France, who would be replaced by the so-called "Citizen King," Louis-Philippe (1773–1850), symbolizing the aspirations of a rising bourgeoisie. These were the forces that provided the backdrop for Marx's formative years, where literature and politics, fueled by wine and spirited debate, will serve as both a personal pleasure and a symbol of his shifting views on society and capitalism.

Marx, coming from a bourgeois family that owned vineyards, was at times "under the influence" of, as well as influenced by, wine as the culture associated with it affected his early attitudes toward leisure and class. From his early days in Trier to his later intellectual battles in Paris and London, wine was a staple in Marx's world—a marker of refined tastes but also one that led to his penchant for excess. The young idealist in Marx gazes out at this world caught between the collapse of the old order and the rise of a new one, mirroring the existential and moral crisis captured in Dante's *Divine Comedy*. Just as Marx observes the alienation and upheaval of his time, so Dante begins "in the middle of the journey of his life," only to find himself "lost in a dark wood."[165] The descent that follows, shaped in the spirit of Dante's allegory and guided by the poetic tradition of Virgil, mirrors Marx's own role as a modern Virgil[166]—a figure leading others through the dark labyrinth of society's virtues and vices, exploitation, and eventual collapse.[167]

Alien Nation

In 1815, when the Rhineland was reattached to the Prussian Crown, Karl's father, Heinrich Marx, addressed a memorandum to the governor-general respectfully asking that the laws applying exclusively to Jews be annulled.[168] This act of advocacy reflected Heinrich's desire for integration and equality in a society that marginalized Jews. In this estate-based society, most Jews lived under extremely precarious conditions due to the regulations of the guilds, which excluded Jews, who were barred from practicing certain trades. Furthermore, certain prohibitions against land ownership made it difficult, but not impossible, for Jews to make agricultural purchases. Economic survival was an ongoing struggle for many, shaping the worldview of young Karl Marx, whose family navigated these limitations while aspiring to a more equitable future. These restrictive conditions planted the seeds for Marx's later profound critique of inequality and alienation. It is in this milieu with a partial alien status that the young Karl Marx on May 5, 1818, enters our stage through the German town of Trier in a world symbolized by tradition and exclusion.

David McLellan describes Marx's family situation: "Thoroughly Jewish in their origins, Protestant by necessity yet living in a Catholic region, Marx's family could never regard their social integration as complete."[169] Yet Marx was surrounded by a family steeped in rich intellectual traditions and one that, in terms of income, belonged to the upper 6 percent of the total population, owning multiple plots of land among which included Rhineland vineyards. This afforded him the comforts and opportunities not available to most of his peers. The family house, which was approximately twenty feet wide and flush with the sidewalk, had eight rooms and a kitchen on the two main floors and three more small chambers under its mansard roof. There was also an outbuilding with four rooms and a scullery in the rear. It was a solid middle-class house that represented the Trier bourgeois average.

As to his own upbringing, Marx's father, Heinrich, would write to the young Karl: "I received nothing from my parents apart from my existence—although not to be unjust, love from my mother, Eva Lwow."[170] Karl's parents, especially his father, understood very early the promise of their son's considerable talents and intellect. According to his granddaughter Eleanor, there was a picture of her grandfather that her father always carried with him: "The face appeared quite handsome to me, the eyes and forehead were the same as those of the son, but the section around the mouth and chin was more delicate; the whole face was of an expressly Jewish, but beautifully Jewish, type."[171]

Heinrich was "a real eighteenth century 'Frenchman,'" who "knew Voltaire and Rousseau by heart"[172] so he would know his rights and freedoms. Biographer Franz Mehring writes that Heinrich Marx was a "Prussian patriot," adding "though not in the humdrum sense the word has today," but rather in terms of "having an honest belief in the 'Old Fritzian' enlightenment"—a reference to the rationalist and reformist ideals associated with Frederick the Great of Prussia, who championed religious tolerance, legal reform, and Enlightenment governance.[173] Some authors copy the part about the "Prussian patriot" but leave out the specification.[174]

Karl's mother, Henriette Pressburg, who had received a considerable dowry, was a loving and supportive presence. Together with Heinrich, she nurtured a household in which Marx's curiosity and intellect could flourish. Her father, Isaak Pressburg, served as both a *Vorleser* ("reader") and *Gazzan* ("cantor") in the Jewish community of Nijmegen. He was also active as a textile merchant, money changer, and lottery-ticket seller, and is believed to have become quite wealthy. In 1814, he was able to secure exemptions from military service for both of his sons by paying for replacements.[175]

Marx's father was exposed to the best intellectual minds of the time and to Trier's history. With the great migrations across Germany and the decline of Roman power, Trier—then known as Augusta Treverorum[176]—became an obscure township, only to flourish again in the Middle Ages under the rule of prince-archbishops. The city's cathedral, built on the ruins of a Roman palace, claimed to house sacred relics such as one of the nails of the cross, a portion of the crown of thorns, and the holy coat—the seamless garment worn by Christ before the Crucifixion. During the summer, pilgrims traveled to Trier for the ceremonial showing of the holy coat. Although the Reformation swept through much of Germany, Trier remained predominantly Catholic.

Heinrich committed to instilling in his son the importance of intellectual and moral development, ensuring that he received an education that exposed him to Enlightenment ideals: "French Revolutionary and Enlightenment philosophers believed in the inherent goodness of men and held that they would create a better society if they were freed from leaders who kept them ignorant to retain control. In this new order, achievement would be based on merit, not birth—a doctrine with enormous appeal to an emerging business class."[177] The French Revolution, which promised "Liberty, Equality, and Fraternity,"[178] a pivotal moment in history, brought forth a wave of philosophical and political ideas that significantly influenced the time. One of the foremost thinkers was Jean-Jacques Rousseau (1712–1778), whose concept of the "general will"[179] emphasized collective sovereignty and the idea that true freedom is found in the participation of citizens in the formation of the laws that govern them. Rousseau's belief that society corrupts the primitive goodness of man,[180] giving them their chains, resonated with Marx, who viewed class struggle and alienation as products of oppressive societal structures.[181] Another key figure was Maximilien Robespierre (1758–1794), who led the Reign of Terror for a time—only to become one of its final victims. His downfall epitomized the brutal irony captured in the phrase later coined about such movements: "The revolution eats its own."[182] Robespierre asserted that the revolution must defend itself against its enemies, encapsulating the tension between revolutionary ideals and the harsh realities of governance. Robespierre's radical interpretation of democracy and his commitment to social justice influenced Marx's understanding of the need for a dictatorship of the proletariat,[183] which would serve to dismantle oppressive systems and ensure that liberty and equality were extended to all members of society.

Marx's studies also included the writings of Henri de Saint-Simon (1760–1825) and Charles Fourier (1772–1837),[184] who introduced socialist ideas based on the Bible,[185] deeply impacting Marx's thought. In the book of Acts, we read that "all who believed were together and had all things in common; they would sell their possessions and goods and distribute the proceeds to all, as any had need,"[186] a vivid depiction of the early Christian community that resonates profoundly with the later ideals of socialism and communism. Acts goes on:

> Now the whole group of those who believed were of one heart and soul, and no one claimed private ownership of any possessions, but everything they owned was held in common. With great power, the apostles gave their testimony to the resurrection of the Lord Jesus, and great grace was upon them all. There was not a needy person among them, for as many as owned lands or houses sold them and brought the proceeds of what was sold. They laid it at the apostles' feet, and it was distributed to each as any had need.[187]

Like the early Christians, Fourier's vision of phalansteries and Saint-Simon's planned economy rested on the belief that communal living and shared resources were not only just but also essential for human flourishing. Yet, while the motivations differ—rooted in divine revelation for the early Christians and secular rationalism for the socialists—the parallels are striking. Both movements challenged the legitimacy of wealth concentration, insisting that the true measure of a society lies in how it cares for its most vulnerable. For Fourier and Saint-Simon, as later for Marx, the Acts passages served as a potent reminder that alternative ways of organizing economic life were not only possible but had been practiced, albeit within a religious framework.[188]

The tension, however, lies in the divergence of spiritual and material motivations. While the Christian community's vision sprang from their faith in the Resurrection and their eschatological hope for the kingdom of God, Fourier and Saint-Simon[189] sought to ground their ideals in human progress and reason. What the early Christians saw as a divine mandate, Fourier and Saint-Simon interpreted as the inevitable next step in human history. Marx would later strip these ideas of their spiritual core entirely to reframe communal ownership not as a moral choice but as a necessity driven by historical materialism. Still, the echoes of Acts reverberate. The vision of a society where "there was not a needy person among them" challenged the selfish individualism of modern industrialization and serves as a reminder of humanity's capacity for shared purpose. Whether seen through the lens of faith or politics, these early practices reveal an enduring truth: the ideals of justice and equality are not bound to one era or ideology but arise whenever human beings seek to transcend their baser instincts. Yet history shows that such ideals flourish only under voluntary, often religious conditions—within small, purpose-driven communities. When transplanted into large secular systems, they often collapse under the weight of human nature or require coercion to survive.

Marx's father, Heinrich, was a respected lawyer, and "for many years *bâtonnier* of the *barreau* there; that is to say, the president of the bar in Trier."[190] Heinrich Marx believed in God but adhered to an enlightened Deism. He recommended to Marx a "pure faith in God," which "Newton, Locke, and Leibniz"[191] had believed in.[192] Heinrich Marx's enlightened Deism, rooted in rationalism and the philosophical ideals of the above-named thinkers, set the tone for a pragmatic approach to faith in the Marx household. This perspective underscores an emphasis on reason and universal principles over dogmatic allegiance, fostering a worldview in which all faiths were equally respected—and equally questioned. His Jewish heritage, steeped in centuries of faith and resilience, clashed with the pressures of assimilation and modernity. Baptized into the Lutheran Church by his father, Heinrich, Marx spent his formative years marked by a dual estrangement—from his spiritual heritage and from the society that rejected it.

Edgar von Westphalen described Heinrich as "a Protestant à la Lessing,"[193] which meant that he was prepared to conform to the outward forms of the Church but did not believe that any faith was superior to any other, that in his view Stoicism, Judaism, Christianity, and Hinduism were all equally valid and equally vulnerable. Given his family and cultural milieu, it comes as no surprise that Marx's relationship with faith was fraught with tension. The decision to convert to Lutheranism, driven by necessity rather than faith, left a young Marx alienated from both his Jewish roots and his familial ties. That emerges clearly in a letter from Heinrich sent in November of 1835 to his son, who was studying at the University in Bonn at the time: "I have always been a faithful member of the Church, and I do not think you can be a true man without it. You, on the other hand, have been led astray, and it seems to me that you are pursuing an unworthy course. I have done everything for you, and yet you reject the religion in which I have placed my faith. I do not know how this will end, but I fear it will not be for the better."[194]

Union with Christ

Heinrich's conversion from the faith of his ancestors to a more socially acceptable religion set a precedent in the young man's mind—one that would evolve into his wholesale rejection of religious belief altogether. There is no reason to think that he suffered any qualms of conscience when he became a Protestant. "Like the poet Heine, who spoke of baptism as 'an entrance ticket to European culture,'"[195] Heinrich appears to have regarded his apostasy as a relief from the burdens of the rabbinical tradition that dominated his youth: "His outlook on life is well summed up in the advice he had given to Karl: 'A good support for morality is a simple faith in God. You know that I am the last person to be a fanatic. But sooner or later a man has a real need of this faith, and there are moments in life when even the man who denies God is compelled against his will to pray to the Almighty.'"[196]

Heinrich was, perhaps unknowingly, echoing the thoughts of Thomas Aquinas, the architect for Dante's *Divine Comedy*,[197] when he warned his son Karl about the consequences of turning away from

God: "To be deprived of the vision of God is a punishment exceeding all pains of hell."[198] Although Marx's father had a complex relationship with religion, he took his religious duties seriously, ensuring that all his children went through the proper stages of Christian education and received the appropriate sacraments. This included confirmation, and on March 23, 1834, Karl Marx, at fifteen, was confirmed and received the gift of the Holy Ghost.[199]

This marked an outward adherence to Christian tradition, but it also hints at the tensions that would later define his relationship with religion and identity. For him, this ritual may have been a symbolic gesture, concealing his deep alienation from both religious dogma and his Jewish heritage. As he matured, his alienation expanded beyond personal faith to a broader critique of society, fueling his growing discontent with existing structures of power and tradition. This transformation was not only intellectual but also deeply personal. This duality—outward compliance with religious norms and inner skepticism—planted the seeds of Marx's eventual rejection of organized religion. This delicate balance between societal expectation and personal conviction extended into his closest relationships to shape the way he navigated his ideology, his personal allegiances, and his developing *Weltanschauung*.

Mary Gabriel writes that "in 1832 Marx at fourteen attended the state-run Friedrich Wilhelm Gymnasium along with the Baron Ludwig Westphalen's youngest son, Edgar, whose family were neighbors. Though Karl had shown an aptitude for Greek, Latin, and German,[200] he was weak in math and history, and did not stand out particularly among his classmates. He had a lisp, which he struggled to overcome and which may have made him shy."[201]

We know from the earliest reports that during his years at the Trier Gymnasium, Marx developed a reputation for his keen intellect and sharp tongue. His early writings, including satirical poems and lampoons, displayed a biting wit that impressed some and unsettled others, earning him respect but little affection among his peers.

According to his neighbor and biographer John Spargo, he enjoyed playing with the girls: "They were older than we boys and wanted everything to go their way, and I liked not that girls should boss boys. So once I teased him about it—told him that he was a baby to play with girls. Then it was that we fought and he gave me a black eye and I gave him a bloody nose in return."[202] Hugo Wyttenbach, school headmaster and a friend of the Marx family, was a key influence. A staunch liberal, he found himself under police scrutiny after the 1832 Hambach demonstration for press freedom. Authorities feared he was spreading subversive ideas, and this led to a school raid where banned speeches and anti-Prussian poetry were discovered. Though Wyttenbach kept his position, a Prussian informant, Vitus Loers, was installed as his assistant. Closely tied to the Rhineland liberal movement, Wyttenbach had co-founded the Trier Casino Club—a literary society tolerated but heavily surveilled by the state. His defiance made a lasting impression on young Karl, who learned early the cost of challenging authority: "Marx's education at a leading liberal university sharpened his intellect and curiosity, yet also exposed him early on to an institutional tension: the clash between academic freedom and authoritarian oversight—a conflict that mirrored the broader ideological struggles of his era. It was also a time to further focus on his stature and ambition. Marx's classmates at the Trier Gymnasium respected his intellect but were wary of his sharp satirical verses, which revealed an early flair for ridicule and critique.[203] Karl Marx's education at Bonn and Berlin sharpened his intellectual curiosity, placing him at the intersection of law, philosophy, and radical critique. In a letter dated November 10, 1837—sent from Berlin to his father—Marx reflects on a pivotal turning point: "There are moments in one's life which are like frontier posts . . . marking the completion of a period but at the same time clearly indicating a new direction."[204]

When it came time to writing his Latin essay on the topic of whether the reign of the first Roman emperor, Caesar Augustus, was a "happy period" for the new empire and erstwhile republic, he concluded that it was.[205] Marx's remarks from his arbiter were varied but telling: "Verum quam turpis litera!!!" ("What shameful handwriting!!!").[206] And as far as philosophy and religion were concerned, "his knowledge of the Christian faith and morals is fairly clear and well grounded; he knows also to some extent the history of the Christian Church."[207] In 1835, Marx wrote his youthful essay "Union of the Faithful with Christ" as part of his graduation requirement, which was in many ways quite profound: "Thus the history of nations teaches us the necessity of the Union with Christ. To be sure, even when we study the history of the individual and the nature of man, we always see a divine spark in his breast, an enthusiasm for the Good, a striving for perception, a longing for truth—but the sparks of the eternal are smothered by the flame of lust."

Marx's passage highlights humanity's pursuit of goodness, truth, and understanding, yet acknowledges how these aspirations are corrupted by sin and worldly distractions, rendering individuals incapable of fulfillment without Christ. Whether this reflects genuine spiritual insight or a skilled academic exercise, it foreshadows the key themes, ambitions, and contradictions that would shape his life. His early engagement with theological ideas, despite his later radical departure from them, reveals a tension between spiritual contemplation and revolutionary zeal, offering insight into the complexities of his intellectual and ideological evolution:

> The enthusiasm for virtue is stifled by the tempting voice of sin, which is made ridiculous when the full power of life is felt. The striving for perception is replaced by the inferior striving for worldly goods; the longing for truth is extinguished by the sweet-smiling power of the lie; and so man stands, the only creature that does not fulfill its goal, the only member in all Creation not worthy of the God that created him. But the benevolent Creator does not hate his handiwork; he wanted to elevate it to his own level, and He sent us his Son, through whom He calls

to us: "Now ye are clean through the word which I have spoken unto you. Abide in me, and I in you [John 15:3–4]."[208]

The essay explores union with Christ as a reconciliation of opposites—ego and altruism, reason and revelation, virtue and sin, individual and collective, mind and senses, and the father-son bond—all unified through the vine and branches metaphor in Paul's Roman epistle[209] and through Christ's teachings in the Gospel of John ("I am the true vine, and my Father is the husbandman" [Jn 15:1]; "I am the vine, ye are the branches" [Jn 15:5]). Paul's image of grafting addresses alienation and reconciliation—key themes in Marx's later writings. The wild olive shoot (Gentiles) is alienated from the cultivated olive tree (Israel), but through divine intervention, it is brought into the same root, sharing in its nourishment and vitality. This mirrors the structure of Marx's essay, where he describes humanity's alienation from God and its ultimate reconciliation through union with Christ.

Marx's analysis of the union with Christ is remarkable for its theological depth and rhetorical power. He writes: "Before we consider the Reason and Essence and the effects of the Union of Christ with the faithful, let us see whether this Union is necessary, whether it is determined by the nature of man, whether or not it may in itself achieve the goal for which God has created him out of the Void."

From the outset, Marx frames the question of divine union as a universal and existential necessity, drawing not only from scriptural authority but also from human history and the nature of man. He observes that even the most advanced cultures, the "greatest men," and the "most splendid arts" fail to shake off the chains of superstition and egoism without the redemptive guidance of Christ. He laments: "Even their virtues were more the product of a rough kind of greatness, of unrestrained egoism, of a passion for fame and bold deeds, than a striving for true perfection."

The essay demonstrates an extraordinary grasp of philosophical and theological concepts for someone so young. Marx contrasts the "divine spark" within humanity—a yearning for truth and virtue—with the corrupting forces of sin and worldly ambition. "The sparks of the eternal," he writes, "are smothered by the flame of lust . . . the longing for truth is extinguished by the sweet-smiling power of the lie." His vivid language captures the internal struggle of humanity, which stands as "the only member in all Creation not worthy of the God that created him." The metaphor of the vine and branches illustrates the necessity of this divine union. Drawing directly from John 15:5–6, Marx writes: "The branch cannot bear fruit of itself, and likewise, says Christ, you can do nothing without Him." This analogy, both poetic and profound, becomes the central image through which Marx explores the interconnectedness of humanity and the divine. "If the branch were sentient," Marx imagines, "how joyously would it look to the gardener who tends it, who anxiously clears it of weeds and ties it to the vine from which it derives nourishment and sap for its beautiful blossoms?" He paints a vision of humanity's dependence on Christ not only for salvation but also for its ultimate fulfillment and flourishing. Reading this work today, one cannot help but marvel at the intellectual capacity and spiritual imagination of a seventeen-year-old Marx.

In an era where such depth of thought would be considered exceptional even among most adults, Marx displayed a precocity that hinted at his future intellectual achievements. If one were to end the tale here, they might be tempted to see Marx as a young man embarking on a deeply personal Christian journey, on which he would navigate the flaws and perils of faith with the sincerity of an educated believer. The theological musings of young Marx stand in stark contrast to the ideological trajectory he would soon pursue. The themes of alienation and reconciliation, so beautifully woven into this essay, would reappear in his mature works, but in a radically different context—stripped of their spiritual foundation and reinterpreted through the lens of materialism. The union he envisioned here, grounded in divine love and mutual dependence, would be transformed into a call for class struggle and revolution. As we glimpse into the mind of a young Marx, we see him standing at the crossroads of faith and reason, unaware of the path he would soon walk down.

Why does a young man who articulates such a profound understanding of divine union ultimately turn away from it? What internal struggles, external influences, or intellectual developments led Marx to completely reject the faith he so eloquently analyzed? The answers to these questions are as complex as the man himself and form the foundation of his tragic journey—a journey that mirrors the vine cut from its branches, withering apart from the source of its vitality, now alienated. It is obvious that from an early age, Marx's command of language and thought forecast a series of themes, ambitions, and personal struggles that would define his journey and spark his performance on the world stage—but not without his Beatrice, Jenny von Westphalen.[210]

The Road to Revolution

In the year 1835, Karl Marx left the comforting confines of Trier to embark on a journey that would see him both physically and ideologically alienated from the familiar world of his upbringing. This departure marked his entry into the intellectual and social maelstrom that would shape his revolutionary ideas and eventually fracture the very foundations of his identity. At the University of Bonn, Marx entered alongside his father's hopes for him to practice law—a secure and prestigious profession. But the seventeen-year-old found himself drawn to a vastly different life, one steeped in intellectual rebellion, indulgent socializing, and spirited drinking. His time there marked the beginning of a shift away from the sheltered world of Trier, plunging him into youthful excess and ideological exploration—a stark departure from his early years. Yet, this departure was more than just the beginning of a physical journey—it was a severance from the only world Marx had ever known.

In leaving, Marx was stepping away from not only his father's hopes and the confines of his upbringing but also those he loved and admired. Among those left behind was Jenny von Westphalen, his childhood sweetheart and intellectual confidante. Jenny, with her profound intellect and unwavering commitment to the ideals of justice, had been his anchor, both emotionally and intellectually. Their relationship, built on mutual admiration and shared ideals, was a symbol of Marx's connection to his own moral compass—a moral center that would be tested in the chaos of the years to come. In this moment of departure, Marx was not just leaving Trier, but also the world of security and familiarity that Jenny, with her quiet strength, represented. She was not merely a lover; she was a reflection of the world Marx had known, a world of bourgeois respectability and intellectual promise. Jenny's absence would echo through his life, a constant reminder of the contradictions between his personal desires and his revolutionary destiny. As Marx ventured into the unknown, this break with Jenny and the world of his upbringing became symbolic of his rejection of the established order—a rejection that would soon deepen into a full ideological fracture. He was now, in many ways, alone, cast into the swirling currents of an era in which the old world was rapidly giving way to the new, and the path ahead, though filled with promise, was fraught with uncertainty.[211]

Marx's first year at university involved alcohol.[212] "The seventeen-year-old who left Trier declaring himself ready to sacrifice all for the good of mankind rented the most expensive student apartment available, joined the university's Poetry Club, and became president of the bourgeois Tavern Club."[213] Rehearsing for his role as the New Moses,[214] he grew a wispy beard, wore his black curly hair long and disheveled, and on one occasion was imprisoned overnight for drunken rowdiness. Biographer and scholar Michael Heinrich comments on Marx's appearance at some length:

> No one, perhaps with the exception of his [future] wife Jenny, ever accused young Marx of being handsome. One Marx

> biographer quoted a resident of Trier as saying Karl was "nearly the most unattractive man on whom the sun ever shone." He was compact as a boxer, coarse-featured, unshaven, and unkempt. He wore a dark frock coat of relatively good quality but often failed to button it correctly. His black beard had grown past the point of respectability and in the social code of mid-nineteenth-century Prussia it announced its bearer as an extreme radical, as did the cigars he smoked—in public. (Gentlemen smoked pipes in the privacy of their homes.)[215]

Marx was threatened with arrest for carrying a pistol and allegedly fought saber duels[216] against members of a rival aristocratic club. He also "spent freely amid his champagne-quaffing fellow students. The few letters he sent home were generally appeals for money as he sank deeper and deeper into debt."[217] These youthful excesses were more than mere indulgences; they were symptomatic of a deeper discontent brewing within Marx that foreshadowed the ideological battles that he would wage against the ruling classes. Even in these formative years, Marx was drawn to oppose authority, privilege, and the structures that upheld them. His father's admonitions reveal an emerging pattern: Marx's defiant spirit, sharpened in beer halls and fencing halls alike, would soon find its true battleground in the realm of philosophy and politics, while, at the same time, his growing debts and extravagant habits reflected the contradictions that would mark his life. He positioned himself as a champion of the working class, yet he relied on family wealth and borrowed funds to sustain his lifestyle. This tension—between the revolutionary theorist and the dependent son—would follow him well into adulthood to mirror the economic struggles that he would later diagnose in capitalism itself.

As Marx transitioned from rowdy student to radical thinker, his instinct for rebellion would soon be channeled into something far more potent than tavern quarrels: a taste for a revolutionary critique of the entire social order. Marx also brought with him to Bonn his family's taste for wine into a more rebellious context and a new cause.

These early tavern days hinted at Marx's underlying tension with Prussian rule and his awareness of social divisions, as his clashes often involved aristocratic students loyal to the government.

While at Bonn, Marx's youthful indulgence became notorious. He spent many nights drinking heavily in local taverns, engaging in brawls with other students[218]—a behavior that both alarmed his father and symbolized the tensions between discontented bourgeois students and Prussian loyalists. In 1836, according to Marx's record of studies issued by the university, "he was sentenced to one day's imprisonment for drunkenness and causing a disturbance at night; in moral and economic connections, nothing else discreditable to him is known."[219] As the old political and legal systems were swept away in the wake of Napoleon's reorganization of Europe, the political powers of the monarchy and the aristocracy, on which the churches had often relied, were drastically reduced. Commercial and industrial elites gradually replaced the aristocracy as political and cultural leaders. While the roots of capitalism, competition, and profit-seeking long predate the Industrial Revolution, the rise of industrial capitalism marked a dramatic shift in scale and social impact. Mass production and expanding markets disrupted traditional ways of life, including the small-scale economies often tied to local religious and moral frameworks. For Marx and other critics, this shift seemed to erode belief in the transcendent, and Christian theology—once central to Western moral life—appeared increasingly irrelevant in a world driven by mechanized labor and material gain.[220]

And yet his biting critiques must have not been so threatening given that "most students had grown up in households with service staff (in the household of Karl's parents, there had been only two maids), and many had become accustomed to behaving in a 'lordly' way. Frequently, a certain academic arrogance was added to this: one felt far superior to the 'philistines,' that is, to normal citizens, artisans, and merchants, not to speak of the common people, the 'rabble.'"[221]

The level of entitlement was evident when we learn that Marx's mother Henriette once demanded "that Karl not only make sure that his room is scrubbed weekly (by the landlords, apparently), but that he should also 'have a weekly scrub with sponge and soap'"[222]—a needed admonition that would play out in Marx's life. Spargo commented that "everybody thought that he would soon become a great man." Spargo's father was puzzled when:

> Heinrich Marx came in one day and spoke very sadly that Karl had wasted all his time at Bonn and learned nothing, other than getting into a bad scrape and spending a lot of money: "My Karl—the child in whom all my hopes were centered—the brightest boy in Treves[223] is a failure." He said that, instead of studying hard to be a Doctor of Laws, as he ought to do, Karl was wasting his time. "He writes such foolish letters that I am ashamed of him," said the old man. For Heinrich, his son, "wastes his time writing silly verses and romances and then destroying most of them; talks about becoming a second Goethe, and says he will write the great Prussian drama that will revive dramatic art."[224]

Karl in return would write to Heinrich: "The inn meals [were] not more extravagant, more indigestible, than the store of fantasies I carried with me, and, finally, no work of art was as beautiful as Jenny."[225] Marx wrote love poems to Jenny, and they "settled into their long-distance romance tormenting each other in letters by describing their insecurities and jealousies, and melodramatic accounts of ill health designed to stir the lover's sympathy." Their correspondence "overflowed with the ratcheted-up anxiety of unconsummated passion, and in the style of great tragedians, they seemed to relish each new injury."[226]

Karl's early intellectual influences, like Heinrich's, included French Enlightenment thinkers such as Voltaire and Rousseau, who shaped his views on society, religion, and human nature. Voltaire

(1694–1789), the *nom de plume* for François-Marie Arouet, criticized the Church and Christian dogma while maintaining a belief in a supreme being whose moral laws should guide human behavior, ensuring a tolerable coexistence. Voltaire's famous satire *Candide* (1759) critiques blind optimism, organized religion, and societal norms, providing an intellectual foundation for Marx's later exploration of morality and authority. In one pointed passage, Candide asks: "Do you believe . . . that men have always massacred each other as they do today . . . liars, cheats . . . hypocrites, and fools?" On the surface, this recalls the biblical Fall of Man, but Voltaire reframes it as a permanent feature of human society—not a theological condition but a social and historical one. Marx would absorb this critique, stripping it of its metaphysical frame and recasting human corruption as the product of material inequality and class exploitation.[227] Rousseau (1712–1778), on the other hand, emphasized the inherent goodness of man and the corrupting influence of society: "Man is born free; and everywhere he is in chains."[228] His works, such as *The Social Contract*, advanced the idea that legitimate political authority arises from the general will of the people. Rousseau's critique of inequality and his vision of a society based on collective sovereignty resonated with Marx's later focus on class struggle and the need for revolutionary change.[229]

Together, the works of Voltaire and Rousseau offered a blend of Enlightenment rationalism and revolutionary idealism that Marx would integrate and transform within his materialist critique of society. While Rousseau's moral influence was toward tenderness, sentiment, and the restoration of family life and marital fidelity, the moral influence of Voltaire was toward humanity and justice, toward the cleansing of French law and custom from legal abuses and barbaric cruelties; he, more than any other individual, spurred on the humanitarian movement that became one of the credits of the nineteenth century. Voltaire shared in begetting the French Revolution by weakening the respect of the intellectual classes for the Church and the belief of the aristocracy in its feudal rights. But after 1789, Voltaire's political influence was overwhelmed by Rousseau's. Voltaire seemed too conservative, too scornful of the masses, too much of the seigneur. Robespierre rejected him, and for two years the *Social Contract* was the Bible of the French Revolution.[230]

Bonaparte felt the two influences in reverse order: "Until I was sixteen," he recalled, "I would have fought for Rousseau against the friends of Voltaire; today it is the opposite. The more I read Voltaire, the more I love him. He is a man always reasonable, never a charlatan, never a fanatic."[231] After the restoration of the Bourbons, the writings of Voltaire became an instrument of bourgeois thought against the revived nobility and clergy. Between 1817 and 1829, there were twelve editions of Voltaire's collected works, and in those twelve years, over three million volumes by Voltaire were sold. Historian William Durant comments that post–*Communist Manifesto* (1848) all revolutionary movements "have followed Rousseau rather than Voltaire in politics, Voltaire rather than Rousseau in religion."[232]

Amid the study of foreign revolution and coming new ages, a poet was emerging in the young Marx, but his stay in Bonn would soon come to an end. Marx's father had enough of his "wild rampaging," as he called it, and only one year later decided that Karl with his "solipsistic self-absorption"[53] should transfer to the more serious "University of Berlin,"[54] for he complains: "He spends more money than the sons of the very rich, and I fear that he has got into bad company and formed evil habits."[55]

As for Jenny, Marx's father—aware of their uncertain future—believed it wise to separate the young lovers for the time being. He chose the University of Berlin, "his Prussian patriotism having perhaps influenced his choice of Berlin in addition to the fact that the new university did not foster the 'glorious college days' tradition that, for his prudent parent, Karl had supported quite enough at Bonn." Other "universities are positively Bacchanalian compared with this workhouse" in Berlin.[233] Soon, Karl transferred and traveled alone by carriage or train to mark a significant step in his academic career.[234] In Berlin, Marx would study in the shadow of towering figures of German idealism such as Kant, Fichte, and Hegel, in an environment ripe with embers still burning from the Revolutionary Wars and French Enlightenment. As we will see, his journey from carefree student drinking to advocating for small-scale vintners echoes a deeper ideological transformation.

RING 2

The Ring of Alienation (1832–1844)

"A being only considers himself independent when he stands on his own feet, and he only stands on his own feet when he owes his existence to himself."[235]

—*Karl Marx*

As Marx entered Berlin, the city was alive with the intellectual fire of the times. Though Hegel had died in 1831, his presence still loomed over the academic world like a philosophical god, a towering figure whose ideas shaped every corner of the city's thought. Berlin was a place where the spirit of Hegel's philosophy—his dialectical method—reigned supreme. Hegel's legacy was one of intellectual gravity, casting a long shadow over all who studied philosophy. The dialectic, a process of thesis, antithesis, and synthesis,[236] was how the world's progress unfolded[237] and should be understood and interpreted.[238] It was a method that transformed every subject it touched into a dynamic, ever-evolving narrative of contradictions and resolutions. Marx, coming into this intellectual crucible, was drawn into the orbit of Hegel's ideas, even as he began to push back against them. In this tension, Marx would begin to build his own system, one that was not merely academic but deeply rooted in the struggle for social change and the material forces that shaped human history.

As Marx would later observe, Hegel and Feuerbach each sought, in their own way, to translate the ethical and spiritual vision of Christianity into secular, philosophical terms—stripping away its divine framework while preserving its humanistic aims. Their work paved the way for Marx to reframe Christian moral structures within a materialist worldview. However, this intellectual excitement carried with it the seeds of discontent. Even as Marx's mind absorbed the grand dialectics of Hegel, still echoing its roots in Christian theology, there was an undercurrent of alienation and a growing realization that the traditional academic world could not offer the answers he sought. Marx, deeply dissatisfied with the abstract and idealistic nature of the philosophical debates surrounding him, would soon turn his focus toward a more practical critique of society. It was in this ferment of thought—between Hegel's dialectical method and Feuerbach's materialism—that Marx and Engels began constructing a system meant to replace classical understandings of alienation. In earlier theology and philosophy, alienation had been seen as a spiritual or existential rupture—the Fall being the seminal biblical story of humankind's break with its origins, a separation from one's full being and the source of being itself. For Marx, however, alienation was not primarily metaphysical but material. It was the estrangement of human beings from the products of their labor, from their creative essence, and from one another, caused by the structures of capitalist production.[239] As Marx famously wrote: "Religion was therefore a form of alienation which prevented people from realizing their true nature, or 'species being,' as Feuerbach called it."

At this early stage, Marx was still developing his materialist philosophy, with the seeds of his critique of capitalism and class struggle being planted. Yet, unwittingly, as we shall see, he was not replacing the divine narrative behind history but rather reframing it—offering a new narrative that would cast the dark powers and principalities as the driving forces within the mechanisms of the capitalist system, a system that ground humanity under its relentless, human-made forces.[240] This was not merely a scientific project but one that was, in many ways, deeply poetic, if not prophetic.

Marx would immerse himself in the world of poetry, as the illusions of youthful idealism began to wane. The grand visions that once seemed within reach would soon be confronted by personal hardships and disillusionment that would reshape his path. At the same time, instead of the budding philosopher, he would become the budding poet. By "the end of the [first] term, according to his Father Heinrich, he was devoted to the 'Dance of the Muses and Music of the Satyrs,'—the domain of real poetry opened up before his eyes like a far-off fairy palace and all his own creations fell to nothing."[241] But beneath the surface of his poetic fervor, the foundations of his world were already beginning to crack. The pursuit of poetry, once a source of boundless inspiration, would also face the harsh realities of personal loss to force him to reckon with a world far more unforgiving than the idealized visions of his early musings. Before long, what was familiar and expected, the security of family, the comforts of home, and, to some degree, the romantic ideals of his youth would slip from his grasp and lead him to follow a path that would ultimately define his life and legacy.

The Peculiar Demon

This period marks a shift in Marx's creative expression. No longer merely a student grappling with philosophy, he immersed himself in dark, Gothic themes, experimenting with poetry, drama, and even a novel. His poem "Scorpion and Felix," written in a haze of intoxicated whimsy, bore the imprint of Laurence Sterne's *Tristram Shandy*, blending satire with absurdity. Yet beneath its playful surface, his early writings revealed a fascination with chaos, destruction, and rebellion—themes that would later find a more serious form in his revolutionary ideology. This phase of Marx's life—a mixture of rebellious whimsy and earnest philosophical exploration—marks the transition from the idealistic musings of his youth to the more radical and intellectual awakening that defined his years at Berlin. His poetry and dramatic works from his youth often included demonic imagery, themes of defying God, and existential despair. He was deeply influenced by Romantic literature, which frequently dealt with horror, the supernatural, and rebellion against divine authority.[242]

Beginning in 1836, he engaged with dark, rebellious themes, even casting himself as a Faustian figure when he maniacally conjures "the powers of darkness." He started writing about the "prince of darkness"[243] beating time, an eerie foreshadowing of the intellectual and spiritual alienation that would mark his five years in Berlin and show his distance from his youthful Christian writings. Author of *The Devil and Karl Marx*, Paul Kengor records: Marx's radical critique of religion extended beyond mere atheism; his writings often evoked themes of darkness and destruction that some, like Kengor, interpret as reflective of a deeper rebellion against divine order.[244] He traces Marx's philosophical and personal journey as one that became increasingly aligned with nihilistic and destructive forces. Kengor points out that Marx's favorite line from *Faust*—"Everything that exists deserves to perish"—reflects a deep-rooted desire to tear down not just the political and economic structures of the time but the spiritual foundations of society itself. This interpretation adds a disturbing layer to Marx's revolutionary ideas, suggesting that his desire for destruction was not merely theoretical but deeply personal.

Was Marx privately entangled with his own existential suffering, or with some kind of possession? Heinrich Marx poignantly reminded his son of the importance of personal joy and familial harmony, cautioning that "you may never know the simple happiness and family joys, nor bring happiness to those around you."[245] Marx's early works reflect this inner turmoil, as he conceived of existence as inherently painful, to the point where nonexistence seemed preferable to suffering. Marx's poem "The Fiddler"[246] concerns a man who carries a fiddle and saber, who plays so that "the soul's cry" is carried "down to

Hell." He states that "with Satan [he] [had] struck [his] deal" and is now bound to him:

> He chalks the signs, beats time for me,
> I play the death march fast and free.

Here, he makes a Faustian bargain with the devil—the fiddler must play "till bowstrings break my heart outright."[247] Marx writes: "The sword—the prince of darkness sold it to me,"[248] imagery reflecting a Faustian bargain, where he sees himself as an instrument of darkness who is willing to wield destructive power to achieve his ends. Though not a Romantic by creed, Marx was undeniably a child of the Romantic age, haunted by its dreams and consumed by its obsessions—satanic seduction, the allure of curses, rebellion against divine order, and the ruin of the world. These were not mere metaphors for Marx; they were the contours of his inner landscape—visions and nightmares that drove him deeper into darkness in pursuit of his revolutionary ends.

Throughout his writings and letters, Marx often identified with Aeschylus, Prometheus, Faust, and Satan, those who symbolized defiance and the rejection of any authority. Terry Eagleton discusses the appeal of the tragic hero and thinker Walter Benjamin's view thereof:

> Walter Benjamin has a typically idiosyncratic view of the transitional nature of tragedy. The tragic hero, he argues in *The Origin of German Tragic Drama*, finds himself suspended between the old regime of myth and the gods and the birth of a new community, one which his sacrificial death will help to usher in. Belonging fully to neither order, and eventually crushed to death between them, he is caught between the language of ancient law and superstition and the as yet inexpressible discourse of the ethico-political future. As a sacrificial victim, the tragic hero is a remnant of the ancient régime, but he also represents a principle which is capable of bringing it low, and as such foreshadows an emancipated future.[249]

Some scholars have pointed to these references as evidence of Marx's attraction to dark, rebellious figures, while others argue that these were symbolic critiques of the oppressive systems he opposed. For example, in *Oulanem*,[250] an early dramatic work, Marx writes: "I wish to avenge myself against the One who rules above."[251] We can investigate the literary life of Marx with two plays that Karl wrote as a student: They were well named, for there is no attempt to disguise the raw savagery and the yearning for catastrophic destruction in the poet's mind. A crazed musician in the style of the virtuoso Paganini (1782–1840) and his reputation as possessed by the devil summons up the Prince of Darkness, a lover offers a poison cup to the beloved, and both run headlong to their deaths in a satanic rejection of the world.[252] Marx, in the same vein, succeeds in conveying an authentic frisson, the terror at the heart of terror. He is not playing games.[253]

As for "The Player,"[254] this unnerving poem describes a violinist who, in a delirious frenzy, summons up the powers of darkness with his furious strings. In this ballad, the performer, who seems to be Marx himself, plays so frenetically that there can be only one outcome: he destroys himself. When an onlooker asks the violinist why he must perform this way—it is believed that the onlooker was Jenny—a perturbed Marx answers that he cannot help himself and that he will stab her with his "blood-dark sword" before his violin and his heart burst:

> O player, why playest thou so wild?
> Why the savage look in thine eyes?
> Why the leaping blood, the soaring waves?
> Why tearest thou thy bow to shreds?[255]

Marx answers for himself in the next phase, and the player misuses this elegant art, the graceful sound of the violin. He uses it not to elevate the passion or romantic intensity as would Wagner, Verdi, or Beethoven[256] elevating to the heavens so passionate a love or longing that reaches for the divine, but for something quite the opposite—there's no final chorus and no *Ode to Joy.*[257] He denies God's knowledge. He thinks not of bowing a final heavenly chord but thrusting a blood-dark sword through the hellish vapors that fill his brain:

> Look now, my blood-dark sword shall stab
> Unerringly within thy soul.
> God neither knows nor honors art.
> The hellish vapors rise and fill the brain.

"It is an ominous and deeply disturbing poem," concedes Payne, "for a man does not write such things unless he is on the verge of madness or despair."[258] In his poem "Invocation of One in Despair," Marx plots his wrath:

> So a god has snatched from me my all
> In the curse and rack of Destiny.
> All his worlds are gone beyond recall!
> Nothing but revenge is left to me![259]

By contrast, some of Marx's poetry reflects the suffering for the object of desire, such as Dante's Beatrice, Goethe's Gretchen, or in this case, Jenny: collections captioned with "Book of Love" and "Book of Songs," they are devoted to Karl's love for her. He draws strength from this relationship but at the same time fears losing her. In the first poem, "Die zwei Himmel" (or "The Two Skies/Heavens"), he writes at the end: "If you break the bond, I will plummet / the flood envelops me, the grave swallows me / both heavens have been submerged / and the bleeding soul has withered away."[260] Strangely, back on March 2, 1837, Heinrich wrote of a shadow hanging over Jenny:

> I notice a conspicuous countenance in Jenny. She, who gives herself so completely to you with her childlike, pure disposition, reveals at times, involuntarily and against her own will, a kind of fear, a foreboding fear, which does not escape me and which I do not know how to explain, and which she has tried to

> destroy every trace in my heart as soon as I pointed it out to her. What is it, what can it be? I cannot explain it to myself, but fortunately my experience does not allow me to be easily misled.[261]

While Marx is later celebrated for his incendiary rhetoric and revolutionary ideas, these poems seem to indicate more than passion: they indicate an obsession with the forces of self-destruction or self-condemnation:

> Thus heaven I've forfeited,
> I know it full well.
> My soul, once true to God,
> Is chosen for hell.[262]

Eventually, Marx would put down his poet's quill and give up his vision. In his own words: "Suddenly, as if by a magic touch—oh, the touch was at first a shattering blow—I caught sight of the distant realm of true poetry like a distant fairy palace, and all my creations crumbled into nothing. . . . A curtain had fallen, my holy of holies was rent asunder, and new gods had to be installed."[263] The new gods were Hegel, Bauer, and Feuerbach, the latter's name ironically meaning "stream of fire."[264]

As early as 1838, biographer John Spargo reported: "Karl came home that Easter, looking pale and worn and thin. I was shocked when he came to see me, so grave and sad was he. He had given up all hopes of being a great poet then and was now determined to get a Doctor's degree and become a professor at the University."[265] Perhaps this was his moment: Marx's ideological fall marks a profound loss of identity—a moment when he, like many before him, seemed unmoored from any stable sense of self, unsure of his place in the world. This mirrors a familiar pattern among thinkers and revolutionaries who abandon established moral and philosophical foundations and find themselves adrift in uncharted intellectual territory.[266] In the case of Marx, according to Franz Mehring, with all his brilliance, he "lacked the creative genius of the poet, who creates a world out of nothing."[267] David McLellan adds that his poems of this period "reveal a cult of the isolated genius and an introverted concern for the development of his own personality apart from the rest of humanity."[268]

This early introspection, rooted in a sense of isolation and individual genius, found resonance in Goethe's works, particularly *Faust*, which mirrored the very struggles Marx was experiencing. This moment could be seen as Marx's Faustian turning point, where he ceased to view social power as something separate from himself and to see it as being intertwined with political power. It was only through the attainment of this political power that he believed true human emancipation could be realized. The tension between personal ambition and collective responsibility, so central to *Faust*, would now shape Marx's critique of human striving within the constraints of a capitalist society. Although he immersed himself more deeply in philosophy and abandoned the writing of poetry, his deep feelings were not lost. The urgency and rhythm of his verses found new life in a thunderous prose that would reverberate with the same reckless abandon. Erupting passages that clanged like metal, like the sound of a medieval battlefield, were crafted with deliberate artistry—an elegy to his poetic past. To the very end, Marx remained, as one observer put it, "something of a poet."[269]

Blaise Pascal once famously wrote: "The heart has its reasons which reason knows nothing of,"[270] yet in Marx's naked expressions of youth, we witness raw emotion unfiltered, his truest desires being revealed. Sometimes naïve in expression or amateurish in form, the core sentiments of Marx's early poetry were quite clear. During these years, Marx seems to have reveled in the horrors he depicted. Whether these early musings were only rebellious explorations, his dark apocalyptic messaging would evoke a vision of destruction—not just of ideas, but of entire classes of people.

Weapons of Weariness

By 1838, Heinrich Marx's declining health cast a shadow over the household, yet he remained preoccupied with Karl's future. Confined to his sickbed—suffering from what was likely tuberculosis or a liver condition—he was surrounded by illness and grief. Three of his daughters were also sick, and the family was still mourning the recent death of young Eduard. Amid this gloom, Jenny von Westphalen occasionally visited to read aloud, her lively presence offering a brief light in the midst of so much sorrow. Jenny's kindness provided a rare solace amid the turmoil and shared hardships of these years, which not only deepened the bond between Karl and Jenny but also left an indelible mark on his outlook, as he observed firsthand the fragility and struggles of family life.

On February 10, 1838, two months after he had taken ill, Heinrich Marx wrote his last letter to his son. He needed to be brief. He spoke once more of Karl's peculiar attitude to money, "whose worth to a father of a family you do not seem to have grasped,"[271] and he wondered how his son could go on spending money so recklessly when it was obvious that there existed no fathomless treasure chest that could be looted at leisure. He wrote: "I am not blind, and I lay down my weapons only out of weariness. Nevertheless you must believe and never doubt that I carry you in my innermost heart, and you are the greatest hope of my life."[272]

He also said: "I should like to see in you what perhaps I could have become, if I had come into the world with equally favorable prospects."[273] Heinrich had written to Karl, when he was seventeen, in 1835, to express his aspirations that he achieve the successes he could not, given his less advantageous circumstances. He acknowledged the "potential unfairness of placing such expectations on his son but attributes it to the natural inclinations of a father's hope."[274] It was this prevailing spirit that he would transfer to Karl as he took a final breath on May 10, 1838. His death marked a turning point, both emotionally and financially, for a now twenty-year-old college student: "Without his father's financial leniency, Marx faced a stark reality—his mother, struggling to provide for six other children, refused to subsidize his mounting expenses. This newfound hardship deepened his resentment toward economic constraints and fueled his growing conviction that systemic change, rather than individual fortune, dictated the course of human lives."[275] As Manus McGrogan explains: "With his mother now in control of the family finances, her frequently penniless son would often write to her requesting sums of money."[276] As Marx matured, his feelings toward his mother soured, yet in his younger years, he held an idealized view of her. While at university, he referred to her as his "angel mother" and praised her as a "great and wonderful woman." She was a meticulous housekeeper, frugal with money, and dedicated wholly to her family, though largely unaware of the wider world beyond her domestic sphere—a woman solid in her ways but lacking imagination: "She was a good housekeeper, careful with money . . . who lived entirely for their family and have little inkling of anything that happens outside, solid and unimaginative."[277] Biographer Jonathan Sperber claims that Heinrich Marx wanted a career and participation in public life but that his "'Dutch wife' and her 'very household-oriented version of female Jewish piety' did not fit."[278] Given the new limitations and possibly as a forecast of his own future, Marx wrote in an essay: "Our relations in society have to some extent already begun to be established before we are in a position to determine them."[279] And also:

> The career a young man should choose should be one that is most consonant with our dignity, one that is based on ideas of whose truth we are wholly convinced, one that offers us the largest scope in working for humanity and approaching that general goal towards which each profession offers only one of the means: the goal of perfection. If he works only for himself, he can become a famous scholar, a great sage, an excellent imaginative writer [Dichter], but never a perfected, a truly great man."[280]

Marx's five university years in Berlin were shaped by his engagement with the Young Hegelians, a group of radical intellectuals who sought to push Hegel's philosophy beyond its original boundaries.[281] In fact, some accuse Marx of becoming so preoccupied with the Young Hegelians and his new doctoral thesis that in 1838 he did not attend his father's funeral—a decision often cited as evidence of his selfishness and disregard for family obligations.

Gabriel in her *Love and Capital* challenges this claim: "Some biographers have accused Marx of inexcusable callousness toward his father, claiming he did not attend his funeral because he said he had better things to do. That is a misrepresentation of events. Having just left Trier, Karl did not return for the funeral because it would have been impossible to make it there on time, and in any case, he had said his good-byes."[282]

Remember, "throughout his life Marx carried a daguerreotype image of his father in his breast pocket, and at Marx's own death forty-five years later, Engels would place the worn photo in Marx's grave."[283] Even during Karl's forays into his (ominous) poetry, "Heinrich Marx obviously wanted to support his son, even if the latter took a path different from the one he wanted."[284] Karl's sister Laura told biographer Franz Mehring: "I must tell you that my father treated these verses very disrespectfully; whenever my parents spoke of them, they laughed heartily about these follies of youth,"[285] though Heinrich had guided Karl to have two poems published.

With the death of his father, Karl "lost his most important familial contact"[286] along with any intention to earn a degree for a legal or administrative career. Marx seems to have moved on while Jenny grieved the loss of Heinrich: "I still can't get my bearings, still can't bear the thought of an irreplaceable loss with calm and composure; everything appears so cloudy to me, so ominous, the whole future so dark."[287] This cast a shadow over their shared future, and it deepened her sense of uncertainty. Her words, filled with sorrow and foreboding, reflect a world suddenly unmoored—a sentiment that resonated deeply with Karl, who was already navigating his intellectual transformation. As he processed his own emotions, he turned increasingly to literature as an outlet, channeling his thoughts into the macabre and the fantastical.

The Trumpet of the Last Judgment

One of Marx's most provocative anti-Christian acts of youthful rebellion was riding a donkey in a mock parody of Jesus's entry into Jerusalem, a direct act of blasphemy and ridicule or a final gesture of defiance, as Marx joined Bruno Bauer in what biographer Jonathan Sperber describes as a "public, atheist provocation."[288] During the Easter season of 1842, Bruno Bauer (1809–1882)—a German theologian, philosopher, and key figure in the Young Hegelians movement—traveled with Marx to the nearby village of Godesberg, a popular excursion spot near Bonn, where they famously rented donkeys. Bauer was known for his radical critique of Christianity, not merely analyzing it but openly rejecting its authority and historicity. His so-called "historical skepticism" referred to his belief that the biblical accounts, especially the Gospels, lacked reliable historical foundations. The Young Hegelians, including Bauer and eventually Marx, applied Hegel's dialectical method to religion and to politics, aiming to strip away tradition and ideology in order to expose the power structures underlying them. According to Sperber, this incident spread by word of mouth around Bonn and would later be fondly recalled by Bauer, who sought to justify his act—not by defending Christian miracles, but by framing his blasphemy as a critique of superstition. Like Jefferson and Dickens, Bauer wished to preserve Christianity's ethical influence in society while stripping it of its supernatural claims. This not-so-lighthearted episode in Godesberg underscores a deeper intellectual current running through Marx's and Bauer's relationship. Their excursions were not merely youthful revelry but part of an ongoing engagement with the major theological debates of their era—chief among them the question of whether religion could survive as a moral force in a disenchanted world. Marx did not study directly with Hegel, but after Hegel's death, he studied with the above-mentioned Bauer, one of Hegel's pupils and a leader of the circle of the Young Hegelians, a group to which Marx attached himself. Alongside Bauer, Marx also engaged with the work of Ludwig Feuerbach, whose materialist critique of religion—and rejection of Hegel's idealism—deeply resonated with him. Whereas Hegel conceived of reality as the unfolding of a universal spirit,[289] Feuerbach argued that religious belief was merely a projection of human qualities onto an imagined divine being. He emphasized the human being as a concrete, sensory, and social creature—not an abstract or spiritualized entity. This anthropocentric view provided Marx with crucial insights for his own shift toward historical materialism. By the early 1840s, Hegelianism itself had become a target of religious orthodoxy, with critics accusing it of fostering atheism and undermining traditional Christian doctrine. In his own difficult-to-understand jargon, Hegel himself stated: "Science [Wissenschaft, Hegel's philosophy] has achieved . . . that the miracles of Christ . . . are known as the equally necessary self-exposition [Selbstdarstellung] of the personality of Christ as are the teachings [Christian dogma]."[290] Bauer's fascination with the miraculous, filtered through his Hegelian framework, reflects an attempt to secularize Christianity—recasting its supernatural elements as symbolic expressions of historical consciousness rather than divine intervention.

Marx, however, would soon move beyond such speculations. While he had once followed Bauer's radical critiques of religion, his intellectual path would diverge toward a more materialist view. Bauer sought to reinterpret religious dogma, without miracles, through the lens of Hegelian dialectics, whereas Marx would ultimately reject both the miraculous and the dialectical rationalization of religion, seeing in it not a self-exposition of spirit, or disclosure of revelation, but an ideological construct masking deeper social and economic realities.

Bauer and Marx's time together in Bonn and their shared irreverence for religious orthodoxy would give way to profound ideological differences and foreshadow the break that was soon to come for Marx. Bauer's commitment to Hegelian philosophy and his attempt to reinterpret religious narratives through the lens of dialectical reason became too nuanced and sophisticated. Marx, more rigidly, began to move in a more reductionist direction, growing more skeptical of the speculative nature of such arguments. What had started as a shared irreverence for religious orthodoxy in Bonn soon revealed a deeper personal divide. While Bauer sought to explain away the miraculous as symbolic expressions of historical consciousness—denying their supernatural content because they did not comport with reason—Marx went further. He judged even this symbolic interpretation as an evasion of material realities. For Marx, religion, miracles included, was not merely misguided philosophy but also an ideological construct serving the political and economic interests of the ruling class. Bauer's interpretation of Christ's miracles as expressions of "historical consciousness" reflected his broader attempt to reinterpret Christian belief through a Hegelian lens. By historical consciousness, Bauer meant the evolving awareness of humanity coming to understand itself through history—religious narratives included. Rather than affirming the supernatural, Bauer argued that reason and science required us to see such miracles as symbolic projections of human development. As he put it, "Christ's personality cannot present itself other than through miracles"—not because the miracles are real but because they function as necessary expressions of his cultural role. This marked a clear break from the traditional Christian understanding of faith and reason as complementary, a position later affirmed dogmatically by the First Vatican Council in *Dei Filius* (1870) in response to such philosophical reinterpretations.[291] This tension came to a head in November 1841, when Otto Wigand published *The Trumpet of the Last Judgment against Hegel, the Atheists and the Anti-Christs*, a scathing anonymous pamphlet that condemned Hegelian philosophy as an irredeemable assault on Christianity:

> The hour has now struck in which the last, the worst, and the proudest enemy of the Lord will be brought to earth. This last enemy is also the most dangerous; these "Wild Men"—these people of the Antichrist—have dared to declare the non-existence of the Eternal Lord, and this in the full light of day, in the market, before all Christian Europe, in the light of the sun which has never shone upon such wickedness.[292]

Written in the prophetic style, the tract warned of the consequences of Hegel's ideas, citing his own works as evidence of their heretical nature.

The pamphlet was a direct challenge to the Young Hegelians, including Bauer, signaling the growing backlash against their radical interpretations of philosophy and history.[293] It created a great sensation, particularly as in the beginning, the orthodox mask actually deceived the public; even the philosopher and political writer Arnold Ruge was taken in by it. In reality, the author of *The Trumpet of the Last Judgment against Hegel, the Atheists and the Anti-Christs* was Bruno Bauer, and "he intended to continue the work together with Marx and to prove on the basis of Hegel's aesthetics, his philosophy of law, etc., that the Young Hegelians and not the Old Hegelians had inherited the real spirit of the master."[294] Bauer again prophesies: "It is my desire that this history of Philosophy should contain for you a summons to grasp the spirit of the time, which is present in us by nature, and—each in his own place—consciously to bring it from its natural condition, that is, from its lifeless seclusion, into the light of day."[295] *The Last Trumpet* was eventually censored, and Wigand failed to publish it ever again; in any case, Marx came to disagree with Bauer and the rest of the Young Hegelians about the usage of Hegel's dialectic. From 1841, the young Marx broke away from German idealism and the Young Hegelians. He only needed his degree, which meant completing his doctoral thesis.

Marx biographer Francis Wheen writes: "*The Difference between Democritean and Epicurean Philosophy* looks remarkably like a self-portrait: Cicero calls him a *vir eruditus*. He is competent in physics, ethics, mathematics, in the encyclopedic disciplines, in every art."[296] Marx's doctoral thesis itself was controversial, in particular among the conservative professors at Berlin, so Marx submitted his thesis to the more liberal University of Jena.[297] It was yet another weapon to undermine the roots of Christianity in classical Greek philosophy.[298] In that spirit of true enlightenment and for the one who had helped inspire that spirit, Marx dedicated his thesis to Ludwig van Westphalen:

> May everyone who doubts of the Idea be so fortunate as I, to be able to admire an old man who has the strength of youth, who greets every forward step of the times with the enthusiasm and the prudence of truth and who, with that profoundly convincing sun-bright idealism which alone knows the true word at whose call all the spirits of the world appear, never recoiled before the deep shadows of retrograde ghosts, before the often dark clouds of the times, but rather with godly energy and manly confident gaze saw through all veils the empyreum which burns at the heart of the world. You, *my fatherly friend*, were always a living *argumentum ad oculos* to me, that idealism is no figment of the imagination, but a truth.

In a deleted paragraph of this dedication, Marx had originally added that he hoped to be in Trier again soon and "to roam again at your side through our wonderfully picturesque mountains and forests."[299] Clearly, Marx's words carry the profound anguish of a son who has lost not just a father figure but a true mentor—a loss that echoes through his soul. Ludwig would not have only been grateful but proud of this new vision, which, on paper, opens with: "Greek philosophy seems to have met with something with which a good tragedy is not supposed to meet, namely, a dull ending. The objective history of philosophy in Greece seems to come to an end with Aristotle."[300] Democritus, often considered the father of atomism, posited that all things in the universe are composed of indivisible particles—atoms—that move and interact according to chance, devoid of any higher purpose or divine order.[301] But then it was Epicurus who "was the true radical Enlightener of antiquity; he openly attacked the ancient religion, and it was from him, too, that the atheism of the Romans, insofar as it existed, was derived. For this reason . . . among all church fathers, from Plutarch to Luther, Epicurus has always had the reputation of being atheist philosopher par excellence, and was called a swine."[302]

For this reason, for his being what today we might refer to as a "hippie,"[303] Epicurus became a figure of intense controversy, maligned by Church Fathers from Tertullian and Clement of Alexandria to Basil of Caesarea and Augustine. His reputation as a "swine,"[304] as Marx pointedly notes, was less a reflection of his philosophy and more a projection of the unease that his ideas caused among those invested in a divinely ordered cosmos. One can imagine the indignation of a medieval theologian or even a devout Renaissance scholar confronting Epicurus's assertion that the gods, if they existed at all, were indifferent to human affairs. Epicurus offered no comforting metaphysics—only the stark and disconcerting claim that the universe was governed by atoms in motion, and that the perception of the senses was tantamount to reality. His atomism posed a profound challenge not only to theological frameworks but also to the philosophical idealism of Plato and Hegel. Even thinkers within the Christian tradition, like Thomas Aquinas—who began with the natural world of sensory experience—would have rejected Epicurus's view as incomplete, proposing instead that the material world pointed beyond itself to a divine source, a *prima causa* who set the atoms in motion. Marx's doctoral thesis, completed *in absentia*, focused on the differences between the atomistic materialism of Democritus and the hedonistic materialism of Epicurus, both of which profoundly shaped his worldview.[305] Most significantly, Marx highlights how Epicurus introduced a break in the chain of material cause and effect—what he saw as a crucial opening for human freedom and independent will, in contrast to Democritus's rigid determinism. It was essential that Marx find human agency in his determinist view to promote change, let alone a new age.[306] He writes: "Epicurus introduced the concept of the swerve as a way to reconcile materialism with human agency. This seemingly minor adjustment opened the door to discussions of autonomy within material frameworks."[307] Marx, at this point, not a complete determinist, argues that "the distinction between necessity and chance is crucial for understanding freedom," or in the case of Epicurus, the possibility of social adaptation. By engaging with the pre-Socratics, Marx began laying the foundation for his later philosophical project—a rejection of metaphysical and religious explanations of existence in favor of materialism. This intellectual journey eventually led him to confront and reject Hegel's Idealist framework and offer a vision of the world rooted in tangible reality, one that opposed the abstractions of the Hegelian "Mind," and beyond the Bauer synthesis.

It was Ludwig Feuerbach, however, who would remain the key figure with whom Marx would align himself for much of his early intellectual development, despite the significant distinctions that would eventually emerge between their views. Feuerbach's materialism, which focused on religion as solely a human projection and on the sensory world, provided Marx with a critical bridge between Hegel's dialectics and his own conception of history and society.[308]

After Marx had been late in finishing his dissertation, "he probably did not want to wait longer for the exam."[309] He turned in his thesis on April 15, 1841, and received his doctorate in philosophy just over a week later.[310] "The doctorate was originally conceived for candidates who were already working or had already submitted a scholarly work and wished to retroactively obtain a doctor title," and he was graded as "eminently worthy."[311] The dissertation,[312] though intellectually rigorous, "revealed his grounding in ancient philosophy and his growing critique of religion,"[313] but did not lead to the professional success that Marx had hoped for. In his defense, he would write: "Who would want to have to talk always with intellectual skunks, with people who study only for the purpose of finding new dead ends in every corner of the world!"[314] This professional disappointment only deepened Marx's sense of alienation: "His Abitur essay from 1835 demonstrates that the seventeen-year-old Marx still believed in a God. From the preface to his dissertation from March 1841, in contrast, it becomes evident that he now took a decidedly atheist position."[315] The sense of alienation was heightened in Marx's personal case by his subsequent inability to obtain a teaching post in a university system that had "no room for dissident intellectuals"[316] who were deeply ideological. His exclusion from academic positions due to his controversial views only reinforced his belief that existing institutions were designed to stifle dissent rather than encourage true intellectual freedom.[317] For Marx, now, the task ahead was not to defend the acknowledged advances of capitalism but to push beyond it—to expose its limits and envision a world where its promises could be fully realized in a revolutionary paradigm.

No longer the academic philosophical theorist, Marx was, according to his own beliefs, the activist he needed to be. Saul Padover says that "Marx's university years were defined by intense intellectual curiosity and a rebellious spirit."[318] According to family accounts and letters, Marx was known to be a difficult, often depressive figure, who displayed "excessive self-centeredness" and bitterness toward the world. Marx's personal life, so far filled with failed ambitions, alienation, and perpetual dependence on others, reveals a man who had been at war not just with society but with himself. His fascination with figures of rebellion, defiance, and darkness may not necessarily imply actual Satanism, but it certainly points to the shadows within his psyche:[319] perhaps an unconscious acknowledgment of the pacts he had made and the betrayal that awaited him. As he once wrote of the tension between human ambition and divine order, Marx's life, marked by this relentless pursuit of self-constructed glory, would continue to unfold as a slow descent into revolution—a tragic spiral from which he would struggle to escape. His fate, increasingly entwined in the web of ideology and human conflict, led him toward a final confrontation with the consequences of his own choices, a moment in which he faced the irreversible nature of his intellectual and personal destiny.

Just as Dante used vivid imagery to depict the deserved punishments of the damned, Marx turned to similar language to expose and condemn the injustices of his own age. He saw these images not merely as literary devices but as a moral reckoning—tools to call out exploitation, demand reparation, and provoke a change in human behavior. This sense of righteous fury helped set the stage for what Marx envisioned as an impending upheaval—not a divine reckoning, but a revolutionary reckoning that would shatter the capitalist order. As William Clare Roberts explains:

> Marx enters the "dismal science" of economics in the same way that Dante enters Hell, to face the truth without flinching, to know the truth, to know how bad things can be as a result of the wrong actions of individuals. Dante and Marx are operating in accordance with a standard of the true, the good and the beautiful, but with a different metaphysics. Dante's Christian metaphysics locate Heaven beyond Earth, Marx's metaphysics are naturalist.

While Dante's metaphysics elevate truth and redemption to the realm of the divine, Marx's naturalist framework seeks salvation within the material conditions of earthly existence.[320] As the night settled over Berlin, the last echoes of the university's halls faded into silence. Marx sat alone in his dimly lit room, the weight of his intellectual transformation bearing heavily on him. It was the night before he would leave the secure walls of academia, a transition not just in his physical journey but in his deeper engagement with the world's profound contradictions. In that quiet moment, Marx found himself contemplating the foundations of his new worldview. His entrance into the "dismal science" of economics was not unlike Dante's descent into hell—both facing the truth of the world in its most brutal form, without flinching, without the solace of divine intervention.

Roberts is right. Marx, like Dante, operated under the assumption that there exists a higher moral standard—the true, the good, and the beautiful. But while Dante's foundation was rooted in divine order, Marx's metaphysical ground was entirely different: he sought transcendence through history and revolution, not through grace or revelation.[321] While Dante's Christian metaphysics elevated truth to a divine realm, Marx's materialist framework sought redemption in the tangible, earthly world. The flickering candlelight cast long shadows across his study as he pored over his thoughts, glass of wine in hand. It was in this darkened room, consumed by ideas of revolution, that Mephistopheles—cloaked in shadow—entered, his presence felt more than seen. Behind Mephistopheles, Dante stands in a nearby alcove to listen. The air grew heavier, charged with the tension of Marx's unrelenting intellectual pursuit. The stage was set, not for divine judgment, but for a confrontation with the very forces of history itself:

Mephistopheles:
Ah, young Karl, a mind that burns too bright!
You seek the secrets that gods keep hidden.
The alchemy of gold? Nay, far beyond—
A new world wrought from reason's forge.
But tell me, child of earth, at what cost?

Marx (startled, looks up):
Who speaks? An echo of my own doubts?
Or a specter sent to mock my labor?

Mephistopheles:

Neither ghost nor doubt, but a guide, if you wish.
I see the furnace of your soul, young man,
Your thirst to unravel the world's great lie.
You would tear down the heavens, remake the earth—
But shall your new Eden bear no serpent?

Marx (defiant):

No serpent, no gods, no chains of the mind!
A paradise born of men's hands alone!

Mephistopheles (chuckling):

So sure you are, yet blind to your own folly.
Beware, Karl Marx, of the fire you stoke.
For what begins as justice may end in ashes,
And your dream of freedom may bind more chains.

BOOK TWO

Revolutionary in Purgatory

(1842–1864)

"Much like the souls in Dante's Purgatorio, who must shed their sins before they are allowed into Paradise. It is only through revolution that the working class can be cleansed of its oppression."[322]

—Karl Marx

RING 3

The Ring of Exile

(1842–1845)

"The weapon of criticism cannot, of course, replace criticism by weapons; material force must be overthrown by material force."[323]

—Karl Marx

Karl Marx arrived in Paris in 1843, a city teeming with revolutionary energy, where exiles, radicals, and intellectuals debated the fate of Europe in crowded cafés, underground meeting halls, and dimly lit salons. In some shadowed corner place, Henri Murger created his *La Bohème*, which later became the basis for the opera by Puccini, the story of the bohemian lifestyle, artistic rebellion, poverty, and the struggles of young intellectuals who rejected bourgeois values.[324] Paris was then the epicenter of European dissent, home to exiled revolutionaries, socialist theorists, and clandestine networks that sought to upend the old order.

For Marx, it was an immersion into the heart of radical thought—a world where utopian socialists, anarchists, and republicans debated culture and politics in every available venue.[325] Marx came into contact with various revolutionary socialists and workers' organizations that engaged in protests against the ruling classes, and while he was not always directly involved in violent protests, he supported the revolutionary sentiment. His arrival marked a new turning point:

his ideological development no longer under the watchful eye of Prussian officials, he took refuge in the vibrant intellectual scene, connecting with figures such as Pierre-Joseph Proudhon, Mikhail Bakunin, and Heinrich Heine, all of whom contributed to his evolving worldview. Yet, the most consequential meeting of all was with Friedrich Engels—a moment that would solidify Marx's path toward communism.

Throughout the period 1842–1845, Marx's life continued a descent from youthful idealism toward a deeper, more methodical understanding of the world, but it was also a time of extreme personal suffering that took a toll on his family's health. During these years, in the midst of political unrest and growing intellectual momentum, Marx and Friedrich Engels began forging the ideas that would define their shared revolutionary path.

Engels and Marx had met briefly the previous year at the offices of the *Rheinische Zeitung* in Cologne. At the time, their encounter had been polite but unremarkable—Engels was still formulating his ideas on political economy, while Marx remained skeptical of his perspectives. But now, in Paris, their second meeting would prove fateful, as they forged a partnership that would shape the ideological battles of the modern world. The *rencontre* took place in the bustling Café de la Régence, a legendary haunt of philosophers, revolutionaries, and chess masters, located near the Palais-Royal. The café had long been a gathering place for Europe's brightest minds, from Voltaire and Rousseau to Napoleon, and now, amid the flickering candlelight and the scent of strong coffee and tobacco, it became the setting for one of history's most consequential collaborations.

Beyond the café, their collaboration deepened in Marx's cramped and book-laden apartment on Rue Vaneau, where they refined their ideas into articles, essays, and eventually a shared manifesto. Engels, fresh from his observations of industrial England, was already formulating his critique of capitalism, and he brought with him vivid accounts of Manchester's factories—describing the choking soot, the relentless machinery, and the desperate conditions of the working poor. Marx, having steeped himself in Hegelian philosophy and political economy, was eager to engage with Engels's firsthand experiences. They spoke for hours, debating late into the night, their conversation animated by the clinking of glasses and the murmurs of other exiled radicals discussing the latest uprisings across Europe. Over the following months, they made the café their regular meeting place, to sketch out the framework of what would become historical materialism. Their discussions covered everything—the failures of previous socialist movements, the lessons of the French Revolution, and the necessity of proletarian revolution. Between sips of black coffee and swirls of cigar smoke, they envisioned a world where the working class, long subjected to exploitation, would rise to reclaim history.

Marx, despite his deep theoretical background, had yet to fully develop a materialist critique of history. Engels, with his sharp observations and clarity of expression, helped push Marx toward grounding his ideas in the realities of economic production. As Engels later recalled, their discussion "immediately found us in agreement in all theoretical fields."[326] The two men fed off each other's energy—Marx with his uncompromising logic and encyclopedic knowledge, Engels with his pragmatism and experience among the workers. They agreed that the driving force of history was the material conditions of human life, in particular the economic relationships between the ruling class (the bourgeoisie) and the working class (the proletariat). In the years to come, their major literary efforts would design polemical works such as *The Holy Family and The German Ideology*,[327] along with Marx's *On the Jewish Question*[328] and *Economic and Philosophic Manuscripts of 1844*.[329] The growing awareness of the brutal realities of industrial capitalism would deepen his convictions. His early philosophical discoveries gradually gave way to an unyielding focus on the structural forces driving human suffering—a transformation mirrored by the physical and emotional hardships his family endured that would blend to fuel his scathing commentary.

The Exile's Crucible

Amid personal losses, economic instability, and recurring health crises, Marx's commitment to his vision of revolutionary change only intensified to shape the trajectory of his work: The *Rheinische Zeitung* was launched on January 1, 1842, with four hundred subscribers. Marx began writing for it four months later. Marx's involvement with the paper often put him at the center of revolutionary agitation, especially as he wrote articles criticizing Prussian authorities, landowners, and aristocracy. His writing on the "freedom of the press" was critical of both the Prussian government and liberal opponents, setting the stage for more active protests. "The press is the chief organ of the revolution, it is the voice of the masses, of the oppressed."[330] "For his first article he returned to press freedom, prompted by a debate on the issue in the Rhineland Diet."[331] It was on November 16, 1842, that Marx had first encountered Engels, who visited the office of the *Rheinische Zeitung* on his way to England, traveling to Manchester to work at Ermen & Engels, a textile firm partly owned by his father. This was part of his family's business interests in the industrial sector.[332] At the *Rheinische Zeitung*, Marx made an immediate impression on the resident intellectuals, among them the paper's radical editor. Gustav Mevissen (1815–1899), one of the financial backers of the *Rheinische Zeitung*, described Marx as "a sturdy man of twenty-four who had thick black hair protruding from his cheeks, arms, nose and ears; domineering black eyes, impetuous, passionate, full of boundless self-assurance, but also serious and learned, a restless dialectician who, with his restless Jewish perspicacity, carried out every phrase of the Young Hegelian doctrine to its final conclusion."[333]

Arnold Ruge, one of the prominent Young Hegelians, initially studied theology and philosophy before becoming a staunch advocate for radical democracy and freedom of thought. He coedited the influential journal *Deutsche Jahrbücher* and later collaborated with Karl Marx on the publication of *Deutsch-Französische Jahrbücher* in 1844. Ruge was sixteen years older than Marx, but like Bruno Bauer, he had the greatest respect for the capacities of the younger man, as did lead writer Moses Hess, a well-established communist. As biographer Francis Wheen explains, "his very first article was a lacerating assault on both the intolerance of Prussian absolutism and the feeble-mindedness of its liberal opponents."[334] It was here that Marx continued honing his criticism of political and economic systems, which would lay the foundation for his later revolutionary work.[335] It was the Doctor's Club, home of Cologne's intelligentsia, whose members were awestruck by Marx's intellectual prowess, force of conviction, and hirsute appearance. He was described in a friend's poem as that "swarthy chap from Trier"[336]—thick black hair sprouted from his head and cheeks, earning him the nickname "Moor" and adding to his aura of philosophical gravitas.[337] Also, as the new Moses, Marx shifted his focus from merely drinking wine to championing the struggles of wine-growers, particularly those of Germany's Moselle Valley. Small vintners faced economic hardship due to abrupt changes in Prussian policy, which had once protected them but now left them vulnerable to competition.

Karl Marx was installed as the editor of the *Rheinische Zeitung* in 1842 and took on one of his first major investigative pursuits: the economic crisis facing the vineyards. The small wine-producers in the Moselle region of Prussia had been devastated by a combination of poor harvests, heavy taxation, and restrictive trade laws. Marx sought to expose what he saw as systemic exploitation,[338] writing passionately about the economic plight of the vintners and their struggle against both landlords and state bureaucracy.[339] Marx argued that the crisis was emblematic of broader injustices within the Prussian economic system, where the state, rather than protecting its citizens, reinforced class inequality.[340] His articles accused the authorities of prioritizing the interests of large landowners and the wealthy elite, leaving small farmers to suffer. The controversy drew significant attention and criticism from Prussian officials, who considered Marx's tone dangerously radical. Despite Marx's efforts to rally public support for reforms, the Moselle vintners' plight persisted, with minimal changes to their economic conditions. These articles, however, marked an early example of Marx's ability to blend journalism with a scathing critique of economic systems, foreshadowing the revolutionary lens he would bring to his theoretical work.

The plight of the Moselle vintners marked Marx's shift from pure political interests to a social and economic commitment to the working class.[341] It captured his growing belief that social and economic conditions were not immutable but shaped by policies and power dynamics. He recognized that the vine-growers were crushed by a sudden reversal in Prussian trade policies. For years, the Prussians had imposed tariffs that shielded them from outside competition, but in the 1830s, they reversed course, opening the market and devastating small producers. This illuminated for Marx the critical role of government policy in shaping economic outcomes and the importance of addressing the needs of affected communities in the face of such transitions, which were not uncommon in the modern world's rapidly changing economy.[342] By the time Marx removed to back to Cologne in 1845, the plight of these winemakers had become a focus of his editorials. Marx argued that the Moselle crisis was not "a natural phenomenon"[343] but rather the result of material conditions shaped by Prussian policies—a viewpoint that would move him "from pure politics to economic relationships and so to socialism."[344]

After the Moselle crisis, Marx then turned his attention to one of the most pressing legal debates in the Prussian Rhineland: the *Thefts of Wood* controversy. This debate centered on new laws that criminalized the collection of fallen wood from privately owned forests—a right that poor peasants had traditionally exercised for survival. "These laws are mere tools in the hands of the oppressors, designed to keep the peasantry in shackles."[345] Marx's analysis of these laws marked a crucial turning point in his intellectual development, as he began to explore the ways in which legal structures served the interests of the ruling class at the expense of the poor.[346] From December 12 to April 22, Engels too wrote (anonymously) articles for the *Rheinische Zeitung* to also make his case.[347] Marx's focus shifted from abstract political theory to the tangible economic and social conditions shaping society. His articles were filled with fiery critiques of the Prussian government and the capitalist system, and his tone became increasingly confrontational. Marx began to see revolution not as an abstract ideal but as a concrete necessity, a means of transforming society and liberating the oppressed.

Engels, meanwhile, was undergoing a similar transformation. Born into a wealthy industrial family, he had firsthand experience of the exploitation of the working class,[348] which deepened his commitment to socialism[349] and revolution and fueled the articles he wrote anonymously for the *Rheinische Zeitung*. However frenetic with new writings or causes, Marx's (and Engels's) newfound platform did not last long. In 1843, the Prussian government shut down the *Rheinische Zeitung paper*, citing its revolutionary content as a threat to the state; the last issue was published on March 31, 1843: "Marx resigned from the paper on March 17. He hoped his departure might save it. It did not."[350] In any case, Marx was ready to sever the connection and move forward, though he had severely strained his editorial patience. According to biographer Franz Mehring, "Marx was never an accommodating author either for his collaborators or his publishers, but none of them ever thought of ascribing to neglect or laziness what was caused only by an overbrimming richness of ideas and a self-criticism which was never satisfied."[351]

While Engels was still formulating his ideas, Marx's earlier partnership with Arnold Ruge had already ended. Their collaboration was short-lived due to ideological differences, with Ruge favoring reformist approaches while Marx pushed for revolutionary upheaval.

As Marx's ideas gained prominence, Ruge's influence waned, ultimately being overshadowed by Marx's legacy. In regard to the newspaper, Marx told Ruge: "I had begun to be stifled in that atmosphere. It is a bad thing to have to perform menial duties even for the sake of freedom; to fight with pinpricks, instead of with clubs. I have become tired of hypocrisy, stupidity, gross arbitrariness, and of our bowing and scraping, dodging, and hair-splitting over words." In his cancellation, Marx adds, "The government has given me back my freedom."[352] Marx's paper was shut down, but in his mind, he was freed from the restrictions of working for an employer.

And so Marx once again was without work or income. "This was to be a theme in the decades to come; Marx would spend his life stressing the primacy of economics but was chronically irresponsible when it came to his own finances."[353] From July 12 to August 21, 1845, Marx and Engels journeyed to England, not merely as an intellectual excursion—it was an initiation into the brutal realities of industrial capitalism. The theories they had debated in Paris found their stark confirmation in the relentless churn of England's factories, where wealth and destitution coexisted in a cruel paradox. The beating heart of industrial capitalism was a place where progress had been forged in fire and steel—but at what human cost? The relentless hum of machinery, the blackened skies over London, and the ceaseless march of laborers through soot-choked streets revealed a world transformed by the factory system. For Marx, this was no mere economic phenomenon; it was the very crucible in which modern class struggle was being shaped. Here, in the belly of industrialization, the proletariat toiled under conditions that embodied the alienation and exploitation he had long theorized. Now, confronted with the grim reality, Marx and Engels would sharpen their critique, to refine the ideas that would soon shake the world. As they crossed the English Channel, they were stepping into a world where the specter of economic progress masked a far grimmer reality.

The Infernal Machine

England, the heart of industrial capitalism, served as a living laboratory for Marx as he witnessed firsthand the conditions that Engels had so powerfully described in his book *The Condition of the Working Class in England*.[354] The stark reality of overcrowded slums, brutal factory conditions, and grinding poverty reinforced Marx's conviction that capitalism was inherently exploitative. For Marx, the six weeks in England further solidified his belief that the working class was not just a victim of capitalist exploitation but the engine of revolutionary change. "As in the later fiction of Charles Dickens, it is crime which what lies at the root of achievement."[355] The observations he made during this period deepened his understanding of how economic forces shaped social relations and solidified his historical dialectic as one of class struggle. It was then that Marx began to crystallize the ideas that would later culminate in *The Communist Manifesto* and eventually *Das Kapital*. The partnership with Engels, strengthened by shared experiences in England, became the bedrock of their revolutionary mission, with Engels providing not only financial support but also the empirical insights that would shape Marx's theoretical framework: "Only in England has industrial development in all its aspects been fully elaborated; only in England, therefore, can the consequences of the industrial system be studied in all their relationships. In no other country has the war between the two classes which divide modern society—proletariat and bourgeoisie—been fought out so openly and so ruthlessly."[356] This period stands as a testament to how collaboration and firsthand observation can forge the foundation of revolutionary thought, setting the stage for Marx's lifelong quest to understand—and ultimately overthrow—the capitalist system.

Their collaboration deepened as they moved through the industrial landscapes of England, with Engels's firsthand observations enriching Marx's theoretical insights. Together, they began to forge their ideas, bridging the philosophical roots of Hegelianism with the harsh realities of the working class. This partnership marked the transition from abstract critique to a jointly held concrete vision of historical materialism grounded in class struggle. Thereafter, Marx and Engels worked together for the rest of Marx's life so that the collected works of Marx and Engels are generally published together, almost as if they were the output of one person.[357] Important publications, such as *The German Ideology*, were a joint effort. Engels said that "with Marx I had a certain independent share in laying the foundation of the theory, and more particularly in its elaboration."[358] However, he added:

> But the greater part of its leading basic principles, especially in the realm of economics and history, and, above all, their final trenchant formulation, belong to Marx. What I contributed—at any rate with the exception of my work in a few special fields—Marx could very well have done without me. What Marx accomplished I would not have achieved. Marx stood higher, saw further, and took a wider and quicker view than all the rest of us. Marx was a genius; we others were at best talented. Without him the theory would not be by far what it is today. It therefore rightly bears his name.[359]

Their collaboration on *The German Ideology* reflected the intellectual struggle and purification of ideas,[360] much like Dante's ascent in *Purgatorio*: "We were once all straying in the wood, before that she turned our steps to the straight way."[361] This passage reflects being lost in confusion before reaching clarity and truth, mirroring how Marx and Engels refined their revolutionary ideas through struggle and debate. Their revolutionary vision was dangerous, but to them it offered the promise of a transformed world. Marx's financial struggles during this period were well-documented, and the support he received from Engels would stretch well beyond the monetary kind; their cause furthered a deep bond between the two men. However, that was not enough to shield them from the toll that this isolation took on their personal lives. Before his name would echo through revolutions and classrooms, Karl Marx was, at home, a husband and father. Yet, the same intensity that fueled his intellectual and political life often eclipsed the quiet demands of domesticity. His wife, Jenny von Westphalen, came from a prominent Prussian family and had given up a life of relative comfort to follow Marx into exile, financial ruin, and social stigma. Their marriage, once filled with shared intellectual passion, became marked by long separations, emotional strain, and relentless poverty. Together, they would bear seven children, only three of whom would survive into adulthood. The Marx household, whether in Brussels, Paris, or London, was a place of ideological fire—and chronic deprivation. However, that was not enough to shield them from the toll that this isolation took on their personal lives. Jenny and their children lived in poverty, and the strain of Marx's political activism often left little room for family life.

Engels, too, experienced a form of isolation, though his financial situation was far more stable than Marx's. His break with his family, particularly his father, Friedrich Engels Sr. (1796–1860),[362] over his socialist commitment, left him estranged from his bourgeois roots. In many ways, Engels's support for Marx during this period can be seen as an expression of his revolutionary commitment; it demonstrated his dedication to the cause as it led him further away from the life he was born into. Engels remained closely intertwined with the Burns sisters, Mary and Lydia (commonly called Lizzie), working-class women from Manchester. Around 1842, Engels met Mary Burns, a fiery Irishwoman, who shared Engels's concern for the oppressive conditions of industrial capitalism. Mary Burns and Engels maintained a "non-traditional" relationship,[363] choosing not to marry despite societal expectations. The Burns sisters provided Engels with a unique perspective on the struggles of the working class, which he so vividly chronicled in his writings. One of his most passionate quotes comes from his *The Condition of the Working Class in England*, based on his firsthand observations: "The workers sink deeper and deeper, while the few capitalists become richer and richer, and every crisis demonstrates the powerlessness of the bourgeoisie to govern the world, which has been abandoned to its greed."[364] His connection to the Burns sisters provided him with a personal connection to the working-class struggles he and Marx sought to analyze. This intimate perspective deepened their understanding of class dynamics beyond mere theoretical abstraction.

Those six weeks in England marked a crucial phase in their intellectual development, as they immersed in the study of the latest economic theories and firsthand observations of industrial capitalism at its peak. England, as the birthplace of the Industrial Revolution, offered a living laboratory with workers, political activists, and reformers that would solidify their belief in the necessity of revolution. Marx and Engels also studied the latest English books on economics and gained insight into England's economic and political life. Immersed in the bustling streets of London and the industrial centers of England, they studied the economic theories and political trends up close, particularly the works of Adam Smith (1723–1790) and David Ricardo (1772–1823).[365]

In addition, Marx and Engels connected with leaders of the Chartist movement, the foremost working-class political organization of the time. Feargus O'Connor (1796–1855), a charismatic figure and leader of the Chartist newspaper *Northern Star*, championed direct action and land reform to promote economic independence.[366] The prominent Chartist leader Ernest Jones (1879–1958), a Welsh neurologist and psychoanalyst, renowned for being the first English-speaking practitioner of psychoanalysis and a close associate of Sigmund Freud's,[367] took a more intellectual approach, blending legal expertise and poetic talent to advocate for socialism. Jones emphasized the connection between economic and political salvation. Both leaders contributed to shaping Marx and Engels's understanding of working-class struggles and their vision for democratic reforms. The focus of leaders like O'Connor on practical reforms and Jones's emphasis on broader systemic change provided insights that strengthened Marx and Engels's conviction in the revolutionary potential of the working class.

They also engaged with members of the League of the Just, a secret society advocating social justice. These meetings not only solidified Marx's and Engels's shared vision but also immersed them in the bustling realities of industrial England and the stark contrasts of wealth and poverty they sought to dismantle in this infernal machine. Engels, in his seminal book *The Condition of the Working Class in England*, reports: "The middle classes have a truly extraordinary conception of society. They really believe that human beings . . . have real existence only if they make money or help to make it."[368] The more they witnessed, the clearer it became: the industrial system was not a mere malfunction; it was an infernal engine, feeding on the blood of the masses to fill the pockets of a privileged few, turning the city into a hellish mockery of what it should have been. Engels's description echoes the way Charles Dickens would have written it: "It was a town of red brick, or of brick that would have been red if the smoke and ashes had allowed it; but as matters stood, it was a town of unnatural red and black like the painted face of a savage. . . . The giant city, with its bed of filth, its mire, its lies, its corruption, and its soul-consuming madness"[369] was "long past the point of salvation, trapped in its own self-damnation."[370] It was a place "where every soul's hope was drained, and no compassion to be found. It was the very image of Hell itself."[371] Amid the smoke-choked alleyways and overcrowded tenements, the world witnessed a scathing analysis—an exposé that would become a foundational text in Marx's developing ideology.

Engels provided a searing account of the living and working conditions that justified a revolution; he exposed the horrific realities of industrial capitalism, painting a vivid picture of the suffering endured by the proletariat. He wrote about the working class ground down by relentless exploitation. He observed: "The proletarian is practically regarded as a mere chattel, to be used and abused at will, a passive instrument of production."[372] In Manchester, Birmingham, and Leeds, he noted the labyrinth of dark, narrow streets in working-class districts, where the air was "polluted by the effluvia of stagnant pools and open drains."[373] Entire families were crammed into brick facades, with rooms in damp, unventilated tenements, as hidden caverns, their health eroded by hunger and disease. In his words: "Everywhere barbarous indifference, hard egotism on one hand, and nameless misery on the other." The factories stood like infernos, with their scorching fires and relentless machinery, each flame a symbol of the souls lost to the brutal fires of industrialization. Engels detailed the long hours worked by men, women, and children in hazardous conditions,[374] where machinery maimed with ruthless efficiency, and wages barely kept families alive. "The toil in the factories is exhausting, the air poisonous, the surroundings repulsive,"[375] he lamented, emphasizing how industrial capitalism stripped workers of their humanity and treated them as mere appendages to machines. One might envision Charlie Chaplin's satirical *Modern Times*, where the protagonist's transformation mirrors the very gears of the factory itself—until, like a cog in the machine, he is ingested, transformed, and expelled, reduced to nothing more than a commodity. All the while, dizzy and unbalanced, he teeters on the precipice of disintegration, emblematic of the soul-crushing effects of mechanization.[376] Marx came to view the alienation of labor not merely as a structural defect of capitalism, but as a moral and existential crisis that reduced the worker to a mere instrument, estranged from both the product and the act of labor itself.[377] The suffering documented by Engels was more than a statistical reality—it was a living indictment of a system that reduced human beings to commodities; it fueled Marx's conviction that capitalism was unjust and inherently unsustainable. It was against this backdrop of shared outrage and intellectual alignment that Marx and Engels forged their revolutionary partnership; it would transcend mere critique to lay the foundation for a transformative political ideology. "It was in this period, in the spring of 1845," as Engels himself would later note, that Marx wrote his *Theses on Feuerbach*,[378] continuing the arguments he had pursued in the *Economic and Philosophic Manuscripts of 1844* to their logical conclusions: "The less you eat, drink, buy books, go to the theatre or to balls, or to the pub, and the less you think, love, theorize, sing, paint, fence, etc., the more you will be able to save and the greater will become your treasure which neither moth nor rust will corrupt—your capital. The less you are, the less you express your life, the more you have, the greater is your alienated life and the greater is the saving of your alienated being."[379]

This moment marked the crystallization of their shared vision, a turning point that would propel them toward the creation of a movement that sought worldwide transformation. The partnership between Marx and Engels became a crucible for their revolutionary thought, with Marx's book *Theses on Feuerbach* serving as a pivotal articulation of their emerging ideology: "The philosophers have only interpreted the world, in various ways; the point, however, is to change it."[380] This collaboration not only deepened their intellectual synergy but also planted the seeds of communism, as Engels recognized the transformative potential of Marx's concise yet groundbreaking arguments.

In his essay *On the Jewish Question* (1843),[381] Marx examined the nature of political emancipation and the role of religion, namely the Jews, in the state, critiquing the limitations of bourgeois democracy.[382] He argued that while the state formally abolished social distinctions, it did so only in a superficial manner:[383] "Political emancipation is, of course, a big step forward. True, it is not the final form of human emancipation in general, but it is the final form of human emancipation within the framework of the prevailing social order."[384] This early work signaled Marx's shift toward a more radical critique of political structures. Yet, it was in his *Economic and Philosophic Manuscripts* that his ideas fully crystallized. In these manuscripts, Marx articulated his theory of alienation, arguing that human history was fundamentally shaped by labor and production, framing it in almost poetic terms: "The entire so-called world history is nothing but the creation of man through human labor, the emergence of nature for man; he has therefore the evident and irrefutable proof of his self-creation, of his own origins."[385] Here, Marx abandoned any notion of human essence as a static concept. Instead, he contended that human nature itself was a product of historical and social conditions—a radical departure from the idealist traditions of German philosophy. This shift in thinking was formalized in *Theses on Feuerbach.* But perhaps of most significance was the fact that Marx dismantled the notion that human essence was something innate or metaphysical, arguing instead that it was a construct shaped entirely by social relations: "The essence of man is no abstraction inherent in each single individual. In its reality, it is the ensemble of social relations."[386]

The Garden of Alienation

As the mythological figure Prometheus snatched fire from the gods to bring knowledge to humanity, Marx positioned himself as a revolutionary hero rejecting all established systems of thought and belief in favor of a radically new vision for society, not being aware how flawed was his radical proposal.[387] Prometheus, Marx's self-proclaimed prototype, is a revolutionary figure—bringing knowledge and empowerment to a transformed humanity but having to suffer for it at the hands of the ruling powers, much like the Messianic figure meant to suffer.[388] Marx might have seen Prometheus as the intellectual who arms the proletariat with the fire of revolutionary consciousness, and reinforces his critique of capitalism as a Sermon on the Mount that speaks of human needs and the plight of alienated individuals. Ultimately, it sows the seeds of a war to come: "The socialist doctrine is not merely an economic theory; it is a messianic prophecy that promises ultimate salvation through the destruction of capitalism."[389]

After the trip to England in August of 1845, Marx and Engels co-authored *The German Ideology*,[390] which articulated the concept of historical materialism: "The production of ideas, conceptions, and consciousness is directly interwoven with the material activity and the material conditions of life. The ruling ideas are nothing more than the ideal expression of the dominant material relationships."[391] However, as the weight of revolutionary expectations from 1848 cracked his idealism, "the realization of historical inevitability"[392] began to take hold. The revolutionary prophet, Marx, the guiding figure of his age, came to offer a new path to salvation from societal oppression. He posited that, like the Jews in Egypt, laborers were enslaved under capitalism and that only by crossing over to communism would they be truly free. Marx explains: "Communism is for us not a state of affairs which is to be established, an ideal to which reality [will] have to adjust itself. We call communism the real movement which abolishes the present state of things."[393] Marx's bohemian vision of communist society here was one in which "the productive forces of the individual will be so developed that he can hunt in the morning, fish in the afternoon, rear cattle in the evening, and critique after dinner, just as I have a mind to, without ever becoming a hunter, a fisherman, a shepherd, or a critic."[394] This aspirational dream reflects Marx's own desire as a poet, but also to avoid the hard time and space decisions, and the compromises and responsibilities of this life. Marx further explains: "Communism is the genuine solution of the antagonism between man and nature and between man and man,"[395] the same vision prophesied in Hebrew Scripture where 'the wolf shall live with the lamb'[396] . . . 'neither shall they learn war anymore.'"[397] "It is the true solution of the struggle between existence and essence, between objectification and self-affirmation, between freedom and necessity, between individual and species above all its solves the eternal plight. Communism is not an economic aspiration only but the solution to the riddle of history which knows itself to be this solution."[398]

At the heart of the Marx's eschatological story, humankind suffers with "the problem of alienation," which is "an atheistic version of the selfsame religion's metaphysical grievance at the entire created universe."[399] In the same way the Bible begins with the Fall, strives to overcome sin, and culminates in the Apocalypse with the return of the Messiah,[400] Marx's vision begins with the worker's "chains,"[401] those bound with alienation given their status, and then reaches the final age of communism ushered in with the "dictatorship of the proletariat."[402] As one observer put it: "This is the final irony: Marxism as messianism. If all of previous history is the history of class struggle, then communism, ushering in a classless society, is surely the end of history and the beginning of a new age. And this is the core religious nature of Marxism: the promise of secular redemption, of the de-alienation of man. For this purpose nothing less than a powerful determinism will avail."[403] Earlier messianic movements could invoke the supreme authority of God, from Scripture, or from divine providence. In a secular age, devoid of any higher revelation, only a materialistic determinism—"historical materialism," as Engels put it—could serve to validate a doctrine as radical, as presumptuous, as this. And it is this real movement toward this idyllic end that is thought to justify the harsh realities of the present—the brutalities of revolution[404] and the tyrannies of communist regimes."[405]

As we will see, their radical ideas alienated them from mainstream society and even from many of their contemporaries in the socialist movement. Without the Christian nemesis in a Satan or devil, the story would need to form new groups, and new opposition. As George Orwell would later show in *Nineteen Eighty-Four*: what is also needed is new "enemies" and "hate-figures," those "dedicated to the overthrow of the State . . . the indispensable figure on whom hatred could be focused."[406] Marx's directed hate is toward the capitalists or the landowners, "abstract mythical faceless terms that cast a sinister shadow,"[407] much like the white supremacists, misogynists, or racists who are weaponized today.[408] As Marx wrote: "The weapon of criticism cannot, of course, replace criticism by weapons; material force must be overthrown by material force."[409]

His growing conviction that only revolutionary action could dismantle the oppressive forces of capitalism fueled his attempt to galvanize the working class, an effort that came to an abrupt end with the first and last, and double, issue of the *Deutsch-Französische Jahrbücher* in Paris in late February 1844, a short-lived, radical intellectual journal founded by Marx and Arnold Ruge, a fellow German political thinker that predated the convictions brought about after visiting England. The ending further put him at odds with both the Prussian government and the intellectual circles in which he had once moved. Marx often wrote with a vitriolic passion against adversaries, and the *National Zeitung* exposed his intense disdain. The judgment might have passed with the final issue, where he writes: "We have no compassion and we ask no compassion from you. When our turn comes, we shall not make excuses for the terror."[410] He goes on: "the royal terrorists, the terrorists by the grace of God and the law, are in practice brutal, disdainful, and mean, in theory cowardly, secretive, and deceitful, and in both respects disreputable."[411] He collected letters and affidavits to support his contentions with an almost fiendish cunning.[412]

Marx brimmed with extensive quotations from literary giants such as Dante, Shakespeare, Virgil, Schiller, and Byron to fortify his polemics and lay his ideological adversaries to rest.[413] Each of these figures reflects an aspect of Marx's evolving identity, shaping his intellectual foundation, reinforcing his personal values, and illustrating the character he aspired to embody. By embedding these references throughout his private journey, he made sure these influences could serve as thematic markers, tracing the development of his ideals and underscoring the enduring connections between his inspirations and his life's work. Marx and Engels indeed referenced Dante's *Divine Comedy* and often made comparisons between the ruling bourgeois class and those damned in Dante's *Inferno*, but this specific quote does not match a direct citation from their letters. It's possible that the sentiment was paraphrased or summarized based on their ideas, but it doesn't appear to be a verbatim excerpt from their correspondence.[414] In this, Marx mirrored Dante's tragic figures, whose unyielding ambitions often led them deeper into alienation and self-fulfilling prophecy. "The worker becomes all the poorer the more wealth he produces, the more his production increases in power and scope. What the capitalist is, the worker must become: alienated from the product of his labor, from his own life, and from other people,"[415] with "mindless factory work."[416]

Although Marx and Engels shared a deep sense of alienation, their responses were shaped by contrasting personal experiences and ideological frameworks. For Engels, alienation was often tempered by the privileges of wealth and social standing, allowing him to observe capitalist injustice from a certain remove. For Marx, however, alienation was not merely a theoretical concept—it was lived reality. As he wrote about estranged labor and commodified man, his own family endured poverty, illness, and social isolation. Alienation was both the subject of his economic critique and the shape of his daily existence: long nights of writing in damp lodgings, children buried before their time, and a wife worn thin by years of sacrifice. His philosophy emerged not just from books but from hardship—a fusion of thought and suffering that animated his vision of revolutionary change.[417] For Engels, it was more visceral, rooted in the tension between his wealthy bourgeois upbringing and his commitment to the working class, to stem of abuses of early capitalism in England, before child labor laws or any workers rights, serves the radical action, like Jesus overturning the money changers.[418] Ultimately, their commitment is also the greatest flaw, an all-consuming passion and uncompromising zeal that must define progress by violence and war. Though it defies the more scientific approach to history, Marx's projection onto the future operates within a "morphic"[419] vision, which assumes historical development follows a deterministic and inevitable path toward a perfect society—a clear change from the "swerve" concept he developed in his dissertation on Epicurus.[420] The implications of this morphic vision is a series of phases or stages—each one leading inevitably to the next, much like that of Hegel or the Christian millenarian and dispensationalist movements of the time, which continue to shape religious and political thought today. The same patterns can be seen in political movements driven by historicist philosophies, where, as the twentieth-century philosopher Karl Popper[421] warns: "The doctrine that history follows a predetermined path has led to some of the greatest ideological disasters of modern times."[422] Whether in religious or secular contexts, these rigid historical frameworks tend to justify extreme measures in pursuit of an imagined future, often at the expense of present realities. Throughout history, such ideologies—whether in the form of Marxism, religious millenarianism, or other revolutionary doctrines—have often culminated in totalitarianism: systems that subsume the individual into a grand narrative and view alienated persons not as ends in themselves but as instruments to be sacrificed for the so-called "greater good," whether in a secular or religious context. Marx's apocalyptic vision is marked by the tension between theoretical ideals and real-world execution, resulting in a historical clash marked by violence, repression, and the betrayal of one's own principles. Raymond Williams speaks in *Marxism and Literature* of how all societies are made up of

> the residual, the dominant and the emergent; but one must grasp this model dynamically, since the dominant may be about to become residual, the emergent may be moving into the ascendant and the new may recapitulate the old. There are times, however, when consciousness of this change is keener than usual—when an age may actually feel itself in middle march or *medias res*, shaped by what lies behind it yet driven on by what is still to come, tugged by the tidal influence of both eras and anxiously or excitedly aware of its own experience as open-ended. There are periods such as the late eighteenth or early twentieth centuries in which the ground can be felt shifting beneath one's

> feet, as various seismic rumblings announce the arrival of some apocalyptic rough beast.[423]

Marx aspired to be the Darwin of history, and sought to overturn traditional religion, but unwittingly, he projected the same prophetic impulses as those of the Scriptures such as Jeremiah and Isaiah, or figures like Jesus and Paul—men who confronted the fallen nature of humanity while advocating for transformation.[424] It is this eschatological framework that best helps contextualize Marx's thinking. Like the biblical narrative of the Fall and redemption, Marx envisioned a story of man's descent into alienation and his eventual rise—not through divine grace, but through economic revolution. In this vision, man becomes a kind of new Adam, reborn not in Christ but in his role as the laboring agent of historical transformation. Just as Paul describes Jesus as the "second Adam,"[425] Marx reimagines humanity's salvation through material struggle rather than spiritual renewal.[426] While Christianity ushers in a new creation by reconciling humanity to God,[427] Marx positions the proletariat as the faithful or collective redeemer, tasked with reversing the alienation caused by capitalist structures.[428] This recasting of the Fall in the Garden transforms the messianic narrative into an economic framework, or "principalities or powers,"[429] where Paul's second Adam restores spiritual harmony.[430] In contrast, Marx's vision sees the proletariat as the agents of a revolutionary transformation, to birth a new socio-economic order free from exploitation.[431] In Marx's framework, the proletariat assumes the role of the "second Adam," symbolizing the culmination of human suffering and struggle under capitalism. Much like Christ, who, according to Paul, "bears the sins of humanity"[432] to inaugurate the Kingdom of God, the "dictator of the proletariat"[433] carries the new messianic role to unburden and redeem those suffering with alienation. Marx's Edenic inversion of Paul's eschatological vision replaces spiritual salvation with a purely historical and materialist kingdom. As Paul writes: "For as all die in Adam, so all will be made alive in Christ."[434] Marx reinterprets this transformative hope into a revolutionary struggle, where salvation is achieved not through divine fulfillment but through the proletariat's overthrow of oppressive systems. The Fall is no longer the result of the spiritual imperfection (*hamartia*)[435] but the laborer forced into an estranged role. In this new grand narrative,[436] Marx secularizes and transforms the redemptive arc of Pauline theology, recentering it on the economic rather than the spiritual plane.[437] In doing so, he ignores the warning against any attempts to "immanentize the eschaton."[438] As Marx wrote: "The philosophers have only interpreted the world in various ways; the point, however, is to change it."[439]

A core principle, perhaps *obiter dicta*, for Marx comes from another pre-Socratic, Heraclitus, who undergirds the view of perpetual change in his claim that "you cannot step into the same river twice, for other waters are continually flowing on."[440] On the contrary, Paul spoke from the revelation of ancient wisdom: "For as all die in Adam, so all will be made alive in Christ,"[441] reflecting their shared vision of humanity's transformation. He said that "there is no longer slave or free,"[442] or in our case "bourgeois or proletariat," albeit through profoundly different means. Marx condemns capitalism's relentless pursuit of profit, as does Jesus in His warning of the "love of money,"[443] to take an ethical stance against the rich man's[444] fetishization of life.[445] "Money, like metaphor, is a magical power which can transmute anything into anything else, as Timon of Athens protests in a passage which attracted the attention of Karl Marx ('Thus much of this will make black white, foul fair, / Wrong right, base noble, old young, coward valiant…')."[446] For Marx, if money is the fuel, "revolutions are the locomotives of history."[447]

Getting back to Paul, in his writings of redemption through Christ, he claims that "creation itself will be liberated from its bondage to decay"[448] in the new kingdom. This convergence on the need for ethical considerations highlights both Paul's and Marx's recognition of the moral implications of societal transformation. Paul also acknowledges the limits of historical understanding, writing that "now we see in a mirror, dimly,"[449] a statement that reflects his humility before the unfolding of divine truth. Marx, by contrast, sought clarity through material analysis, believing the path to human redemption lay not in revelation but in revolution.[450] Marx emphasizes that "men make their own history, but they do not make it as they please." Paul, too, acknowledges that "when the fullness of time had come, God sent forth his Son."[451] The Apostle witnessed the Roman roads that bridged the ancient world to new industry, setting the stage for a shift from the master-slave economy to the feudal order of the medieval age. Dante's Florence emerged amid early banking and burgeoning economies, precursors to the Industrial Revolution that would unfold in Marx's nineteenth century. All were acutely aware that history was not static but in constant flux, with the cost of global transformation marked by upheaval. Marx declares: "There is a spectre haunting Europe—the spectre of communism," where Paul threads the needle to balance immanence with transcendence while waiting for "the perfect"[452] in the Kingdom of God,[453] "giving what is Caesar's to Caesar and what is God's to God."[454] However, Marx dismisses the redemptive power of shared suffering as a means to greater insight, but still offers the same promises. Walter Kaufmann, philosopher and literary critic, explains: "Many admirers of Marx are also very much like religious believers. They have not become Marxists by way of a thorough study of Marx and of rival thinkers whom they gradually discover to be inferior to him. On the contrary, they are Marxists first, and it is emotionally important for them to belong to this tradition. The study of Marx comes afterward and is usually no more scholarly in nature than was Kierkegaard's study of Christianity."[455]

Dante Alighieri's *The Divine Comedy* delves deeply into themes of alienation, particularly the soul's estrangement from divine grace due to sin. In *Purgatorio* Canto XIX, Dante encounters a soul who reflects on his earthly life, stating: "For till then I was a soul in misery, alienated from God and covetous of all earthly things."[456] This acknowledgment underscores the recognition of personal alienation resulting from material desires and the subsequent journey toward reconciliation. "The little that we know of Dante's Life corresponds well enough with this Portrait and this Book. He was born at Florence, in the upper class of society, in the year 1265. His education was the best then going; much school-divinity, Aristotelean logic, some Latin classics, no inconsiderable insight into certain provinces of things: and Dante, with his earnest intelligent nature, we need not doubt, learned better than most all that was learnable."[457] Dante's lament for the decline of Florence[458] as metaphor for all of humankind captures the danger of unchecked ambition and internal strife, to offer a poignant cautionary parallel of the fallout of Marx sewing discord. Alice Turner, in her *History of Hell*, writes: "Writing his great poem in exile, Dante was concerned with history, with Florentine politics, with the corruption of the clergy, with the moral position of his contemporaries, and most of all with the state of his own psyche."[459]

Dante also depicts the punishment of the sowers of discord: "And so, you see, in me the penalty, in me who, while alive, set neighbors on to fight and brother against brother's kin."[460] In their actual worlds, Marx and Dante were exiles, which "gives them an independence from the societies in which they find themselves, and a moral and epistemological capacity to see through the dominant assumptions and norms of an age. It clears their sight and their moral and intellectual vision, they can see more clearly, more 'objectively,' than those with a stake in the prevailing society,"[461] though they reach very different conclusions.

The period from 1842 to 1845 marked a critical phase in Karl Marx's transformation, as youthful idealism gave way to hardened revolutionary conviction. What began as a journalistic venture in Cologne turned into a direct confrontation with the Prussian state, and by 1845 would end in Marx's banishment from Paris. He would enter the next stage of his journey in a pattern of exile that would become emblematic of his life. Marx's ideological commitments had set him on an irreversible course. His exile was not merely geographical but intellectual—he had severed himself from the institutions that might have tempered his radicalism and refined a totalizing worldview in which revolution was the only option, as necessitated by his own reductionist beliefs. Marx, now fully convinced of his role in history, was, with Engels, ready to chart the course of the coming upheaval. Soon, in the *Communist Manifesto* of 1848, the world would hear his call to arms.

RING 4

The Gospel of Revolution (1845–1848)

"We have no wealth but Karl's ideas, no security but his pen—what kind of inheritance is that for our children?"[462]

—Jenny Marx

Karl Marx was officially expelled from Paris on January 24, 1845, under pressure from the Prussian government. The bitter winter air likely stung his face as he boarded the train, his breath visible in the cold as he left behind the bustling streets of Paris, once the center of his intellectual ambitions. With Jenny and their first child, Jenny Caroline, he traveled toward Brussels, a city that now loomed as both a refuge and a new battleground. The journey by train was long and uncertain, a stark contrast to the vibrant cafés and salons of Paris, where his ideas had once flourished. This expulsion marked a pivotal moment in Marx's life. It forced him to leave the intellectual hub of Europe and relocate to Brussels, where he hoped to continue his revolutionary work under more stable conditions. Marx's expulsion was the culmination of increasing pressure from the French government, which was growing uneasy about his radical activities and inflammatory writings, particularly through his work in collaboration with Arnold Ruge on the *Deutsch-Französische Jahrbücher*. The Prussian government had been exerting diplomatic pressure on France to silence Marx, whose critiques of both Prussian autocracy and the broader capitalist system had made him a target. This political crackdown left Marx with no choice but to leave Paris.

So it was on that fateful day in January of 1845, under pressure from the Prussian government, that Marx was officially forced to move, carrying with him the embers of an intellectual revolution that would soon ignite across Europe. The upheaval brought significant personal strain to Marx's family life. Financially, the family was struggling, and the move only deepened their precarious situation. Marx's political writings had alienated potential benefactors, leaving the family reliant on the modest inheritance from Jenny's aristocratic family and occasional loans from friends like Engels. In the days leading up to his departure, Marx's Paris apartment was a scene of chaos, as the family packed up their belongings and said hurried goodbyes to comrades.

Despite the tension, Marx reportedly expressed defiance, viewing the expulsion as further evidence of the growing fear among Europe's ruling classes: "We have no compassion, and we ask no compassion from you. When our turn comes, we shall not make excuses for the terror."[463] He saw the move to Brussels not as an end but as an opportunity to regroup and expand his revolutionary work. Indeed, Marx's writings from that period (most famously the *Economic and Philosophical Manuscripts of 1844*, which most explicitly elaborated his theory of alienation) reveal a line of thinking that could have initially led him down several paths, including the study of law, religion, the state, natural philosophy, or political economy. He chose the last track as the predominant focus of his studies for the rest of his life. In addition, he closed the chapter on his role as editor of the newspaper *Rheinische Zeitung*, on whose pages he fought for freedom of expression against Prussian censorship.[464] Marx seemed unable to penetrate the truths of religion and philosophy, which left him dealing solely with economic and social causes of social reality, and this, in turn, prompted him to critically study political economy.[465]

Upon arriving in Brussels in February 1845, Marx immediately set about securing permission to reside in the city. Belgium at the time offered relative freedom for political exiles, and Marx saw it as a strategic base from which to continue his critiques of European monarchies and capitalist structures. In the months that followed, he worked tirelessly to deepen his collaboration with Engels, who joined him in Brussels in the summer. Together, they would begin developing the ideas that would culminate in *The Communist Manifesto*, as Brussels became the intellectual and political incubator for Marx's evolving revolutionary ideology.

Ascent through Revolution

Earlier, in April 1845, Engels and Marx established contacts with democrats and socialists, and their life in Brussels was relatively calm. A few years later, Jenny looked back at a period of relative tranquility and remembered her excursions to "the pretty cafés"[466] and her contentment amid the small community of German exiles. "The small German colony lived pleasantly together,"[467] she wrote, and never again would she speak in this way about German exiles.

Meanwhile, Moses Hess and his wife came to live in Brussels and became instrumental in shaping Marx's early development, particularly through Hess's role in articulating the materialist conception of history. The two met in 1845, while active in revolutionary and intellectual circles. A co-founder of the Communist League alongside Marx and Engels, Hess contributed to the formation of early socialist theory. His work, especially *The Holy History of Mankind* (1837), which critiqued organized religion and centered human emancipation, left a lasting impression on Marx. Though he remained committed to socialism throughout his life, Hess eventually broke with Marx's emphasis on class struggle, favoring instead a more ethnic nationalism and a proactive use of the state—evident in his proto-Zionist vision of Jewish restoration as laid out in *Rome and Jerusalem* (1862).

By this time, the Marxs had been cut off from support from the Westphalen family, given the excessive spending and lack of economic progress. In April 1845, when Jenny was pregnant with her second child, Laura, the Baroness von Westphalen, in part to offer some support without direct funding, sent her own trusted maid, Helene Demuth, to help her. Jenny and Karl knew Helene from their youth, and she would remain with the Marx family for nearly forty years. Much of Jenny's contentment during those early months in Brussels came from the presence of this young peasant woman who was sweet-tempered, sensible, and completely reliable, but also known for her firm controlling hand.[468] According to biographer Robert Payne, "Jenny had been terrified at the thought of a second child, but now the fear left her."[469] Helene Demuth "did the shopping, washed the children, prepared the meals, and saw that the bills were paid if there was any money to pay them," and she describes the home, "when there was no money, she would wander down the street to the pawnbroker at the corner. It was a squalid, dirty, miserable place, but all of them came in time to have a feeling of belonging."[470] Again, Marx was bailed out by the kindness of others, in this case with a basic domestic laborer, whom we will learn was never paid.[471]

The toll of defeat and exile weighed heavily on Marx during these years. His political isolation was compounded by financial difficulties, as his revolutionary activities left him without a stable source of income. Despite the financial support that Engels continued to provide, the family suffered greatly during these years, as Marx's political ambitions left little room for personal stability. Marx, in the heart of Europe, could observe firsthand the accelerating forces of industrial capitalism, the widening gap between the bourgeoisie and proletariat, and the deepening class struggles that would shape his critique of political economy.

But stability would not last. Marx's time in Brussels marked a geographical shift and a shift in his intellectual trajectory away from the immediate pressures of revolutionary fervor in other parts of Europe.

Marx found the space to critically reassess and refine his ideas. In collaboration with Engels, he began to articulate a comprehensive materialist conception of history to ground his critique of capitalism in the interplay of economic forces and class dynamics. The Brussels years became a crucible for Marx, forging the theoretical tools that would soon shape his enduring critique of the modern world, but this period also underscored Marx's increasing alignment with Engels, whose insights and shared vision became indispensable to Marx's intellectual evolution. Their long walks through the streets of the city were filled with intense discussions that shaped their collaborative works.

Engels had an unparalleled ability to distill complex ideas into compelling prose, making him essential not just as a theorist but also as a cowriter who brought clarity and accessibility to Marx's often dense arguments. In this way, Engels was far more than an intellectual peer; he was the practical, financial, and creative force that allowed Marx's revolutionary vision to flourish. Engels's arrival in Brussels in April 1845 provided Marx with more than just an ideological ally—it gave him a collaborator whose analytical rigor and firsthand observations of industrial England helped crystallize Marx's own economic theories. Their partnership, akin to Dante's reliance on Virgil, served as a guiding force, helping Marx navigate the complexities of revolutionary thought. Just as Dante, in the *Inferno*, humbly acknowledges his not being Aeneas or Paul—Marx too, in this period, was still shaping his own intellectual identity, but was he aware that he was not the sole prophet of a new world or "end of days"?[472]

In Brussels, Marx's prophetic vision gained clarity, and the intellectual groundwork for his later successes—and eventual failures—were firmly laid. Here, away from immediate political persecution, he moved beyond the radical democratic ideals of his youth toward the fully articulated theory of historical materialism. As Europe, in 1845, filled with the murmurings of revolt, inched toward the upheaval of 1848, the longing for home and belonging intertwined with the growing realization that home, for Marx, could only ever exist in the triumph of his revolutionary ideals. With this fusion of personal and political desire, the next chapter of his journey—the build-up to the 1848 revolutions—loomed ever closer, like a storm gathering on the horizon. With a relationship grounded in mutual respect, Marx and Engels became one of the most significant collaborations in modern history, and the pillars for a movement that would challenge the very fabric of industrial society.

Marx would also delve deeper into his critique of Hegelianism and refine the materialist conception of history that would define his later work.[473] However, he was still settling his account with Hegel and the Young Hegelians in his writings, as he criticized them for limiting the horizon of their critique to religion and for not taking up the critique of the state and civil society as paramount. As a result, colleagues and mentors began to remark on Marx's emerging ideas—often with an inflated sense of their potential impact, mistaking his early theories for signs of lasting influence. In an earlier letter, Arnold Ruge would inquire: "Your critique of Hegel is brilliant, but how do you address the people's material conditions?"[474] Marx and Engels's collaboration flourished during this period as their partnership was evolving. Marx began to view history through the lens of class conflict, recognizing the modern proletariat as the revolutionary force capable of overturning the capitalist order through controlling the means of production. As we have seen, their observations of the squalid living conditions of workers in England, vividly described in Engels's *The Condition of the Working Class in England*, informed much of their critique of capitalism. But Engels's contributions extended beyond research. When Marx faced near-destitution, it was Engels who sent money to sustain Marx's family, ensuring that he could continue his intellectual pursuits. He became involved with socialist groups and began drafting his seminal work, *The German Ideology* (1845 and 1846), in collaboration with Engels. This text, although unpublished during their lifetimes, was instrumental in articulating their materialist conception of history, emphasizing the economic base as the foundation of societal development: "The mode of production of material life conditions the general process of social, political and intellectual life. It is not the consciousness of men that determines their existence, but their social existence that determines their consciousness."[475]

Brussels, in 1845, was not merely a waypoint for Marx but a crucible in which his ideas began to coalesce into the revolutionary framework that would later dominate his writings. On December 1 of that same year, Marx renounced his Prussian citizenship due to mounting persecution by the Prussian police, and by early 1846, Marx and Engels set up the Communist Correspondence Committee in Brussels with a view to organizationally unite the socialists and politically aware workers of different countries, paving the way for the establishment of an international proletarian organization.

In the years 1846 and 1847, Marx and Engels entered a period that would significantly shape the trajectory of revolutionary thought in Europe. German political activist Wilhelm Weitling would make a good point when he told Marx that "talk was cheap": "Your intellectual rigor is unmatched, but revolution requires action, not just theory."[476] And Marx did indeed take action. He worked on organizing the Communist Correspondence Committee in January 1846 to establish communication and foster international collaboration among the growing socialist movement. During this period, Marx's intellectual environment was characterized by a continuous flow of ideas, debates, and theoretical advancements. Marx's work with the committee marked the beginning of his deeper engagement with the broader European socialist landscape. It was time to write the manifesto.

The Ghost in the Manifesto

As 1846 unfolded, Marx and Engels found themselves immersed in a whirlwind of intellectual fervor; their days spent in animated discussions, scribbling notes, and challenging each other's ideas, all in pursuit of a revolutionary vision. By autumn, their collaborative efforts had crystallized into a clear conviction: the proletariat must rise against the chains of capitalism. Marx, a natural storyteller,[477] fond of Shakespeare, used the metaphor of the "specter," as depicted in *Hamlet,* to parallel the "specter of communism"[478] that he and Engels described in the *Communist Manifesto*. Hamlet's lament, "The time is out of joint: O cursed spite, That ever I was born to set it right,"[479] is a verse that mirrors Marx's own perception of his role in addressing the tumultuous transformations of the modern world.[480] The play, for him, embodies the conflicts inherent in societal evolution.[481] Once again, he likewise used the imagery of ghosts or haunting to represent societal rot and the rise to transformative action. For Marx, Hamlet was not simply a tragic figure; he was a symbol of the modern man caught in the contradictions of his time,[482] torn between the decayed remnants of feudalism and the burgeoning forces of capitalism. In this context, Hamlet can be seen as a figure navigating his own purgatory and confronting the moral ambiguities of his existence.[483] Similarly, Marx viewed the capitalist stage as a purgatorial phase, where the contradictions of the system would eventually lead to its dissolution and the emergence of a new societal order. Thus, the stage of capitalism, much like a tragedy, would be unmasked as a spectacle where appearances deceive and the true actors—laborers—are rendered invisible, with a "refusal to let any comfort, faith, or joy deafen our ears to the tortured cries of our brethren."[484] Marx's analysis reveals the illusory nature of capitalist structures, much like Hamlet's realization of the deceptive façades within the Danish court. Both highlight the necessity of piercing through appearances to confront ghostly truths, to set the stage for transformative action. For Marx, Hamlet embodied the tensions of history itself—a single figure caught between fading feudal loyalties, rising bourgeois ambition, and the stirrings of proletarian unrest. In him, Marx saw a living paradox, a man whose internal conflict mirrored the larger contradictions of a world in transition. In Marx's analysis, Hamlet's paralysis—the hesitation to act despite the moral clarity of his mission—mirrored the struggles of the working class in the face of systemic oppression. Just as Hamlet wrestled with the burden of avenging his father and restoring order to Denmark, so too did Marx believe that the proletariat needs to be avenged and therefore bore the responsibility of dismantling capitalism to reshape society. This literary parallel allowed Marx to frame the modern struggle in universal terms, drawing upon the emotional and symbolic weight of one of the greatest tragedies to convey the urgency of revolution. Hamlet's call to action—to "pull back the curtain" on the corruption of his society—was an apt metaphor for the role of the revolutionary in exposing and confronting the systemic contradictions of the modern world.

In this way, Shakespeare's tragedy became a stage on which Marx could interpret the present and envision the future, offering a bridge between the cultural legacy of the past and the revolutionary potential of his time. This connection between theory, art, and history exemplified Marx's ability to intertwine the intellectual and the emotional, making his vision not only a matter of reason but also of human passion and moral necessity.

In *German Ideology*, Marx and Engels elaborated on their materialist conception of history, providing a comprehensive critique of the philosophical and political ideas that had dominated European thought. As 1845 drew to a close, their intellectual efforts continued unabated. Despite challenges in finding a publisher because of political repression and censorship, Marx and Engels remained undeterred, confident that their work would eventually find an audience. At home, Jenny, heavily pregnant and worn down by the grinding poverty that had come to define their lives, gave birth to their son Heinrich on October 15, 1846. His arrival brought a moment of joy, though it was quickly overshadowed by the harsh realities of their situation. The family's financial struggles were dire, with Jenny often left alone to bear the brunt of keeping the household afloat while Marx poured his energy into his work.

The birth of Heinrich was yet another reminder of the unstable balance that Marx had to maintain between his revolutionary ideals and the practical need to support his growing family. Despite these challenges, Marx and Engels were entering a crucial phase of their partnership. By December 1846, they had begun drafting the framework for what would soon become *The Communist Manifesto.* The document began to crystallize their critique of capitalism, their rejection of transcendence in favor of idealized socialism, and their insistence on the necessity of class struggle to achieve a truly just society. For Marx, this project was not only an intellectual endeavor but also a potential breakthrough that could establish him as a leading voice in the socialist movement—and one that might finally provide the stability and recognition his family so desperately needed.

The following year, 1847, would prove transformative for Marx and Engels. They forged alliances with revolutionary thinkers and labor leaders, many of whom were also struggling under the weight of industrial capitalism's injustices.[485] These efforts culminated in their involvement with the Communist League, an international network of workers and intellectuals committed to revolutionary change. The league's congresses in London in June and November 1847 provided Marx and Engels with the platform to present their ideas to a broader audience and solidify their leadership within the movement. Marx grappled with the pressing need to turn theoretical work into tangible action. The social and political upheavals of the time provided a fertile ground for revolutionary thought, but they also demanded clarity and direction. In this context, Marx's collaboration with Engels deepened, as the two men shared not only an intellectual vision but also a personal determination to effect change. Engels' financial support and strategic insights were indispensable, for they allowed Marx to focus on his writing and organizational efforts. The world around them was teetering on the edge of revolution. Across Europe, industrialization was transforming economies and societies, creating deep divides between the working class and the bourgeoisie. Marx famously declared in *The Communist Manifesto*, "The history of all hitherto existing society is the history of class struggles."[486] For Marx, this was the central lens through which to interpret human history—one that reduced cultural, religious, and even existential dimensions to expressions of material conflict. Yet, non-Marxist historians have long pointed out that for much of history, most people—regardless of class—were united not by political rivalry but by a shared struggle for survival.[487]

The conditions Marx observed during his travels to Paris, Brussels, and London were stark: crowded tenements, exploitative labor practices, and the growing discontent of workers who were beginning to organize in response. These real-world events lent urgency to Marx's work and shaped the ideas that would become central to *The Communist Manifesto*. Amid these developments, Marx's personal life remained fraught. Jenny's health remained fragile after Heinrich's birth, and the family's poverty was a constant source of strain. Marx knew that success in his revolutionary efforts was not only a matter of ideological commitment but also of survival for his family. The stakes were higher than ever as 1847 progressed, with the growing anticipation of a broader revolutionary wave. By the end of the year, Marx and Engels had completed the first drafts of their *Manifesto*, setting the stage for what would become one of the most influential political documents in history. Their ability to tie the personal struggles of the working class to the broader historical forces at play would cement their place in the annals of revolutionary thought, even as they, given their views, continued to live on the margins of society.

Engels also took on a more active role in the League of the Just, a revolutionary socialist group based in Paris, and traveled between Brussels and Paris, strengthening their ties with the league, which helped them to guide its reorganization into the Communist League. Eventually, in June 1847, the Communist League held its First Congress in London, where Engels represented their shared ideas, advocating for the league to adopt a more defined communist agenda. The

League of the Just was reorganized under Engels's influence, and its members embraced the communist slogan "Workers of the world, unite!"[488] This marked a significant shift in the group's focus, as it moved from vague socialist goals to a more radical, Marx-inspired agenda.

The summer and fall of 1847 were consumed with preparations for the Communist League's Second Congress. Marx and Engels worked together drafting materials and refining the league's ideological framework. Engels continued to travel, spreading revolutionary ideas and gathering feedback from various socialist groups. In November, the Communist League's Second Congress convened in London. Both Marx and Engels attended and were tasked with drafting what would become *The Communist Manifesto*. The congress also solidified the principles of revolutionary socialism, marking a critical moment in the development of Marxist thought.

Redemption in Revolt

As 1847 drew to a close, Marx and Engels began drafting what would become the world-renowned pamphlet. Marx, taking the lead in writing, synthesized their ideas into a cohesive document that called for the overthrow of the existing capitalist system and the establishment of a classless,[489] stateless society.[490] *The Communist Manifesto* would "clarify the struggles of the proletariat"[491] and serve not only as a revolutionary document but also as a rallying cry for workers and revolutionaries across Europe. Marxist historian Eric Hobsbawm succinctly summarizes the document's impact: "Marx's genius lay in connecting the personal struggles of laborers with the grand sweep of historical development."[492] Biographer Schlomo Avineri adds: "*The Communist Manifesto* was not just a revolutionary document but a philosophical intervention in its own right."[493] It was not merely a call to arms but a profound condemnation of the evils wrought by capitalism.

Marx and Engels issued a call for uprisings during the 1848 revolutions in Europe. They urged workers to rise against the bourgeoisie by offering a diagnosis of the present as well as a vision for the future. "Workers of the world unite, you have nothing to lose but your chains!"[494] Hobsbawm captures this duality when emphasizing Marx's ability to blend the intimate with the universal, while Avineri underscores the manifesto's philosophical depth, elevating it beyond a mere revolutionary tract. The phrase "All that is solid melts into air"[495] crystallizes the document's critique of capitalism's disruptive power. Marx's imagery once again draws from literary tradition to capture the instability and impermanence of human structures under industrialization. In his view, the system does not merely evolve—it dissolves: age-old institutions, customs, and beliefs are stripped away, revealing the naked mechanisms of production and profit. Later economists, such as Joseph Schumpeter, would famously describe this process as "creative destruction," recognizing capitalism's inherent dynamism—the same forces that dismantle the past also unleash human ingenuity and material progress. Yet as critics like Christopher Lasch have noted, this progress often comes at the cost of tradition, family, and cultural cohesion. For Marx, this radical transformation was inevitable. For modern critics, the question is how to harness innovation without sacrificing the moral and institutional foundations of society. This idea, both poetic and incisive, underscores the manifesto's resonance as a critique of the modern condition. Siegbert Prawer, author of *Karl Marx and World Literature*, writes, "the revolutionary fervor of 1848 was matched by Marx's literary references, grounding his political ideas in cultural heritage."[496]

Through his adopted poetic lens, Marx here reframes the brutality of capitalist upheaval as a paradoxical opportunity: a moment of disintegration that also holds the seeds of revolutionary potential and a new age. By first stripping away the supposed myths that sustain the status quo, capitalism inadvertently lays bare the conditions for its own overthrow, making the manifesto as much a prophecy of transformation as a critique of exploitation. This juxtaposition of Hamlet's introspection and Marx's critique highlights a shared recognition of impermanence and the transformative potential within decay. Similarly, Marx observes that the very structures of capitalism are in a constant state of flux, something that will lead to their eventual dissolution, "all that is solid melts into air"[497] thus capturing the ephemeral nature of societal constructs under past economic paradigms. By the end of 1847, the foundation had been laid for what would be one of the most influential political documents in history, setting the stage for the revolutions of 1848 and the long-term impact of Marxist theory on Europe and, inevitably, global politics. As the new year dawned, the political landscape in Europe was shifting, and 1848 would prove to be a pivotal year for Marx, Engels, and the movement.

The political climate in Europe made it ripe for revolution, with discontent brewing among the working class and growing unrest in many parts of the continent. King Louis-Philippe, born on October 6, 1773, in Paris, ascended to the throne as king of the French in 1830 following the July Revolution. His reign, often characterized by conservative policies and limited political reforms, lasted until he was forced to abdicate on February 24, 1848, amid widespread social unrest. Following his abdication, the Second French Republic was established, marking a significant shift in France's political landscape. The provisional government of the Second Republic came into existence on February 24, 1848, the same day Louis-Philippe abdicated.

These course-altering political events provided Marx with a real-world context to analyze the dynamics of class struggle and the role of the state in suppressing or facilitating revolutionary change. In his book *The Eighteenth Brumaire of Louis Bonaparte*, Marx examined the events leading up to and following the 1848 Revolution, offering insights into the interplay between political power and class interests. The revolution and the subsequent establishment of the Second Republic also provided Marx with a profound case study on the dynamics of political authority and the prerequisites for a successful proletarian uprising.

These events underscored the intricate challenges at the heart of revolutionary movements—struggles that Marx would continue to dissect throughout his writings. In this spirit, he echoed Shakespeare's Hamlet: "O cursed spite . . ."[498] As Marx wrestled with the burdens of historical change, his predicament mirrored a deeper dramatic archetype. As Marx biographer Terry Eagleton observes, drawing from Heidegger, "Great tragedy, then, is a revolutionary act of world-founding; and the unhappy fate of such world-founders, prophets out of joint with their times who are destined for martyrdom, is often enough the subject-matter of the drama itself."[499] This sentiment mirrors the revolutionary fervor of 1848, a period when the old order seemed misaligned, and individuals felt destined to rectify societal imbalances. On February 21, 1848, as Europe teetered on the brink of widespread revolution, Marx and Engels published the *Communist Manifesto* in Germany. They declared: "The history of all hitherto existing society is the history of class struggles." This proclamation not only critiqued existing power structures but also served as a clarion call for the proletariat to recognize their role in reshaping the world. Thus, both Hamlet's introspection and Marx's manifesto grapple with the imperative to confront and amend a disordered world, highlighting the enduring struggle "to set things right."[500] Marx saw human society as structured around the struggle of classes and their eventual purging and transformation.

During this period, his financial struggles and detachment from family responsibilities deepened his disconnect from the world.[501] His family struggled in squalor while Marx philosophized from a position of intellectual superiority, and this discontent helped fuel his political radicalism.[502] Marx's writings moved from poetic musings on suffering and rebellion to philosophical critiques of society. He famously embraced the idea of the "abolition of everything"[503] focusing on the destruction of societal structures, including family—with Engels referring to women at home as "glorified prostitutes"[504]—religion,[505] and property,[506] all of which he viewed as tools of oppression. Marx, in the *Communist Manifesto*, wrote: "Abolition of the family! Even the most radical flare up at this infamous proposal of the Communists. . . . On what foundation is the present family, the bourgeois family, based? On capital, on private gain. In its completely developed form this family exists only among the bourgeoisie. But this state of things finds its complement in the practical absence of the family among the proletarians, and in public prostitution."[507] This radical critique culminated in calling for the overthrow of existing conditions. The *Manifesto of the Communist Party* was written in expectation of the coming revolution. A short pamphlet originally published in 1848, it is the classic text for understanding Marx's and Engels' action-orientated political thought. The work is radical, contentious, and short, with ten basic tenets:

1. Abolition of property in land and all rents of land to public purposes.
2. A heavy progressive or graduated income tax.
3. Abolition of all right of inheritance.
4. Confiscation of the property of all emigrants and rebels.
5. Centralization of credit in the hands of the State by means of a national bank with State capital and an exclusive monopoly.
6. Centralization of the means of communication and transport in the hands of the state.
7. Extension of factories and instruments of production owned by the State, the bringing into cultivation of wastelands, and the improvement of the soil generally with a common plan.[508]
8. Equal ability of all to labour. Establishment of industrial armies, especially for agriculture.
9. Combination of agriculture with manufacturing industries; gradual abolition of the distinction between town and country, by a more equable distribution of the population over the country.
10. Free education for all children in public schools. Abolition of children's factory labour in its present form. Combination of education with industrial production.[509]

Above all, the *Manifesto* is a political mandate, with the prophetic vision for the clash of a final holy war. The bare bones of Marxist theory are presented in clear, coherent text. The bourgeoisie (capitalist class) and the proletariat (the dispossessed and working classes) are set up as clear and opposing forces.[510] Marx recognized that capitalism, by its nature, tends toward expansion: it seeks new resources, new labor, and new markets to sustain its momentum. As he and Engels wrote in the *Communist Manifesto*, the bourgeoisie "must nestle everywhere, settle everywhere, establish connections everywhere." This tendency toward international trade, however, was not the same as modern globalism. In Marx's time, international trade existed alongside national policies—such as tariffs—that protected domestic industries and reinforced national sovereignty. What Marx astutely diagnosed was capitalism's dynamic logic: it unleashes human productivity and technological advancement, but can also result in instability, exploitation, and dislocation when unchecked. He saw a contradiction at the heart of the system: workers generate wealth, yet often remain impoverished, while capitalists appropriate the surplus.[511] Still, this is not an inevitable outcome of capitalism itself—it is a reflection of choices made within the system. Henry Ford, for instance, famously raised his workers' wages so they could afford the very cars they were building—a move rooted not in socialism but in practical capitalism. As modern economies grow, workers are not always pauperized; many become consumers and beneficiaries of a rising middle class. While collective bargaining played a role in this process, the real strength of capitalism lies in its capacity to elevate living standards through innovation, competition, and expanding opportunity—when accompanied by policies that protect national interests and preserve social cohesion.

Marx and Engels detail the "revolutionary role in history" of the bourgeoisie. They claim that the colossal forces of capitalist production far exceed the marvels of the "Egyptian pyramids, Roman aqueducts, and Gothic cathedrals."[512] The *Manifesto* claims that the bourgeoisie have uniquely demonstrated what human activity can accomplish and how the latter "produces their own gravediggers."[513] Here, "gravediggers" metaphorically refers to the proletariat, who, through their growing awareness and unity, are seen as the force that will eventually overthrow the bourgeoisie.[514] As Marx foretold, the bourgeoisie, like the skull of Yorick, have long since forgotten their inevitable end, yet in their triumph, they unwittingly nurture the very force—the gravediggers—who will bury their reign. The more proletarian workers are brought together—through the concentration and growth of industry—the more their capacity for revolutionary unity increases. "Workers of the world," Marx claims à la Rousseau, have "nothing left to lose but their chains."[515] At the same time, given their *Manifesto*, "they have a world to win."[516]

Proletarian Purgatory

Winning meant the next morph from a capitalist society to that of socialism and eventually communism: "Agrarian feudalism and monotheistic religion, as he saw it, were superseded by urban capitalism and scientific on philosophical reason. In a real sense capitalism provided the basis of a new society founded on reason."[517] Marx and Engels also draw upon the idea of a spiritual and social reckoning in discussing the revolutionary upheaval. They frame capitalism's end in a way that evokes Dante's vision of retribution and judgment: "The class struggle, as in Dante's Hell, divides the damned from the chosen, the oppressed from the oppressor, the rich from the poor, the exploiter from the exploited."[518] The *Manifesto* pamphlet quickly gained traction, resonating with the aspirations of workers, intellectuals, and radicals who sought to challenge the existing order. Marx's call for proletarian revolution, the abolition of private property, and the overthrow of capitalist structures struck a chord with many, particularly as the revolutions of 1848 unfolded.[519]

In the months that followed the publication, Marx's ideas gained increasing prominence. In France, the February Revolution inspired workers' uprisings, and the new government found itself struggling to reconcile the demands of the working class with the demands of the bourgeoisie. Engels traveled to Paris in the wake of the revolution, where he worked alongside other revolutionaries to spark further action. Marx, too, became involved in the political fires of the period, using his position to further advocate for revolutionary socialism. He was briefly involved with the resurrection of *Neue Rheinische Zeitung* (*New Rhenish Newspaper*) as a platform for his ideas and a tactical rallying point for revolutionary forces.

As for the written document itself, critics would fire back. Pierre-Joseph Proudhon (1809–1865), for example, asserts in a letter sent to Marx: "Your communism is authoritarian, and your critique of property lacks nuance."[520] The revolutions of 1848 tested Marx's theories in practice. The June Days Uprising in France highlighted the struggles of the working class but ended in violent suppression[521] and the rise of Louis-Napoléon Bonaparte, later known as Napoleon III. He was born on April 20, 1808, and died on January 9, 1873. The nephew of Napoleon Bonaparte, he rose to prominence as the first president of the French Second Republic from 1848 to 1852. Following the *coup d'état*, he declared himself emperor of the French and ruled as Napoleon III from 1852 to 1870.[522] Marx famously analyzed Louis-Napoléon's rise in *The Eighteenth Brumaire of Louis Bonaparte* (1852), framing his rule as a "farce" when compared to his uncle's "tragedy."[523] For Marx, Louis-Napoléon's reign epitomized the contradictions inherent in capitalist society, where popular support was manipulated to maintain bourgeois power while revolutionary movements were systematically suppressed. This critique not only reflects Marx's broader analysis of class struggle but also highlights the interplay between political leadership and the socioeconomic forces of the era.

Ferdinand Lassalle, the German political activist and early advocate for workers' rights, challenged Marx's approach, arguing that laborers required leadership grounded in their daily hardships—not abstract promises of a distant utopia. While the revolutions failed to deliver immediate change, they confirmed Marx's belief in the inevitability of class struggle. Despite setbacks, the year solidified Marx and Engels's ideas in the political discourse of their time and beyond. They would continue to inspire generations of revolutionaries in the struggle for a more just and egalitarian world. Prior to the *Communist Manifesto*, Marx's thought was still deeply derivative—borrowing from ancient materialists, classical economists, and modern philosophers, but his unique contribution lay solely in his prophetic vision of a revolutionary future. As a new *Weltanschauung*, however, Jeffrey Burton Russell adds: "Marxism, like any other system, is based upon unproven a priori assumptions, some of which involve severe internal contradictions. Marxism is best understood as a kind of religion based on faith,"[524] and not a philosophy but a "social practice."[525]

As far back as 1838, Marx "announced that Prometheus was the chief saint and martyr in the human calendar, because he had defied the Gods on behalf of man."[526] "I gave men knowledge; I taught them to think, and for this, I am bound in chains."[527] Marx, too, saw himself as a bringer of enlightenment, a liberator of humanity from the ignorance of capitalism. In this sense, his journey mirrors Lucifer's defiant rejection of all spiritual realities in favor of human autonomy. Marx's vision of a future communist utopia—a classless, stateless society—was not merely an economic or political proposition but a messianic promise, a secular apocalypse[528] in which humanity would be liberated from the chains of exploitation and oppression.

As Robert Payne remarks: "Sooner or later the real man emerges from behind the screen of propaganda, and as the reader will see, he is far more interesting, more human and more vulnerable than the figure enthroned on the Communist altars."[529] Paul Johnson adds: "No political writer has ever excelled the last three sentences of the Manifesto: 'The workers have nothing to lose but their chains. They have a world to gain. Workers of the world, unite!'"[530]

Karl Marx was not alone in his Promethean Spirit within the revolutionary culture of his time. The rhetoric of radical minions often invoked the figure of Satan not as an embodiment of evil but as a symbol of defiance against authority. For Marx and many of his contemporaries, rebellion was more than atheism—it was a driving force, a defiant spirit that cast Satan not as a villain, but as a symbol of radical upheaval. Marx's early writings, with their fiery language and relentless yearning, reflect this deeper alignment with the mythic tradition of revolt. Pierre-Joseph Proudhon, one of the first anarchist thinkers, openly called upon Satan in his writings: "Aid me, Lucifer, Satan, whoever you are, demon opposed to God according to the faith of my fathers! I will speak for you; and I ask nothing from you."[531] In another passage, he glorifies Satan as the necessary force against divine tyranny: "Come, Satan, come, slandered by priests and kings! Let me embrace you, let me clutch you to my breast! . . . What would justice be without you? An instinct. Reason? A routine. Man? A beast."[532] Russian anarchist leader Mikhail Bakunin took this further, declaring that Proudhon "adored Satan and proclaimed Anarchy."[533] Bakunin himself believed that invoking the devil was essential to the revolutionary cause: "The Evil One is the satanic revolt against divine authority, revolt in which we see the fecund germ of all human emancipations, the revolution. . . . In this revolution we will have to awaken the Devil in the people, to stir up the basest passions. Our mission is to destroy, not to edify."[534]

The comment was not merely rhetorical. Many radicals did not simply reject religion but inverted it, turning the Holy Family's cross upside down to make Satan a hero against an oppressive God. This anti-theism fueled the revolutionary drive not only to dismantle religious belief but to overturn all associated institutional structures. Moses Hess, the man who introduced Karl Marx to communism, expressed his own existential torment upon becoming an atheist: "I became an atheist. The world became a burden and a curse to me. I looked at it like a cadaver."[535] Hess would later boast about his influence on Friedrich Engels, writing: "He parted from me as an over-zealous Communist. This is how I produce ravages."[536] The spirit of Lucifer, as a figure of rebellion, destruction, and defiance, became an ideological tool to drive not just Marx but an entire generation of radicals who sought to tear down the old world by any means necessary. "The 'European fraternal union of peoples' cannot be achieved by mere phrases and pious wishes, but only by profound revolutions and bloody struggles."[537] Bakunin was both dismissing of Engels and darkly revealing of Marx when he wrote: "While Mr. Engels, his devoted friend, was just as intelligent as [Marx], though not as erudite, he made up for that by being more practical, and no less adept at political calumny, lying and intrigue."[538] Marx, in his role as liberator, would also connect the idea of the slave and chains to religion itself, when he said:

> Criticism has plucked the imaginary flowers from the chains not so that man may bear chains without any imagination or belief, but so that he may throw away the chains and pluck living flowers. The criticism of religion disillusions man so that he may think, act and fashion his own reality as a disillusioned man come to his senses; so that he may revolve around himself as his real sun. Religion is only the illusory sun which revolves around man as long as he does not revolve around himself.[539]

What did any of this have to do with the politics and economics of the real world? Just as the origin of Marx's philosophy lay in a prophetic vision, so its elaboration was an exercise framing an apocalypse. "What it needed, however, to set Marx's intellectual machinery in motion was a moral impulse."[540] By June 1848, Marx's role as the new Moses—a revolutionary intellectual—had launched. His fervent revolutionary ideals were both nurtured and challenged by his contemporaries. The promised land of 1848 did not result in the sweeping transformations that Marx and Engels had hoped for, and their peers knew it. As Lassalle stated in his earlier critique, "the workers need leadership that speaks to their immediate struggles, not just future visions."[541] Influential figures like atheist Moses Hess encouraged his revolutionary passion but warned him not to forget spirituality. Hess cautioned: "Your atheism disregards the moral strength religion provides in mobilizing the oppressed."[542] He admired Marx's passion for revolution but expressed reservations about Marx's staunch atheism. Hess cautioned that dismissing the moral and spiritual dimensions of human existence could alienate potential allies among the oppressed, who found solace and strength in their religious faith. He believed that religion provided a moral framework that could be harnessed to mobilize the masses against oppression and so would communism.

This perspective highlighted a fundamental tension in Marx's approach: while he sought to rally the proletariat to overthrow existing societal structures, his rejection of religion risked alienating those for whom faith was a source of comfort and motivation. As 1848 approached, Europe was a tinderbox of social and political unrest, and Marx, fueled by the belief that the proletarian revolution was imminent, published *The Communist Manifesto.* The timing seemed prophetic, as revolutionary waves swept across Europe shortly after its publication. In France, the February Revolution led to the abdication of King Louis-Philippe and the establishment of the Second Republic. Inspired by these events, similar uprisings erupted in the German states, the Austrian Empire, and parts of Italy.[543] Even so by the end of 1849, the revolutionary fervor had been effectively extinguished, and the old regimes had largely restored their power.

The aftermath of the 1848 revolutions was a profound disappointment for Marx. The proletarian uprising he had anticipated failed to materialize. The working class, instead of rising as a unified force, remained fragmented and often at odds with allies. Marx's belief in the imminence of a proletarian revolution seemed more distant than ever.

In the wake of these disappointments, Marx's financial struggles deepened, leading to periods of further destitution for his family. Despite this, Marx delved deeper into economic theories and refining his critique of capitalism. He recognized that the path to revolution was more complex than he had initially envisioned. The working class was not a monolithic entity, and the dynamics of class struggle were intricate and multifaceted. "Marx is a dialectician for whom the working through of conflict involves irreparable loss. Those who perished in the class struggle will not be requited by whatever successes their descendants are able to chalk up."[544] He began to appreciate the need for a more nuanced understanding of societal structures and the factors that could galvanize the proletariat into a cohesive revolutionary force.

This period of introspection and analysis led Marx to refine his theories, laying the groundwork for his later works. Marx's experiences during and after the 1848 revolutions underscored the importance of a scientific approach to understanding society—a method that combined empirical observation with critical analysis. He realized that spontaneous uprisings, while significant, were insufficient to overthrow entrenched systems of power. A successful revolution required a deep understanding of economic structures, class relations, and the development of class consciousness among workers. As we will see, the period following the 1848 revolutions was a time of profound disillusionment and reevaluation for Marx. The setbacks he experienced forced him to confront the limitations of his earlier revolutionary optimism. His next evolution would require a shift—not just toward grand visions for a passing world, and a new one to come—in the subterranean struggles of his own home, where the seeds of his greatest insights would be sown in the shadows of personal and intellectual upheaval.

RING 5

The Dispossessed (1848–1851)

"There is only one way in which the murderous death agonies of the old society and the bloody birth throes of the new society can be shortened, simplified and concentrated, and that way is revolutionary terror."[545]

—Karl Marx

Dante wrote: "And what a bitter path it is to climb and cross the mountain of exile."[546] These words resonate deeply, as the ambition that had once guided Marx was now feeling more like a burden than a beacon. Marx's journey, marked by unfulfilled aspirations and profound personal loss, mirrored the struggles of a man caught between the hope of redemption and the reality of human frailty.[547] This experience of exile marked a turning point in Marx's descent, forcing him to confront personal tragedies like the edge of financial ruin. The revolutionary cause that once seemed so vivid and attainable began to fade into the shadows of disillusionment. Marx's writings grew more pessimistic, reflecting the weight of his ideological frustrations and wavering commitment to the movement.

In March 1848, Karl Marx, after his exile from Brussels, returned to Cologne, where he had initially begun his editing work with the original *Rheinteng Zeitung*; it was a city teeming with revolutionary fervor. The atmosphere was charged with the aspirations of various social strata that included middle-class liberals advocating for constitutional governance and civil liberties and working-class citizens demanding significant improvements in their living conditions.

This convergence of diverse demands created a complex and dynamic environment, as Marx seized this opportunity to influence the revolutionary discourse by launching the *Neue Rheinische Zeitung*, a daily newspaper that became a prominent voice for radical perspectives. He used his platform to rally support for a proletarian uprising, positioning himself at the center of revolutionary fervor sweeping across Europe. But his leadership style was anything but collaborative. At the paper, contributor Pavel Annenkov (1813–1887) observed, Marx embodied "the personification of a democratic dictator."[548] Engels himself admitted that "the editorial constitution [of the *Neue Rheinische Zeitung*] was the simple dictatorship of Marx." Yet, Engels insisted that this dominance was "self-evident, undisputed, and gladly recognized by all of us."[549] Marx's commanding presence and unshakable confidence ensured that the paper became the most influential German publication of the revolutionary years.

Despite Marx's forceful leadership, the revolutionary tide in Cologne—and across Europe—was beginning to wane. The initial fervor that had fueled uprisings was dissipating, met with crackdowns, exhaustion, and the gradual reassertion of state power. The question was no longer how to ignite revolution but how to sustain it in the face of growing resistance. The initial unity among various revolutionary factions fractured, leading to internal conflicts, as conservative forces exploited these divisions, systematically dismantling any revolutionary gains. By May 1849, the counter-revolutionary resurgence had gained the upper hand, resulting in the suppression of radical activities. As a result, Marx, facing political persecution, was expelled from Prussia on May 16, 1849, compelling him to seek refuge once again in Paris.

This period marked a profound personal and ideological crisis for Marx. The failure of the anticipated proletarian revolutions, coupled with his expulsion and the collapse of his new publication, led to significant disillusionment. These events not only challenged his revolutionary optimism but also precipitated a period of introspection and personal turmoil, setting the stage for subsequent developments in his life. During Karl Marx's tenure in Cologne from March 1848 to May 1849, he also faced significant challenges that profoundly impacted his psychological state. The swift suppression of revolutionary movements across Europe led to increased governmental repression. Marx and his associates were subjected to police harassment, and he faced multiple legal charges, including inciting armed rebellion, though he was acquitted each time. His expulsion from Cologne was a profound personal and ideological setback for him, contributing to a period that would see him in deep psychological distress.[550] These post-manifesto years paralleled the struggles of Dante's souls in Purgatorio, caught between aspirations and failures. His revolutionary fervor, like Dante's fire, sought to burn away societal injustices, though the path was fraught with disillusionment, setbacks, and the harsh realities of unfulfilled ideals.

Marx's evolving ideas mirror the seven deadly sins, with pride leading to his most profound struggles and realizations. The *Communist Manifesto* reflected his hope for a purifying revolution, but 1848 revealed the profound obstacles to systemic change. Marx employs Dante to express his outrage at and condemnation of iniquity and exploitation, "in order to establish some point of rectification through punishments that fit the crime, demand justice and urge appropriate modification of behaviors."[551] In the same way that Dante enters his own purgatory, to face the truth about himself without flinching, to know how dire things can become as a result of the wrong actions by individuals. Though with vastly different metaphysics, they are both operating in accordance with their distinct understandings of justice.

In 1844, writing from Brussels, Marx confided in Jenny that exile had stripped away any illusion that ideas alone could change the world—he now believed that theory had to be fused with real-world force. At this point, he had reunited with Engels, and together they were beginning to shape the revolutionary framework that would soon take form in *The Communist Manifesto.* The letter to Jenny reflects a critical moment of personal and political awakening—a brief period of hope when the revolutionary ideas he had been developing for years seemed poised to spark real-world transformation. His return to Cologne that year marked the beginning of his editorial work with *Neue Rheinische Zeitung*, a revolutionary newspaper that placed him in direct opposition to the monarchy and ruling elites. Marx's outspoken criticism and incendiary journalism eventually led to his arrest and expulsion. As one historian notes, "Marx's editorial work put him directly in conflict with the forces of reaction, culminating in the shutdown of his paper."[552] The eventual defeats were a significant blow to Marx's hopes for immediate change and solidified his status as a political exile.[553] On November 7, 1848, with a diminished voice, Marx wrote: "The very cannibalism of the counterrevolution will convince the nations that there is only one way in which the murderous death agonies of the old society and the bloody birth throes of the new society can be shortened, simplified and concentrated, and that way is revolutionary terror."[554]

The Last Threshold

Engels, whose guidance remained steadfast, had emphasized the importance of workers' unity: "The *Communist Manifesto* must emphasize workers' unity across borders." However, Marx's focus on long-term revolutionary goals often left him disconnected from the movement's immediate struggles—a critique voiced by contemporaries. In 1846, tailor and activist Wilhelm Weitling, who would represent a more utopian and working-class perspective, accused Marx of being out of touch with the lived realities of the proletariat. "The scientists," Weitling wrote, "have done nothing for us workers; we have had to help ourselves." Similarly, in 1847, Pierre-Joseph Proudhon warned Marx that "to be feared by the masses and hated by the powers, it is not enough to be right in theory—you must also be useful in practice. . . . Property is theft, but your methods seem overly theoretical for practical change."[555]

Marx's work, which had increasingly focused on the material conditions of society, continued to evolve as he engaged with critiques and correspondences that sharpened his theories. Philosopher and economist Victor Considerant (1849) challenged Marx: "Your critique of capital is sharp, but where is the room for individual freedom?"[556] This echoed a broader concern: Marx's growing focus on economic systems often overlooked the moral and spiritual dimensions that others, like Moses Hess, had cautioned him about as early as 1844. These tensions between materialism and human freedom would persist throughout Marx's intellectual life. By 1850, Marx's revolutionary ambitions would face stark limitations, though his theories clashed with contemporaries like Mikhail Bakunin (1814–1876) and Louis Blanc (1811–1882), a French socialist. Bakunin, a prominent Russian revolutionary[557] anarchist and a significant rival to Karl Marx within the First International, criticized his centralized vision of revolution, arguing: "You overestimate the role of the state in revolutionary movements." Blanc similarly challenged Marx's economic focus, stating in 1851: "Socialism must balance justice with practicality, which your theories sometimes neglect."

As authors Boris Nicolaievsky and Otto Maenchen-Helfen clarify: "Marx dreamed of building a better society out of the old one. Bakunin was the master of annihilation. He dreamed of destroying society and starting the process all over from the smoldering embers."[558] Amid these ideological struggles, Marx's personal life continued to unravel. In 1849, following his expulsion from France and the collapse of the 1848 revolutions, the Marx family was once again uprooted—this time relocating from Paris to London. The city, though foreign and unforgiving, would become their final refuge. For Marx, who had visited briefly before, it was already etched in his mind as the modern industrial metropolis, pulsing with capital and contradiction.

As Marx had discovered on his earlier trips, it was the heart of the infernal machine, where the smokestacks of industry rose like black towers over a hellscape of child labor, poverty, and ceaseless toil. His family's move in 1849 began their longest and final exile.[559] Though Marx, outside of his home, seems to have engaged in a confrontative, contentious style, he was remembered at home as "a loving, gentle and indulgent father. 'Children should educate their parents,' he used to say. There was never even a trace of the bossy parent in his relations with his daughters, whose love for him was extraordinary. He never gave them an order, but asked them to do what he wished as a favor or made them feel that they should not do what he wanted to forbid them."[560] The Marx family had affectionate nicknames for one another. Jenny was called "Möhme," while their daughters were "Jennychen" (or "Qui-Qui"), "Kakadou" (also "The Hottentot"), and "Tussy" (sometimes "Quo-Quo"). Edgar was known as "Moosh," and their maid, Helene Demuth, was "Lenchen." All the Marx daughters were named after their mother, Jenny. Out of the seven children, only three survived into adulthood: Jenny Caroline (1844–1883), Jenny Laura (1845–1911), and Jenny Julia Eleanor (1855–1898). The others—Edgar (1847–1855), Henry Edward Guy ("Guido") (1849–1850), Jenny Eveline Frances ("Franziska") (1851–1852), and an unnamed infant (died July 1857)—all passed away in childhood.

Friedrich Engels was referred to as "General," and Karl Marx himself was strangely called "Old Nick," a British term for Satan, though the origin of this nickname remains unclear. Marx encouraged his children to call him "Old Nick,"[561] possibly as a playful reference to his own perceived mischievous or rebellious nature. However, the reason Marx chose this nickname remains curious in light of his early poems. Marxist Scholar and biographer Marcello Musto notes that Marx signed letters to his family as "Old Nick,"[562] to indicate his amusement with the diabolic association.[563] Biographers have noted that Karl Marx's family and close friends referred to him by various nicknames, but Old Nick was used as late as 1869, decades after his youthful poems.

London, the world's largest city at the time, welcomed thousands of political refugees, but life in the English capital was challenging. Karl's early aspirations, fueled by his academic pursuits in Germany, had now given way to a more radical vision. The intellectual excitement that had once defined his relationship with Hegel's work, along with Bauer's and Feuerbach's, was now fueled by a growing disillusionment with the limits of Western thought in its entirety. Jenny Marx wrote to Karl in 1849: "Your ideas may change the world, but they leave our family in despair."[564] This despair was not unfounded. By November of that year, the family was evicted from their Chelsea home for nonpayment of rent. Jenny recounted the humiliation: "Five months later, they were turned out onto the pavement before the entire mob of Chelsea." The beds were "sold to pay the butcher, milkman, chemist, and baker."[565]

Their move to a boarding house in Leicester Square did little to alleviate their "plight." The cramped, unsanitary conditions added to the family's misery. Jenny was already worn down by the perpetual cycle of poverty, and "Lenchen," their housekeeper, found herself struggling to provide even the basics for the children. In the chaos of their daily lives, Jenny still managed to keep up appearances, keeping her dignity in the face of humiliation. Karl, meanwhile, often retreated into his work, to furiously correspond with Engels, while his family bore the brunt of their material deprivation, which would continue through 1851. Despite her best efforts, Jenny's resilience could not shield her from the weight of their misfortunes. Each day brought new humiliations: debts unpaid, possessions pawned, and the haunting specter of hunger. While his family fought to survive, Marx sharpened his critique of the world that had failed them, pouring his frustrations into the written word. These moments also saw Marx still grappling with the failure of revolutionary movements.

The aftermath of these revolutions also led Marx to refine his focus on political economy, laying new groundwork for *Das Kapital*. As Marx continued to dismiss any transcendence in his material new world order, his own health deteriorated, and his once grand vision was now burdened by the harsh realities of life in exile. The Marx family continued to rely heavily on the generosity of Engels and the small contributions Jenny could secure through pawning their belongings. In Marx's words: "Every day my wife says she wishes she and the children were safely in their graves, and I really cannot blame her, for the humiliations, torments and alarms that one has to go through in such a situation are indeed indescribable."[566] These moments exposed the growing gap between his ideological aspirations and the grim realities of his personal life. Far from prompting honest self-reflection, these hardships led Marx to dig deeper into abstraction and theory—often at the expense of practical engagement. The world around him was not merely indifferent but increasingly hostile, and yet Marx misread this resistance not as a call for reconsideration but as confirmation of his convictions. This blind spot would haunt him for years to come.

Despite these challenges, Marx struggled upward, yearning for ideological salvation, much like Dante's pilgrim, who endured penance while grappling with despair.[567] Marx's dream of a proletarian revolution had been deferred, and he found himself increasingly entombed from the political establishment and other socialist thinkers who began to question the viability of his radical vision.

The Ruins of Revolution

Marx had believed that the 1848 revolutions were the first step toward overthrowing the capitalist order. The counter-revolutionary forces crushed these movements, exposing the limitations of his vision. Marx was politically forsaken. In a cruel irony, the man who had written about the plight of the proletariat was unable to provide for his own family, despite Engels's continued financial assistance. Evictions, mounting debts, and malnutrition still defined their daily existence.[568] Amid these challenges, a bright moment occurred with the birth of their son, Henry Edward Marx, known as "Guido" or "Föxchen," on November 5, 1849, it was clearly a moment of joy to Karl and Jenny—though their moment of light would quickly dim when sadly, while still an infant, Guido died in 1850, before reaching his first birthday. He was one of several Marx children who would die young due to poor living conditions and a lack of adequate medical care, further devastating Jenny, who was already suffering from illness and exhaustion. Biographers have speculated that his death was due to scarlet fever, a common and often fatal illness for children during that time: given the unsanitary conditions of the flat in Soho, malnutrition and disease were likely factors, but the precise cause is uncertain. Guido's passing was a precursor for others to come, which would further break their spirits and[569] cast an even darker shadow over an already struggling household.[570] Marx lamented in a letter to Engels, acknowledging the grim realities of their existence.[571]

Though Karl deeply grieved Guido's death, his response was to retreat further into theory, burying himself in research. He confided to Engels: "Just a line or two to let you know that our little gunpowder plotter, Föxchen, died at ten o'clock this morning. Suddenly, from one of the convulsions he had often had. A few minutes before, he was still laughing and joking. The thing happened quite unexpectedly. You can imagine what it is like here."[572] Along with the deep mourning, the family continued to live in neglect,[573] with more furniture sold off to pay bills and bailiffs seizing what little remained. Jenny's letters paint a harrowing picture of their lives: the family surviving on bread and potatoes, Marx refusing to work, and his children ailing from malnutrition.[574] Marx writes: "The situation has become unbearable. I live in a constant state of anxiety, not only because of the political oppression I face but because I cannot pay for our survival without constant help."[575] Despite everything, Marx continued to procrastinate on his writing. He blamed his failures on external factors—capitalism, the bourgeoisie, and even his children's illnesses—rather than his irresponsibility.

A chain-smoker, Marx also struggled with bronchial issues[576] as would his children:[577] "The sad irony was that as much as he loved his family, he did not seem to consider that they, too, needed a revolutionary change. Like an artist single-mindedly dedicated to his vision, Marx expected his wife and children to fall into place behind him because they also recognized the significance of his work. He believed that they, too, must be ready to sacrifice for his goals. Lovingly and without hesitation, they did."[578] With that said, Marx's indifference to his family's suffering stands in stark contrast to the revolutionary fervor with which he approached his intellectual projects in November 1849. In letters from this period, Marx references his hardships, though he rarely lingered on personal tragedies. His focus remained on his intellectual work. Engels expressed concern about the family's situation in his letters to Marx, but even he could do little beyond sending financial aid when he could, but it was clear that Marx's professional life was costing his family: "The revolution must begin, but first I must feed my children."[579]

Despite writing passionately about the conditions of the working class and the exploitation of the proletariat, Marx struggled to escape the grinding poverty that many of his fellow workers experienced. His great intellectual legacy has often been characterized by loss, desperation, and dependency on the charity of his closest friends. Engels's support was not just a lifeline for Marx's intellectual work, it also kept his family alive during some of their darkest moments. Marx knew it and acknowledged as much: "I live in a state of extreme poverty and am totally dependent on the charity of others. Your support is, for me, not just a financial lifeline but an intellectual one."[580] The family's debts continued to mount even with these contributions, along with Marx's continued spending.[581]

Between December 1851 and March 1852, he composed *The Eighteenth Brumaire of Louis Bonaparte* to analyze the 1851 coup in

France. The essay was first published in May 1852 in the German monthly magazine *Die Revolution*, edited by Joseph Weydemeyer in New York. In this work, Marx dissected the events leading up to Louis Bonaparte's rise to power, providing a critical examination of class struggles and political dynamics in mid-nineteenth-century France.

The Eighteenth Brumaire of Louis Bonaparte, a political essay, demonstrates Marx's ability to intertwine politics with literary and historical analysis, showcasing his distinctive style of using artistic expression to illuminate the mechanisms of power. Marx's literary references throughout the text reveal his acute awareness of both the historical process and its tragic nature: "In Marx, we find not only an economist but a storyteller who understood the tragic nature of human enterprise under capitalism."[582]

Remember, Marx wrote: "Hegel remarks somewhere that all great world-historic facts and personages appear, so to speak, twice. He forgot to add: the first time as tragedy, the second time as farce." This observation underscored Marx's understanding of historical events as cyclical and repetitive, marked by diminishing grandeur. These were accompanied by other evocative comments, such as: "history resembles the theater; it repeats its scenes, but with a grotesque exaggeration of the characters."[583] As seen already, these literary flourishes were not merely rhetorical devices; they reflected Marx's view of tragedy as an interplay of human agency with inherited structures, and the role it would play for self-understanding and ultimate purpose. "Tragedy, then, is a form of reason beyond all reason. It is a model of the dialectical knowledge of humanity."[584]

Central to Marx's processing was his assertion: "Men make their own history, but they do not make it as they please; they do not make it under self-selected circumstances, but under circumstances existing already, given and transmitted from the past." This encapsulated Marx's belief in the material conditions that shape human action—history was neither an inevitable march of progress nor a simple sequence of individual choices. Instead, it was a dialectical process in which inherited structures largely constrained the possibilities of the present, even as they provided the raw materials for a future world.

However, as he charted the cycles of revolution, he too was ensnared by the ghosts of past failures, unable to escape the very patterns he diagnosed. Derrida argued that the intellectual committed to justice must become attuned to the lingering voices of history—those ghostly presences that speak through others, through the self, and through the fractured boundary between the two—calling us to reckon with what has been silenced or forgotten. Each exile, each setback, each betrayal reinforced his own entrapment within history's relentless repetition. The struggle to break free from the burdens of the past became not just a theoretical problem but an existential one. Yet, as he dissected the contradictions of capitalism with intellectual precision, his own life began to mirror those same contradictions. He was no longer just a critic of economic oppression; he was its casualty. While he called for the liberation of the proletariat, his own household was drowning. His wife and family, once the foundation of his ideological resolve, were now dismissed and stood as further proof that the weight of history presses not just upon his ideal theories but upon his real existence.

Gathering Shadows

While Marx was writing some of his most scathing critiques of capitalism, his revolutionary zeal was taking its toll. The stark contrast between his intellectual pursuits and personal responsibilities grew more apparent. In 1851, Marx's focus remained on the grand theory of history rather than on immediate relief for those around him. For Marx personally, the weight of history was not only theoretical but also profoundly lived. Amid these financial woes and the strains of exile, Marx fueled the flames of despair through an act of betrayal. It involved none other than the family's trusted lifelong caregiver;

Helene "Lenchen" Demuth managed the house, cared for the children, and was a trusted part of the family.

In the early summer of 1851, Jenny wrote in her autobiography that "an event occurred that I do not wish to relate here in detail, although it greatly contributed to an increase in our worries, both personal and others."[585] It was "only the recent chance discovery of a letter brought it to light."[586] This letter was written by Louise Freyberger, who later kept house for Engels, on the death of Helene Demuth, to whom she had been very close. To the shock of those who knew the Marxes, in the summer of 1851, Lenchen gave birth to Karl's son, Henry Frederick ("Freddy"). Always ready to come to the rescue, Engels claimed paternity to shield Marx from scandal. Wilhelm Liebknecht, a close friend of Marx, remarks on Helene: "Marx submitted like a lamb to her dictatorship . . . yet he had shattered Jenny's trust forever." "Freddy," the new son, was adopted and raised by a working-class family in East London.

As one could well imagine, Jenny's faith in her husband was irreparably damaged. This moment of personal failure further deepened Marx's descent and exile—not only from nations but from the devoted muse he had cast as the guardian of his ideals, making his betrayal not just personal but profoundly sacrilegious. The affair remained a closely guarded secret within the family. It was only later revealed in Jenny's documents that according to her, Engels had "saved Marx from a difficult domestic conflict." The revelation of the letter was a source of scandal at the time, as both Marx and Engels were committed to maintaining a certain degree of respectability—not to mention hypocrisy—within their intellectual and socialist circles.

Engels was aware of the potential damage that the illegitimate birth could cause, particularly in the context of Victorian moral standards. Marx was Victorian, too, and somewhat prudish in his attitude toward conventional morality, though he would spend hours in the British Museum searching for some small erotic bauble to present to Engels. He also enjoyed singing student songs about the downfall of young maidens—he could not keep a tune in his head, so he would simply shout the song—and he liked to tell dirty stories in the political clubs and saloon bars. That said, in the presence of women and children, he would blush like an English governess if there was so much as a whisper about sex.[587] At such times, he would squirm in his chair, look anxiously around, ponder various courses of action, his face growing redder and redder as he became more flustered. Finally, there would come from somewhere in the depths of his being a harsh command for silence. For Engels, these personal sacrifices to protect Marx were just part of his unwavering commitment to their shared ideological cause. He believed Marx's theories were crucial for the future of the working class and feared that any scandal could undermine both Marx's reputation and the revolutionary movement. Engels's loyalty exemplified his dedication to ensuring the success of Marx's ideas, even at his own significant personal cost.

While there are indeed some rumors and speculations about their relationship, most biographers treat the matter with great caution. Here's what is known: Helene Demuth was the Marx family's housekeeper and lived with them for many years, particularly in their years of exile in London. She had a close and complicated relationship with Marx. Her role went far beyond that of a traditional servant. As Robert Payne describes it, "she cooked, cleaned, made the beds, swept the floors, sewed their clothes, fed the children, prepared all the meals, lit all the fires, did all the washing, and carried the coal into the house."[588] "When money was scarce, she even pawned the family's belongings, a task Marx himself could not face. He exploited her shamelessly, as he exploited nearly everyone who came in contact with him."[589] Yet, their relationship was complex. Helene, known as a "dictator"[590] of the household, held Marx in no particular awe, knowing his weaknesses and flaws intimately. Payne writes that "the great revolutionary has fathered a bastard on a house servant would have been fodder for satirical poems and whispered jokes among his detractors."[591] Paul Johnson summarizes the reaction Marx might have faced had the affair become public: "Marx was saved from disgrace not by his own integrity, but by Engels' willingness to bear the shame in his stead."[592]

Privately, for Jenny, who was pregnant at the time, the birth of Marx's bastard son led to a hysterical collapse and long months of nervous prostration.[593] She had possessed an infinite trust in her husband, whom she had always regarded as a heroic figure waging a selfless war on behalf of the dispossessed; now, she knew that he too had all the frailties of ordinary mortals. In *Wilhelm Meister's Apprenticeship* by Goethe, whom Jenny thought of as a model for Karl, the protagonist embarks on a journey seeking artistic and personal fulfillment, often facing disillusionment and the harsh truths of life. Though in the book, "Wilhelm Meister is a young, aspirant actor, it becomes the archetype of his capacity to wound those he loves."[594]

Marx, like Wilhelm, sought to construct a world of intellectual and political transformation, yet in his most private moments, he succumbed to the same human frailties he condemned in others. The gap between his theoretical convictions and his personal life widened, leaving behind not just ideological contradictions but deep wounds in those closest to him. And Jenny's journey with Marx led her from admiration to a painful recognition of his human frailties, mirroring the themes of shattered ideals and personal growth found in Goethe's narrative.[595] If he had fathered a child with almost any other woman, she might have been more tolerant, but that it was her beloved Lenchen was almost beyond endurance. For the rest of her life, the mere presence of the maidservant would remind her of her shame.[596]

In a letter to Engels, Marx speaks of the sobbing that continued all night and the recriminations of the daytime. "And you know I am naturally not very long-suffering and even a bit hard, and so it happens that from time to time I lose my equanimity."[597] Marx unburdened himself in a long letter to his friend Joseph Weydemeyer. He spoke of "the unspeakable infamies which my enemies are spreading about me"[598] and how they were all gleefully crying "Marx is finished."[599] "Of course, I should laugh at all this filth," he continued. "I should not let it interfere with my work for a moment, but you understand, my wife is ill, and she has to endure the most unpleasant bourgeois poverty from morning to night, and her nervous system is disturbed, and she gets none the better because every day some idiotic talebearers bring her all the vaporings of the democratic cesspools. The tactlessness of these people is sometimes colossal."[600] So it was, and it may sometimes have occurred to him that he had only himself to blame for the misfortunes that were raining down on him.[601]

His own "colossal tactlessness"[602] had led him from one disaster to another. The evidence of his failure lay all around him—in his "abysmal poverty, his wife's nervous prostration, his friends in jail, his ineffectiveness as a revolutionary, his unwanted child."[603] Some commentators have insinuated that Karl Marx, given his superior status, took advantage of Lenchen, or even raped her,[604] but this accusation is not supported by clear evidence.

This period of Marx's life underscores the relentless personal and ideological contradictions he navigated. His public pursuit of salvation clashed starkly with the private exploitation and tragedies within his home. It reflects the broader contradictions of a man whose ideals often stood at odds with his actions. Marx handled the problem by going into seclusion, and that meant the British Museum's reading room.[605] He first visited the British Museum's reading room in 1849, shortly after his arrival in London, and by 1850, it had become his primary refuge. Beneath its soaring, cathedral-like dome, supported by elegant columns and lined with towering bookshelves filled with centuries of accumulated knowledge, Marx found himself in an intellectual fortress. The circular design of the room, reminiscent of a royal war chamber, exuded an air of strategy and power. Scholars and statesmen alike had once gathered there, poring over books like generals studying maps before battle. Here, amid the hushed reverence of history's greatest works, Marx stationed himself daily, buried in research, wielding his pen like a weapon, and drafting the ideological blueprints for what he hoped would be a climactic event. He became a regular visitor to the British Museum for the next thirty years, but the most concentrated period of research took place between 1851 and 1857. During this time, Marx immersed himself in economic theory, history, and political economy, laying the intellectual groundwork for what would become *Das Kapital.* Although the first volume—eventually published in 1867—was largely completed with Engels's help, the subsequent volumes remained in draft form at Marx's death and were compiled and edited by Engels in the years that followed.[606]

Marx maintained a rigorous schedule. Every day, from nine o'clock in the morning to seven o'clock at night, he gathered in his arms a bunch of books and periodicals and vanished into the reading room, where he studied economics for his long-projected *Critique of Political Economy*. He read interminably, copied out lengthy extracts from all the English economists and sociologists, dipped into Roman and medieval history, and studied banking and agricultural chemistry. By the early 1860s, Marx was immersed in English reading—more, he claimed, "necessary for his own book," though it also served to "drown out the sound of the ever-encroaching world outside." His daughter Laura, then nineteen, had become his full-time assistant at the British Museum, often working alone when he was too unwell to join her. With her striking auburn hair and stylish dress, she drew attention even in the staid Reading Room. One admirer reportedly sent word: "Tell her that I have three-hundred-fifty pounds a year, also forty acres of land and that I shall call on her one of these days . . . I was afraid of the Papa." Prior to their marrying, we can hear in Marx's words to Paul Lafargue [Laura's admirer], who was born in Cuba to French and Creole parents, the caution he might have issued to himself with Jenny some years earlier: "If you wish to continue your relations with my daughter, you will have to give up your present manner of 'courting.'"[607] Ironically, given his own failings,

Marx remained the protective father for his daughter: "You know full well that no engagement has been entered into, that as yet everything is undecided. And even if she were formally betrothed to you, you should not forget that this is a matter of long duration. To my mind, true love expresses itself in reticence, modesty and even the shyness of the lover towards his object of veneration, and certainly not in giving free rein to one's passion and in premature demonstrations of familiarity."

In another letter, Marx warned him "Should you plead in defense your Creole temperament, it will be my duty to interpose my common sense between your temperament and my daughter. . . . I probably don't need to explain this any further."[608] Just as Dante's tempest symbolizes the uncontrolled forces of passion,[609] Marx, despite his revolutionary fervor, found himself advocating for measured restraint when it came to his own family.

This contrast between rational control and unchecked passion reflects Marx's broader philosophical paradox—while he championed radical upheaval, he still sought order and discipline in his private life. In this way, his personal admonitions to Lafargue stand in ironic juxtaposition to his revolutionary call for the working class to break free from societal constraints.[610] Marx's betrayal of his wife within his own household echoes his overall blindness to the ways in which ignoring human frailties can undermine the most ambitious visions. The scandal involving Helene Demuth was not merely a private failing but a deeply symbolic moment that underscores further dissonance between Marx's ideals and his personal life.

Dante describes in his journey a place for those overcome by lust, forever tormented by swirling winds—symbolic of passions that sweep away reason. Just as Dante's sinners in the second circle of hell are swept away by uncontrollable forces, Marx's actions reveal the tension between his revolutionary ambition and the human vulnerabilities he could not escape. These lapses of character, combined with his family's persistent struggles, intensified the emotional and moral pressure bearing down on him. This episode in Marx's life stands as yet another layer in his personal descent, where the lofty ideals of a secular utopia were increasingly overshadowed by the stark realities of human frailty.

By 1851, Marx had not only been exiled from multiple nations but was becoming an exile unto himself. The man who had once proclaimed the future of the proletariat was now struggling to feed his own family. Dante wrote: "And what a bitter path it is to climb the mountain[611] of exile."[612] These words resonate with Marx's fate. His revolutionary ambitions had led him to a moment of darkness.

Looking ahead, this period marks the midpoint of Marx's journey. We close on 1851. Marx's exile was no longer just political—it was existential. Exiles that began in the realm of the political, dictated by revolutions, expulsions, and ideological battles, now pushed Marx over borders and into deeper isolation. Each step of Marx's journey mirrored the outer circles of Dante's *Inferno*—his exiles were tangible, geographic, and material. He lost his homeland, his newspaper, his revolutionary hopes, and most of his financial security. Though he openly rejected faith, the weight of exile still carried an almost prophetic quality, paralleling the displacement of the Jewish diaspora—a people marked by a long history of being outsiders.

For Marx, exile was not just physical but ideological. He severed ties not only with his birthplace but with the very traditions and beliefs that had shaped his ancestors. His path reflected a deeper pattern of disillusionment—first with religion, then with revolution, and ultimately with the very utopian vision he had spent his life constructing. Like the souls in Dante's *Inferno*, trapped in delusions of their own making, Marx's exile was as much the result of his own choices as of external forces. Though this chapter ends in 1851, by the midpoint of his life—age thirty-five in 1854—the greater suffering was no longer political banishment but the crushing weight of his personal and ideological contradictions, many of which were already well underway. If the outer circles of hell were reserved for political exile, the inner circles—the final rings of Marx's journey—were constructed from his inability to see the cost of his own obsessions. Marx's blindness to (intimate) human frailty—the suffering of wives, children, friends, and caretakers—ensured that, even in moments of intellectual triumph, he remained imprisoned within his own purgatory. In *Purgatorio*, the flames serve as both punishment and purification, a path toward ascent for those willing to humble themselves. But for Marx, there was no ascent—no recognition, no repentance, no outstretched hand to those he left in suffering. His exile was not merely from nations and governments; it was from the very essence of human tenderness and connection. As he wandered deeper into the inferno of his own making, the flames did not cleanse—they consumed, leaving only the embers of a man who, in seeking to liberate the world, had bound himself in chains.

RING 6

Barricades to the British Museum

(1851–1857)

"The tradition of all dead generations weighs like a nightmare on the brains of the living."[613]

—Karl Marx

The clang of the barricades had faded.[614] The revolutions that once promised a new dawn ended in failure, only to leave Karl Marx not in the streets of Paris or Cologne but in a different kind of exile—the cold, smoke-filled libraries of London. He had exchanged the immediacy of revolutionary struggle for something deeper, more consuming: the slow, solitary labor of theorizing a world yet to come. The revolutions of 1848 had revealed to Marx an unsettling truth: the bourgeoisie, rather than being swept aside by revolutionary fervor, had instead co-opted and suppressed the uprisings to solidify their own power. Rather than believing that spontaneous revolts would bring about socialism, Marx began to view revolution as something that required both strategic organization and a clearer understanding of the mechanisms of state power.

In *The Eighteenth Brumaire of Louis Bonaparte*, he reflects on how the revolutionary forces of 1848 had ultimately paved the way for a new form of authoritarian rule, writing.[615] This period marked a shift in his thinking—from seeing revolution as inevitable to understanding it as a process that needed not only economic foundations but also political strategy. His descent continued, though no longer through the physical tumult of revolution, no longer with the clang of barricades. Now, the descent was internal, into the depths of thought, where the fires of ideology burned without relief. Marx had entered a different kind of banishment, not merely from nations but from relevance. He was not in Paris, as agitator among the workers, nor in Cologne, rousing his compatriots. He was in the silence of London, where the weight of his own ruins had settled upon him like a heavy smog. His battlefield was no longer the streets but the pages of his unfinished manuscripts, and his war was waged against the very logic of history itself.

London was not just a geographic exile; it was an intellectual one. Cut off from the revolutionary activity on the continent, Marx increasingly lived in the world of ideas, deep in the reading room of the British Museum; his wife saw their exile as a form of slow death. In a letter to a friend, she lamented: "We are in such a dreadful position that if we don't get help soon, we shall be utterly lost."[616]

The Marx family's financial struggles were compounded by illness and ongoing personal tragedy. In one of his more reflective moments, Marx acknowledged the toll it had taken, writing: "History does nothing, it does not possess immense riches, it does not fight battles. It is men, real, living, who do all this."[617] Marx's banishment forced him to reconsider the relationship between theory and reality. He now saw more clearly than ever that revolution was not merely an economic inevitability—it was a deeply human struggle, with all its attendant suffering and sacrifice.

The previous years had been characterized by political disillusionment, financial instability, and emotional suffering, and 1852–1857 continued on the same path, though "exile forced Marx into a dual role as both an activist and a theoretician."[618] In his relentless study of old worlds, he had grown deaf to his own. As he chronicled capitalism's crimes, his wife, Jenny, begs for money for their child's burial. Marx was staring into the abyss of economic theory, mapping out the horrors of exploitation with mathematical precision, but what he failed to see was how his stubborn thoughts had also trapped him—and from this damnation of the mind, there seemed to be no return.[619]

Overthrowing Heaven

For Karl Marx, capitalism was more than an economic system; it was moral deception—a great lie perpetuated by the ruling class, sustained by faith and social order. Christianity, with its doctrines of humility, sacrifice, and mercy, was the ideological twin of capitalism, a theology of submission meant to pacify the working class. In *The German Ideology*, he had declared that morality itself was an illusion, a fiction crafted by the ruling class to maintain their power. Now, he sought not just to overturn capitalism but to destroy the very moral order that sustained it.

Alienated from both revolution and domestic stability, Marx poured himself into analysis, mapping the forces that shaped history while feeling increasingly powerless within them. He filled his *Excerpt Notebooks*, copying passages from Adam Smith and David Ricardo, as well as historians, philosophers, and political theorists.[620] These notebooks, often overflowing with underlined sections and marginalia, reveal his evolving engagement with figures like Aristotle, Machiavelli, and Hegel. He also studied anthropological and ethnographic accounts, including Lewis Henry Morgan's *Ancient Society*, which influenced his later ideas on historical materialism and primitive communism. His growing frustration with the political landscape in Britain is evident in his frequently expressed disdain for the reformist movements that sought to work within the capitalist system rather than overthrow it.

His engagement with classic British economics during this period marked a critical phase in his intellectual journey. Immersing himself in Smith and Ricardo, he began to draft his ideas on value, labor, and capital. Both foundational figures in classical economics acknowledged potential pitfalls within capitalist systems, particularly Smith in his *The Theory of Moral Sentiments* with concerns of the moral consequences of unchecked capitalism. Smith, often regarded as the "father of modern economics," knew the human foibles of wealth and virtue, and wrote: "The beggar, who suns himself by the side of the highway, possesses that security which kings are fighting for."[621] He emphasized that the individual "intends only his own gain, and he is . . . led by an invisible hand to promote an end which was not part of his intention,"[622] and that the division of labor was there to lay the groundwork for capitalist economic theory. Marx critiqued Smith's optimism about free markets, arguing that they masked the exploitative nature of wage labor and the alienation of workers.[623] For Marx, the division of labor, rather than fostering societal growth, created inequalities that concentrated wealth and power in the hands of a few.

Ricardo, one of the most influential classical economists, is best known for his contributions to economic theory, particularly in *On the Principles of Political Economy and Taxation* (1817). This work further influenced Marx through the trade theory and labor theory of value, and used the metaphor of the invisible hand: "This pursuit of individual advantage is admirably connected with the universal good of the whole. By directing that industry in such a manner as its produce may be of the greatest value, the individual labors to render the annual revenue of the society as great as he can. He intends only his own gain, but he is in this, as in many other cases, led by an invisible hand to promote an end which was no part of his intention."[624] Economic historian R. H. Tawney once remarked, with some irony, that "the true descendant of the doctrines of Aquinas is the labour theory of value."[625] His comment reflected a moral critique of modern capitalism, not a celebration of Marx's economics. Still, Tawney's observation points to deeper tensions and overlapping concerns: both scholastic economic thought and Marx's critique of industrial capitalism were concerned, in different ways, with justice in exchange, the dignity of labor, and the problem of exploitation.[626] Yet there are important discontinuities. While classical liberal economists like Adam Smith introduced new insights into how wealth is created, they remained indebted to the moral tradition of natural law, particularly on trade and commerce. In contrast, Marx, despite his legitimate objections to the inequities of his time, represented a far more radical break—rejecting both theological tradition and liberal economics alike. On the continuities between scholasticism and liberal economics, the work of Alejandro A. Chafuen offers essential insight.[627] "The last of the Schoolmen was Karl Marx."[628] Ricardo expanded on Smith's ideas, asserting that value is determined by the labor required to produce goods and analyzing wealth distribution among landowners, capitalists, and workers. Marx adopted and refined Ricardo's theory, introducing the concept of "surplus value" as the source of capitalist profit. However, he criticized Ricardo for failing to fully grasp the systemic exploitation inherent in capitalism. While Ricardo saw potential for stability within capitalist systems, Marx believed their contradictions would inevitably lead to collapse.

Marx developed his own critique of capitalism, emphasizing its excesses and potential unsustainability, which "remains one of the most penetrating analyses of the system's contradictions, though its predictive power has waned."[629] The contrasting views of Smith and Ricardo highlight the complexities of early economic thought. Smith offered a vision of economic growth, while Ricardo provided a structured analysis of value and distribution. Marx, however, focused on the darker implications of these systems, highlighting how they perpetuated inequality and exploitation. Yet, he failed to recognize the moral constraints that had previously prevented these systems from self-destruction, as discussed in Smith's *The Theory of Moral Sentiments.*

Marx overlooked the reality that capitalism's abuses were tempered—never eliminated, but restrained—by the ethical structures of faith, particularly the Christian tradition. It was a delicate balance: commerce with a conscience. In essence, Smith argued that "to feel much for others and little for ourselves, that to restrain our selfish, and to indulge our benevolent affections, constitutes the perfection of human nature."[630] He understood that markets, like men, required moral discipline to function justly. Smith's *The Theory of Moral Sentiments* placed sympathy and duty at the heart of economic life, arguing that commerce alone could not sustain a civilization—it had to be undergirded by a moral ethos, and he believed that "how selfish soever man may be supposed, there are evidently some principles in his nature, which interest him in the fortune of others, and render their happiness necessary to him, though he derives nothing from it except the pleasure of seeing it."[631]

But Marx, ever the iconoclast, rejected this entirely. To him, morality was not a safeguard; it was an illusion. Wielding religion was not just another weapon to pacify the oppressed; it dulled their awareness of the material forces shaping their suffering. In stripping faith from history, he also stripped capitalism of its moral counterbalance, leaving behind an unstoppable engine of exploitation, devoid of any internal mechanism for restraint.[632] A fitting quote to illustrate this perspective comes from Marx himself: "Capital comes dripping from head to foot, from every pore, with blood and dirt."[633] Even the philanthropy of industrialists, the reforms that sought to ease working conditions, the social policies designed to blunt the sharp edges of economic disparity—these, in his eyes, were mere deceptions, palliative measures meant to disguise capitalism's true nature.

By rejecting moral restraint, by severing the ethical from the economic, Marx unleashed the same unyielding spirits he condemned in capitalism. The struggle for supremacy had not been abolished—it had only been baptized in revolutionary fervor. Where capitalism had wielded gold as its scepter, socialism would forge the hammer of the state into a weapon of absolute control.[634] Compliance would no longer be dictated by market forces but by the relentless will of the party. The battle lines had shifted, but the war for domination raged on. The chains of exploitation would not be shattered; they would be recast in the fires of ideological purity, their weight no lighter under the banner of the proletariat. The dictatorship of the bourgeoisie would not be eliminated but merely replaced by the dictatorship of the proletariat, and the price of that transformation would be the very freedoms Marx once claimed to defend. This was the inescapable paradox at the heart of his vision.

And so, his revolution remained incomplete, not because it failed to diagnose the ailment of the age, but because it failed to see that no system—capitalist, socialist, or otherwise—could be sustained without an ethos beyond mere material struggle. History had proved it time and time again—revolutions tend to consume their own children, a la Trotsky and Robespierre; empires collapsed under the strain of their own excess, and ideologies, in their untempered pursuit of purity, become indistinguishable from the tyranny they seek to overthrow. The dream of 1848 had not just failed, it had been obliterated, and in its place stood an unshakable reality: the revolution had no army, no government, and no real base of power. Marx, once riding the clouds of a coming revolutionary storm, now found himself an exile—disconnected from the very movements he had fought to lead. The world moved on, while he sat in the British Museum's grand reading room, surrounded by the works of the great economists, philosophers, and historians. The weight of these failures haunted him: the revolutions had come, and they had been crushed. As he saw it, the bourgeoisie had adapted, strengthened themselves, and consolidated. The workers had fought and bled—and lost.

One evening, "on the long walk back to Soho someone sang or Marx recited passages from *The Divine Comedy* or played the part of Mephisto in Goethe's *Faust* (which Liebknecht[635] said he did not do very well, because he exaggerated considerably). . . . Marx had begun instilling a love for literature and language in his children at the earliest age. He often read them passages from the *Divine Comedy*, including the line: 'Here must all distrust be left; all cowardice must here be dead.'"[636] This quote reflects the courage and resolve that Marx admired and sought to impart to his children[637]—and possibly himself.

During this period, the family suffered yet another devastating loss. Jenny, as his wife and closest confidante, still bearing the brunt of their suffering, chronicled their plight in letters. Jenny wrote to friends begging for financial assistance.[638] The weight had become unbearable. They lost their third child, Franziska, in March 1852. It was one of the deepest blows Marx and Jenny would endure. Only a toddler, she succumbed to what was likely a respiratory illness, exacerbated by the cold, damp conditions of their Soho home. With no money for medical care, Marx could only watch as his daughter wasted away. Jenny wrote of the night they spent sleeping on the floor with their remaining children, unable to provide their daughter with a proper burial.[639] She had to beg for funds to afford a coffin. For three days, the child was between life and death, suffering terribly:

> Our three living children lay down by us and we all wept for the little angel whose livid, lifeless body was in the next room. Our beloved child's death occurred at the time of the hardest privations, our German friends being unable to help us just then. Anguish in my heart, I hurried to a French emigrant who lived not far away and used to come to see us, and begged him to help us in our terrible necessity. He immediately gave me two pounds with the most friendly sympathy. That money was used to pay for the coffin in which my child now rests in peace. She had no cradle when she came into the world and for a long time was refused a last resting place. With what heavy hearts we saw her carried to her grave.[640]

The event left the Marx family in a state of deep emotional and psychological turmoil. Karl's response to her death was muted. Jenny faced further health challenges, and Marx himself struggled with his own deteriorating health. Yet this did not stir Marx to abandon his work, nor did it soften him; it steeled him. There was no turning back now. The fires of ideology had burned away too much.

Marx's London years sharpened his critique of capitalism as a self-perpetuating system of exploitation. His metaphor of capitalism as a "vampire" that feeds on the living was one of the most vivid descriptions of this mechanism. This vision of industrialization was not unlike Dante's *Inferno*, where sinners are trapped in cycles of torment from which they cannot escape. Marx's observations in the slums of London reinforced this imagery, the Manchester's slums where "streets are generally unpaved, full of holes, filthy, and strewn with refuse."[641] For Marx, these conditions were not aberrations but the logical outcome of industrialization. He saw the factory system as a monstrous creation, one that enslaved workers while enriching the bourgeoisie. In *The Communist Manifesto*, he earlier wrote: "Modern industry has converted the little workshop of the patriarchal master into the great factory of the industrial capitalist. . . . Masses of laborers, crowded into the factory, are organized like soldiers."[642] This hellish vision of capitalism as an infernal machine would fuel his most important theoretical works. They were tools that he could use to draft his own version of socio-political *Sturm und Drang*.[643]

History: Tragedy or Farce?

While Marx had inspired movements across Europe with his revolutionary ideas, the struggle to make those ideas resonate with both his contemporaries and his own family underscored a persistent tension in his life and work. His criticism could just as easily apply to Marx's ability—or inability—to balance his intellectual pursuits with the immediate needs of those closest to him. He had once believed history moved in predictable stages, but here he saw its cyclical cruelty.

The revolutionary fervor had collapsed into counter-revolution, and Marx was left to pick apart the corpse of failed radicalism. The weight of history was suffocating, pressing down upon him, upon Jenny, upon their children.

He was also deeply involved in his writings on history and economics, but his situation in London meant that he had little opportunity to engage directly with revolutionary movements in Europe. Instead, Marx turned his attention to writing the critique of Louis Bonaparte, Napoleon III, which "marked his transition to political historian."[644] Marx analyzed Bonaparte's rise to power, framing it within his broader theory of historical materialism, which viewed historical events as the product of class struggles: "The class struggle is the motor of history, but it requires conscious action."[645] Marx's increasing awareness of the complexities of political power, which he viewed as emblematic of the contradictory nature of bourgeois society, deepened his critique of the existing system. The fact that Bonaparte was able to gain power despite the revolutionary fervor of 1848 showed Marx that the state was not simply an instrument of the bourgeoisie but a much more complicated institution, subject to manipulation and control by various social forces (he observed that "all revolutions perfected this machine instead of breaking it"). He grappled with the challenges of understanding political power without direct involvement in the revolutionary movements that he once believed would bring about change.

Marx began to more systematically develop his theories on the state, the economy, and historical change, and his intellectual output remained prolific. According to biographer Saul Padover, Marx's exile functioned not only as a personal hardship but also as a powerful stimulus, sharpening his critique of capitalism and compelling him to clarify his revolutionary vision from the margins of society. In his book *The Poverty of Philosophy* (1847), Marx wrote: "The social principles of Christianity preach the necessity of a ruling class and the resignation of the oppressed."[646] This critique aligned with his broader theory of ideology, which argued that the ruling class controls not just the economy but also the cultural and intellectual institutions that shape public consciousness. The so-called benevolence of industrialists—building schools, endowing charities, funding hospitals—was, in Marx's view, a way to pacify workers without addressing the fundamental injustices of capitalism. As he wrote earlier in *The German Ideology*: "The ideas of the ruling class are in every epoch the ruling ideas: that is, the class which is the ruling material force of society is at the same time its ruling intellectual force."[647] It is an argument that remains relevant in modern discussions about corporate social responsibility. In his 2023 book *Technofeudalism: What Killed Capitalism*,[648] Yanis Varoufakis argues that the rise of tech giants like Amazon,[649] Google,[650] and Apple have led to a new economic system resembling medieval feudalism, where these companies act as modern-day lords, and users function as digital serfs. Large tech firms today often donate millions to charitable causes while simultaneously exploiting workers in developing countries or engaging in monopolistic practices that undermine competition. Marx would have seen these gestures not as genuine commitments to social justice but as ideological distractions—what he called the "opium" of bourgeois morality—meant to preserve the status quo and forestall systemic reform. But one doesn't need to be a Marxist to recognize the contradiction. As Adam Smith warned, free markets require moral administration; without it, economic power becomes concentrated, virtue is reduced to performance, and the wealth capitalism generates no longer serves the common good.[651]

Despite the mounting challenges, this period marked yet another turning point in his theoretical work, setting the stage for his more in-depth scrutiny of capitalism. "The bourgeoisie cannot exist without constantly revolutionizing the instruments of production,"[652] he would later write, demonstrating how even in exile, his ideas continued to evolve, sharpened by adversity and the stark realities of industrial modernity. We can hear Marx's growing frustration with a system that not only perpetuated economic exploitation but also distorted the fundamental social relations that bind people together.

The greed of the bourgeoisie, in Marx's view, was not just a matter of economic exploitation—it was a moral failing, a form of greed that dehumanized the working class and left them alienated from their labor.[653] According to economist Richard Wolff: "Greed is not the cause of capitalists' behavior; it is a quality they acquire in accommodating to and internalizing the requirements of competitive survival within the capitalist system."[654] Capitalists are not inherently greedy; rather, they become so in order to survive in the cutthroat and exploitative environment that capitalism creates. This moral degradation of the bourgeoisie, Marx suggests, is not just a byproduct of their economic position but a sign of the deepening alienation that capitalism engenders in both the working and ruling classes.[655]

Capitalists increase profit not merely by extracting more surplus from workers but by reducing labor costs—often by relocating production overseas to countries with lower wages and fewer labor protections. This became especially pronounced in the United States after 1991, with the mass exodus of manufacturing jobs to China. The same output could be maintained—or even increased—at a fraction of the cost, not because productivity rose, but because wages and benefits were drastically reduced. In many cases, corporate virtue signaling, particularly around social justice causes, has served to obscure these exploitative practices.[656] Immigration of lower-wage workers has long been a feature of capitalist societies, used to meet labor demands or, more cynically, to suppress wages. In the United States, corporations have often favored illegal immigration or temporary work visas as tools to avoid hiring American workers who expect higher pay and benefits. Historically, legal immigration was encouraged to fuel economic growth, and many of those workers eventually joined the middle class. But with the rise of globalization in the 1990s—ushered in by policies under George H. W. Bush and others—the focus shifted. Instead of integrating labor into a rising national economy, corporations increasingly sought to displace domestic labor with cheaper alternatives, whether abroad or at home. Switching labor sources—from men to women, adults to children, or one ethnicity to another—became a familiar strategy in pursuit of lower costs and higher flexibility.[657] Marx's theory of alienation, which he had begun to develop in his earlier writings, became more sharply defined in this context. Alienation, for Marx, was not just an economic condition, it was also the condition of human existence under capitalism. The exploitation of labor meant the reduction of human beings to mere commodities. A worker, alienated from the product of his labor, was also alienated from his own humanity. This sense of alienation was something Marx felt deeply on a personal level during these years of exile, as his own sense of isolation and despair mirrored the alienation he saw in the working class. Without any promises for teaching positions, Marx turned once again to journalism, to wield his pen as a weapon against the injustices of his time.

Slow Descent into Battle

In 1853, Marx began to write for the *New York Tribune*, one of the most widely read newspapers of the time. His journalism provided a vital source of income during a time when his political and economic theories were still gaining traction.[658] His articles dissected European politics and exposed the economic motives behind the Crimean War.[659] In one of them, he wrote that "the working men pay the cost in blood and taxes"[660] as a way to condemn Britain's and France's imperialist ambitions. Marx's critiques were razor-sharp, but his role as a journalist was tinged with frustration—he was observing history, not shaping it.[661] Marx began by writing primarily about England—a subject he knew intimately—but by 1853, with the approach of the Crimean War and rising tensions among the continental powers, he broadened his scope to include European affairs as well, where the dominant topic was the approach of the Crimean War.[662] For Marx, the war was not about defending the rights of the Ottoman people or protecting Christian minorities but was rooted in a long-standing rivalry for economic and political dominance. Moreover, Marx emphasized the exploitation of the working class, who were the ones sent to fight. He stated: "The masses are sacrificed in these conflicts, while the ruling class reaps the benefits of expanded imperial control."[663] He saw the war as another example of how the working class was exploited for the interests of the capitalist class, who benefited from the political outcomes of imperial wars, while the workers bore the brunt of the physical and economic costs. In his reflections, Marx observed that "the war is but the continuation of the struggle between the bourgeoisie and the proletariat, but conducted by other means."[664] He viewed the war as a symptom of a broader pattern of capitalist rivalry, where nations used military conflict as a way to maintain and expand their capitalist economies.

As he dissected the Crimean War, he exposed its true nature, stripping away the patriotic veneer: "History does nothing," Marx wrote. "It does not possess immense riches, it does not fight battles. It is men, real, living, who do all this."[665] His words remind readers that behind every act of war stood those who stood to gain and those who were made to suffer. His articles incisively cut through the rhetoric of war to expose its underlying economic and imperialist motives: "While the aristocracy reaps the glory, the working men pay the cost in blood and taxes."[666]

Marx's reflections on geopolitics and imperialism remain strikingly relevant today, particularly in light of current global conflicts. In one article, Marx noted: "The real question at issue is not the fate of Turkey, but the maintenance of the balance of power in Europe, and more particularly, the neutralization of the Black Sea."[667] He observed, "It is curious to observe the contrast between the profound discontent excited by the war among the people of England and the enthusiastic war-cry raised by the press on behalf of the aristocracy and the moneyocracy."[668] These words, written during the Crimean War, shed light on the complex interplay of imperialism, nationalism, and class interests that Marx believed shaped international conflict. The underlying causes of the Crimean War that Marx analyzed—imperialism, national struggles, and class exploitation—are disturbingly relevant today in the ongoing Russia-Ukraine conflict.[669] The imperial maneuverings surrounding the Crimean War—so central to Marx's analysis in the 1850s—find echoes in the current conflict between Russia and Ukraine. Then, as now, great powers exploited smaller nations in pursuit of broader strategic aims. While today's war is often framed as Russian aggression, many scholars argue that it was also provoked by Western ambitions in Russia's sphere of influence, particularly through NATO expansion and political encroachment near Russian borders. Regardless of where one stands on the question of culpability, the results reflect a pattern Marx identified long ago: elites manipulating national identities and geopolitical fears for economic and strategic gain, with ordinary people paying the cost. In this light, Marx's critique of power structures remains a useful lens for understanding the dynamics that continue to shape global affairs.[670] For Marx, the Crimean War also highlighted the fragility of alliances between major powers and the volatility of a global system driven by capitalist interests.[671] He observed: "The history of this war is the history of alliances made and unmade, of treaties signed and violated, and of promises given and recalled."[672] These contradictions, he argued, revealed the inherent instability of imperialist diplomacy. The war's importance to Marx lay in its embodiment of the systemic flaws he sought to expose—how ruling elites mobilized resources and people to wage wars that ultimately benefited the wealthy while devastating the working classes. These articles not only cemented Marx's reputation as a sharp political commentator but also demonstrated his ability to connect contemporary global events to his broader theories of historical materialism and class conflict: "Marx's articles were not merely a means of earning his living: in spite of his low opinion of his own work, he consistently produced highly persuasive pieces of journalism and, in the words of the *Tribune*'s editor [Horace Greeley] 'not only one of the most highly valued, but one of the best-paid contributors attached to the journal.'"[84]

"His greatest gift was as a polemical journalist. He made brilliant use of epigrams and aphorisms."[673] Greeley played a pivotal role in Marx's financial survival. Despite their ideological differences, Greeley valued Marx's analysis. "Go West, young man, go West. There is health in the country, and room away from our crowds of idlers and imbeciles," Greeley famously declared in his support for Manifest Destiny. But for Marx, there was no frontier escape—only the daily struggle.[674]

Unlike most reporters and commentators, Marx was far removed from the conventional sources of news and so made much more use of official reports and statistics, which gave his articles added depth and contributed to his later works. Some of his press articles on India,[675] for example, would be incorporated almost verbatim into *Das Kapital.* Considering the strong personal views, his articles were remarkably detached and objective. In many areas—opposition to reactionary European governments, for example—he saw eye to eye with the paper and could express himself forcefully, and where there was a divergence, he contented himself with the straight facts.[676]

Marx's reflections on history and class struggle mirrored a deeper, almost Dantean descent into the archives of human civilization. His studies in the museum were not mere academic pursuits but a relentless excavation of the economic and social forces that shaped the world. Just as Dante's journey through the underworld revealed the consequences of moral failings, Marx's historical materialism exposed the cycles of oppression that weighed upon society. He asserted that "the tradition of all dead generations weighs like a nightmare on the brains of the living."[677] A similar sentiment is found in Dante's warning: "Consider your origin: you were not made to live like brutes, but to follow virtue and knowledge."[678] In both cases, history is not a passive record but an active force pressing upon the present, demanding reckoning and transformation.

As always, the British Museum was Marx's second home. The grandeur of the reading room, with its high-domed ceiling and eternal bookshelves, stood in stark contrast to his cramped lodgings in Soho. Those who encountered him there recalled his intense focus, his desk piled high with papers and ink-stained notes. "He devoured books like a hungry man at a banquet," one acquaintance remarked.[679]

Yet, even as he defended the values of Western European civilization against what he saw as the "Asiatic barbarism" of Russia, as always, his own household remained in turmoil. Even though he was the best paid writer at the Tribune, the fees were meager and provided little relief, and as Marx immersed himself ever deeper in economic theory, their financial struggles persisted. Engels's letters during this time reveal his deep concern for his friend's well-being: "You must take better care of yourself and Jenny," he urged, but Marx was consumed by his work, unwilling or unable to focus on anything else.[680]

He continued his correspondence with Engels, who provided both moral and financial support: "The cost of living here is exorbitant, and despite my most frugal living, I find myself in constant debt. The only solution is to rely on your generosity, which I deeply regret."[681] Engels, himself disillusioned by the failed revolutions of 1848, in 1853 urged Marx to shift his focus toward a more scientific critique of capitalism, to encourage him to make his theories more accessible to workers. In his letters to Engels, Marx frequently discusses his views on religion, often showing contempt for both Christianity and Judaism. Marx argued that religion was a hindrance to human emancipation and that it perpetuates false consciousness: "I know that the first question I shall have to answer is: 'Is the God of the Bible the true God?'" Engels urged Marx: "Your exploration of capital must connect more explicitly to the struggles of the proletariat."[682] To which Marx would say: "Yes, and the Bible contains everything that is useful to humanity. But it is not the Bible that we need, it is a revolution that we need."[683]

London had become his prison as much as his sanctuary. He no longer directly inspired men to action. He largely was a man at his desk, suffering chronic illness, tormented by debt, increasingly dependent on Engels for survival. As Jenny contracted smallpox and their remaining children grew up in hardship, Marx spent his days at the museum and his nights in the cramped, smoky rooms of Soho, where a growing despair and intellectual brilliance coexisted in equal measure.

Self-Imposed Damnation

By 1857, Karl Marx had become a man locked in the labyrinth of his own making. His theories had grown more intricate, his vision more uncompromising. The exile had hardened him, shaping his mind into a weapon against capitalism. But at what cost? Marx, in his polemical writings, would frequently invoke Dante's language to describe the moral degradation he saw in the capitalist class. In one letter to Engels, he writes that "the English working class has undergone no Dantean Hell yet," referring to certain factories as "perfect gates of hell."[684] One could imagine over the factory entrance the writing etched into the soot-laden brick: "Lasciate ogne speranza, voi ch'intrate" ("Abandon all hope, you who enter here").[685] Marx implies that the working class, while suffering, had not yet fully descended into the kind of hellish torment needed to truly see the revolutionary light.

In the broader context of Marx's life and work, this ring—a descent into the heart of economic theory—parallels Dante's journey through the *Inferno*. Just as Dante encountered the souls suffering for their moral failings, Marx scrutinized the structures of capitalism, exposing its exploitation and its moral corruption. Adam Smith's warnings about the corruption of the wealthy in *The Theory of Moral Sentiments* served as a stark reminder that even the proponents of free markets recognized the ethical dangers of unrestrained capitalism: "The rich man glories in his riches, because he feels that they naturally draw upon him the attention of the world."[686] In *The Wealth of Nations*, Smith cautions against the potential conflicts between business interests and public welfare: "The interest of [businessmen] is always in some respects different from, and even opposite to, that of the public. . . . The proposal of any new law or regulation of commerce which comes from this order . . . ought never to be adopted till after having been long and carefully examined . . . with the most suspicious attention." The interplay between Smith's cautionary insights and Marx's apocalyptic zeal underscores the moral urgency of their respective critiques. As readers journey with Marx through his intellectual evolution, they witness the building blocks of his prophetic vision. Each step, from his early economic studies to his *magnum opus*, reveals a relentless drive to tear open the veil for a new Eden.[687]

The echoes of Dante's *Divine Comedy* remind us that this journey was not just economic but profoundly moral, grappling with the fundamental question of what it means to live in a just society which naturally is an echo of Plato's *Republic* and the meaning of justice.[688] Marx's path mirrored Dante's descent into the icy cold of intellectual isolation, where the only escape was to push forward, ever deeper into the abyss of theory. In exile, he had lost so much—his homeland, his wealth, a daughter, and two sons. But he had gained something, too: clarity. He now saw capitalism not just as an economic system but as a totalizing force, shaping every aspect of human life. And he was determined to expose it. Dante, as he emerges from the inferno, writes: "We came forth to see again the stars."[689] For Marx, there were no stars yet, only a dark sky.

The years 1851 to 1857 had stripped away everything except the work itself. And so he wrote. He refined. He burned away the last remnants of his former self, forging a vision that would shape the world long after he was gone. Yet, as he stared into the abyss, as he mapped out its horrors with mathematical precision, he never saw the abyss staring back at him. Marx's tragedy was not just that he misread history but that he failed to see himself within it. Tragedy, at its core, is not just a narrative device but shapes perception and transforms reality into something more than a sequence of events. It lends weight to moments of upheaval and defines characters through the inexorable logic of their downfall. Marx understood this implicitly. He wielded literary references to cast his historical materialism in dramatic form,[690] shaping revolution not as mere historical process but as an existential journey. But still, he did not see the nature of the human dilemma.

Marx saw in tragedy an opportunity for escalation, a tool for permanent revolution rather than a final reckoning. Marx was not merely a theorist; he was a dramatist of history, shaping his vision in a way that made it impossible to resolve, ensuring that the fires of struggle would never be extinguished. In this sense, his dialectic was not just a theory of material conditions but a script—one designed to keep the stage set for perpetual upheaval. He had sought to liberate humankind, but in doing so, he had become a prisoner of his own final act, his own *denouement.* His descent was complete—not into the hell of capitalism, but into a hell of his own creation. He had seen too much, and yet he had seen nothing. And in that myopia, he would never find his way back. He never understood that his banishment was more than political. It was spiritual. It was absolute.

RING 7

The Gathering War (1857–1864)

"I am engaged on a work which I have not yet completed. I regard it as the most terrible missile that has yet been hurled at the heads of the bourgeoisie."[691]

—*Karl Marx,* Letter to Kugelmann, *December 1862*

The first great economic crisis of industrial capitalism erupted in 1857, and Marx saw it not as a passing disaster but as proof that history was bending to his vision. The world convulses. From economic collapse to the cannon fire of the American Civil War. History was moving in violent strides, confirming Marx's long-held beliefs. He watched from exile, ink staining his fingers, his mind ablaze with the conviction that the old world was crumbling under the weight of its contradictions. Yet, as the world moved closer to his vision, his own life spiraled deeper into struggle.

The Panic of 1857 had shattered global markets, sending financial shockwaves through Europe and America, and in its wreckage, Marx saw proof that capitalism was unsustainable. He had thrown himself into the *Grundrisse*, a proposed book that was a furious attempt to map the logic of capital in its entirety, but the text remained a raw, sprawling monolith—brilliant, but chaotic. His thoughts were expanding, but his resources were dwindling.

As Marx wrote his *Das Kapital*, the air was thick with ink and desperation. Marx sat in his crumbling London apartment; for two decades, he had wandered the dark forests of exile, each step leading him deeper into the purgatory of obscurity and intellectual torment. Behind him were six rings of descent—his youthful fire in Germany; his exile in Paris; his ideological wars in Brussels; the gluttonous excess of revolutionary thought in Paris; the political exile in London; and the suffering of personal loss. Each had stripped him further of his humanity, and now, in this seventh ring, the abyss had opened completely. Banks collapsed, markets froze, and the poor drowned in misery. To Marx, this was clearly the harbinger of capitalism's doom. He threw himself into his *Grundrisse*, an unfinished skeleton of what would become *Das Kapital*, only two years after his son Edgar's death.

Marx's personal grief fueled his intellectual fire as he sought to understand and explain the suffering. Jenny would write: "I see the toll your work takes on you, yet I believe in your mission."[692] Marx responds: "Jenny, you have endured so much for my work; I fear I can never repay you."[693] The suffering he witnessed and experienced became fused with his economic critiques, driving him to dissect the global economic crisis with unparalleled vigor. It was as though the anguish in his personal life found a parallel in the systemic failures he sought to address through his writing.

Still, during these years, Marx contributed to various publications, developing his economic theories and becoming more involved in the International Workers' Association (IWA). Marx's writing and activism set the stage for some of his most significant intellectual contributions. His analysis of the crisis appeared in the American, British, and German press, further establishing his reputation as an economist and political thinker. During the period between July 1857 and March 1864, Marx immersed himself in understanding the fundamental laws of capitalist economics and war and how to turn his knowledge into a secular apocalypse.

Mystical Materialism

By June 1858, he completed *Grundrisse: Foundations of the Critique of Political Economy*, a manuscript, not a formally published book during Marx's lifetime. It was written in 1857–1858 as a series of notebooks in preparation for *Das Kapital*.[694] Though referred to as an essay, *Grundrisse* is more accurately described as a set of draft writings containing Marx's extensive explorations into capital, labor, production, and historical materialism, many of which laid the foundation in his great work. As he had written for the *Rheinische Zeitung*, *Deutsch-Französische Jahrbücher (1844)*, and *Vorwarts* (1844),[695] and in the *New York Daily Tribune* (1852, 1857–1858), Marx authored several articles for the *New American Cyclopaedia* to expand his influence among world revolutionaries, with his mind focused on unveiling a new vision for social transformation. The faces of his children faded into the shadows, and his wife's despair was drowned out by the scratch of his pen. He could not see that the revolution he envisioned would not resurrect them.

As Marx began to crystallize his understanding, he plummeted further into the complexities of human systems and their moral failings. It is here, in this intellectual crucible, that Marx's prophetic vision of a mystical materialism began to take shape, charting a path from the pre-Socratics through Hegel and the Millenarians, all the way to the current injustices, furthering his unyielding belief in revolution. Marx's call for a materialist analysis of history began to crystallize, and his writings influenced contemporary uprisings such as those in France and Italy: "The contradictions in the economic structure must inevitably lead to revolution."[696]

Other revolutionary leaders stand as a cloud of witnesses to the new faith as they come to Marx. Giuseppe Garibaldi (1807–1882) an Italian revolutionary, military leader, and nationalist who played a crucial role in the unification of Italy, wrote: "Your ideas inspire revolutionaries in Italy, but clarity is needed on tactical steps."[697] This was a sentiment that reflected a broader tension between doctrine and praxis.[698] Garibaldi's words reflect both admiration for Marx's intellectual framework and a subtle critique of its practical applicability.[699]

Unlike Marx, Garibaldi was deeply rooted in direct action and military strategy, which made his perspective uniquely pragmatic. His caution to Marx underscores a significant tension: while Marx was crafting theoretical critiques of capitalism, figures like Garibaldi were in the trenches, navigating the complexities of real-world revolution. Adding to these critiques, Ferdinand Lassalle (1825–1864), a prominent German socialist and future founder of the first modern socialist political party, echoed a similar concern in 1858: "We need to make socialism accessible to the masses."[700] His comment reflects the growing recognition among Marx's contemporaries that the abstract and highly theoretical nature of Marx's writings risked alienating the very audience he sought to mobilize. While Garibaldi emphasized tactical clarity, Lassalle pointed to the need for broader communication and accessibility, emphasizing that revolutionary ideals must resonate with the workers on the ground.

In the same period, Moses Hess, one of Marx's early collaborators and a key figure in the development of socialist thought, added another layer of critique. Amid the global financial crisis of 1857, Hess remarked to Marx: "The world is changing rapidly; your analysis must adapt to the industrial age."[701] Hess's observation heightened the urgency of updating Marx's critiques to reflect the evolving realities of industrial capitalism and the increasingly interconnected global economy. The financial crisis exposed significant vulnerabilities in the capitalist system, vulnerabilities that Marx had begun to address in his *Grundrisse*. "As soon as labour in the direct form has ceased to be the great well-spring of wealth, labour time ceases and must cease to be its measure, and hence exchange value [must cease to be the measure] of use value."[702] It's a typical passage in Marx's dense prose—abstract, theoretical, and impenetrable to most working-class readers, which ironically distances him from the very people he sought to liberate. Still, the point he's making is significant: under industrial capitalism, wealth is no longer created primarily by direct human labor but increasingly by machines, automation, and capital itself. As a result, the old metric—labor time—no longer functions as the true measure of value, even though the system still pretends it does. For Marx, this disconnect revealed a deeper contradiction in capitalism that would eventually bring about its collapse. Marx's analysis reflects his effort to adapt his critiques to the changing realities of industrial capitalism and the increasingly interconnected global economy. Yet Hess's words suggest that even close allies felt that Marx needed to remain more attuned to the immediate challenges of his time.

Wilhelm Liebknecht, another influential German socialist and a close confidant of Marx, offered a more complex response during this period. He reflected a shared concern among Marx's allies that his focus on long-term revolutionary goals often left urgent worker needs unaddressed: While he valued Marx's intellectual contributions—especially as they related to his groundbreaking economic theories—he also recognized the growing frustration among workers who sought actionable guidance in the face of daily struggles. These voices from Marx's contemporaries highlight a pivotal tension in his life and work. Garibaldi's call for tactical clarity, Lassalle's plea for accessibility, Hess's demand for adaptability and religious sensibilities, and Liebknecht's dual critique of inaction and praise for economic insight illuminate the deeper challenge Marx faced: translating his sweeping theoretical vision into a viable political movement. Ironically, as democratic reforms began to improve conditions for workers, they weakened the revolutionary momentum Marx had predicted and, in doing so, exposed the limits of his theory in practice.

While Marx's intellectual brilliance was widely acknowledged, the critiques from even his closest allies underscored the difficulties of turning his sweeping vision into a movement that could effectively address the rapidly changing realities of the nineteenth century. Marx began to redirect his focus toward a more systematic exposition of his economic theories, but also one with the persuasive force of a great literary work in the form of an apocalyptic biblical narrative. Marx's book *A Contribution to the Critique of Political Economy* (1859) reveals a dimension of his thought that some commentators have described as a form of "mystical materialism,"[703] a unique synthesis of materialism, dialectical philosophies, with eschatological over tones.[704]

As we've seen earlier in *The Essence of Christianity*, Feuerbach argued that theology is essentially anthropology—that is, the divine is a projection of human qualities.[705] Engels noted that Feuerbach's work had a profoundly "liberating effect" on both him and Marx, breaking the spell of Hegelian idealism and grounding their philosophy in material reality.[706] Hegel's dialectical method profoundly influenced Marx, but Marx sought to reorient it from its idealist framework to a materialist one. In *Das Kapital*, Marx will state his intention to "discover the rational kernel within the mystical shell" of Hegel's dialectics, aiming to turn it "right side up again."[707] Marx moves beyond Hegel, imbuing material conditions with a near-transcendent significance, suggesting a "swerve" that empowers human agency, fostering development and the potential for transformation—a mystical perspective that attributes this power to material forces.[708]

Marx integrates the materialist philosophy he inherits from thinkers like Feuerbach with the dialectical methodology of Hegel and an inherent self-revealing spirit, but his thought is also rooted in the deep millenarian movements[709] of the nineteenth century,[710] which dates back to medieval thinkers[711] like Joachim of Fiore,[712] the eschatologist source behind Dante's *Divine Comedy*, whose vision of history—divided into three distinct ages culminating in a final era of spiritual fulfillment—anticipates themes that would echo through later philosophical and theological systems. His model influenced thinkers like Hegel, who reimagined historical development as a dialectical unfolding of *Geist*, or spirit, across successive eras. Marx, in turn, would adapt this framework into a materialist conception of progress—still marked by an eschatological urgency, though stripped of its theological core. The structure of Joachim's vision, emphasizing historical rupture and ultimate transformation, finds resonance in both *The Divine Comedy* and Marx's revolutionary imagination. In Joachim, we glimpse the roots of the millenarian impulse that would pass through Dante's moral cosmology and into the radical philosophies of modernity. Hegel's Lutheran background and belief in the progressive revelation of truth further served as a conduit through which these spiritual frameworks were secularized and politicized—ultimately shaping Marx's own historical vision.

This notion of progression, where each phase connects deeply with the material world, resonates with Marx's own analysis of how material conditions shape human society. Marx takes this further, asserting that money becomes the ultimate binding force in capitalist society. As he states, "If money is the bond binding me to human life, binding society to me, connecting me with nature and man, is not money the bond of all bonds? Can it not dissolve and bind all ties? Is it not, therefore, also the universal agent of separation?"[713] This reflection shows Marx's awareness of the almost mystical power that capitalist societies give to material things, highlighting the contradictions in his claims of pure materialism or determinism. Philosopher Leszek Kołakowski observed that Marx's worldview elevated material conditions to such prominence that they assumed a nearly theological status. In this framework, human consciousness becomes a reflection of material forces, and history itself unfolds through a fixed, necessary sequence—a kind of secular providence guiding the course of events.[714] Similarly, Georg Lukács, in *History and Class Consciousness*, notes how Marx's materialism "elevates the material to the level of the universal, making it the sole vehicle of human liberation," that its "materialism does not view history as a passive reflection of economic forces,"[715] and that "by grasping the totality of capitalist society, Marxist thought transcends empirical observation and reveals the real movement of history—the dialectical unfolding of necessity." It provides what Lukács describes as the "rational kernel within the mystical shell"[716] of Hegelian thought—replacing spiritual determinism with the inexorable logic of class struggle. For Marx, these material realities are not static but dynamic, shaping and reshaping human history through a series of economic dualities from the ancient master–slave dynamic, through the feudal lord–serf relationship, to the modern bourgeois–proletariat divide, history reveals a progression of class structures—from feudalism to capitalism—each shaped by shifting forms of economic power and exploitation. The essence of the new secular apocalypse he envisioned—a world where class struggle resolves in the establishment of communism—was grounded in this mystical faith, similar to that found in the world of Hegel and Fiore: "After the age of the Father and the age of the Son, there will come the age of the Spirit, in which mankind will reach a new stage of universal brotherhood, free from the institutions and constraints of the past."[717]

While Marx claims to reject metaphysical interpretations of history, his materialism takes on a quasi-mystical quality by positioning economic forces as the hidden drivers of human development and societal transformation,[718] with the dualism in words such as "base"[719] and "superstructure,"[720] to explain how economic relations underpin ideological systems. However, he was receiving criticisms from figures like Pierre Leroux, a French philosopher, political economist, and journalist, who took issue with Marx's atheistic framework. In 1859, Pierre Leroux criticized Marx for disregarding the role of religion in people's lives, arguing that such a stance risked distancing the working class, many of whom still drew deep meaning and moral grounding from their faith. Marx's rejection of religion, while consistent with his materialist philosophy, created a barrier between his ideas and the deeply spiritual lives of many workers.[721] In his 1859 preface, Marx describes this process with near-religious certainty, asserting that "the material productive forces of society come into conflict with the existing relations of production"[722] in a way that is both predictable and inexorable.[723] This deterministic perspective assigns a type of agency to historical materialism itself, as though it operates as an unseen hand guiding humanity toward salvation, "with history itself as the divine force leading to an inevitable proletarian paradise."[724] Yet, for all his rejection of religious eschatology, Marx could not entirely escape its shadow.[725] His vision of historical materialism is a prophecy of an end-times struggle, an Armageddon in which the old world is consumed and a new, purified order emerges.[726] Even Marx himself acknowledged this undertone, invoking Dante's *Inferno* in the preface to *Das Kapital* as if to warn readers of the consuming fire they were about to enter.

The Secular Apocalypse

At the entrance to science, as at the entrance to hell, the demand must be made: "Qui si convien lasciare ogni sospetto / Ogni viltà convien che qui sia morta" ("Here must all distrust be left behind; / All cowardice must die here"). These words, inscribed above the gates of Dante's hell, serve to forewarn those embarking on a perilous journey—a fitting metaphor for Marx's own descent revealed how his ideas, while cloaked in the cold logic of economic theory, were rooted in mystical origins. His vision merely transposed it into "an eschatological dream clothed in pseudo-scientific terms."[727] Instead of divine providence guiding history toward an ordained end, Marx forged a mysticism that clothed itself in the garments of science, as did Smith's *invisible hand*[728] or Hegel's *world spirit*.[729] Marx's materialism functioned as its own guiding force, an inexorable logic shaping the course of civilization. This was no mere economic theory—it was religious doctrine. Philosopher and ethicist Alasdair MacIntyre, in his *Marxism and Christianity*, writes: "Only one secular doctrine retains the scope of traditional religion in offering an interpretation of human existence by means of which men may situate themselves in the world and direct their actions to ends that transcend those offered by their immediate situation."[730] Both Marxism and Christianity are "conscious of the appalling price that an unjust world must pay for its redemption."[731] Written in exile, in the dim glow of the British Museum's reading room, Marx's final work was not just an analysis but a prophecy: a messianic materialism that sought to erase the past and rebuild history in a purified form. The revolution he envisioned was more than political; it was eschatological. In his rejection of the old theology, Marx unknowingly embraced its structure. His apocalypse mirrored the Christian end times; his proletarian deliverance echoed the promise of the kingdom of heaven. His doctrine required a faithful remnant—the revolutionary vanguard—to suffer and sacrifice, awaiting the final victory. "The proletariat, as defined by Marx, is the equivalent of a chosen people, destined to bring about a final reckoning that will transform society forever."[732]

Meanwhile, across the Atlantic, the American Civil War was winding down, and Marx's mind burned with the realization that history was aligning with his vision. The old world was dying, and the new world was being born in blood. In Abraham Lincoln, he saw a reluctant revolutionary, a statesman unwittingly carrying forward the historical dialectic, shattering the remnants of feudalism and unleashing industrial capitalism upon the world. This was the inexorable march of history, the revolutionary transition from one stage to the next, the kind of upheaval Marx had so long predicted and sought to cultivate. His writings for the *New York Tribune* captured his growing excitement and his feverish belief that the workers of Europe must recognize in America's war the battle cry of their own struggle. "Labor cannot emancipate itself in the white skin where in the black it is branded,"[733] he declared.

His pen, his greatest weapon, had long been confined to theory, to polemics aimed at shaping the consciousness of the revolutionary class. But now history itself had become his instrument. The battles he once chronicled from afar were now shaping the movement that bore his intellectual imprint. Revolutions stirred across Europe, workers' uprisings flared and faded, and for the first time Marx was not simply interpreting history—he was attempting to seize it, to mold it, to give it form. But history does not pause for its scribes. Engels worked to organize and mobilize workers in industrial settings, and while Marx himself was not always on the ground, his writings and strategic advice played a role in these actions, particularly in framing the factory system as a mechanism that would eventually galvanize workers into conflict with the bourgeoisie. By the 1860s, Marx was no longer just a writer: he was also making a mark as a leader. The formation of the IWA, or the First International, was a moment of vindication, the realization of a lifetime's labor. Here, at last, was the embryonic force that could transform the world, the tangible manifestation of the workers' solidarity he had prophesied. It was no longer just a dream; it was a movement. A congregation assembled beneath the banner of revolution, looking to him for guidance.

Yet leadership is not victory. The IWA, though grand in vision, was fractured in spirit. It was a congregation of disparate voices, conflicting ideologies, and rival visions of socialism. Marx battled not only external enemies but internal schisms, engaging in polemical wars that turned comrades into heretics. His struggle against Pierre-Joseph Proudhon—whom he dismissed in *The Poverty of Philosophy*—and later, Mikhail Bakunin, was not just a theoretical dispute; it was a battle over the soul of the revolution. Anarchism, reformism, state socialism—these were the factions vying for control, and Marx, with the same iron grip he once used to rule over the *Neue Rheinische Zeitung*, sought to purge his movement of what he saw as impurities. His excommunications were brutal. Bakunin was cast out, labeled a saboteur and a counterrevolutionary. But the expulsion of enemies did not bring unity—only deeper fractures. The movement grew, but its foundation was unstable, the ground beneath Marx's feet shifting even as history seemed to be racing toward his vision of the future.

But at what cost? His movement had followers, his ideas had spread, and yet he remained a man alone, exiled from the revolution he so desperately sought to ignite. Jenny Marx bore the weight of his ambitions, as their home knew more hunger than triumph. Yet Marx would not relent—he could not relent. In this period of upheaval, his writings on the American Civil War and the IWA's struggles revealed a man whose mind remained sharp even as his body weakened. His analysis of global events showed a growing reputation not just as a thinker but as a voice for change. He was no longer merely the theorist of alienation—he was becoming the prophet of revolution. But if he was to lead his disciples "pointing toward the promised land,"[734] he first had to bear the full weight of exile.

By the 1860s, Marx had assembled all the building blocks of his revolutionary doctrine. His materialist mysticism, forged in the crucible of exile and intellectual struggle, had become his first principle—his *prima philosophia*.[735] He had rewritten the Genesis story, not as a tale of divine creation, but as the moment capitalism emerged and severed humankind from its own nature. Alienation, the condition that had once described fallen man in the theological sense, was now repurposed as the fundamental crisis of industrial society.[736] And the *only* salvation, the only resolution to history's ceaseless contradictions, was communism: not as a mere political program, not as an economic structure, but as the end of history itself—the moment at which all suffering would be resolved, all estrangement abolished, and the long march of human struggle would finally reach its conclusion.

Marx was not merely writing about this transformation—he was *prophesying* it. His philosophy had taken on the tone of the great eschatological narratives of the past, but where the ancients had placed their faith in divine justice, Marx had placed his in historical inevitability. The revolution was no longer an event to be debated, no longer the dream of political radicals: it was a certainty, an apocalypse inscribed into the very logic of history.[737] The dialectic was marching forward, unstoppable, indifferent to the will of humans. And Marx? He was its prophet, its Moses standing at the edge of the Red Sea to call the faithful to cross over.

The revolutionary fire had been kindled in 1848, but it had burned out before reaching its full potential. Now, as he wrote furiously in London, Marx believed the conditions were aligning once more. The old world was collapsing—the cracks were appearing in the walls of empires, and the masses were restless. The IWA was the first sign, the first tangible proof that the workers of the world could unite. This was no longer just theory. It was happening. But who was the messiah of this new order?

Marx had spent most of his Faustian spirit willing himself past what he considered the superstitious, the backward, the unenlightened. He had cast himself as the destroyer of old illusions, the breaker of chains, the slayer of gods and kings. In his vision, history had been shackled for too long by myths—Christianity, the invisible hand, bourgeois morality[738]—stories that had kept the proletariat in bondage.[739] He had burned through these deceptions one by one, leaving only the cold steel of materialism. But had he burned away something more? Had he, in his relentless drive to destroy, lost the very human element that gave revolution its meaning?

Even his most devoted allies had felt his wrath—Engels, his loyal patron, had been berated and belittled when he dared to contradict Marx's conclusions. Mikhail Bakunin, the great anarchist, had once been a fellow traveler in the revolution, but Marx saw in him only a threat to his control of the movement. When he expelled Bakunin from the IWA in 1872, it was not a matter of mere disagreement; it was an excommunication. The Church of Marxism had no room for heretics. But this was the paradox: his messianism had no Christ. There was no grace in his vision, no redemption, no kingdom of heaven where the poor would inherit the earth. Instead, the path to the new world ran through fire. The ruling class would not simply fade away—it had to be crushed. The revolution would not be a peaceful unfolding—it would be a war, a great conflagration, a reckoning written in blood. The old world had to burn.

And so, did Marx simply want to see the world burn? For all his talk of liberation, his writings crackled with a certain apocalyptic rage, a fury directed not merely at capitalism but at existence itself. His denunciations were not just critiques—they were curses, litanies of destruction, aimed at every institution that had ever given men structure, meaning, or comfort. The family, the state, religion, even history itself—all were to be overturned. Marx, like the great fallen angel of John Milton's *Paradise Lost*, had set himself against the order of the world. "Everything that exists deserves to perish," he had once quoted from Goethe's *Faust*, a line that could just as easily have been spoken by Satan himself. In his quest to unshackle humankind, had he become something else entirely? He was a liberator, yes—but also a destroyer; he was a prophet, yes—but of an apocalypse that cared little for those caught in its flames.

For all his grand designs, for all the thunder of his manifestos, Marx's own life was a ruin. His family suffered in ways that would have been unthinkable for a man who claimed to be leading the cause of the working class. Jenny suffered alongside him, growing weaker as the years passed. His children were raised in squalor. One by one, they died young, victims of the very conditions Marx had sworn to abolish. His home in London was no revolutionary command center—it was a place of illness, hunger, and despair. Even in his middle age, when his ideas were beginning to spread across Europe, when the seeds of revolution were sprouting in Germany and France, Marx himself had been left behind. The world was surging toward the storm he had predicted, but the storm no longer needed him. Would he have been satisfied with this? Or would it have infuriated him? Would he have rejoiced in the knowledge that history was moving toward his vision, or raged at the fact that he would not be the one to lead it? Would he have felt triumph or bitterness? The revolution was coming, but it would be carried out in his name. His theories would be twisted, repurposed, and wielded as weapons by those who would never understand the depths of his vision. The prophet had laid the foundation, but the kingdom would not be his to rule.

And in the end, what did he have left? Not the passion of the poet, not the rapture of the messiah, not even the satisfaction of seeing his enemies fall. He had only the embers of his own destruction—the burning ruins of a life spent in struggle, a movement that had consumed everything around him, leaving only a small, exiled man in London, struggling to maintain what little remained. The revolution was his child, but like all children, it would grow beyond him. And Marx? He would fade, not in the blaze of revolution, but in the slow, painful collapse of a body and mind worn down by years of battle spent trying to remake the world. But in the end, the world had remade him.

Permanent Exile

November 30, 1863, brought the death of his mother, Henriette, during an already turbulent period in Marx's life. Her passing deepened his sense of personal loss at a time when his political writings were beginning to gain wider public attention. Henriette's death followed a long period of estrangement; her pragmatic, bourgeois values had long clashed with her son's radical ideals and uncompromising devotion to theory over stability.[740] In a letter to his eldest daughter, Jenny Caroline, Marx reflected on his mother's pragmatic concerns, recalling her words: "If only Karl had made Capital, instead of just writing about it."[741]

Henriette's death, though overshadowed by the towering legacy of Marx's ideas, serves as a window into the emotional and familial toll of his revolutionary ambitions, reminding us that even the most influential figures are not immune to the fragility of human existence. His father, Heinrich Marx, once wrote to him about his mother to express both admiration and concern for her quiet endurance: "Your dear mother's love and devotion are beyond words, though I fear she suffers too much in silence."[742] If his mother's quiet endurance shaped his early years, perhaps it led him to develop a blindness to the suffering of others. As biographer Mary Gabriel explains:

> There were many instances in Marx's life in which he showed himself to be a deeply self-centered man. Even in respect to those he loved most, he was at times maddeningly blind to their feelings and needs. January 1863 was one such time. On the seventh of that month, Engels wrote Marx a brief note to say that Mary Burns, his companion of two decades and the woman he called his wife, had died: "Last night she went to bed early and, when Lizzy wanted to go to bed shortly before midnight, she found she had already died. Quite suddenly. Heart failure or an apoplectic stroke. . . . I simply can't convey how I feel. The poor girl loved me with all her heart." Marx responded the next day. To even the surprise of Engels who really knew Karl, "the first two lines of his letter expressed his surprise and dismay about Mary, and then he devoted the next thirty-one lines to his own financial problems."[743]

Or perhaps Engels was supposed to have found solace in Marx's similarly compassionate sentence in which he said: "Instead of Mary, ought it not to have been my mother, who is in any case a prey to physical ailments and has had her fair share of life?"[744] For Engels, this was a tragedy and something that would transform his life: "One can't live with a woman for years on end without being fearfully affected by her death. I felt as though with her I was burying the last vestige of my youth. . . . I'm glad that, in losing Mary, I didn't also lose my oldest and best friend."[745]As is obvious, Marx shows a lack of empathy for others, even for one who would support him to his grave. Though Engels might have wanted to depart at that point, he too had signed the pact with the revolution and even personal hurts could not prevent the mission: "Engels waited nearly a week before he responded, and when he did, it was in the imperious Prussian tone, 'You will find it quite in order that, this time, my own misfortune and the frosty view you took of it should have made for me to reply to you any sooner. All my friends, including philistine acquaintances, have on this occasion, which in all conscience must needs afflict me deeply, given me proof of greater sympathy and friendship than I could have looked for. You thought it a fit moment to assert the superiority of your dispassionate turn of mind. So be it then!'"[746]

Engels's second letter "had been an eye-opener," Marx admitted, and he had now decided to act on a conclusion reached months before. "The only way for the family to survive would be for Marx to file for bankruptcy, send his two eldest girls out to be governesses, send Lenchen into service elsewhere, and move with Jenny and Tussy into a city-operated lodging house where Wilhelm Wolff had once lived when down on his luck."[747]

At this point, it was Marx's turn to play the role of provider—but was he capable? Engels, who remained a partner at the Manchester firm Ermen & Engels, described how he quietly diverted funds: he redirected a company payment, making the bill payable to Marx instead. The result was one hundred pounds—enough to keep the family in their home and allow the girls to return to school. Yet this act of generosity underscored a growing emotional distance. Engels, who had quietly orchestrated the support, confided that "the loneliness was unbearable."[748]

As Engels continued his support, Marx seemed increasingly distant, caught in a web of personal and ideological struggles. Much like Dante's damned, who are defined by their inability to escape their sins, Marx appeared trapped in his own intellectual labyrinth—forever bound by the very ideas that had once promised liberation.

The contradictions inherent in his vision—the utopian hope for communism juxtaposed with the harsh realities of material conditions—would turn his fires inward. But while Marx struggled with depression, digestive problems, and the effects of years of stress and financial anxiety, his theories were beginning to have a lasting impact on socialist movements, even though he was still far from the influence or power he had envisioned in earlier years.

In his essay *Karl Marx: His Life and Environment*, Isaiah Berlin notes: "For a great part of his life his mind dwelt on fantasies of power. At moments of depression, he would buoy himself up with the hope of becoming the revolutionary dictator of Germany, and he would discuss quite seriously with Engels how the next crisis would inevitably bring him to a position of supreme power."[749] Even on a trip to the opera with the king of Prussia, where he hoped to ask for the return of his citizenship, Marx remained deeply immersed in his ideological battles, with little relief from his personal struggles. Biographer Robert Payne observes: "It seems never to have occurred to him that the Germans might not want him."[750]

Marx's attempt to regain Prussian citizenship, despite his lifelong denunciations of monarchy and the state, was a striking contradiction to his high ideals. According to Shlomo Avineri, the Prussian authorities were wary of his revolutionary activities and rejected his application.[751] Marx had already alienated himself from many former allies because of his relentless polemics and ideological purism.[752] With each severed alliance, Marx drifted further into exile—not just from his homeland but from the revolutionary movement.

Despite his failures, in 1864, Marx pivoted toward building the IWA, a move that signaled his full commitment to an internationalist revolutionary agenda: his exile was no longer just political—it had become existential. With his homeland rejecting him and his family ties fraying, he was condemned to a fate akin to Dante's lost souls, wandering without hope of return. Unlike Dante, whose exile led him to "seek the stars," Marx doubled down on his revolutionary vision, forsaking all but the material struggle. Where Dante had his Beatrice, a symbol of redemption and love,[753] Marx had Jenny, but turned to a relentless force he believed would vindicate him. Marx's permanent exile in London meant a final judgment that severed any lingering ties to his homeland, but it also pushed him further into the shadows, stripping him of his political agency. And so, in this underground world of socialist organization, where revolutionaries whispered his name in reverence, his ideas gained a momentum that outstripped his personal influence. His followers saw in him a prophet of upheaval, but what had once been a concrete political movement was now something more—a doctrine, an eschatology, a vision of the end and rebirth of the world.

Marx's body bore the weight of his contradictions: the festering sores that erupted over his skin seemed less a mere affliction and more a manifestation of his own moral losses. Cast out from his homeland, denied the recognition he craved, and severed from the levers of political power, he descended into a different kind of underworld—one not of fire and torment but of ink and shadows, where his words would forge a new kind of inferno. The underground was no longer merely a refuge; it was becoming his kingdom, a realm where exiles and radicals clung to his doctrine like scripture, awaiting the day when the old world would burn and the new would rise from its ashes.

His next stop, then, was an imagined scene in the underground, as Marx walks into a dimly lit chamber, the air thick with the scent of coal and steam stretching deeper into darkness. A faint, hellish glow pulses from a grating below, though Marx does not yet see it for what it is. Books and scattered papers lie at his feet—his imagined blueprint for a new world. He is then met by Dante and Hamlet, two familiar figures, who provide insight into Marx's life course and character.

Dante (*stepping forward, arms crossed*):
This place is not thine home, yet here thou dwell'st.
Still penning laws for ghosts, still chasing fire.
Tell me, Karl, dost thou know where thy feet now tread?

Marx (*gripping a page, scoffing*):
Where history is written!

Where men forge their own salvation!
Each word a hammer, each page a stone—
With these hands, I build the new Jerusalem!

Hamlet (*laughing darkly from the shadows*):
Aye, Jerusalem, but built on what?
The bones of kings? The prayers of beggars?
Or merely the echoes of thine own despair?

Marx (*turning sharply*):
I see no ghosts here, only cowards.
The world will not shift by whisper nor doubt—
It must be forced into shape, beaten like iron!

Dante *(softly, shaking his head):*
And dost thou think thy hammer strikes free?
Or is thy hand already bound to fate's wheel?
Step forward, if thou wouldst know.

(Marx hesitates. The tunnels ahead seem no longer to be tunnels but a vast, open chasm, their depths unknowable. A faint wind stirs, carrying the distant wail of unseen voices. A tremor runs beneath his feet—barely felt, but growing.)

Hamlet *(mocking, with a smirk):*
Still so sure, my would-be king?
Or doth a shadow lengthen at thy heel?

Marx (*clutching his manuscript, pressing forward*):
The shadow is history, and I its author.

Dante (*watching as Marx steps closer to the abyss, voice barely above a whisper*):
Nay, Karl.
It is judgment.

(The glow from below intensifies—not the light of revelation, but the flickering of unseen flames. Marx, still blind to its meaning, walks on. The wind rises, carrying the faintest of whispers: a name not yet spoken, a truth not yet seen.)

BOOK THREE

Author in Hell

(1864–1883)

"The bourgeoisie, like Dante's damned, will not escape their judgment. For their actions, they will face the inferno of their own making, their systemic oppression reflected in the suffering of the workers they exploit."[754]

—Karl Marx

RING 8

The Underworld of Capital (1864–1867)

"The power of Dante's thought is that it speaks to the conditions of humanity, and he shows how ambition, greed, and betrayal create a hell of our own making."[755]

—Karl Marx

Beneath the streets of London, something stirs. In 1863, the first subterranean railway in the world began to burrow through the city, an iron serpent tunneling beneath the empire. Smoke and steam billowed from its tunnels, the air thick with soot, its passengers traveling deeper underground than ever. An iron labyrinth of smoke and steam lurks beneath the city. Meanwhile, Karl Marx undertakes his subterranean journey. Still secluded in the British Museum's reading room, he excavates the inner workings of capitalism to dismantle its mechanisms with the precision of an engineer mapping an unseen world. The underground, yet another sign of the industrial age, both literal and symbolic, came to define the life and work of Karl Marx. Much like Dante's descent into the *Inferno*, Marx plunged deeper into an economic underworld, each revelation drawing him further into the tensions of his time. The striking difference, however, is that "Dante has already admitted, before he enters Hell, that Aeneus and Paul—two mortal humans—have gone down and returned safely."[756]

While condemning labor exploitation, Marx survived on the financial support of Friedrich Engels, a benefactor whose wealth was derived from the system Marx sought to dismantle. And his own life mirrors the suffering he chronicled: illness, poverty, and debt tighten their grip, even as his intellectual output reaches its peak with *Das Kapital*. Marx went further into the abyss of his scholarly ambitions. His body was weakening; his mind, however, continued to sharpen like a blade, chiseling through the contradictions of capitalism with relentless fury. Completing the first volume of *Das Kapital* was not merely an academic achievement but an exorcism: he attempted to wrench history into alignment with his vision.

Like the underground railway, *Das Kapital* is a vast machine of economic thought, its components—commodities, surplus value, capital—grinding forward in relentless motion. But where the locomotive carries passengers to new destinations, Marx's great work charts a different course: a passage into the depths of a system he believes is destined for collapse. Much like Dante's *Divine Comedy*, *Das Kapital* becomes an inferno, mapping capitalist exploitation's moral and spiritual torments. The ruthless dynamics of capital are portrayed as a relentless, vampiric force that feeds on human labor and perpetuates its cycle of destruction. Marx's work can be seen as creating monumental intellectual and emotional power, reflecting his growing understanding of capitalism's impact on human beings. As William Clare Roberts discusses in his analysis of Marx's style, the latter imbued *Das Kapital* with a creative narrative energy that recalls Dante's allegorical journey through hell, purgatory, and paradise. Marx's "Inferno" is the capitalist system itself, where every aspect of human life is twisted and commodified, and the worker is eternally chained to the system's insatiable demand for labor.

The year 1864 was marked by continued hardship, but it also brought moments of triumph. His world was on fire—his health was collapsing, his finances remained dire, and his ideological wars had left him increasingly isolated: "Toward the end his life he suffered from progressive paranoia, and he would talk about the great revolutionary movements he still controlled, when in fact he had no organized following at all."[757] The revolution he envisioned grew more distant, but he had already convinced himself that his actual battle was yet to come: *Das Kapital* would be his final, irrefutable testament.

In Marx's case, it was perhaps not a steep climb but a deeper dive into the underworld both literarily and figuratively: the London underground, or "Tube," began operation. But given his financial difficulties, "it is plausible that he primarily relied on walking."[758] The meaning of the underground could also have been how Marx conceived of modern humans living in the underbelly of the capitalist cityscape. Peter Ackroyd's *London Under* (2011) firmly puts the underground on the literary map as an enduring site of fascination,[759] as he plumbs the murkier depths of the city for "forgotten things, discarded things."[760]

Authors have long drawn from real cities[761] to create fictional settings that mirror their essence. Dante Alighieri's *Divine Comedy* reflects his native Florence, populating its realms with contemporary Florentines, embedding his personal and political experiences within the city's landscape. Similarly, Johann Wolfgang von Goethe's *Faust* mirrors Weimar's intellectual and cultural milieu, where Goethe spent much of his life. William Shakespeare often set his plays in Italian cities, such as Verona in *Romeo and Juliet* and Venice in *The Merchant of Venice*. While these plays are set in Italy, they capture social dynamics and human experiences relevant to Elizabethan England. They all transform real cities into fictional landscapes that explore universal human experiences, much as Marx did for London. Marx wrote: "Man is at last compelled to face with sober senses his real conditions of life, and his relations with his kind."[762] And so how much more to enter as the poet of the underground! "The feuilleton writers repeat this as though something were degrading in it for me. Fools, this is my glory, because truth is here," as Dostoyevsky writes in *Notes from the Underground*.[763]

The Descent Beneath the Surface

In his critique, Marx mirrors Dante's structure not merely by describing levels of torment but by situating his readers within an intellectual journey that demands they face the true horrors of capitalist exploitation. Just as Dante's work is a moral quest to navigate the path of sin and redemption, Marx's *Capital* is a relentless intellectual pursuit to expose and ultimately transform the system that enslaves the working class. With the precision of a theologian outlining the punishments of the damned, Marx meticulously details how capital, much like the damned souls in Dante's circles, is bound by its laws of perverse accumulation, an endless cycle of destruction and renewal that traps both the worker and the capitalist in a doomed state of perpetual suffering.[764]

Marx's *Das Kapital* is a product of genius, imagination, and suffering; it is not a mere economic text but a gospel of historical inevitability, his own *Inferno*, mapping the torments of capitalist exploitation with the precision of a theologian. In his own words: "Capital is the great engine of exploitation, a relentless force that grows stronger the more it feeds on the sweat and blood of the worker. It is the unholy law of accumulation, where each drop of labor is extracted as tribute to a system that knows no mercy."[765] He *labors* over every page, turning London's reading rooms into his catacombs, where he pores over financial records like a priest deciphering scripture. Each formula, each footnote, is a brick in a vast intellectual fortress, but like the builders of Dante's eighth ring, he is constructing a system so weighty that it threatens to collapse under its contradictions. Marx now sees capitalism's expansion as a doomed train hurtling toward disaster, not merely as an economic system but as a hellish mechanism of suffering and exploitation. He writes: "Accumulation of wealth at one pole is, therefore, at the same time accumulation of misery, agony of toil, slavery, ignorance, brutality, mental degradation, at the opposite pole."[766] It aligns with the infernal descent—Marx's growing belief that capitalism naturally creates a world of haves and have-nots. The capitalist, in his system, is no less damned than the exploited laborer, each trapped in a cycle of production and alienation that neither can escape. But Marx, like Faust before him, is consumed by his desire for power over history. He believes that in exposing capitalism's inner workings, he will break its hold on the world.

By now, Marx has sacrificed everything for his vision. His wife, Jenny—once his Beatrice, now frail—endures the poverty of exile alongside him. Engels, his eternal benefactor, continues to fund his work, though even *he* is growing weary of Marx's unceasing demands. Marx's daughters, particularly Eleanor, watch as their father sinks further into isolation, his body ailing, his spirit consumed. Their commitment to the cause was unwavering. Marx later assures his son-in-law Paul Lafargue, "I do not regret it," speaking of his devotion to the revolutionary struggle. "If I had to live my life over again, I would do the same. I would not marry, however. As far as it lies within my power, I wish to save my daughter from the reefs on which her mother's life was wrecked."[767] (His concerns about his daughters were well-founded; they all had unhappy lives, one dying shortly before him and the two who survived him committing suicide.)[768]

The Marx family's survival was a testament to Jenny's unyielding strength and determination to hold it together. The revolution that Marx had once believed in so fervently now seemed distant, almost unattainable. His faith in the revolutionary cause began to waver, and his writings were more pessimistic: "The factory workroom is a prison; its overseer is the armed sentinel, its workspace a torture chamber."[769] He evokes a vision of hell when describing the plight of the working class: "In the factory system, the worker is completely alienated from the product of his labor and is as helpless as a damned soul in Dante's Hell, having no control over his creation."[770]

By 1864, as the American Civil War neared its end, Marx had extensively analyzed the conflict, linking it to his class theory and viewing it as part of the broader struggle for freedom and the abolition of feudal-like structures in the United States.[771] In a letter to

Engels dated January 23, 1862, he remarked: "The American war is a great revolutionary event, it is the final struggle between the slavery system and the free labor system, and it will have consequences that will affect the whole world."[772] This highlights his view that the abolition of slavery was a moral imperative and a critical turning point in the global economic system.[773] He saw slavery as deeply intertwined with capitalism,[774] particularly in the southern United States, where the plantation economy was essential to global markets: "The worker is compelled to sell himself piecemeal. He is enslaved, but a temporary one."[775]

Marx emphasized in his writings that this upheaval was essential for progress toward a more equitable economic order. His true happiness lay in fighting against injustice, as shown in his lifelong commitment to class struggle and social reform. From his early days at the *Rheinische Zeitung* to his writings for the *Communist Manifesto* and now with *Das Kapital*, Marx's "happiness" was embodied in the intellectual and practical fight against oppression. His confrontational nature was evident in his many disputes with political figures and fellow intellectuals. This preference supports his belief that true happiness comes from actively challenging the status quo.

By the late nineteenth century, the Second Industrial Revolution was reshaping society. Steel, electricity, and petroleum fueled unprecedented growth, while empires expanded their reach into Africa and Asia. Otto von Bismarck's eventual unification of Germany and establishment of the Third Republic in France signaled profound political shifts. In the United States, Reconstruction struggled to heal the wounds of the Civil War. Richard Wagner's operas dominated the musical world, and in 1867, Fyodor Dostoevsky's novel *Crime and Punishment* plumbed the limits of the human soul without God. Yet, this was also a time of profound transformation: while factory workers often labored under harsh conditions and colonial subjects faced systemic exploitation, the British public increasingly demanded change. A series of reforms—including the Factory Acts of 1833, 1844, 1847, and 1850—sought to improve labor conditions, particularly for women and children.[776] Rather than revolutionary upheaval, England witnessed a gradual evolution, as both major political parties responded to mounting social pressures with legislative remedies.[777] For Marx, these years were marked by personal despair and a grim determination to see his *magnum opus*, *Das Kapital*, through to completion. Engels was eager to see it completed and expressed his investment in its writing: "I have sacrificed my health, happiness, and family to finish this work—let us hope it is worth it."[778] The first volume of *Das Kapital: Kritik der politischen Ökonomie* was published on September 14, 1867. It was subtitled *The Process of Production of Capital* and was the only one Marx published during his lifetime. It offers a critical analysis of political economy, focusing on the capitalist mode of production.[779] To help the cause, Engels would also write reviews to help popularize the work, but despite the book's intellectual success, it did not sell well. Marx lamented: "Every beginning is difficult, but science must forge ahead, even when the world is slow to understand."[780]

The Descent into Contradiction

Karl and Jenny Marx had seven children, yet by 1867, only three had survived: Jenny Caroline (b. 1844), Laura (b. 1845), and their youngest, Eleanor Marx (b. 1855), all of whom were living with their parents at the time.[781] Eleanor would later become involved in the socialist movement.[782] Jenny Caroline was a steadfast presence in the Marx household, offering support and companionship to her parents. Just a year younger, Laura shared her sister's resilience, later becoming an essential link between the Marx family and the socialist movement. Eleanor emerged as a revolutionary figure in her own right, embodying her father's ideals.

Marx advocated for revolutionary action as conditions worsened for the working class in industrial Europe, seeing Paris—long a symbol of popular uprising—as the potential flashpoint that could ignite a broader global workers' movement. In 1866, Paul Lafargue, a young French socialist born in Santiago de Cuba, was compelled to leave France due to his political activism and settled in London. There, he became actively involved with the First International and frequently visited Karl Marx's home, where he met Laura. The two developed a close relationship, leading to their marriage at St. Pancras registry office in April 1868. Karl Marx had mixed feelings about the union. In a letter written on August 28, 1866, he expressed concern over Lafargue's political activities, ironically advising his daughter Laura to ensure that Paul avoids dangerous political work. Despite his reservations, Marx maintained correspondence with the couple, offering guidance and support.[783]

The further he plunged into *Das Kapital*, the more he mirrored the system he sought to dismantle. His life was marked by blind moral failings that revealed the paradox of his revolutionary ideals. In Marx's case, his sins were not theological transgressions but lived contradictions, each shaping the reality he refused to acknowledge. Marx's intellectual arrogance alienated even his closest allies. Once a confidant, Ferdinand Lassalle broke from Marx after enduring his scathing attacks, with Marx dismissing him and ridiculing his aspirations for leadership.[784] Wilhelm Liebknecht, despite his loyalty, found himself repeatedly undermined by Marx's domineering presence.

Marx's letters reveal a seething bitterness toward those who gained influence while he struggled in obscurity. When Mikhail Bakunin's anarchist ideas began to eclipse Marx's influence within the First International, Marx responded by challenging Bakunin's ideology and skillfully maneuvering behind the scenes to consolidate power. His efforts culminated in Bakunin's expulsion at the 1872 Hague Congress,[785] a decisive moment that revealed Marx's growing intolerance for rival revolutionary visions and underscored the deep fracture between authoritarian socialism and anarchist decentralism.[786] He said he "should be driven out of the International for his destructive influence and lack of intellectual rigor."[787] The rise of Social Darwinism during this period only intensified these prejudices, particularly among Western elites. Violent ideologies, especially those that claim moral superiority, often attract individuals whose pride blinds them to their moral failings. As history would later show—from Marx's contemporaries to figures like Che Guevara—revolutionary fervor can mask deeper pathologies, including racism, chauvinism, and authoritarian ambition.

His vitriol was not limited to ideological enemies; even former allies suffered his scorn. In *Herr Vogt*, his response to the journalist Karl Vogt, Marx used language that drips with venom, portraying his opponent as a deceitful coward:[788] "Vogt is the lowest of vermin, and his writings are nothing more than the desperate lies of a man too foolish to understand his own mediocrity."[789] His resentment extended even to Engels, who offered financial stability and a pragmatic approach to politics that Marx lacked. Engels remarked in frustration that Marx could not be persuaded to undertake "a respectable trade" and instead spent his days in the reading rooms of the British Museum, buried in theory while his family suffered:[790] "For the last ten years, I have paid for his bread, his books, and his cigars, yet he cannot lift a hand to help himself."[791] Despite his socialist ideals, Marx's habits often strained his closest relationships, revealing a disconnect between his political philosophy and his private life. While he denounced exploitation in theory, he frequently relied on the financial support of Engels and others, refusing regular employment even when his family suffered. This tension between principle and practice has led some to argue that Marx was not merely inconsistent but embodied a deeper flaw within his ideology—the temptation to justify dependency as a form of resistance. Historically, this tendency has produced dangerous outcomes. In Stalinist Russia, for example, the successful kulaks—independent peasant farmers—were vilified as enemies of equality and purged under the guise of socialist justice.[792]

Marx's call for revolutionary upheaval was never merely theoretical—it demanded, in his own words, a "ruthless criticism of all that exists,"[793] including the overthrow of the ruling bourgeois class. This was not an appeal to dialogue or reform but to force. In his framework, the bourgeoisie, as a class, had to be abolished for history to advance. And under such a radical mandate, human destruction becomes not just likely but inevitable. This logic came into sharp focus during the Paris Commune of 1871—a moment Marx hailed as a prototype of proletarian government. Initially, the Commune succeeded with surprisingly limited violence, but this was less the result of a peaceful uprising and more a product of circumstance: France's army was preoccupied with the Franco-Prussian War, and power in Paris was momentarily unguarded. When retaliation did come, it was brutal. The Versailles government responded with overwhelming force, leading to the execution of thousands of Communards. Marx interpreted the Commune as confirmation of his theory: the state, in the hands of the ruling class, would never surrender without bloodshed. But this view also cemented the tragic trajectory of his vision—a revolution that demands the dismantling of existing structures through violence sets the stage for cycles of repression. The very system he condemned for its cruelty would be mirrored, in a darker form, by the regimes that rose in his name.

Engels eventually grew weary of Marx's relentless financial demands. Though Marx often complained of creditors and hardship, he showed little restraint in spending, relying on Engels's steady support while continuing to indulge in personal comforts. Friends like Wilhelm Wolff also contributed, only to be met with entitlement rather than gratitude. At the same time, Marx's personal life reflected contradictions that mirrored the very bourgeois failings he denounced. The secret of his illegitimate child, Freddy, remained hidden behind a public lie—Engels falsely claimed paternity to protect Marx's reputation, a deception that outlived them both. Even as Marx railed against hypocrisy, he embodied it in private. From the late 1850s on, wine became a symbol of his lingering nostalgia and revolutionary pride. When asked about happiness in 1865, Engels answered on Marx's behalf with a toast to *Chateau Margaux 1848*—a vintage as indulgent as it was ironic. In the end, Marx imagined himself the architect of a new world, yet he remained shackled to old comforts, private dependencies, and personal contradictions. He wrote of a workers' paradise, yet his home was a site of grief and turmoil. The very system he condemned—namely, exploitation, dependency, cruelty—was reflected in his dealings with those closest to him. Marx's intellectual output during these years remained prolific despite the turmoil in his personal life. His writings, driven by his critique of the existing social order, laid the foundation for the future of revolutionary thought, with works like *The Communist Manifesto* emerging as powerful calls for change.

These years of intellectual labor would be some of the most productive in Marx's life, and his contributions to the socialist movement during this period helped shape the future of revolutionary theory. *The Communist Manifesto*, written in 1848, was the clarion call for a new revolution, a herald of the epoch to come; it "proclaimed the spectre of communism haunting Europe, reflecting the revolutionary aspirations of the proletariat."[794] Marx's theories, notably those developed between 1864 and 1867, marked a decisive break from the philosophical legacies of Aristotle, Aquinas, and even Hegel.[795] His critique of Hegel's philosophy, which goes as far back as his 1843 work *Critique of Hegel's Philosophy of Right*, exemplifies this departure.[796] While Aquinas emphasized natural law and moral order rooted in logical arguments, he also knew that "when we speak of God, we do not know what we are talking about, but he fills a large number of volumes with such talk, even so."[797] Marx replaced that vision with a wholly materialist conception of history and human nature. Unlike Aquinas, Marx did not ground human dignity in the *imago Dei* nor preserve a teleological account of virtue or community.[798] Instead, he subordinated ethics to a historical struggle, viewing morality as a superstructure determined largely by class relations. While both Aquinas and Marx were deeply concerned with justice, their foundations—divine order for one, economic determinism for the other—could not be more opposed.

Furthermore, Marx's critique of classical political economy, "its faulty architectonics"[799] and its labor theories of value, proposed by Adam Smith and David Ricardo, led him to develop the concept of surplus value.[800] He portrayed Smith's "invisible hand"[801] and other concepts in *The Wealth of Nations* as tools for capitalist class oppression.[802] This concept highlighted the exploitation inherent in capitalist production, where the laborer's work generates value exceeding their compensation, enriching the capitalist class.[803] However, *The Wealth of Nations* was more nuanced and cautious, with Smith arguing that the free market promotes society's general welfare through the principle of enlightened self-interest, known as the "invisible hand." Smith famously wrote: "It is not from the benevolence of the butcher, the brewer, or the baker, that we expect our dinner, but from their regard to their own interest. . . . By pursuing his own interest, he frequently promotes that of society."[804] Marx, however, saw the market as a system of exploitation, pure and simple.

In his chapter on capital accumulation in *The Wealth of Nations*,[805] "Smith emphasized the need for saving and frugality as keys to economic growth, in addition to stable government policies, a competitive business environment, and sound business management."[806] Marx's economic heresy lay in his rejection of the classic liberal idea that individual self-interest could lead to collective prosperity. For Marx, the market was not a neutral mechanism for allocating resources but a tool solely for class oppression. Many later perceived his *Critique of Political Economy* as a monumental work. Students in communist countries studied it intensely, treating it as if it held the key to ending the world's miseries. Marx's view of the market solely as an instrument of oppression set him apart from classical thinkers who saw economic systems as part of a broader moral and philosophical order.

Unlike Aristotle, who believed in *oikonomia*—the household economy governed by ethical considerations—or Aquinas, who integrated economic justice within a theological framework, Marx dismissed these perspectives as ideological constructs meant to justify existing hierarchies.[807] Instead, he argued that "the mode of production of material life conditions the social, political and intellectual life process in general."[808] In this view, Marx belongs to the camp of thinkers who, faced with the disconnect between theory and lived reality, seek to reshape the world rather than adjust their ideas to fit it. This captures the revolutionary impulse at the heart of Marx's system: interpreting and transforming the world. Whether one sees this as bold idealism or a hubristic war with reality depends on one's philosophical commitments. In any case for many, it captures the epistemological confidence—and perhaps the risk—embedded in Marx's refusal to yield theory to the conditions of the present world.

The consequences of Marx's "rupture from reality" were profound. By 1867, Marx had fully articulated a vision that radically departed from the intellectual traditions that had shaped Western thought for centuries. Marx developed his alienation and mystical materialism theories here and transformed political revolution into a secular apocalypse. Paul Johnson explains:

> The style of Marx's writings is not that of the investigator . . . he does not quote examples or adduce facts which run counter to his own theory but only those which clearly support or confirm that which he considers the ultimate truth. The whole approach is one of vindication, not investigation, but it is a vindication of something proclaimed as the perfect truth with the conviction not of the scientist but of the believer. . . . In this sense, then, the "facts" are not central to Marx's work; they are ancillary, buttressing conclusions already reached independently of them.[809]

In Marx's view, traditional Western philosophy had failed because it remained trapped in the realm of ideas, disconnected from the material realities of life. Thus, Marx positioned himself not just as a philosopher but as a revolutionary theorist whose ideas were meant to reshape the world. Payne argued that he dismissed "history, philosophy, economics, God, love, sex, the subtle loyalties and traditions which have always worked on men. They no longer existed for him. He was wiping the slate clean, reducing the world to what he regarded as the essentials. There remained 'practical man,' devoid of mystery and almost of substance."[810] This radical simplification was not merely theoretical; it was a call to revolution, an effort to reconstruct society from its very foundations: "The proletariat will use its political supremacy to wrest, by degrees, all capital from the bourgeoisie."[811] Marx sought to expose the ways in which capitalism fragmented human existence, to present a vision of salvation that demanded not just individual transformation but the restructuring of society.

This shift reflected Marx's deeper philosophical aim—to strip away the illusions of tradition and replace them with the concrete realities of revolutionary action. His approach sought not merely to critique the past but to rewrite the terms of human existence fundamentally, positioning material conditions, not divine will or natural law, as the actual engine of history. In doing so, he severed humanity from the notion of a transcendent purpose, replacing it with the idea of self-creation through struggle. In this view, the essence of being human—the creative, intellectual, and spiritual capacity—was subordinated to the system's needs. In *Das Kapital*, Marx compares the worker's plight to Faust's pact with Mephistopheles, suggesting that pursuing material gain under capitalism leads to spiritual and existential disillusionment. As Marx describes, capitalism compels the worker to "sell not only his labor power, but also his soul."[812]

Marx's emphasis on scientific rationalism and materialism reflects a modern iteration of the Faustian desire to prioritize empirical understanding over spiritual considerations.[813] This focus can lead to a detachment from moral grounding, echoing Faust's journey into moral ambiguity. By concentrating solely on economic structures, Marx's approach as an ideologue risks overlooking the more profound human need for spiritual fulfillment and ethical connection. This intellectual trajectory invites reflection on the consequences of seeking salvation or knowledge without a corresponding ethical framework. One sympathetic commentator observed in the introduction to a modern edition of *Das Kapital*: "Marx sought to liberate humanity, aware that 'the machine does not free the worker. It enslaves him.'"[814]

This intellectual journey, grounded in the material world, also highlights the absence of a moral or spiritual foundation in Marx's vision. Just as Faust's ambition led him to a tragic end, so did Marx's rejection of ethical considerations, which resulted in profound disillusionment. Though revolutionary in scope, his pursuit of human liberation lacked the deeper ethical anchor that might have tempered the harsh features of his revolutionary ideals.

"The story of Faustus is that of the most brilliant man of his age who gained a great reputation for learning until the moment when: 'swol'n with cunning, of a self-conceit, his waxen wings did mount above his reach, and melting, heaven conspir'd his overthrow.'"[815] The super-intellectual Faustus is not physically powerful or a leader of men. He is essentially weak and is caught by his ambitions.

The Final Descent

Biographer Saul Padover writes: "*Das Kapital* was not just an economic treatise but a moral condemnation of exploitation."[816] Rather than functioning as a straightforward manual, the book unfolded as a dense, unwieldy text—its arguments grinding slowly and forcefully, like an overloaded millstone determined to pulverize capitalism—shaped by the contours of Dante's comedy to show the material fall of mankind. Moreover, Marx's academic rigor often made his works dense and inaccessible. He tended to obscure rather than clarify. The reader who does not know his Dante by heart may swiftly glide over the quotates from the *Paradiso or Inferno*. One scholar notes: "Marx, like Dante, saw history as a grand, unfolding drama—but where Dante's vision was eschatological, Marx's was dialectical."[817] In this sense, *Das Kapital* was not just a critique of economics but also the entire philosophical foundation of Christian morality and liberal capitalism based on economics. And yet, as the ink dried, the revolution did not come. The first volume of *Das Kapital* landed with barely a ripple, largely ignored outside radical circles, though it would be reprinted and eventually gain global traction. Marx had expected the book to set the world ablaze, to rouse the proletariat to action. As Marx waited for the firestorm that never came, his body betrayed him, and Jenny, the steadfast companion of his exile, fell gravely ill. Their surviving daughters—Jenny, Laura, and Eleanor—watched as their father, the self-proclaimed architect of revolution, faded before their eyes. Marx referred to this work as the culmination of his life's efforts, writing to Engels: "*Capital*'s unveiling will be my life's most enduring contribution to science."[818] The publication of *Das Kapital* represented both a personal and intellectual high point for Marx. It solidified his position as a towering figure in the critique of political economy. Still, the weight of his earlier failures and the slow progress of revolutionary movements tempered any sense of celebration.[819]

The first volume is published. Its impact will come, but not in his lifetime. His final years are marked by loss, regret, and an increasing sense that his great work, which had cost him everything, may not be enough. Marx's rejection of an essential human nature in favor of historical materialism marked a seismic shift in Western thought, challenging centuries of philosophical and theological consensus. While thinkers like Augustine and Descartes[820] sought to uncover an immutable human essence through divine revelation or rational introspection, Marx reduced human identity to its socioeconomic conditions. In doing so, he dismantled the classical idea of humanity as possessing a fixed nature, replacing it with a vision of human beings as products of economic forces. The implications of this shift were profound. "Marx treats capitalism as an economic system in which not only are entrepreneurs and proletarians assigned roles that, in place of their wills, determine how they behave, but these roles are represented as being fixed and unalterable."[821] By severing humanity from a transcendent essence, Marx laid the groundwork for a worldview in which human nature was seen as malleable, subject to social constructs rather than bound by divine law or innate reason. As classicist and cultural critic George Steiner writes: "The role of the deities in Greek and Roman tragic theater is of the essence; they manifest the intrusion of mortal men and women into a spider's web of non-human, superhuman agents and voyeuristic watchers whose exact legitimacy and powers may be in question, but whose appalling proximity to fallen mankind is palpable."[822] This perspective fueled the development of the modern social sciences, inspiring thinkers who saw ideology, economics, and power dynamics as the true engines of human behavior. It also provided a theoretical basis for radical political movements that sought to reshape society by altering its economic structures, assuming that by changing material conditions, one could change the very nature of humankind.

This rejection of essence came with consequences. Where is the human agency to effect change? In seeking to liberate humankind from metaphysical constraints, Marx unwittingly left the next century grappling with the dangers of a world where the boundaries of human nature could be redrawn with industrialized war and genocide. This radical departure from the metaphysical traditions of the West would have profound implications for how future generations understood human existence.[823] While Marx and his followers sought to reshape society through revolution, rejecting the existing moral and social frameworks, we must ask: What have we learned from the catastrophic consequences of that ideological zeal? As historian Eric Hobsbawm observed: "Marxism retains an almost religious faith in the ultimate triumph of the proletariat, much like the messianic visions of the Abrahamic faiths."[824]

Marx compares capital accumulation to the sins that Dante's sinners in hell are punished for, especially those in the rings of fraud and treachery. The allusion to moral degradation and blood-soaked sins has echoes of *Inferno*.[825] Marx uses Dante's vivid language to describe the consequences of capitalism and to echo the eschatological urgency of his historical vision.[826] According to Marx, in *Das Kapital*, the value of a commodity was determined by the amount of socially necessary labor time required to produce it. However, under capitalism, Marx argued, workers are not paid the full value of their labor. Instead, the capitalist extracted surplus value from workers' labor, which became the source of profit. This central tenet of Marx's economic theory—the "exploitation" of labor—became the foundation of his critique of capitalism. Modern economists, particularly those of the Austrian School, have soundly countered this view. Eugen von Böhm-Bawerk, for example, argued in *Karl Marx and the Close of His System* that Marx failed to resolve the internal contradictions of his own value theory and that the labor theory of value could not adequately explain prices in a functioning market.[827] In his seminal *Human Action*, Ludwig von Mises dismantled the idea that labor determines value, asserting instead that value is subjective and grounded in consumer preferences, not in the amount of labor expended.[828] While less concerned with technical economics, Friedrich Hayek warned of the broader consequences of central planning built on flawed economic theories like Marx's, noting that attempts to enforce economic equality through control of production would lead inexorably to tyranny.[829] These criticisms reveal theoretical flaws and the potential for dangerous applications when theory is divorced from human nature and empirical reality.[830]

Marx's rejection of the liberal tradition was not merely theoretical; it had profound ethical and spiritual implications. His view of history as a materialist struggle clashed with religious and moral frameworks emphasizing human dignity and transcendence. This tension between Marxist materialism and Christian thought was addressed early in Catholic social teaching[831] and later articulated by modern figures such as Martin Luther King, Jr., who, in a 1953 sermon, declared: "Communism and Christianity are at the bottom incompatible. One cannot be a true Christian and a true Communist simultaneously. . . . They represent opposed ways of looking at the world and transforming the world. . . . We must try to understand Communism, but never can we accept it and be true Christians."[832]

Engels, Marx's patron and enabler, had reached his limit.[833] As *Das Kapital* made little impact, Engels grew weary. "How long must I fund a man who refuses to work outside of theory?" he lamented in letters.[834] According to Payne:

> Engels himself would say that Marx had perhaps gone too far in emphasizing the role of economics in the development of human society, but by that time it was too late. A new generation of revolutionaries had arisen who accepted as an article of faith that man was an economic animal and all his activities were dictated by economic laws. It was a simple belief, and the fact that it was demonstrably untrue carried little weight with them.[835]

Marx argued that the political and economic structures of the West were not natural or inevitable but historically contingent and ripe for overthrow. Engels made the point that "if some younger writers attribute more importance to the economic aspect than is its due, Marx and I are to some extent to blame. We had to stress this leading principle in the face of opponents who denied it. We did not always have the time, space or opportunity to do justice to the other factors that interacted upon each other."[836] This transition reflected Marx's growing realization that economic forces alone did not uniformly disrupt primitive communities. Instead, "what did destroy them was the consciously formulated policies of the state or an occupying power."[837] The first volume of *Das Kapital* emerged as a work of transition to capture Marx's evolving understanding of the interplay between economic and political forces even as he was in the process of writing it. This new dynamic underlined Marx's shift in his writings from abstract philosophical structures to a more grounded and complex analysis of historical causation.[838]

Despite the publication of *Das Kapital* in 1867, Marx found little respite from the hardships that had defined his life. The book, though intellectually groundbreaking, did not bring immediate recognition or financial security, leaving him increasingly entombed as he continued his work. Jenny, whose health further faltered under the weight of their struggles, remained Karl's closest confidante.[839] As Marx himself battled chronic illness, the years following *Das Kapital* forced him to confront the limitations of both his circumstances and the revolutionary change he had long envisioned. As Marx sat in the reading rooms, the subterranean trains rumbled beneath his feet—a haunting specter of the industrial world he sought to dismantle. Marx, like Dante's damned, was trapped in the economic hell he had so meticulously described, unable to escape the cycle of expectation and disillusionment. And so, in the depths of London, he lingers as the iron serpent burrows beneath the empire, and beneath it, his mind tunnels deeper to exhume the mechanics of history.

Critics, too, had begun to emerge.[840] Marx, however, was unmoved. He dismissed them as apologists for capital, incapable of seeing the inevitable course of history. He believed in the iron laws of dialectical materialism,[841] the inexorable march toward proletarian revolution. But in the quiet of his home, where Jenny coughed in the next room and creditors banged on his door, the question loomed: *What if he was wrong?* Marx, sinking deeper into sickness and obscurity, remained trapped by the strain of his contradictions.[842] The specter of revolution still haunted his thoughts, but the fire of his ambition had burned too long, too bright, and now, at the very end, it flickered and began to fade, and Marx's final years embodied this paradox. He envisioned himself as a revolutionary force reshaping history, yet his world was crumbling. He demanded radical change while clinging to personal dependencies. He wrote of a workers' paradise, yet his own home was a site of grief and turmoil, as the apocalypse tarried. By the time *Das Kapital* was published in 1867, Marx had already lost more than he had gained. His intellectual fortress stood complete, but at the cost of his health, friendships, and family. As his body ached and his spirit faded, the underground train of his thought moved ever deeper—not toward revolution, but into the abyss of his contradictions. Marx, as with Dante's damned souls, was left in his own inferno, with self-imposed chains—trapped, waiting, unable to escape.

RING 9

The Eternal Descent (1867–1883)

"My dear Engels, my health is utterly broken, my strength is gone, and my life has become a burden to me. I fear I shall never finish what I have begun."[843]

—Karl Marx

The final years of Karl Marx's life bring us to the last ring of his journey—an isolation that mirrors Dante's ninth ring of hell, where movement ceases and souls are entombed in ice. The first installment of his *magnum opus*, *Das Kapital*, had been published in 1867, but the volumes that were to follow remained unfinished. In 1875, Marx composed what would later be published as *Critique of the Gotha Program*—initially a private letter addressed to the German socialists during their convention. In it, he challenged what he saw as compromises with bourgeois reformism. The following year, the dissolution of the First International signaled the death of his dream for a unified revolutionary movement. The ensuing years brought declining health, the deaths of his closest family members, and a growing sense of disillusionment. *Das Kapital* was meant to be his *magnum opus*—the culmination of decades of economic study, polemical writing, and revolutionary ambition. Although only the first volume appeared during his lifetime, Marx regarded the work to be the foundation of a larger system still to come. Ironically, the years following its publication marked not a triumphant ascent but the beginning of his final descent. A smoldering bitterness replaced the revolutionary fire that burned so brightly in his youth. *Das Kapital* was meant to be his great weapon, a torch of knowledge that would ignite the proletariat's uprising. Instead, it became the very thing that shackled him—an eternal labor he would never complete.

His life after 1867 unfolded much like the early stages of Dante's journey through hell. The vineyards of Moselle, where his father had once dreamed of a prosperous future for his son, had long since faded from view. The friendships and alliances that had once sustained him were strained, fraying under the weight of his relentless ideological pursuits. He was increasingly at odds with the world, a thinker whose uncompromising critique of capitalism had alienated him from political opponents and many who might have been his allies. And yet, there was the work. Though Marx's unequivocal support for the Paris Commune of 1871, in which workers and revolutionaries in Paris briefly seized control, was for Marx the magic moment: "The Commune marks the first real proletarian government."[844] *The Civil War in France* (1871) is a clear example of Marx's ongoing advocacy for violent revolutionary action. His physical exile and ideological isolation deepened after the Paris Commune. "The working class," Marx wrote, "did not expect miracles from the Commune. It did not demand of the government that it should perform feats of magic. It was fully conscious that it was engaged in a war against a hostile class."[845] In his political analysis, Marx uses the Paris Commune of 1871 as an example of the potential of proletarian rule and its failures. The lessons of the Paris Commune deepened Marx's conviction that capitalism could be truly overthrown only by establishing a proletarian state. Yet, as time wore on, his focus shifted from immediate revolutionary action to the complexities of capitalist economics, as he continued writing the second and third volumes of *Das Kapital*, which reflected not only the evolution of his economic theory but also the unrelenting intensity of his intellectual labor, even as the political program he once championed began to fade into a more abstract, theoretical realm.

The Unfinished Work

As mentioned, Marx dedicated his final years to completing the remaining volumes of his economic treatise. His days were once again spent in the reading rooms of the British Museum, his body weakened by illness,[846] yet his mind still clinging to the belief that the revolution would come. *Das Kapital* had laid bare the mechanics of capitalism, revealing what he believed to be the inevitable contradictions that would lead to its collapse, but what was it for Marx? Engels, his longtime collaborator, continued to offer financial support, but Marx's stubbornness and idealism meant that he often rejected offers of help in favor of working in solitude. Still, his reliance on Engels grew stronger, while his self-image as an independent intellectual began to weaken. After the failure of the Paris Commune in 1871, Marx's revolutionary confidence faltered. He no longer seemed confident that history was unfolding according to the predicted pattern—or that he would live to see its fulfillment.

The commune, a brief but explosive experiment in proletarian self-governance, had embodied Marx's ideals—a worker-led uprising against the bourgeois state, seizing control of Paris in a bid to remake society along revolutionary lines. Yet its brutal suppression by the French government, leaving thousands dead or imprisoned, shattered any illusions of an imminent socialist triumph. The streets of Paris, once filled with the promise of a new order, became a graveyard of revolutionary hopes. It was a grim reminder for Marx that history did not bend so easily to ideology. This intellectual failure mirrored the collapse of his ideals: he had envisioned a society liberated from exploitation, but it seemed capitalism, like hell, was an eternal force impossible to escape.

Marx's bitter reflections on the commune mirrored his increasing alienation from the world. His intellectual confidence began to dissolve as his faith in his ideas faltered, and the second volume of *Das Kapital* remained unfinished. He was forced to face the truth of his inability to achieve the material success he had once hoped for. In the late 1850s and early 1860s, chronic illness became a constant in his life. The loss of key allies and friends now compounded the isolation that Marx experienced.

In a critique of *The Gotha Program* (1875), Marx rejects the German Social Democratic Party's moderate approach to socialism and instead advocates for the dictatorship of the proletariat. He argues that the transition from capitalism to socialism cannot occur through gradual reform alone, as it requires revolutionary upheaval. In his view, the program's emphasis on incremental change betrays the radical core of socialist theory. This work reflects Marx's deep disdain for reformism and unwavering commitment to revolutionary transformation. His evolving views on the state, class power, and political authority are sharply articulated here, marking a shift from abstract theory to strategic confrontation. As Marx wrote elsewhere: "Between what is and what ought to be lies the whole tragic history of the human race."[847]

Political critiques or failed organizing efforts, coupled with his deepening personal struggles, further corroded his spirit. Jenny became even more dependent on the physically and emotionally frail Marx. Marx's eldest daughter, Jenny Caroline, was involved in the early stages of her struggles with mental health. Marx's family became even more dependent on Engels, which only heightened Marx's sense of failure as a provider and protector. As Marx became physically weaker, his mind, once sharp and full of revolutionary energy, now felt clouded by an overwhelming sense of futility. Marx was no longer the fiery revolutionary of his youth but a man confronting the reality of his limitations and the failure of his revolutionary vision.

The intellectual vigor that had once driven him to confront the social order now seemed to be a burden that could no longer be carried alone. Engels, his lifelong collaborator, noted Marx's obsession with completing the additional volumes. "Marx worked tirelessly, knowing that history was against him,"[848] Engels wrote. Yet his manuscripts were left in a state of disorder, thousands of pages unfinished. In a bitter irony, *Das Kapital* became Marx's burden, which aimed to liberate the worker from alienation. In the same place where Marx had once written passionately about the future he sought to build, and cradled the lifeless bodies of his children, he realized that those lofty ideals must have seemed hollow, and the weight of his tragedies inescapable.

By the late 1870s, Marx was ensnared in the second and third volumes of *Das Kapital*, which remained unfinished. He was tormented by revisions and rewritings and an obsession with perfecting his argument, as if searching for a final, definitive answer that would never come. The endless revisions of *Das Kapital* became his intellectual purgatory from which there was no escape. His work, once a clarion call for revolution, had become an albatross around his throat with each pen stroke. He and Dante had been exiles in their lifetimes and cast out for their radical ideas. However, whereas Dante's exile ultimately led him to a greater understanding of divine justice and the possibility of redemption, Marx's exile led only to further spite and alienation. His vision of a classless society, once a source of hope, now seemed an impossible dream, fading into the smoke-filled solitude of his London flat.

The Death of Beatrice

Stacks of manuscripts, ash-filled pipes, and worn-out books littered the space, a silent testament to a life spent in relentless pursuit of an idea that seemed always beyond his grasp. His words echoed: "It is a bad thing to perform menial duties even for the sake of freedom; to fight with pinpricks, instead of with clubs. I have become tired of hypocrisy, stupidity, gross arbitrariness, and our bowing and scraping, dodging, and hair-splitting over words."[849] The family's lives were marked by what one observer called "tear-stained ambition."[850]

In the heart of London, he lived out his purgatorial existence: "He said that everything was going splendidly," a contemporary recalled, "but never a word did he say about the terrible poverty and hardship from which they were suffering."[851] His financial patrons likely knew the truth, but revealing the extent of his failure would have been humiliating for Marx and the cause they supported. Marx's loss of his children, especially Edgar, echoes the tragedy of Count Ugolino in Dante's *Inferno*: "I did not weep; so I turned to my sons / And said: 'You must not weep; I'll take the blame.' / It is for your sake that I am in this place, / and so I suffer pain that you cannot imagine." Like Ugolino, Marx bore the weight of choices that cost his family dearly. And yet, he remained insistent that he had only followed the fire that drove him. At the end of Marx's journey—and perhaps our own—we must return to the haunting question posed earlier: Was the calling we followed ever truly inspired, or was it merely a projection of our own desires, cloaked in the illusion of purpose? The true test is not in passion but in discernment—to ask whether what we once heard as a sacred call was, in fact, the echo of ourselves. For Marx, the revolutionary blaze may have raged too hot for him to hear anything else. Meanwhile, Engels, ever the faithful ally, directed his energies toward the ongoing struggle. He lent support to anti-tsarist protests and even financed Russian exiles working to stir revolt—his own way of keeping the revolutionary flame alive.

Marx's writing inspired several revolutionary movements in Eastern Europe: "The revolution in Russia will be inevitable, the monarchy will collapse under the weight of the proletariat's demands."[852] As we follow Marx's journey to its end, we find him plummeting into the lowest rings of his own empty rhetoric, his spirit dimmed, his body ravaged by boils[853] and illness, seeming to mirror the decay of his ideals: "I am not taking arsenic, because it dulls my mind too much and I need to keep my wits about me."[854] His claims that "religious suffering is, at the same time, the expression of real suffering and a protest against real suffering," but is this lament for himself and his mission?

> Everything great glitters, glitter begets ambition, and ambition can easily have caused the inspiration or what we thought to be inspiration. But reason can no longer restrain one who is lured by the fury of ambition. He tumbles where his vehement drive calls him; no longer does he choose his position, but rather chance and luster determine it. Then we are not called to the position where we can most shine. It is not the one which, in the long succession of years during which we may hold it, will never make us weary, subdue our zeal, or dampen our inspiration. Soon we shall see our wishes unfulfilled and our ideas unsatisfied.[855]

Marx suffered the most significant personal loss of all when his wife, Jenny von Westphalen, died on December 2, 1881; his unwavering companion succumbed to liver cancer. She had endured every hardship alongside him, had followed him into exile, and had sacrificed her comfort and stability for his ideals. In the final years of her life, she suffered greatly, her body weakening as she clung to whatever was left of their shared dreams. The woman who had been his "only sweetheart"[856] was now gone, to leave a void that no intellectual pursuit could fill. In the quiet that followed her passing, one can imagine Marx, the revolutionary thinker, grappling with a personal grief that mirrored the classic tragedies—a love so consuming that its end heralded his descent into the abyss of sorrow. Her death devastated Marx, and his health rapidly declined in the wake of this personal tragedy.[857] His letters following Jenny's death reveal a man shattered by grief. "Without her, I am nothing,"[858] he admitted. Her slow death from cancer was a reminder of the toll that his cause had taken on those closest to him. Even Jenny was not spared from the consequences of his relentless pursuits.

Their union, a tapestry woven with threads of intellectual fervor and deep affection, had withstood the tempests of political exile and personal hardship. Jenny, once described as having a "sharply cut, witty and attractive face, a proud bearing and an extraordinarily amiable nature,"[859] was not only Marx's wife but also his muse. Their correspondence reveals a love both tender and tumultuous. In one letter, Jenny confessed: "Oh, Karl, how little you know me, how little you appreciate my position, and how little you feel where my grief lies, where my heart bleeds."[860] Both passion and misunderstanding marked his words; in a letter from 1865, he professed: "I am writing you again, because I am alone and because it troubles me always to have a dialogue with you in my head, without your knowing anything about it or hearing it or being able to answer."

Their daughter Eleanor observed that her parents shared moments of profound closeness, reminiscent of their youthful affection.[861] She noted they appeared as "a loving girl and a loving youth on the threshold of life."[862] When Jenny passed away, Marx was plunged into a profound despair. The woman who had been his "only sweetheart" left a void that no intellectual pursuit could fill. There was no more Beatrice, no Gretchen nor Ophelia, no mirror for self-reflection, as the light would continue to fade.

Marx's statement that weakness is a woman's ideal trait is complex and perhaps ironic, as the women in his life, especially his wife and daughters, were anything but weak. His daughter Eleanor would take on Jenny's role.[863] Marx may be acknowledging the gendered societal expectations of his time, yet his relationships reflect his deep respect for the resilience and intellect of his wife and daughters.[864] Marx's writings reveal a rare voice of vulnerability or even desperation to echo Jenny in her intensity: "Your support means more than words can express in these times of struggle."[865] "Thank you for standing by me."[866] "Exile has been hard on all of us, Jenny, but together we will endure."[867] "Your strength amazes me."[868] "Your unwavering faith in me sustains my work even in the darkest hours."[869] "I fear I can never repay you."[870] "*Das Kapital* is a shared victory—your sacrifices made it possible."[871] "Your presence is a constant source of hope and stability."[872] "Your love and patience are the foundation of everything I have achieved."[873] And, finally, "I would trade anything to ease your suffering."[874] For a fleeting instant, he allows himself the indulgence of nostalgia. But just as quickly, he shrugs it off. He could ill afford regret. He must be right. He has to be: "The moment you are absent, my love for you shows itself to be what it is, a giant, in which are crowded together all the energy of my spirit and all the character of my heart."[875] Marx's admission about the toll his ambitions took on Jenny's life offers a rare glimpse into the inner conflict of an unshakable man in his convictions. Jenny was more than a wife and partner; she was his anchor, allowing Marx to endure poverty, exile, and social ostracism. Her unwavering support underpinned his work, yet her suffering often went unnoticed in the shadow of his monumental aspirations.

When Jenny died, the final unraveling of Marx's world began. Engels noted that Marx seemed diminished in her absence, as if the fire that had driven him was now consuming him from within. Her absence illuminated the gaps in his philosophy—an ideology so focused on systems and structures that it often failed to account for the quiet, personal sacrifices, or even presence of those who stood beside him. Jenny's life, in many ways, embodied the very humanity that Marx sought to elevate but often overlooked.

Jenny's death forced Marx to reckon with the personal costs of his unyielding focus. Her life had been a testament to resilience and sacrifice, which Marx celebrated in theory but often took for granted in the actual world. The humanity she embodied—the quiet endurance, the steadfast loyalty—starkly contrasted the grand abstractions that dominated his work. We can imagine in those final moments, hearing in her silence the voice of Ophelia, "There's rosemary, that's for remembrance; pray, love, remember: and there is pansies, that's for thoughts,"[876] Gretchen, "Meine Ruh' ist nur der Tod" ("My rest is only in death),"[877] or Beatrice, "O gracious light! O eternal love! That dost illuminate the heaven, and on earth unfold the depths of thy own being."[878] Did Marx, in his relentless pursuit of historical materialism, fail to see that the most profound truths are not those etched in stone or bound by the immediacy of the physical world? In anchoring his ideology to the imminent, he lost sight of the transcendent—of the love, suffering, and loss, the moral struggle that could not be reduced to economic forces or dialectical struggle. Carlyle emphasized that true knowledge requires a moral connection to the subject—that without a foundation of virtue or sympathy, intellect alone is hollow. To truly understand something, one must not only study it, but care for it in a deeper, ethical sense.[879] Jenny's unwavering devotion and the quiet burdens she bore were not mere reflections of material conditions but expressions of something beyond—something that Marx, in his rejection of the spiritual, could not fully comprehend.

The true revolution was not in restructuring the world but in recognizing that what is most real is often the least capable of being quantified. In his attempt to remake humanity through the stones of the imminent, he missed the tragico-poetic, the eternal, and the truth that cannot be confined to systems or manifestos. Not even Christ, after all, could be trapped in concrete. Jenny's absence left a void that no intellectual pursuit could fill. Marx had spent his life dismantling the illusions of religion, rejecting faith as a means of solace, yet now, in the wake of Jenny's passing, the cold finality of death left him utterly bereft. There was no one to guide him to the other side but only his unfinished works, the ghosts of the past, and the pacts he signed.[880]

The Ghost of Highgate

By the time Karl Marx reached the final stretch, he was little more than a shadow of the man igniting revolutions with his pen. He sat among the wreckage of his life, surrounded by the remnants of a vision that had once seemed destined to change the world. His mind, once so sharp and unyielding, must have been burdened with doubt: Had it all been worth it? Had his sacrifices, labor, and suffering amounted to anything beyond the silence surrounding him? What of his wife and family? Jenny's life was an example of the relational depth and human connection that Marx's theories sought to universalize but could not fully encompass. Her absence revealed the fragility of a life built on relentless purpose, where personal bonds were often subordinated to the demands of an all-consuming mission. Even as Marx pushed forward, his fixation on completing the additional volumes of *Das Kapital* demonstrated the relentless determination that defined his character. This "singleness of purpose,"[881] while a driving force behind his intellectual achievements, came at a significant cost. Yet, this same trait fueled his enduring partnership with Engels and cemented his legacy as one of history's most influential thinkers. This paradox reflected the duality of his life and work.[882]

Few embody "singleness of purpose" as thoroughly as Marx. His fixation on developing his theories and completing *Das Kapital* remained. Engels marveled at Marx's unwavering dedication. But his daughter Eleanor would later remark that her father, once so defiant, seemed to shrink after Jenny's death. Only a year later, in 1883, on a trip to Algiers and having what appears like an uneventful time, he wrote: "Because of the sun, I have done away with my prophet's beard and my crowning glory."[883] Marx scholar Marcello Musto states that he "saw himself taking leave of his familiar look. The New Moses like an actor who has finished performing and is about to remove his makeup, he was bidding farewell to the character who had dictated his image throughout his life."[884]

Marx's beard had, for decades, been a visual and metaphorical extension of his prophetic persona. Like the prophets of old, his wild, patriarchal visage projected an image of authority, rebellion, and a mission to reshape the moral and social order of the world. To shave it in his final years was an act laden with meaning. On the surface, it was a practical concession to the Algerian heat. Still, on a deeper level, it symbolized the stripping away of a lifetime of defiance and the mythos he had carefully cultivated. In removing his beard, Marx seemed to shed the prophetic mantle he had worn for so long, as if the mask of revolution—the fiery ideologue who had thundered against the gods of capital—was finally being laid to rest.[885] In this moment of symbolic surrender, Marx's life comes full circle, from defiance to reflection.

His critique of exploitation in *Das Kapital* now resonates as a cautionary tale, underscoring how even the noblest intentions can falter when divorced from the human realities they aim to transform. The man who sought salvation for others now faced the weight of his ideological and personal entrapments, a poignant reminder of the complexities of revolutionary ambition. The grief did not end there—his eldest daughter, Jenny Caroline, would die in 1883, just months before Marx himself. His final years were spent in increasing solitude. The revolutionary circles that once embraced him had fractured. The utopia he envisioned for the working class had become a distant dream, while the real-world struggle for daily survival consumed those he loved. In his own life, Marx had unknowingly mirrored the alienation he had written about—the isolation of man from his labor, his family, and ultimately, himself.

He died sitting in his chair, his body finally succumbing to the weight of years, the struggles, the relentless toil. The man who had spent his life attempting to reshape history passed away quietly, his mind still burdened by unfinished works. Engels, his most loyal companion, was at his side. "At a quarter to three in the afternoon," Engels solemnly declared, "the greatest living thinker ceased to think."[886] His funeral, attended by no more than eleven people,[887] was a stark contrast to the revolutions he promised. He was buried in Highgate Cemetery, alongside Jenny, under a simple headstone.[888] Ever faithful, Engels spoke at his gravesite: "You were the greatest mind of our time, and your ideas will guide generations."

Yet, the path those ideas would take—through Lenin, Stalin, Mao, and beyond—was something even Marx could not have foreseen. His ideology had not yet led to the global revolution he imagined. Instead, his legacy would take unexpected turns, shaping the tumultuous political upheavals of the twentieth century. In death, Marx became not just a historical figure but a symbol of defiance—a man whose dreams for humanity came at great personal and collective cost, to leave behind a monumental and cautionary legacy. "So long as the great struggle for human liberty endures, Karl's name will live in the hearts of men,"[889] Engels declared. But would it? Or was Marx now just another tragic figure, a man whose ambition had outpaced his humanity, whose vision had led him not to salvation but to the cold solitude of an unfulfilled dream? Friend and biographer Spargo reflects: "While Engels was speaking over the grave, proclaiming what a wonderful philosopher Karl was, my mind was wandering back over the years to Treves."[890] Now his ideas, crystallized in *Das Kapital* and *The Communist Manifesto*, would ignite revolutions, birth nations, and inspire generations—but they would also unleash a scale of human suffering that defies comprehension.[891]

In the quiet solemnity of Highgate Cemetery, Karl Marx's memorial converges earth and ideal, embodying his enduring influence. The rallying call of his life's work is gleaming in gold at the top of the plinth: "Workers of all lands unite."[892] Just below, a tablet commemorates his wife, Jenny von Westphalen; their daughter Eleanor Marx; their grandson Harry Longuet; and Helene Demuth, Marx's longtime confidante and the mother of one of his children. Notably absent are several of Marx's other children, including Laura and Jenny Caroline, whose names are missing from the monument—perhaps a reflection of limited space or the symbolic choices made when the memorial was commissioned in 1956 by the British Communist Party. This tablet captures the intimate ties that made Marx's journey as deeply personal as it was revolutionary, holding his memory and those who supported him and sacrificed with him.

At the monument's base lies an inscription echoing Marx's enduring conviction: "Philosophers have only interpreted the world in various ways; the point, however, is to change it."[893] The monument rises on sloping ground, defiantly facing uphill, a fitting testament to a life dedicated to the laborious ascent to an elusive vision. Marx's life, seen through the prism of Dante's *Divine Comedy,* was a journey through rings of suffering and revelation; yet, unlike Dante, Marx's journey did not end in comedy or redemption[894] but in cold isolation.[895] The Marx we leave behind is a fully tragic figure—a man whose ambition was to reshape the world but who, in the end, left it shackled by the very ideas which he had set out to liberate it from: "Breeding such Faustian aspirations, modernity risks witnessing their ignominious collapse. No historical period has unleashed human powers as abundantly as the modern era, and none is more at risk of being mastered by the forces it unchains."[896]

The pact between Faust and Mephistopheles in Goethe's *Faust* is one of literature's most potent symbols of human desire and moral consequence. Faust, dissatisfied with his life and intellectual pursuits, makes a deal with the devil: in exchange for unlimited knowledge, worldly pleasures, and the fulfillment of his deepest desires, Faust agrees to serve Mephistopheles when he is finally content: "Make a compact with me, that I shall be your servant when the moment comes, when you have enjoyed it to the full, and can say: 'Stop, you are so beautiful.'"[897] This deal, however, is flawed from the outset. Mephistopheles, a cunning trickster, presents Faust with the illusion of fulfillment, offering him power and experiences but withholding the true cost to his soul. Faust's craving for control and infinite knowledge blinds him to the fact that in chasing ultimate satisfaction, he has sold his soul, not for enlightenment or redemption but for the fleeting whims of the material world. The irony of Faust's pact lies in the invisible consequences of his ambition.[898] Just as Faust sought control over his world, Marx sought control over the forces of labor and capital, hoping to remake society. Marx's struggles may have ended, but his ideas were destined to march forward, inscribed into the imaginations of those seeking change. I am not of their number. The plot of *Faust* makes no sense if one cannot conceive, even for dramatic purposes only, that there is a life beyond the grave.

Engels reflects on Marx's enduring legacy:

> As his contemporaries faded into the shadows of memory, Marx became more than a man—a symbol, a name bound to the eternal struggle for human liberty. However, the intimate reflections of those who knew him remind us that behind the towering legacy was a man shaped by friendship, conflict, and the relentless pursuit of an ideal: Aye, and in the distant ages—when the struggle is over, when happy men and women read with wondering hearts of the days of pain which we endure—then Karl's name will still be remembered. Nobody will know then that poor old Hans Fritzsche went to school with Karl; I played with him, fought with him, loved him for nearly sixty years. But no matter; they can never know Karl as I knew him.[899]

Marx's legacy carries the weight of Dante's allegory and the tragic irony of a life spent in pursuit of an earthly paradise that ultimately became its prison.[900]

Marx's legacy, immortalized by those who knew him, carries the weight of reverence and tragedy.[901] Through the lens of Dante's allegory, his life becomes a cautionary tale of ambition unmoored from transcendence, a descent that mirrors the inverse of redemption. Ultimately, the silence surrounding his final days speaks louder than the tributes, a solemn echo of a life spent striving yet never finding peace.[902] Viewed through the lens of Dante's allegory, we see new layers of his decline, a journey that inverts the path toward redemption.[903]

As we close this tale, the silence remains a final testament to a life defined by the relentless pursuit of an ideal haunted by the long shadows it cast, the silence of a divine tragedy,[904] a fitting close to one man's flickers of brilliance absorbed into the darker spaces: "Thus heaven I've forfeited, I know it full well. My soul, once true to God, is chosen for hell."[905] As we leave the grave at Highgate, we are left with the echoes of a legacy of a man who sought to transform the world, but in doing so may have lost himself—a church bell tolls.

No one can determine the fate of a man's soul, but we can evaluate Marx's life by utilizing Dante's inspired allegory. We could also imagine a final trial of Karl Marx, and we, his jury, could watch as he takes the witness stand. Using his *Divine Comedy* as his rule book, Dante is the prosecutor. The grand hall is unlike anything of earthly construction; its architecture blends celestial radiance and infernal shadows. Marble columns rise infinitely into a sky of luminous clouds, while the floor beneath resembles glass, reflecting those below whose sins and virtues are under debate. At the center sits Dante Alighieri, wearing the crimson biretta of a judge, his face both stern and compassionate, etched with the wisdom of a man who has traversed all three realms of the afterlife.

Seated before him is Karl Marx, his figure diminished yet defiant. His unkempt hair and now shaven face reveal a man weathered by exile and humbled by disillusionment. Around the courtroom,[906] luminaries of thought bear silent witness: Shakespeare, with his quill poised, observes with curiosity; Goethe's eyes reflect a deep melancholy; Smith and Ricardo exchange whispered comments; Hegel, Bauer, and Feuerbach sit with folded arms, their gazes inscrutable. Karl's father and mother, and the children he's lost, are there; Jenny, too, looks on. The air hums with an otherworldly tension. In my imagined *Divine Tribunal*, Marx is on trial for his life and the consequences of his vision. Dante asks the first, chilling question:

Dante:
"Karl, did you, in your pursuit of justice, lose sight of the human soul?"

There is silence, as Dante pauses before he continues.

Dante:
"Karl Heinrich Marx, son of Trier, you stand here accused not by man but by the weight of your own life. We are gathered to judge not your soul's eternal destiny—only God may know that—but the legacy of your deeds, your teachings, and their consequences upon humanity."

He gestures toward the court clerk, who begins reading the charges:

Clerk:
"First, the rejection of the divine order: your dismissal of God and faith as 'the opium of the masses,' sowing disbelief and severing man from transcendence. Second, the instigation of class struggle: a doctrine that has fostered violence, division, and despair among peoples. Third, the reduction of human nature: an ideology that stripped humanity of its spiritual and moral dimensions, reducing man to mere material conditions."

The clerk, aware of what comes next, must pause to clear his throat.

Clerk: cont.
"Lastly, the enduring consequences of your legacy: regimes inspired by your ideas have wrought oppression, totalitarianism, and genocide."

The clerk's voice falls silent. Dante steps forward.

Dante:
"Do you deny these charges?"

Marx, ever the dialectician, leans forward in his chair, his voice as gravelly as the earth he believed in.

Marx:
"I deny nothing, for history absolves me. My critique of capitalism exposed its hypocrisies. If others misused my ideas, that is not my burden to bear. My intent was a freedom and what you

might call salvation, to once and for all unshackle man from the chains of exploitation."

Dante tilts his head, his eyes penetrating Marx.

Dante:
"Intent, Herr Marx, is but the seed. The fruit it bears depends on the soil in which it is sown. Did you not foresee the violence that would erupt when you determined there would be an inevitable revolution? Did you not understand that your materialist doctrine left no room for the soul, moral reform, or mercy or forgiveness?"

Marx shifts uncomfortably in his seat.

Marx:
"Mercy and forgiveness are tools of the oppressor, meant to pacify the masses. I sought justice!"

From the gallery, Shakespeare interjects, his voice smooth yet cutting.

Shakespeare:
"And what is justice without mercy? A tyrant's justice, perchance? A tale of sound and fury, signifying nothing?"

The court murmurs. Marx remains silent, his fist clenching the armrest.

Dante continues, his tone softening.

Dante:
"I do not doubt your suffering, nor your desire for a better world. But your vision, Karl, was blind to the human heart. In your rejection of genuine tragedy, you severed yourself from love—the very force that moves the sun and the other stars."

He pauses, reciting the closing lines of his Paradiso:
"L'amor che move il sole e l'altre stelle."

A palpable silence envelops the courtroom.

Dante: cont.
"What remains of you, Karl? Do you see the ruin your vision has wrought, not just in the world but within yourself . . . your family?"

Marx sneaks a glance at his loved ones and lowers his gaze. For a moment, his defiance falters, and then he regathers himself.

Dante: cont.
"In my *Inferno*, those betrayers in the coldest depths of hell are because they chose to be there. They that sought to destroy what they could not possess, to elevate themselves by dragging others down. Tell me, Karl, was envy at the root of your revolution?"

Marx's voice is barely a whisper.

Marx:
"Perhaps . . . envy is the spark that ignites change. Is it not natural to want what others have denied you?"

Dante sighs, heavy with sorrow. He removes his biretta and steps closer to Marx.

Dante:
"A volte il mondo è senza parole."[907]

The court falls silent once more. Slowly, Dante continues.

Dante: cont.
"Karl Heinrich Marx, your ideas brought light to the injustices of capitalism, but they also cast shadows of destruction. For your blindness to the spiritual dimensions of humanity, for your rejection of love and grace, I sentence you to the frozen depths of Cocytus, where the envious and the betrayers reside. May your exile teach others the cost of a world without light."

The judgment echoes through the hall. As Marx is led away, Dante turns to the gallery.

Marx:
"I don't fear your imaginary inferno, nor am I condemned."

Dante:
"Then let this be a lesson, not of condemnation but of reflection. For we all walk the line between hope and despair, redemption and ruin. It is love—sacrificial love —that saves us from ourselves. It's your choice now Karl. Will you receive God's mercy?"

Marx lowers his head, unable to find a new place within himself.

Dante: cont.
"You know my work so well, I don't need to recite anything but only to remind you that some time ago I too was a man of exile, fighting to return home, but that home was not Florence, it was not a place at all.

Marx:
"I know, I know. You 'found yourself within a forest dark, for the straightforward pathway had been lost'."

Dante is slightly impressed.

Dante:
"Yes, you know my work too well, but I'm afraid you still don't understand its meaning: "L'amor che move il sole e l'altre stelle."

With that, Dante's gaze softens—not in absolution, but in a mournful recognition of what Marx could never grasp.

Epilogue:
A Tragic Reckoning

"The criticism of religion is the premise of all criticism."[908]

—Karl Marx

Curiously—or perhaps not so—Marx and his long-time confidant Engels filled their pages with hell and its torments, with the march of history as purgation, but nowhere did they speak of paradise. There was no ascent, no final vision of harmony—only struggle without end, revolution without transcendence. Their silence on *Paradiso* is perhaps the final revelation: they could imagine the fire, but never the light.[909] In the end, there is no heaven for Karl Marx. No redemption, no absolution, no great reckoning in the stars. There is only this eternal image: the same London flat, the same dim candlelight, the same desk; the same ink-stained hands, endlessly scratching at parchment; and the same manuscript that will never be finished. He is alone. There is no Jenny, no children. No laughter. No voices calling his name. The room has been stripped of all warmth, of all trace of family, of all reminders of the life he once knew. The walls are bare, the floorboards splintered. The silverware is gone. The wine bottles, now emptied and scattered at his feet, are relics of memories long past. In a moment of clarity, he notices a half-empty bottle of Moselle wine on the table. The label is peeling, but he recognizes it as a symbol of his homeland and the days when the world held promise.[910]

He has not ascended to the heights of a prophet or the architect of a utopia. Still, instead he finds himself bound to a fate resembling that of Dante's Count Ugolino: left to gnaw upon his creation, condemned to an eternity where the object of his obsession becomes the very instrument of his suffering. Just as Ugolino, imprisoned with his children, was driven to the ultimate horror, starving in the darkness of his ambitions and betrayals, Marx too became a prisoner of his vision: "Then fasting overcame my grief and me."[911] His revolutionary gospel, which promised to free the masses, chained him in solitude, his ideals turned against him,"doomed for a certain term to walk the night, / And for the day confined to fast in fires, / Till the foul crimes done in my days of nature / Are burnt and purged away."[912]

But Marx will not be purged. Like Mephistopheles, he, too, was a man of negation, tearing down the illusions of capitalism, religion, and the old order: "I am the Spirit that denies! / And rightly too; for all that comes to be, / Deserves to perish wretchedly."[913] Back to his flat: he can hear his father's voice in the vineyards of Trier and imagines the long verdant afternoons of poetry and idealism. He remembers Jenny's smile, his children playing at his feet, his once-boundless ambition. For a fleeting instant, he allows himself the indulgence of nostalgia. But just as quickly, he shrugs it off. He cannot afford regret. He must be right. He has to be. He has only his thoughts or a safe bridge for retreat. The ink bleeds onto the paper, an endless river of words. He is writing *Das Kapital*—again. He does not know how many times he has rewritten it, only that he must continue.

A Tomb with a Final View

In his quest to understand and control the world, Marx, like Faust, sought to impose his will upon the natural order, believing that the world would fulfill its potential through revolutionary change. This quest was his attempt to chart a path of moral redemption through the understanding and ultimate overthrow of capitalism, much like Dante's journey to divine enlightenment. Marx's insistence on revolution was a political call and a poetic expression—a defiant rebellion against the forces he saw as unjust and corrosive to human dignity. With its fierce urgency and vivid imagery, Marx's language mirrors the fiery, tumultuous landscape of Dante's hell. It is a work that combines logic and passion, rigor and emotion, as Marx channels his youthful revolutionary fervor into a critique that transcends mere economics.[914]

In many ways, Marx's *Capital* is the ultimate poetic gesture of defiance, a furious challenge to the existing order and a conjured moral vision that left a lasting imprint on the world's intellectual and political terrain. But as Dante shows us in the *Divine Comedy*, the path to hell is often paved with good intentions—a truth Marx failed to calculate in the real-world consequences of his theories. Exiled from Germany, he sought refuge in Paris, Brussels, and finally, London, where he would spend the remainder of his life with poverty, illness, and the unyielding demands of his intellectual pursuits.

His flat in London became his sanctuary: a place where he poured himself into the contours of *Das Kapital*, at a time and place haunted by the unfulfilled dreams that weighed upon him. Here, in the heart of London, he lived out his purgatorial existence. Marx camped each day like a general returning to the battlefield, his battered satchel slung over one shoulder, brimming with the tools of his revolution: notes, borrowed books, and fragments of his monumental *Das Kapital*. The room itself, domed and vast, seemed to echo the weight of his task—to decode the hidden machinery of capitalism and expose its inevitable collapse. Marx's disheveled and worn appearance reflected the long years of exile, poverty, and struggle. His own choices, yet his eyes betrayed a ferocious clarity, that of a man possessed by the need to see the world as it truly was, all part of his role on the world stage, a new Moses come to set the people free.[915]

H. G. Wells sees Marx's untamed beard as analogous to his final work: "It [Karl Marx's beard] is exactly like *Das Kapital* in its inane abundance, and the human part of the face looks over it owlishly as if it looked to see how the growth impressed mankind."[916] The library desk became his refuge, surrounded by political economy and history tomes, his pen moving furiously across the page. Yet, as we return to the silent tomb of his London flat in 1867, we are struck not by the triumph of these ideals but by the somber realization of what his life had truly become. Marx was born into the hope of a nascent earthly paradise, a world where intellectual fervor and revolution promised a new vision of hope and potential. As a young man, he believed deeply in the power of reason to dismantle oppressive structures and pave the way for a just society. From his early times in Moselle, his writings were filled with the optimism of a world reborn, a heaven where the chains of class oppression would be broken and where humanity would stand united in freedom, but also a deep denial of the natural order and Marx's union with Christ. Schwarzwalder comments: "This lovely, if anodyne, statement was drafted by a German boy named Karl Marx. He wrote those words at the age of 17 as part of a high school essay. That he denied the truths they assert, militantly, only a year or two later is not only tragic with respect to his own spiritual life but more than tragic, in fact devastating, for the life of the world he helped create."[917]

As Marx's journey through the rings of his life concludes, we are left with a tragic irony: a man who sought to liberate humanity yet whose vision became a prison of its own. Unlike Dante, who ascended to the light of divine love, Marx remained bound to the shadows of his ideological hell, his legacy a testament to the dangers of radical idealism untethered from moral and spiritual grounding. Marx's life closes not with the crescendo of a revolutionary anthem but with the dim echoes of unresolved contradictions. In the quiet confines of his London flat, the weight of his ambitions, the breadth of his intellect, and the depths of his alienation converge into a solemn epitaph: "Hence! To endless battle, to the striving, / Like a Talisman out there, / Demon-wise into the far mists driving / Towards a goal I cannot near."[918] Like the figures in Dante's *Inferno*, bound by the choices that defined them, Marx's existence serves as a reminder that even the most transformative visions can falter when disconnected from the spiritual truths that bind humanity together.

In Dante's journey, the descent into hell was but the beginning, a prelude to redemption through humility, love, and grace. Marx's descent, by contrast, offers no such resolution. In the silence of his London flat, Marx's thoughts end not in triumph but in anguish, acutely aware of a life filled with demanding burdens and the frailties of human nature. His own words, "Thus heaven I've forfeited," echo like a judgment, not just of his life, but of the movements his ideas would inspire. His confidante Gustav Techow observed that Marx's ambitions were "lacking in nobility of soul,"[919] underscoring the toll of a life spent chasing a dream so grand that it left little room for the personal connections and virtues that sustain the human spirit. His misguided brilliance is undeniable, yet it is haunted by the same human frailties he sought to overcome. In the absence of heaven's light, Marx's life, though monumental in its intellectual scope, becomes a tale of alienation from the divine, humanity, and, ultimately, himself. The fires of his revolutionary zeal are not consuming the structures he sought to overthrow but the foundations of his being.

What does striving for a better world mean if it costs the world its soul?[920] And at what point does the drive or ambition become its form of enslavement? In this narrative, unlike *The Divine Comedy*, where Dante's ascent offers a counterpoint—a journey toward light, love, and redemption, Marx never opened that door, that "mystery."[921] Techow laments: "I am convinced that the most dangerous personal ambition has eaten away all the good in him."[922] For Marx did not need an underworld journey to feel the flames of woe, for they were already present in his life. As Wilhelm Liebknecht later recalled:

> "Oh, I'd put an end to it all, Hans, if I didn't have to finish *Capital*," he said to me once as we walked over Hampstead Heath, he leaning upon my arm. "It's Hell to suffer so, year after year, but I must finish that book. Nothing I've ever done means so

much to the movement, and nobody else can do it. I must live for that, even though every breath is an agony."[923]

Marx's struggle manifested in his family's poverty and more profoundly in the hollow spirit with which he mocked his peers. John Spargo writes: "He laughs at the fools who parrot his proletarian catechism, just as he laughs over the communists à la Willich and the bourgeoisie. The only people he respects are the aristocrats, the genuine ones who are well aware of it."[924] Ugolino cries out: "O thou, who in the world of the living, / On me hast such a heavy penance laid, / Thou shouldst have been so much more kind, / For thou dost gnaw on my own heart and soul."[925] Marx, too, remains bound to his own hellish task: toiling over the pages of *Das Kapital.* In these final years, his room becomes less a place of work and more a prison of his own creation, echoing with the quiet solitude of ideals that have calcified into chains,[926] only to recall his labyrinth of memorized lines from great tragedies with the morals Marx would never fully imbibe. Hamlet knows that actual suffering is self-imposed: "There is nothing either good or bad, but thinking makes it so. To me, it is a prison."[927] His Promethean defiance doomed him to suffer, forever shackled by the consequences of his fire: "I gave men knowledge; I taught them to think, and for this, I am bound in chains."[928] Faust confesses: "What I possess seems far away to me, and what is gone becomes reality."[929] Techow concludes: "In spite of all his assurances to the contrary, and perhaps because of them, I took away with me the impression that the acquisition of personal power was the aim of all his endeavours."

Marx was captivated by Gothic and Romantic literature, especially in his early poetic writings. But these were more than dreamy reveries: at moments, they veer into something psychologically raw and unsettling. In poems like "Awakening," Marx channels what reads like a psychedelic or dreamlike experience, imbued with flashes of poetic insight. That is immediately followed by "Desperate Prayer," where the tone shifts dramatically from melancholy to fury. Romantic affectation gives way to a seething intensity, as he unleashes a vengeful cry—not just against the world, but against the cosmos itself.[930] Yet despite this emotional power, Marx seemed to miss the deeper, tragic warnings at the heart of Romanticism: its emphasis on humility, on limits, and the moral cost of unchecked ambition. Ironically, nine years after Marx's death, Engels encountered a claim that the materialist view of history should be credited to the Prussian Romantic historians. He dismissed it with surprise, calling it "indeed something new to me."[931] The comment reflects how little Marx or Engels ever acknowledged their debt to the Romantic tradition they both—consciously or unconsciously—helped extend.[932] In the end, Karl Marx's personal life mirrors the tragic journeys found in Dante's *Inferno*. His ideals were grand but buried beneath layers of self-deception, personal failure, and a refusal to confront the reality of his circumstances.

Rewrites in Ink and Ashes

In a moment of clarity, Marx is suddenly aware of the passing limits of time. He hears his father's familiar voice, his patterns of speech, and his talk of poetry and idealism: "I will not and cannot conceal my weakness for you. At times my heart delights in thinking of you and your future"[933] and "I always felt the need to surround you with all the love and care of which my heart is capable."[934] Marx remembers Jenny's smile, his children playing at his feet, the myriad nicknames, and his once-boundless ambition.

He quickly returns to his manuscript. He is rewriting *Das Kapital*—again. He does not know how many times he has rewritten it, only that he must continue. It is his purpose. His punishment. Now there is no revolution. No proletariat uprising. No workers' paradise. There is only *the* work. He imagines the endless pages filling the room, his notebooks, his mountains of letters, delivered with spite, warmth, or with passion, but he envisions his youthful writings: "When we have chosen the vocation in which we can contribute most to humanity, burdens cannot bend us because they are only sacrifices for all."[935]

Yet, in that stillness, there remains a question that reverberates beyond the confines of his room: What does it mean to give oneself wholly to a cause, and not to others? Is it due to hurt or something darker? The journey of Karl Marx, like all human journeys, is one of striving, failing, and seeking. Karl Marx and Dante Alighieri were profoundly influenced by the societal decay and corruption of their times, channeling their observations into works that sought to critique and reform their respective societies. Dante's *Divine Comedy* was a reaction to the moral decay he perceived in Italy during the demise of the Holy Roman Empire.[936] This work reflected his spiritual vision for a renewed society rooted in divine justice.[937] In *The Eighteenth Brumaire of Louis Bonaparte*, Karl Marx "sardonically contrasts the noble spirit of the ancient Roman republic with the tawdry attempts of modern bourgeois revolutionaries to tart themselves up in its garments."[938]

Marx saw Europe's social and economic decay as the consequence of capitalism, an empire of profit that he believed was collapsing under its own distortions. Yet what Marx interpreted as decay was, in many respects, the painful but necessary transformation of a pre-industrial order into a modern one—marked not by terminal collapse but by the growing pains of demographic shifts, urbanization, and infrastructural lag, which liberal democracies would eventually address through reform rather than revolution.[939] Where Dante sought a restoration of spiritual order, Marx envisioned a society free from the power that exiled him.[940] The opposing perspectives—one spiritual, one material—frame each man's mission, casting them as interpreters of their fallen worlds. In the end, Marx's intellectual legacy was a tumult of tragic warnings, all signposts pointing to the great idols of power and recognition that consumed it. Perhaps the final verses in his poems are those that address his youthful defiance, words that echo back from the depths of the poet who once sought to cast himself as godlike:

> How you have fallen from heaven, O Day Star, son of Dawn!
> How you are cut down to the ground, you who laid the nations low!
> You said in your heart, "I will ascend to heaven; I will raise my throne above the stars of God.[941]

The words linger like a whispered reckoning, a final response to the young man who once wrote of striding victorious through the ruins of the world.

The Ghost in Exile

The lessons from *Faust* and *Prometheus,* which warn of the consequences of unchecked ambition and the perils of replacing the divine with human reason, are lessons that Marx failed to comprehend fully. Indeed, he not only rejected divine revelation but also cast aside the classical tradition of human reason as embodied in Aristotle and natural law. In doing so, Marx denied the accumulated wisdom of centuries—wisdom that Christian thought would later synthesize through figures like Aquinas. What remained was a reductionist anthropology shaped by Rousseau, Voltaire, and the Enlightenment's break from metaphysics—a view that ultimately failed to grasp the truth of the human person as created in the image of God.[942] And yet, in these quiet hours, his solitude seemed both his strength and his undoing. Here was a man who dreamed of shaping history yet found himself at its margins—a tragic Prometheus, chained not to a rock but to his relentless vision.[943]

"One wonders whether Marx ever thought about the son, now a man, he had abandoned to strangers."[944] His vision of a classless society, once a source of hope, now weighed upon him like a curse, a burden he could neither abandon nor fully realize. Marx himself would write:

> We must seriously ask ourselves, therefore, whether we are really inspired about a vocation, whether an inner voice approves of it, or whether the inspiration was a deception, whether that which we took as the Deity's calling to us was self-deceit. But how else could we recognize this except by searching for the source of our inspiration?[945]

In that prison of a room, tethered to his work desk, Marx endured the eternal gnashing that Dante immortalized—an endless labor undertaken in a world passing him by.[946] While Engels worked tirelessly after Marx's death to publish the remaining volumes of *Das Kapital* and expand on Marx's ideas, the world did not immediately embrace the Marxist vision. The Bolshevik Revolution in 1917, led by Vladimir Lenin, marked the first significant attempt to implement Marxist principles nationally. Although the revolution occurred under conditions Marx never envisioned—within an agrarian society lacking a fully developed industrial proletariat—it was undertaken in his name nonetheless.[947] Lenin adapted Marx's theory to justify a centralized vanguard party that would act on behalf of the working class, a move Marx had not explicitly endorsed.[948] Far from achieving the classless utopia Marx imagined, the revolution gave rise to a one-party totalitarian regime, first under Lenin, and later under Joseph Stalin.[949] The state that emerged not only suppressed dissent and political pluralism but also crushed the very workers it claimed to represent. The purges, forced collectivization, and gulags under Stalin reflected a brutal betrayal of Marx's stated ideals of human liberation and social equality.[950] Yet these developments were not accidental.[951] As historian Martin Malia observes: "It was not Stalin who distorted Marxism; it was Marxism that enabled Stalin."[952] And as Aleksandr Solzhenitsyn famously wrote: "The line dividing good and evil passes not through states, nor between classes . . . but right through every human heart."[953] In this light, Marx's legacy remains inseparable from the revolutions—and the catastrophes—it helped unleash.

This irony reflected the tragic flaw of Marx's own thinking: the belief that revolutionary violence could create a just society, even as it ignored the potential dehumanizing consequences of such radical changes. Marx's legacy continues to be felt, prompting reflection on the costs of revolutionary ideals and the moral compromises that come with them. He is Faust, bound to his contract, unable to break free. He is Hamlet, paralyzed by doubt, unable to act. But above all, he is a man without grace, light, and redemption. The final irony of his life is this: the book he thought would set the world free has enslaved him. There is no escape. There are no stars to guide him: only boundless ink, endless corrections, and the eternal nights.

As we close this tragic tale, darkness fills the space as a final specter to a life haunted by the long shadows it cast. The silence is the end of a divine tragedy, a fitting close to one man's flickers of brilliance absorbed into the darker spaces. As Marx sits alone, the smoke curling around him like a shroud, the weight of his life's work bears down upon him. Marx's critique of religion stands at the core of his broader philosophical break with idealism and the metaphysical traditions of his day. In his *Contribution to the Critique of Hegel's Philosophy of Right* (1844), he famously wrote that "the criticism of religion is the beginning of all criticism."[954] For Marx, religion was not merely a flawed belief system but a symptom of deeper social and material alienation. "Religion is the sigh of the oppressed creature," he continued, "the heart of a heartless world. . . . It is the opium of the people."[955] To Marx, religion offered false comfort and moral justification for systems of exploitation;[956] it was both a psychological balm and an ideological weapon wielded by the ruling class.[957] In rejecting religion, Marx was not only denying metaphysics—he was demanding that people abandon illusion in favor of material, political struggle. Only then, he believed, could true human emancipation begin. He had long declared that faith was a veil over the eyes of the oppressed. "Man makes religion; religion does not make man,"[958] he had once proclaimed, reducing the sacred to a mere construct of human alienation. He had spent a lifetime urging humanity to shed its illusions—"The abolition of religion as the illusory happiness of the people is the demand for their real happiness"[959]—yet, as the ink pools on his unfinished pages, the real happiness he promised remains absent.

Marx had written that "communism begins where atheism begins,"[960] that true liberation required erasing faith altogether. "Religion is the sigh of the oppressed creature, the heart of a heartless world"[961]—yet if this were true, what was left for the heart when that sigh was silenced? His pen scratched the paper, but the words no longer carried force. He had reduced all human suffering to economic struggle, declaring "the religious world is but the reflex of the real world,"[962] yet the real world offered no salvation, only exile, poverty, and loss. He had scorned Christian humility—"The social principles of Christianity preach cowardice, self-contempt, abasement, submission"[963]—but had his relentless pride yielded anything greater as the years passed? Had he conquered the gods or built a new mythology in his image? He had urged humanity to break its chains, writing that "religion is only the illusory Sun which revolves around man as long as he does not revolve around himself,"[964] but in the flickering candlelight, he felt himself trapped in an orbit of his own making, unable to escape. "All that exists deserves to perish"[965]—he had invoked Mephistopheles's words, and now, looking around the empty room, he realized that all had indeed perished. If history were a struggle, then struggle had consumed him. The manuscript before him was a monument to a revolution that would never come. The pen trembled in his grasp, but he could not stop writing. He could never stop writing.

Conclusion: Descent Without Return

"As Dante guides the reader through sin and redemption, I too seek to unveil the hidden struggles within the human condition."[966]

—Karl Marx

To begin: Marx died believing he had failed. His life's work, *Das Kapital*, had not sold well, and his hopes for global revolution had come to nothing. He was ill, bitter, and burdened by personal loss. And yet, the irony of Marx's legacy is that, though he passed into obscurity, his words—however misinterpreted—lived on. *Das Kapital* remains in print; Marxism continues to be taught and debated in universities; and entire regimes have claimed inspiration from his thought. In this way, the life of Karl Marx did not end at his death—it only began to unfold more forcefully. That is why this biography cannot simply end with Marx's passing. The afterlife of his ideas forms the final and perhaps most consequential act of his divine tragedy.

Marx's impassioned rhetoric and radical writings, as confined to our nine rings, would ignite revolutions across the globe. However, as history unfolded, Marx's vision of liberation often gave way to new forms of oppression. Leaders such as Lenin, Stalin, Mao, and countless others would seize upon Marx's political doctrines to establish regimes defined by terror, mass violence, and genocide—ironically replicating the very structures of domination he had sought to dismantle. Reflecting on the aftermath of Marx's journey, we are drawn back to his descent into hell—his katabasis, mirrored in *The Divine Comedy*. Just as Dante's sinners are locked away in the final circle of the *Inferno*, imprisoned by their internal conflicts. His theories, now a labyrinth with no exit, devour themselves, leaving his followers trapped in their own failed vision's cold, inescapable grip.[967]

Marx's tragedy lies not just in the weaponization of his critiques but in his inability to look beyond them—to recognize that human existence, with all its complexity, cannot be reduced to mere economic or political struggles. Reflecting on the profound tragedies that shaped him, it is impossible not to draw parallels to Dante, Shakespeare, and Goethe, whose characters' failings also "miss the mark" (*hamartia*). Dante's *Inferno* probes the depths of human sin and divine justice, portraying souls—even popes—damned for earthly transgressions. Goethe's *Faust* presents a brilliant scholar who, in pursuing forbidden knowledge, makes a pact with the devil, leading to his ultimate downfall. Shakespeare's *Hamlet* wonders: "What is man, that noble mind that is in him, what is he but a quintessence of dust?" "To these phenomena, Dante, a somewhat agonized member of a Church in Crisis, with messages to which most Christians would still rather remain deaf, has eloquent things to say. So Dante lives if only we would read him."[968]

Tragedy or Pseudoscience

Thomas Carlyle in, *On Heroes*, writes: "For the thing that is uttered from the inmost parts of a man's soul, differs altogether from what is uttered by the outer part."[969] As charted through the three major books in the *Divine Tragedy* and their respective rings, Marx's tragedy mirrors the inverse structure of Dante's *Divine Comedy*. Dante rises toward divine grace after confronting his sins, while Marx descends into a cold, deep pseudoscientific moralism. The tragedy here underscores the human ambition, moral compromise, and the catastrophic outcomes that arise when *hubris* divorces itself from the natural order: "Conscious of our frailty, we find in the tragic a critique of hubristic reason, without thereby selling the pass to pessimism or scientific determinism."[970] Marx's life was not just the story of a revolutionary thinker; it was the tragic tale of a man obsessed with a new messianic vision of an apocalyptic future that alienated him from his family and his soul.

Was Marx merely a modern man struggling with newfound self-awareness in an era of industrial change, overwhelmed by the rapid transformations of the world around him?[971] This image—of a man who sought to overthrow the existing order only to become trapped in his ideological prison—captures the paradox at the heart of Marx's life and thought: the search for liberation that ultimately led to personal and moral ruin.

Rather than offering a sweeping ideological indictment or vindication, this work tries to examine the specter of Marx's legacy through the lens of tragedy: how one man's search for justice and liberation helped inspire some of the most profound upheavals in modern history. As a writer, I take Marx unapologetically at his word—that anyone "should merely demonstrate that my views, however one may judge them and however little they agree with the interested prejudices of the ruling classes, are the result of conscientious and lengthy research." My aim has not been to present all the answers, but to trace the contours of a complex life and to show, as best I can, how Marx's revolutionary vision challenged and ultimately betrayed the ideals he claimed to serve. Marx's call for revolution, which initially focused on class struggle, soon morphed into a scapegoating of traditional religion, culture, and political institutions as mere instruments of dark power.

This growing anti-Western sentiment in the modern world distorts Marx's original vision, exaggerating it by broadening its focus beyond class struggle to encompass racial, cultural, gender, and civilizational conflicts. In the wake of the Frankfurt School in exile, the notebooks of Antonio Gramsci,[972] and other modern provocateurs, Marxist critique continued to permeate academia. As classical Marxism faced widespread discrediting due to its real-world consequences, scholars began repurposing its foundational ideas into new modes of inquiry. Postmodern theorists—many of whom could no longer advance a pure Marxist theory—developed alternative frameworks that preserved Marxism's critical thrust against Western institutions, culture, and hierarchy. These strategies, often couched in the language of identity, power, and discourse, expanded the Marxist lens in ways Marx himself may not have anticipated. The evolution of Marxist thought into postmodern critique has drawn rigorous analysis from across the ideological spectrum. Conservative scholars such as Stephen Hicks, John M. Ellis, and Roger Scruton argue that postmodernism emerged as a strategic response to the collapse of classical Marxism—a theoretical rebranding designed to undermine Western civilization through cultural critique rather than economic revolution. Hicks traces this trajectory in his genealogy of skepticism and socialism, Ellis examines its corrosive effect on the humanities, and Scruton profiles the radical theorists who helped engineer the New Left's intellectual framework. At the same time, left-leaning thinkers—including Terry Eagleton and Fredric Jameson—have reflected critically on the postmodern turn. Antonio Gramsci, though writing decades before the rise of postmodern theory, offered a pivotal shift within Marxist thought by emphasizing cultural hegemony over direct political confrontation. Through his *Prison Notebooks*, Gramsci moved Marxist analysis beyond economics alone, laying the groundwork for what would later be called "Cultural Marxism"—a strategy of revolutionary influence through cultural institutions rather than through violent upheaval. While not a postmodernist himself, Gramsci represents an intermediate step between classical Marxism and the cultural strategies later adopted by the postmodern left.[973] While Eagleton critiques postmodernism's retreat from political responsibility, Jameson frames it as the cultural logic of late capitalism—a symptom of economic transformation and a potential lens through which to understand it.

Additionally, key figures such as Michel Foucault, Jacques Derrida, and Jean-François Lyotard laid the philosophical foundation for postmodernism, advancing ideas of discourse, deconstruction, and the end of grand narratives. This convergence of left and right critiques signals that postmodernism is not a closed doctrine but a contested terrain. The debate over its origins and consequences offers insight into the lasting influence of Marxist thought, transformed through the lens of modernity, identity, and power.[974] In *The Communist Manifesto*, Marx called for nothing less than the complete overthrow of all existing societal structures, which would eventually include the state itself and presented evolution not just as desirable, but inevitable—a science akin to biology—and himself as the Darwin of evolutionary history.

In his attempt to replace the tragic-spiritual dimension of the cross with a cold logic and determinism, Marx rejected the *imago Dei*—the divine image in each individual—stripping humanity of its intrinsic dignity: "Behind this model of tragedy lies a theology of the Crucifixion, which Schelling and others project on to ancient Greek tragedy. (It is worth recalling that he, Hegel and Hölderlin all started out as seminarians)."[975] Marx's revolutionary dream downplayed individual essence, to subordinate the person to a collective vision governed by a moral code shaped mainly by historical forces and class dynamics rather than by personal conscience or spiritual dignity. In his final stages, Marx was trapped in an ideological labyrinth where Christian symbols and stories had lost their power and where modern science and Faustian pacts took their place.[976] In this new framework, a moral code emerged, one devoid of redemption and rooted solely in materialism, one that missed the core lesson of the Gospel story, that in dying, one lives. That it is "inevitable that Jesus dies on the cross, not in the sense that his end is predestined, but because juridical murder is the logical fate of those who speak out for justice and fellowship in a corrupt world. Yet Jesus's death, which takes a form reserved by the ancient Roman empire for political rebels, is also portrayed by the Gospel as one in which he freely (though by no means joyfully) acquiesces. Like many tragic protagonists, he makes his destiny his choice. It is clear from his agony in Gethsemane that he does not want to die, but it would make no political or theological sense if he did not."[977]

Katabasis in Apocalypse

Marx's writings not only fail to warn of the dangers of discarding the intangible dimensions of life, but they also helped lay the groundwork for those very dangers by redefining human purpose in purely economic and political terms. Without the possibility of redemption—without the spiritual values that connect us to something transcendent—all journeys lead back to self-absorption. Marx's descent, without a return, led to a material existence that spiraled in an endless loop, forever circling back to emptiness and ultimate disenchantment. The questions and contradictions that plagued Marx's life remain relevant today, making his legacy a testament to intellectual rigor and a cautionary tale that reminds us that even the most sophisticated theories can conceal false premises and that brilliance without truth can lead to ruin.

Like the apocalyptic genre that maps a civilization's beginning, middle, and end, Marx's theory carried a grand narrative.[978] This pseudoscientific eschatology foretold an inevitable societal transformation. Yet, where Christian eschatology promises redemption and grace, Marx's history sought to abolish distinctions of class, ethnicity, and gender, and the state itself would become the divine arbiter. In Marx's utopia, there was no space for the transcendence of the individual or divine grace, only the relentless pursuit of a perfect, material world through violent revolution.

While Marx often borrowed from Christian imagery in his critique of the West, he overlooked the redemptive arc at the heart of the Gospel—the paradox that bearing "the slings and arrows," or "Th'oppressor's wrong, the proud man's contumely" or "the law's delay"[979] can lead to deep revelation. With every hell, there is a paradise: "Only because of our humanity is so disfigured, and our self-delusion so deep rooted, are such baptisms of fire essential."[980] Marx's moral outrage seemed, at times, understandable, as he identified real injustices and inequalities that continue to mark our world. However, his moral framework failed to distinguish between just forms of equality, such as equality before the law or opportunity, and unjust demands for equity as equal outcomes, often requiring coercive measures disregarding merit and undermining freedom. Where Dante's universe is governed by divine love and justice, Marx's world is ruled by mystical materialism. In Dante's *Divine Comedy*, every level of hell, purgatory, and paradise reflects the eternal consequences of human choices, imbued with the possibility of divine grace, which offers a way out of suffering.

Historian Niall Ferguson, often described as a classical liberal, aptly summarizes the situation: "Marx's predictions have consistently failed, yet his critique of inequality and capital accumulation still resonates in a world of growing disparities."[981] While not a conservative in the strict sense, Ferguson represents a skeptical stance toward Marxism that still acknowledges the lasting relevance of its core critiques.

Despite the catastrophic history that followed Marx's ideas, and without absolving him of responsibility, blaming Marx directly for the genocides committed under Soviet or Maoist regimes risks oversimplification. Yet Marxism, by its very structure, contains the seeds of revolutionary violence. While later regimes deviated from Marx's original blueprint—revolutions occurring in largely agrarian rather than industrialized capitalist societies, internal fractures like those between the Bolsheviks and Mensheviks, or Mao's divergence from Stalin—these were not simply distortions. Rather, they were the inevitable consequences of attempting to apply a utopian theory, born in the furnace of industrial capitalism, to the messy, often non-industrial realities of political life.[982] While Marx's ideas undeniably fueled the engines of totalitarian regimes, reducing his work to that of a one-dimensional villain ignores the broader implications of his ideology.

The tragedy of Marxism lies not only in its intellectual roots but in how its revolutionary ideals were transformed into instruments of domination. Marx's critique of Western civilization—initially aimed at exposing economic exploitation—evolved into a totalizing ideology that claimed authority over all domains of life. While Marx did not design the mechanisms of repression later adopted by communist regimes, his writings provided the philosophical scaffolding—rooted in historical determinism, class struggle, and the abolition of traditional institutions—that enabled their rise. The tragic consequences were not mere distortions of Marx's theory, but foreseeable outcomes of applying a utopian doctrine to the irreducible complexity of human society. The very intellectual foundations that sought to redeem humanity gave rise to new forms of suffering and destruction.[983]

The Divine Travesty

Writers, thinkers, teachers, and ministers—believers and non-believers alike—dismiss Marx's work at their peril. Many have labeled it outdated or confined it to a mere economic or philosophical *cul-de-sac*, failing to grasp its enduring power and relevance.

Unfortunately, the generations that followed often perpetuated a dismissal of Marx's insights, whether consciously or out of ignorance, rarely engaging with the full weight of his critique of society and the structural forces that govern it. MacIntyre observes: "Capitalism, taking a variety of forms that range from the corporate capitalism of the United States to the state capitalism of China, seems to be almost unchallenged worldwide—except, of course, by its own self-destructive and disillusioning tendencies."[984] After the shock of 9/11,[985] the 2008 global financial crisis[986] offered a rare moment of reckoning: it jolted the public into confronting that capitalism, so often celebrated as the apex of human progress, is equally susceptible to mismanagement, greed, and shortsighted leadership.[987] In this way, Marx's insights remain uncomfortably relevant.[988] However, such failures reflect the fallibility of human actors and are not necessarily an indictment of the system itself. Every economic model—capitalist, socialist, or otherwise—is vulnerable to mismanagement, exploitation, and corruption. Yet history has repeatedly shown that the alternatives, particularly Marxist regimes, have often produced more devastating consequences when implemented at scale. Acknowledging the legitimacy of Marx's critique does not require embracing his solutions. Instead, it invites a sober reappraisal: to hear the critique, wrestle with it honestly, and then seek our next steps elsewhere, within a framework that still values liberty, accountability, and the dignity of the individual.

Therefore, Marx's legacy remains deeply entangled in policy and protest and in the ideological battlegrounds of the modern university. To quote Robert Payne, "We live in the age of Marx. Nearly half the world, a thousand million people, are ruled by governments which claim to be practicing his teachings and following the path he set for them in *The Communist Manifesto*, *Das Kapital*, and a host of lesser works."[989] Of course, such claims must be qualified. While countries like China nominally adhere to Marxist ideology, their policies often blend state capitalism with centralized authoritarian control, far from Marx's original vision.[990] Whether we like it or not, Marx's analysis continues to permeate contemporary discussions on social justice, economic reform, and critiques of capitalist institutions. His ideas have shaped the language and frameworks through which inequality, power, and labor are debated across disciplines and political movements. To sidestep this influence is to fail to understand the full scope of Marx's impact—not as a relic of a failed ideology, but as an enduring provocation.[991]

Marx's legacy is deeply contentious. Some praise him as the founder of scientific socialism, while others see him as an embittered émigré, trapped in his revolutionary fantasies and distorted ideas about societal progress. More recently, scholars such as Erich Fromm and David Leopold have reinterpreted Marx as an existentialist philosopher, particularly in his early writings, where he critiques alienation, dependency, and the erosion of human freedom in modern life.[992] MacIntyre observes that "Marx's analysis of alienation retains its power, yet his failure to address the moral foundations of community limits its scope."[993] This critique explains how in the hands of totalitarian leaders like Stalin, a former believer,[994] Marxism was warped into a justification for atrocities. The Russian Revolution, which had promised proletarian liberation, soon devolved into a brutal and repressive regime. Marx did not prescribe genocide, but the blueprint of his thought—revolutionary upheaval, centralized control of the means of production, and the abolition of existing social institutions—provided fertile ground for the rise of authoritarianism. That is the tragedy—not only of the ideology's outcomes but its moral blind spots. Dissent was crushed, millions were purged, and an entire generation of intellectuals and political opponents was erased. Taken to their logical and philosophical conclusion, Marx's theories provided a moral framework for radical social engineering, in which those who opposed the revolution were deemed enemies of historical progress. Because Marxism envisions a total reordering of society based on abstract principles and lacks a proper understanding of human nature, it often requires coercion to achieve compliance. As Hannah Arendt warned in her study of totalitarian regimes: "Ideological thinking orders facts into a logical procedure which starts from an axiomatically accepted premise, deducing everything else from it."[995]

Richard Pipes, writing on the Soviet experiment, noted that violence was not incidental but intrinsic to the Marxist project: "The dictatorship of the proletariat was not a provisional institution . . . but the core of Marxist theory."[996] Philosopher Roger Scruton sharpened the point: "Socialism begins with the promise of freedom and ends with the demand for obedience. It is not liberty but its negation, disguised as its fulfillment." In this sense, Marxism is not merely a theory of justice gone awry—it is a system whose utopian demands inevitably produce repression.[997] The tragedies of the twentieth century—from the Soviet gulag to the Cultural Revolution—are not accidental deviations but historical expressions of a deeper philosophical flaw: the attempt to perfect humanity by force.

Similarly, in China, Mao's revolution was inspired by Marxism. Mao led the Chinese Communist Party to victory in 1949, founding the People's Republic of China. Still, his policies—notably the Great Leap Forward and the Cultural Revolution—resulted in one of the deadliest periods of human history. In the Cultural Revolution, intellectuals, political opponents, and everyday citizens were persecuted in the name of Marxist ideals. Mao's words reflected the brutal disregard for human life:

> If we were to add up all the landlords, rich peasants, counterrevolutionaries, bad elements, and rightists, their number would reach thirty million. . . . Of our total population of six hundred million people, these thirty million are only one out of twenty. So what is there to be afraid of? . . . We have so many people. We can afford to lose a few. What difference does it make? The horrific genocides in the Soviet Union, China, and elsewhere were the direct result of the same ideological drive for a perfect society that Marx had envisioned, but which became a deadly fantasy when corrupted by human nature and totalitarian power.[998]

By the end of the twentieth century, the communist Leviathan had consumed itself. The collapse of the Soviet Union in 1991 marked a profound disillusionment with Marxism, revealing that the dream of a classless society had not only failed to materialize but had led to systems of even greater oppression. While socialist movements persist in various forms, they are increasingly tempered by the historical realities of twentieth-century Marxist regimes. Today, the radical fervor that once fueled revolutionary Marxism has largely receded, giving way to a more complex and pluralistic debate about inequality, social justice, and the future of economic life. That debate is not confined to the ideological left. In the United States and parts of Europe, conservative and nationalist economic policies have emerged in response to globalism's failures, championing trade protections, industrial revival, and a renewed emphasis on national sovereignty to support working- and middle-class families. These efforts represent viable, non-Marxist alternatives to address wage stagnation, deindustrialization, and wealth concentration. Still, the relevance of Marx's critique of capitalism endures.[999] His warnings about commodification, alienation, and the corrosive effects of unfettered capital remain points of concern, even among those who reject his solutions outright. The tragedy lies not only in what Marx envisioned but in how his insights were co-opted and misapplied and in the enduring gaps they continue to reveal in the architecture of modern economic life.

Today, there is growing recognition—on both the left and right—that unchecked globalization has eroded working-class prosperity. In response, some nations are reasserting trade protections, pursuing reindustrialization, and rethinking monetary and labor policies. These conservative and nationalist alternatives seek to restore economic sovereignty and defend middle-class interests without resorting to Marxist ideology. Yet, despite the failures of Marxist regimes, Marx's critique of capitalism, particularly his analysis of wealth concentration and corporate dominance, continues to resonate in a world of surging inequality. His warnings about the dehumanizing effects of commodification, alienation, and systemic exploitation remain points of concern, even among those who reject his proposed solutions. The hope for a better world that once animated Marxist revolutionaries has often given way to deep cynicism. The global political landscape is increasingly fragmented, and the quest for justice often leads to temptations for power. The radical ideologies that promised a perfect society have given way to new forms of activism, as identity politics and populism take center stage. Yet, despite the failures of Marxist revolutions, the search for a better society continues. As we reflect on Marx's legacy, we are reminded that the struggle for justice is ongoing. In Marx's view, the "return" is not spiritual but social—a utopian vision of a classless society achieved through revolution.[1000] Dante's architecture is vertical, leading the soul upward toward God; Marx's work is horizontal, focusing on the transformation of society. The clash between the Christian vision in *The Divine Comedy* and Marx's vision in *Das Kapital* is not merely a philosophical dispute, but a battle over the nature of reality, the purpose of life, and the destiny of the human soul. Given Marxism's rejection of transcendence and its grounding in material determinism, its repeated failure should come as no surprise; systems that deny the spiritual dimension of humanity inevitably collapse under the weight of their own illusions.[1001]

In the end, Marx's tragic vision is one where the descent is final—an abyss where revolution consumes its own, and redemption is neither sought nor granted. It is a world abandoned to its illusions, where humans, having cast off the divine, are left to wander in the wreckage of their own making.[1002] For Dante, descent is the necessary threshold to ascent, a harrowing but momentary passage through judgment, suffering, and transformation that leads to the light of redemption. The Christian path does not demand the blood of millions to pave the way for paradise; it offers instead the faith and hope of redemption—an upward climb, not built on ruins, but on love. As the saying goes: "Love conquers all" (*amor omnia vincit*).[1003] Now you must carry the burden alone."[1004]

Bibliography

Books

Ackroyd, Peter. *London Under: The Secret History Beneath the Streets.* London: Vintage, 2011.

Adler, Mortimer J. *Aristotle for Everybody: Difficult Thought Made Easy*. New York: Touchstone, Simon and Schuster, 1978.

Aeschylus. *Prometheus Bound and Other Plays*. Translated by Philip Vellacott. London: Penguin Books, 1961.

Alaimo, Carmen. *Justice and Power in Dante's Divine Comedy*. Cambridge: Cambridge University Press, 2012.

Alighieri, Dante. *Inferno*. Translated by Henry Wadsworth Longfellow. New York: Modern Library, 1867; repr. 2003.

———. *The Divine Comedy*. Translated by Lawrence Grant White. New York: Pantheon Books, 1948.

———. *Hell.* Translated by Dorothy L. Sayers. London: Penguin Books, 1949.

———. *Inferno*. Translated by Elio Zappulla. London: Vintage, 1999.

———. *Purgatory*. Translated by Dorothy L. Sayers. London: Penguin Books, 1955.

———. *Paradise*. Translated by Dorothy L. Sayers and Barbara Reynolds. London: Penguin Books, 1962.

———. "Purgatorio." In *The Divine Comedy*. Translated by Charles S. Singleton. Princeton, NJ: Princeton University Press, 1973.

———. *The Divine Comedy: Inferno*. Translated by Allen Mandelbaum. New York: Bantam Classics, 1982.

———. *The Divine Comedy: Purgatorio*. Translated by Allen Mandelbaum. New York: Bantam Classics, 1982.

———. *The Divine Comedy: Paradiso*. Translated by Allen Mandelbaum. New York: Bantam Classics, 1982.

———. *Inferno*. Translated by Robert M. Durling. Oxford: Oxford University Press, 1996.

———. *Inferno*. Translated by Robert Hollander and Jean Hollander. New York: Doubleday, 2000.

———. *Purgatorio*. Translated by Robert M. Durling. Oxford: Oxford University Press, 2003.

———. *Purgatorio*. Translated by Robert Hollander and Jean Hollander. New York: Doubleday, 2003.

———. *The Divine Comedy*: *Inferno*. Translated by John Ciardi. New York: New American Library, 2003.

———. *Paradiso*. Translated by Robert Hollander and Jean Hollander. New York: Doubleday, 2007.

———. *Paradiso*. Translated by Robert M. Durling. Cambridge, MA: Harvard University Press, 2011.

———. *The Divine Comedy: Hellbound Edition*. Florence: CGR Publishing, 2020.

Alinsky, Saul. *Rules for Radicals: A Pragmatic Primer for Realistic Radicals*. New York: Vintage, 1971.

Allen, Robert C. *The British Industrial Revolution in Global Perspective*. Cambridge: Cambridge University Press, 2009.

Allison, Juliann Emmons, and Ellen Reese. *Unsustainable: Amazon, Warehousing, and the Politics of Exploitation*. Berkeley: University of California Press, 2023.

Althusser, Louis. *For Marx*. New York: Pantheon Books, 1969.

Anderson, Kevin B. *Marx at the Margins: On Nationalism, Ethnicity, and Non-Western Societies*. Chicago: University of Chicago Press, 2010.

Anderson, Perry. *In the Tracks of Historical Materialism*. London: Verso Books, 1983.

Apollonio, Robert. *The Ethics of Dante: A Modern Analysis*. Oxford: Oxford University Press, 2014.

Arendt, Hannah. *The Origins of Totalitarianism*. New York: Harcourt, 1973.

Aristotle. *Poetics*. Translated by S. H. Butcher. London: Macmillan & Co., 1902.

———. *Metaphysics*. Translated by W. D. Ross. Oxford: Oxford University Press, 1924.

———. *Politics*. Translated by C. D. C. Reeve. Indianapolis: Hackett Publishing, 1998.

———. *Nicomachean Ethics*. Translated by Terence Irwin. Indianapolis: Hackett Publishing, 1999.

Aslund, Anders. *Russia's War in Ukraine: The Return of the Russian Empire*. London: Yale University Press, 2023.

Auerbach, Erich. *Dante: Poet of the Secular World*. Translated by Ralph Manheim. New York: New York Review Books, 2007.

Augustine. *Confessions*. New York: Penguin Classics, 1961.

Austin, J. L. *How to Do Things with Words: The William James Lectures Delivered in Harvard University in 1955*. Edited by J. O. Urmson. Oxford: Oxford University Press, 1962.

Avineri, Shlomo. *Moses Hess: Prophet of Communism and Zionism*. New York: New York University Press, 1985.

———. *Karl Marx: Philosophy and Revolution*. New Haven, CT: Yale University Press, 2019.

Aylon, Hélène. *The Divine Comedy Revisited: Art and Theology*. New Haven, CT: Yale University Press, 1995.

Bakounine, Michel. *Oeuvres*, vol. 2. Paris: P. V. Stock, 1907.

Bakunin, Mikhail. *Statism and Anarchy*. Cambridge: Cambridge University Press, 1990.

Balthasar, Hans Urs von. *Theo-Drama: Theological Dramatic Theory*. 4 vols. San Francisco: Ignatius Press, 1988–1998.

Baran, Paul A., and Paul M. Sweeney. *Monopoly Capital: An Essay on the American Economic and Social Order*. New York: Monthly Review Press.

Barbera, Anita. *Dante on Stage: Performative Adaptations of the Divine Comedy*. New York: Palgrave Macmillan, 2019.

Barnett, Vincent. *Marx*. London: Routledge, 2009.

Barolini, Teodolinda. *Dante's Poets: Textuality and Truth in the "Comedy"*. Princeton, NJ: Princeton University Press, 1984.

———. *The Undivine Comedy: Detheologizing Dante*. Princeton, NJ: Princeton University Press, 1992.

Barron, Robert. *Thomas Aquinas: Spiritual Master*. New York: Crossroad, 1996.

———. *The Divine Impossibility and the Mystery of Human Suffering*. Grand Rapids, MI: Eerdmans Publishing, 2018.

Bauder, Harald. *Labor Movement: How Migration Regulates Labor Markets*. New York: Oxford University Press, 2006.

Baumeister, Jens. *How Wine Turned Karl Marx into a Communist*. Trier: Trier Shop, 2018.

Baumgart, Winfried. *The Crimean War: 1853–1856*. London: Arnold, 1999.

Becker, Ernest. *The Birth and Death of Meaning.* New York: The Free Press, 1971.

Belliotti, Raymond Angelo. "Dante's Existential Moral Lessons." In *Dante's Deadly Sins: Moral Philosophy.* Malden, MA: John Wiley & Sons Inc., 2011.

Benjamin, Walter. *The Origin of German Tragic Drama.* London. Verso, 1998.

Benn, Maurice B. *The Drama of Revolt: A Critical Study of Georg Büchner.* Cambridge: Cambridge University Press, 1976.

Berdyaev, Nicholai. *Religion in Life*, vol. 6. Translated by D. A. Lowrie. Nashville: Abingdon Press, 1938.

Berlin, Isaiah. *Karl Marx: His Life and Environment.* 4th ed. New York: Oxford University Press, 1978.

———. *Karl Marx*, 5th ed. Edited by Henry Hardy. Princeton, NJ: Princeton University Press, 2013.

Bigongiari, Dino, ed. *The Political Ideas of St. Thomas Aquinas: Representative Selections.* New York: Free Press, 1997.

Blanton, Ward. *A Materialism for the Masses: Saint Paul and the Philosophy of Undying Life.* New York: Columbia University Press, 2014.

Bloch, Ernst. *The Principle of Hope*, vol. 1. Cambridge, MA: MIT Press, 1986.

Bloom, Harold, ed. *Hamlet.* New York: Chelsea House Publishers, 1990.

Böhm-Bawerk, Eugen von. *Karl Marx and the Close of His System.* Translated by Alice M. Macdonald. New York: Augustus M. Kelley, 1949.

Booker, Christopher. *The Seven Basic Plots: Why we Tell Stories.* London: Continuum, 2004,

Briggs, Asa. *The Age of Improvement, 1783–1867*. London: Longman, 1959.

Bronner, Stephen Eric. *Critical Theory: A Very Short Introduction*. New York: Oxford University Press, 2017.

Buijs, Joseph, ed. *Maimonides: A Collection of Critical Essays*. South Bend, IN: University of Notre Dame Press, 1988.

Cadava, Eduardo, and Sara Nadal-Melsio. *Politically Red*. Cambridge, MA: MIT Press, 2023.

Calan, Ronan de. *The Ghost of Karl Marx*. Illustrated by Donatien Marie. Translated by Anna Street. Zurich: Plato & Co. Diaphanes, 2015.

Callinicos, Alex. *The Revolutionary Ideas of Karl Marx*. Chicago: Haymarket Books, 2011.

Campbell, Scott. *Antifa: Satan's Communists and Anarchists*. S.-P., 2020.

Carlyle, Thomas. *On Heroes*. N.P.: East India Publishing, 2023.

Carver, Terrell. "Introduction." Pages ix–xx in *Marx: Later Political Writings*. Translated and edited by Terrell Carver. Cambridge: Cambridge University Press.

Chafuen, Alejandro A. *Faith and Liberty: The Economic Thought of the Late Scholastics*. Lanham, MD: Lexington Books, 2003.

Chesterton, G. K. *The Outline of Sanity*. London: Methuen, 1926.

———. *In Defense of Sanity: The Best Essays of G. K. Chesterton*. San Francisco: Ignatius Press, 2011.

Chomsky, Noam and Marv Waterstone. *Consequences of Capitalism: Manufacturing Discontent and Resistance*. Chicago: Haymarket Books, 2021.

Clement of Alexandria. *Stromateis 1–3*. Translated by John Ferguson. Washington, DC: Catholic University Press of America, 1991.

Cohen, G. A. *Karl Marx's Theory of History: A Defense*. Expanded ed. Oxford: Oxford University Press, 2000.

Conquest, Robert. *The Great Terror: A Reassessment*. New York: Oxford University Press, 1990.

Cooper, J. C., ed. *Brewer's Book of Myth and Legend*. Oxford: Helicon Publishing Ltd., 1997.

Copleston, Frederick. *A History of Philosophy*, vol. 3: *Ockham to Suarez*. New York: Image Books, 1983.

Cornu, Auguste. *Karl Marx: L'Homme et l'Oeuvre. De l'Hégélianisme au Matérialisme Historique*. Paris: Alcan, 1934.

Courtois, Stéphane, et al. *The Black Book of Communism: Crimes, Terror, Repression*. Cambridge, MA: Harvard University Press, 1999.

Cox, Catherine S. *Dante's Women: Representations and Meanings in the Divine Comedy*. London: Routledge, 1999.

Crenshaw, Kimberlé, et al., eds. *Critical Race Theory*. New York: The Free Press, 1996.

Davies, Brian. *The Thought of Thomas Aquinas*. Oxford: Oxford University Press, 1992.

———. *Thomas Aquinas on God and Evil*. Oxford: Oxford University Press, 2011.

———. *Summa Contra Gentiles: A Concise Translation*. New York: Oxford University Press, 2016.

De Lubac, Henri. *The Drama of Atheist Humanism*. Translated by Edith M. Riley. New York: Sheed & Ward, 1950.

———. *The Drama of Atheist Humanism*. San Francisco, CA: Ignatius Press, 1998.

De Lucca, Diana. *The Language of Dante: Translation and Meaning*. Cambridge, MA: Harvard University Press, 2018.

Del Tondo, David M. *Dante and the Doctrine of the Allegory of Poets*. Oxford: Oxford University Press, 1986.

DeMatteo, Alfredo B. T. H. *The Modern Dante: Philosophy and Poetics in the Divine Comedy.* Chicago: University of Chicago Press, 2015.

Derber, Charles. *Marx's Ghost: Midnight Conversations on Changing the World*. Boulder, CO: Paradigm Publishers, 2011.

Derrida, Jacques. *Writing and Difference*. Translated by Alan Bass. Chicago: University of Chicago Press, 1978.

———. *Limited Inc*. Translated by Samuel Weber and Jeffrey Mehlman. Edited by Gerald Graff. Evanston, IL: Northwestern University Press, 1988.

———. *Specters of Marx*. Translated by Peggy Kamuf. London: Routledge, 1994.

Descartes, René. *Meditations on First Philosophy*. Translated by John Cottingham. Cambridge: Cambridge University Press, 1996.

DeStefano, Angelo. *Post-Colonial Readings of Dante*. Cambridge: Cambridge University Press, 2009.

DeWitt, Norman. *Epicurus and His Philosophy*. Minneapolis: University of Minnesota Press, 1954.

Dickens, Charles. *Oliver Twist*. London: Richard Bentley, 1839.

———. *American Notes for General Circulation*. London: Chapman & Hall, 1842.

———. *Bleak House*. London: Bradbury and Evans, 1853.

———. *Great Expectations*. London: Chapman & Hall, 1861.

———. *Hard Times*. New York: Hurst, 1889.

DiLorenzo, Thomas J. *The Problem with Socialism*. Washington, DC: Regnery Publishing, 2016.

Dole, Andrew. *Reframing the Masters of Suspicion: Marx, Nietzsche, and Freud*. London: Bloomsbury, 2019.

Dotoli, Giovanni. *Dante et la France*. Fasano: Schena Editore, 1994.

———. *Dante e la Filosofia: Interpretazioni*. Rome: Edizioni Universitarie, 2002.

———. *Dante, notre contemporain*. Paris: Hermann Éditeurs, 2012.

Durant, Will, and Ariel Durant. *The Age of Napoleon: A History of European Civilization from 1789 to 1815*. New York: Simon and Schuster, 1975.

Eagleton, Terry. *Marx and Freedom*. London: Blackwell, 1990.

———. *The Illusions of Postmodernism*. Oxford: Blackwell, 1996.

———. *Sweet Violence: The Idea of the Tragic*. Oxford: Blackwell, 2003.

———. *Why Marx Was Right*. New Haven, CT: Yale University Press, 2011.

———. *Tragedy*. New Haven, CT: Yale University Press, 2020.

Egan, Gabriel. *Shakespeare and Marx*. Oxford: Oxford University Press, 2004.

Eliot, T. S. "Dante." In *Selected Essays, 1917–1932*, 237–77. London: Faber & Faber, 1932.

Ellis, John M. *Literature Lost: Social Agendas and the Corruption of the Humanities*. New Haven, CT: Yale University Press, 1997.

Engels, Friedrich. *Ludwig Feuerbach and the Outcome of Classical German Philosophy*. Edited by I. B. Lasker. Moscow: Progress Publishers, 1946.

———. *Anti-Dühring: Herr Eugen Dühring's Revolution in Science*. Translated by Emile Burns. Moscow: Progress Publishers, 1947.

———. *The Condition of the Working Class in England.* Edited by W. O. Henderson and W. H. Chaloner. Oxford: Basil Blackwell, 1958.

———. *The Origin of the Family, Private Property and the State.* New York: International Publishers, 1972.

———. *The Condition of the Working Class in England.* Edited and translated by David McLellan. Oxford: Oxford University Press, 2009.

———. "The Condition of the Working Class in England. 1845." *American Journal of Public Health* 93, no. 8 (2003): 1246–49.

Fahrney, Ralph R. *Horace Greeley and the Tribune in the Civil War.* Cedar Rapids, IA Torch, 1936.

Falconer, Rachel. "Introduction: Descent and Return—The Katabatic Imagination Hell." In *Contemporary Literature: Western Descent Narratives since 1945*, 1–12. Edinburgh: Edinburgh University Press, 2007.

———. *Hell in Contemporary Literature: Western Descent Narratives since 1945.* Edinburgh: Edinburgh University Press, 2005.

Favilli, Paolo. *The History of Italian Marxism: From Its Origins to the Great War.* Leiden: Brill, 2016.

Fedoseev, Petr Nikolaevich. *Karl Marx: A Biography.* Moscow: Progress Publishers, 1989.

Ferguson, Everett. *Backgrounds of Early Christianity*, 3rd ed. Grand Rapids, MI: Eerdmans, 2003.

Ferguson, Niall. *The War of the World: Twentieth-Century Conflict and the Descent of the West.* New York: Penguin Press, 2006.

Feuerbach, Ludwig. *The Essence of Christianity.* Translated by George Eliot. New York: Harper & Brothers, 1957.

Figes, Orlando. *The Crimean War: A History.* New York: Picador, 2012.

Foucault, Michel. *Discipline and Punish: The Birth of the Prison.* Translated by Alan Sheridan. New York: Vintage Books, 1995.

Freccero, John. *Dante: The Poetics of Conversion.* Edited by Rachel Jacoff. Cambridge, MA: Harvard University Press, 1988.

———. *In Dante's Wake: Reading from Medieval to Modern in the Augustinian Tradition.* New York: Fordham University Press, 2015.

Freud, Sigmund. *New Introductory Lectures on Psychoanalysis.* Translated and edited by James Strachey. New York: W.W. Norton & Co., 1965.

Fromm, Erich. *Marx's Concept of Man.* New York: Frederick Ungar Publishing Co., 1970.

Frye, Northrop. *Anatomy of Criticism.* Princeton, NJ: Princeton University Press, 1971.

Fuchs, Christian. *The Digital Economy: The Internet, The Information Society, and the Marxist Perspective.* London: Routledge, 2017.

Gabriel, Mary. *Love And Capital: Karl and Jenny Marx and the Birth of a Revolution.* New York: Little, Brown, and Co., 2011.

Gadamer, Hans-Georg. *Truth and Method.* Translated by Joel Weinsheimer and Donald G. Marshall. London: Bloomsbury Academic, 2004.

García, Eduardo Humberto del Río (RIUS). *Marx for Beginners.* New York: Pantheon Books, 2003.

Garrigou-Lagrange, Reginald. *God: His Existence and His Nature. A Thomistic Solution of Certain Agnostic Antinomies.* Translated by Bede Rose. St. Louis: B. Herder, 1949.

Garza, Christina. *Nature and Civilization in Dante's Divine Comedy.* London: Routledge, 2021.

Gattuso, Reina. "The Struggling Vineyards That Helped Inspire Karl Marx's Communism." *Atlas Obscura*, June 13, 2019. https://www.atlasobscura.com/articles/where-was-karl-marx-born?utm_source=chatgpt.com.

Gay, Peter. *The Enlightenment: An Interpretation*, vol. 1, *The Rise of Modern Paganism*. New York: W.W. Norton, 1966.

Gielkens, Jan. *Karl Marx und seine niederländischen Verwandten: Eine kommentierte Quellenedition.* Trier: Karl-Marx-Haus, 1999.

Gilson, Etienne. *St. Thomas Aquinas*. New York: Doubleday, 1956.

———. *The Christian Philosophy of St. Thomas Aquinas*. South Bend, IN: University of Notre Dame Press, 1994.

Goethe, Johann Wolfgang von. *Faust*, Part II. Translated by Bayard Taylor. Boston: Houghton Mifflin, 1883.

———. *Poetry and Truth*, vol. 1. Translated by John Oxenford. London: H.G. Bohn, 1848.

———. *Faust*. Translated by Walter Kaufmann. New York: Anchor, 1961.

———. *Faust, Part One*. Translated by David Luke. Oxford: Oxford University Press, 1987.

———. *Faust I & II*. Edited and translated by Stuart Atkins. Princeton, NJ: Princeton University Press, 1994.

Goldstein, Philip. "Review of Terry Eagleton, *Criticism and Ideology: A Study in Marxist Literary Theory*." *Symploke* 14, no. 1 (2006): 348–50.

Gonzalez, Mike. *BLM: The Making of a New Marxist Revolution*. New York: Encounter Books, 2021.

Gramsci, Antonio. *Selections from the Prison Notebooks*. Edited and translated by Quintin Hoare and Geoffrey Nowell Smith. New York: International Publishers, 1971.

———. *The Antonio Gramsci Reader: Selected Writings 1916–1935.* Edited by David Forgacs. New York: New York University Press, 2000.

Green, John. *Friedrich Engels: A Biography*. New York: Macmillan, 1979.

Greenblatt, Stephen. *Hamlet in Purgatory*. Princeton, NJ: Princeton University Press, 2001.

Greene, Graham. *The Power and the Glory*. Basingstoke, UK: Macmillan, 1992.

Guillaume, James. *Bakunin on Anarchy*. George Allen & Unwin Ltd, 1971. Accessed via https://www.marxists.org/reference/archive/bakunin/works/various/mebio.htm#:~:text=On%20the%20other%20hand%2C%20Proudhon,head%20to%20foot%20an%20authoritarian.

Hainsworth, Peter, and David Robey. *Dante: A Very Short Introduction*. Oxford: Oxford University Press, 2015.

Hardt, Michael, and Antonio Negri. *Empire*. Cambridge, MA: Harvard University Press, 2001.

Harrison, John F. C. *The Early Victorians, 1832–51*. London: Weidenfeld and Nicolson, 1971.

Harrison, Robert Pogue. *The Body of Beatrice*. Baltimore: Johns Hopkins University Press, 1988.

———. *Forests: The Shadow of Civilization*. Chicago: University of Chicago Press, 1992.

Harvey, David. *A Companion to Marx's Capital*. 2nd ed. London: Verso Books, 2013.

Haug, Wolfgang Fritz. "Philosophizing with Marx, Gramsci, and Brecht." *Boundary 2* 34, no. 3 (2007): 143–60.

Hawkins, Peter S. *Dante's Testaments: Essays in Scriptural Imagination*. Stanford, CA: Stanford University Press, 1999.

———. *Dante: A Brief History*. Malden, MA: Blackwell Publishing, 2006.

Hayek, Friedrich A. *The Road to Serfdom*. Chicago: University of Chicago Press, 1944.

———. *Phenomenology of Spirit* (1807). Translated by A. V. Miller (Oxford: Oxford University Press, 1977.

———. *Lehre von der Religion und Kunst: von dem Standpuncte des Glaubens aus beurtheilt*. Leipzig: Otto Wigand, 1842.

———. *Lectures on the History of Philosophy*, vol. 2. Translated by E. S. Haldane and Frances Simson. London: Routledge and Kegan Paul, 1894.

———. *Elements of the Philosophy of Right*. Translated by T. M. Knox. Oxford: Clarendon Press, 1942.

———. *Lectures on the Philosophy of History* (1837). Translated by John Sibree. New York: Dover Publications, 1956.

———. *Lectures on the History of Philosophy: The Lectures of 1825–1826*. Edited by Robert Brown. Berkeley: University of California Press, 1990.

———. *Early Theological Writings*. Translated by T. M. Knox. University of Chicago, 1996.

Heine, Heinrich. *Lutetia: Berichte über Politik, Kunst und Volksleben*. Hamburg: Hoffmann und Campe, 1855.

Heinrich, Michael. *An Introduction to the Three Volumes of Karl Marx's Capital*. Translated by Alexander Locascio. New York: Monthly Review Press, 2004.

———. *Karl Marx and the Birth of Modern Society: The Life of Marx and the Development of His Work*. Translated by Alexander Locascio. New York: Monthly Review Press, 2019. Online at Libcom.org.

Henderson, W. O. *The Life of Friedrich Engels*. London: Routledge, 1976.

Hibbert, Christopher. *Florence: The Biography of a City*. New York: Penguin Books, 1993.

Hicks, Stephen R. C. *Explaining Postmodernism: Skepticism and Socialism from Rousseau to Foucault. Expanded*. Tempe, AZ: Scholargy Publishing, 2004.

Himmelfarb, Gertrude. *The Idea of Poverty: England in the Early Industrial Age*. New York: Vintage Books, 1985.

Hobsbawm, Eric. *The Age of Capital: 1848–1875*. London: Weidenfeld & Nicolson, 1975. Repr. Barnes and Noble, 1996.

———. *The Age of Empire: 1875–1914*. London: Weidenfeld & Nicolson, 1987; New York: Pantheon Books, 1987.

———. *The Age of Extremes: The Short Twentieth Century, 1914–1991*. London: Abacus Books, 1995.

———. *The Age of Revolution: 1789–1848*. London: Weidenfeld & Nicolson, 1962; repr. New York: Vintage Books, 1996.

———. *How to Change the World: Tales of Marx and Marxism*. New Haven, CT: Yale University Press, 2011.

Hollander, Robert. *Allegory in Dante's "Commedia"*. Princeton, NJ: Princeton University Press, 1969.

———. *Dante: A Life in Works*. New Haven, CT: Yale University Press, 2001.

———. *Dante: A Life*. New York: Farrar, Straus and Giroux, 2021.

Holloway, John and Sol Picciotto, eds. *State and Capital: A Marxist Debate*. London: E. Arnold, 1978.

Holmes, Leslie. *Communism: A Very Short Introduction*. Oxford: Oxford University Press, 2009.

Homer, Sean. *Frederic Jameson: Marxism Hermeneutics Postmodernism*. London: Routledge, 1998.

Hook, Sidney. "Speaking of Books: Karl Marx's Second Coming." *The New York Times Book Review*, May 22, 1966, 2, 44–45. https://www.nytimes.com/1966/05/22/archives/speaking-of-books-karl-marxs-second-coming-karl-marxs-second-coming.html.

Hunt, Tristram. *Engels: A Revolutionary Life*. New York: W.W. Norton, 2009.

Institute of Marxism-Leninism. *Reminiscences of Marx and Engels*. Moscow: Foreign Language Publishing House, 1956.

Jacoff, Rachel, ed. *The Cambridge Companion to Dante*. 2nd ed. Cambridge: Cambridge University Press, 2007.

Jameson, Fredric. *Postmodernism, or, The Cultural Logic of Late Capitalism*. Durham, NC: Duke University Press, 1991.

Jessop, Bob. *The Capitalist State: Marxist Theories and Methods*. New York: NYU Press, 1982.

———. *Intellectuals*. New York: Harper & Row, 1988.

———. *Modern Times: The World from the Twenties to the Nineties*. New York: Harper & Row, 1983.

———. *Birth of The Modern: World Society, 1815–1830*. New York: HarperCollins, 1991.

Jones, Gareth Stedman. *Karl Marx: Greatness and Illusion*. Cambridge, MA: The Belknap Press of Harvard University Press, 2016.

———. *Karl Marx: Greatness and Illusion*. London: Vintage, 2017.

Kain, Philip J. *Hegel and Right: A Study of the Philosophy of Right*. Albany: SUNY Press, 2018.

Kamenka, Eugene. *The Ethical Foundations of Marxism*. 2nd ed. New York: St. Martin's Press, 1972.

Kamenka, Eugene, ed. *The Portable Karl Marx*. New York: Penguin, 1985.

Kaufmann, Walter. *Tragedy and Philosophy*. New York: Doubleday, 1968.

———. *Hegel: A Reinterpretation*. Notre Dame, IN: University of Notre Dame Press, 1978.

———. *From Shakespeare to Existentialism: An Original Study*. Princeton, NJ: Princeton University Press, 1980.

———. *Goethe, Kant, and Hegel*. New Brunswick, NJ: Transaction Publishers, 1998.

Kaufmann, Walter, and James Hughes. *The Future of the Humanities: Teaching Art, Religion, Philosophy, Literature and History*. London: Routledge, 1995.

Kengor, Paul. *The Devil and Karl Marx: Communism's Long March of Death, Deception, and Infiltration*. Gastonia, NC: TAN Books, 2020.

Kierkegaard, Søren. *Philosophical Fragments*. Translated by David F. Swenson and Howard V. Hong. Princeton, NJ: Princeton University Press, 1985.

Kołakowski, Leszek. *Main Currents of Marxism*, vol. 1. Oxford: Clarendon Press, 1978.

Konstan, David. *The Origin of Sin: Greece and Rome, Early Judaism and Christianity*. New York: Bloomsbury Academic, 2022.

Kotkin, Stephen. *Stalin*, vol. 1: *Paradoxes of Power, 1878–1928*. New York: Penguin Books, 2015.

———. *Stalin, Vol. II: Waiting for Hitler, 1929–1941*. New York: Penguin Books, 2017.

Kreeft, Peter. *Summa of the Summa*. San Francisco: Ignatius Press, 1990.

Kroeger, A. E. "The Difference between the Dialectic Method of Hegel and the Synthetic Method of Kante and Fichte." *Journal of Speculative Philosophy* 6, no. 2 (1872): 184–87.

Krylov, Boris. "Preface." In *Karl Marx and Friederich Engels on Literature and Art*, 15–37. Moscow: Progress Publishers, 1976.

Kung, Hans. *Christianity: Essence, History, and Future*. New York: Continuum Publishing, 1995.

———. *Great Christian Thinkers: From the Early Church through the Middle Ages*. New York: Continuum, 1999.

LaCapra, Dominick. *Rethinking Intellectual History: Texts, Contexts, Language*. Ithaca, NY: Cornell University Press, 1983.

Lamb, Peter. *Marx and Engels' "Communist Manifesto": A Reader's Guide*. London: Bloomsbury Academic, 2015.

Lambert, Andrew. *The Crimean War: British Grand Strategy against Russia, 1853–56*. London: Routledge, 2011.

Lansing, Richard. *From Image to Idea: A Study of the Simile in Dante's "Commedia"*. Ravenna: Longo Editore, 1977.

Lansing, Richard, ed. *The Dante Encyclopedia*. New York: Garland Publishing, 2000.

Lasker, I., and S. W. Ryasanskaya. *Marx Engels Selected Correspondence*. Moscow: Progress Publishers, 1975.

Ledbetter, James, ed. *Dispatches for the New York Tribune: Selected Journalism of Karl Marx*. London: Penguin Classics, 2007.

Lee, Hermione. *Biography: A Very Short Introduction*. Oxford: Oxford University Press, 2009.

Lenin, V. I. "What Is to Be Done?" In *Lenin: Selected Works*, vol. 1. Moscow: Progress Publishers, 1963.

Leopold, David. *The Young Karl Marx: German Philosophy, Modern Politics, and Human Flourishing*. Cambridge: Cambridge University Press, 2007.

Lesser, Wendy. *The Life Below Ground*. Boston: Faber and Faber, 1987.

Liang, Qiao, and Wang Xiangsui. *Unrestricted War: China's Master Plan to Destroy America*. Brattleboro, VT: Echo Point Books and Media, 1999.

Liddell, H. G., and R. Scott. *Greek-English Lexicon, Abridged: The Little Liddell*. Oxford: Clarendon Press, 2007.

Liebknecht, Wilhelm. *Karl Marx: Biographical Memoirs*. London: Swan Sonnenschein, 1901.

———. *Karl Marx: Biographical Memoirs*. New York: Greenwood Press, 1968.

Lohmeier, Matthew. *Irresistible Revolution: Marxism's Goal of Conquest & the Unmaking of the American Military*. Self-Published: Matthew Lohmeier, 2021.

Löwith, Karl. *Meaning in History*. Chicago: University of Chicago Press, 1949.

———. *From Hegel to Nietzsche: The Revolution in Nineteenth-Century Thought*. Translated by David E. Green. New York: Columbia University Press, 1964.

Lukács, Georg. *History and Class Consciousness: Studies in Marxist Dialectics*. Cambridge, MA: MIT Press, 1971.

Lyotard, Jean-François. *The Postmodern Condition: A Report on Knowledge*. Translated by Geoff Bennington and Brian Massumi. Minneapolis: University of Minnesota Press, 1984.

———. *The Postmodern Explained: Correspondence 1982–1985*. Minneapolis: University of Minnesota Press, 1997.

MacCulloch, John A. *The Harrowing of Hell: A Comparative Study of an Early Christian Doctrine*. Edinburgh: T&T Clark, 1930.

MacIntyre, Alasdair. *Marxism: An Interpretation*. London: SCM Press, 1953.

———. *Marxism and Christianity*. South Bend, IN: University of Notre Dame Press, 1984.

———. *Whose Justice? Which Rationality?* South Bend, IN: University of Notre Dame Press, 1988.

———. *Three Rival Versions of Moral Enquiry: Encyclopaedia, Genealogy, and Tradition*. South Bend, IN: University of Notre Dame Press, 1990.

———. *A Short History of Ethics*. 2nd ed. South Bend, IN: University of Notre Dame Press, 1998.

———. *The MacIntyre Reader.* Edited by Kelvin Knight. South Bend, IN: University of Notre Dame Press, 1998.

———. *Dependent Rational Animals: Why Human Beings Need the Virtues*. Chicago: Open Court, 1999.

———. *Ethics and Politics Selected Essays*, vol. 2. South Bend, IN: University of Notre Dame Press, 2006.

———. *After Virtue: A Study in Moral Theory*. 3rd ed. South Bend, IN: University of Notre Dame Press, 2007.

———. *Ethics in the Conflicts of Modernity: An Essay on Desire, Practical Reasoning, and Narrative*. Cambridge: Cambridge University Press, 2016.

Malia, Martin. *The Soviet Tragedy: A History of Socialism in Russia, 1917–1991*. New York: Free Press, 1994.

Manzoli, Gregory. *Dante's Political Legacy: Power and Activism*. Cambridge: Cambridge University Press, 2020.

Marlowe, Christopher. *Doctor Faustus*. Edited by David Bevington and Eric Rasmussen. Manchester: Manchester University Press, 1993.

Marsden, Richard. *The Nature of Capital: Marx after Foucault*. London: Routledge, 1999.

Marx, Karl. *A Contribution to the Critique of Political Economy*. Moscow: Progress Publishers, 1859.

———. *Das Kapital: Kritik der politischen Ökonomie*. Hamburg: Otto Meissner, 1867.

———. *Capital: A Critique of Political Economy*, vol. 1: *The Process of Production of Capital*. Translated by Samuel Moore and Edward Aveling. Moscow: Progress Publishers, 1887.

———. *Capital: A Critique of Political Economy*. New York: Modern Library, 1906.

———. *The Letters of Karl Marx*. Edited by Helen Macfarlane. New York: International Publishers, 1934.

———. *Karl Marx: Selected Works in Two Volumes*, vol. 1. Moscow: Foreign Languages Publishing House, 1951.

———. *Theories of Surplus Value*. Translated by Terrell Carver. London: Lawrence & Wishart, 1951.

———. *Economic and Philosophic Manuscripts of 1844* Translated by Martin Milligan. New York: International Publishers, 1964.

———. *The Eighteenth Brumaire of Louis Bonaparte*. Translated by Samuel Moore and Edward Aveling. New York: International Publishers, 1964.

———. *Letters to Friends and Family*. Edited by C. P. Magill. New York: International Publishers, 1965.

———. *Writings of the Young Marx on Philosophy and Society*. Translated by Lloyd D. Easton. Garden City, NY: Doubleday, 1967.

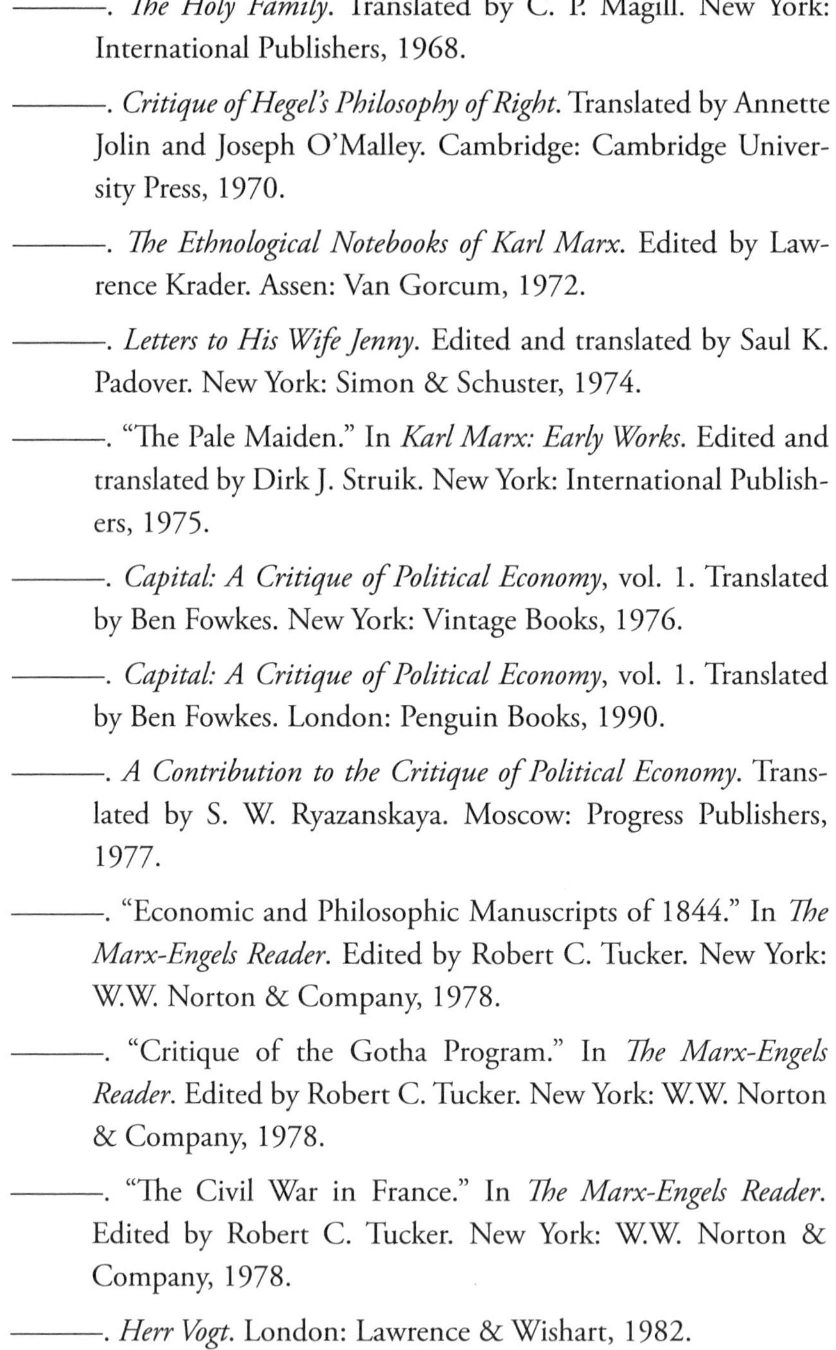

———. *The Holy Family*. Translated by C. P. Magill. New York: International Publishers, 1968.

———. *Critique of Hegel's Philosophy of Right*. Translated by Annette Jolin and Joseph O'Malley. Cambridge: Cambridge University Press, 1970.

———. *The Ethnological Notebooks of Karl Marx*. Edited by Lawrence Krader. Assen: Van Gorcum, 1972.

———. *Letters to His Wife Jenny*. Edited and translated by Saul K. Padover. New York: Simon & Schuster, 1974.

———. "The Pale Maiden." In *Karl Marx: Early Works*. Edited and translated by Dirk J. Struik. New York: International Publishers, 1975.

———. *Capital: A Critique of Political Economy*, vol. 1. Translated by Ben Fowkes. New York: Vintage Books, 1976.

———. *Capital: A Critique of Political Economy*, vol. 1. Translated by Ben Fowkes. London: Penguin Books, 1990.

———. *A Contribution to the Critique of Political Economy*. Translated by S. W. Ryazanskaya. Moscow: Progress Publishers, 1977.

———. "Economic and Philosophic Manuscripts of 1844." In *The Marx-Engels Reader*. Edited by Robert C. Tucker. New York: W.W. Norton & Company, 1978.

———. "Critique of the Gotha Program." In *The Marx-Engels Reader*. Edited by Robert C. Tucker. New York: W.W. Norton & Company, 1978.

———. "The Civil War in France." In *The Marx-Engels Reader*. Edited by Robert C. Tucker. New York: W.W. Norton & Company, 1978.

———. *Herr Vogt*. London: Lawrence & Wishart, 1982.

———. "Inaugural Address of the International Working Men's Association." In *Marx/Engels Collected Works*, vol. 20. London: Lawrence & Wishart, 1985.

———. *Capital, Volume 1*. London: Penguin Classics, 1990.

———. *Early Writings*. Translated Rodney Livingstone and Gregor Benton. London: Penguin Books, 1992.

———. *Selected Writings*. Edited by Lawrence H. Simon. Indianapolis: Hackett Publishing, 1994.

———. *The Eighteenth Brumaire of Louis Bonaparte*, Translated by Terrell Carver. Oxford: Oxford University Press, 1996.

———. "The Class Struggles in France." In *Karl Marx: Selected Writings*. Edited by David McLellan. Oxford: Oxford University Press, 2000.

———. "Debates on the Law on Thefts of Wood." In *Karl Marx: Selected Writings*. Edited by David McLellan. Oxford: Oxford University Press, 2000.

———. "The Eighteenth Brumaire of Louis Bonaparte." In *Karl Marx: Selected Writings*. Edited by David McLellan. Oxford: Oxford University Press, 2000.

Marx, Karl, and Friedrich Engels. *Marx/Engels Collected Works* (*MECW*). 50 vols. Moscow: Progress Publishers; London: Lawrence and Wishart; and New York: International Publishers, 1975–2004.

———. *The German Ideology*. Moscow: Marx-Engels Institute, 1932.

———. *Werke*, vol. 13. Berlin: Dietz Verlag, 1964.

———. *The German Ideology*. Translated by Clemens Dutt, W. Lough, and C. P. Magill. Moscow: Progress Publishers, 1964.

———. *The Communist Manifesto*. Translated by Samuel Moore. London: Penguin Books, 1967.

———. *The Critique of the Gotha Programme*. Moscow: Foreign Language Publishing House, 1959.

———. *The German Ideology*. Translated by Joseph Fracchia and Gregor Benton. New York: International Publishers, 1970.

———. *The German Ideology*. Edited by C. J. Arthur. New York: International Publishers, 1970.

———. *The German Ideology*. Moscow: Progress Publishers, 1975.

———. *The German Ideology*. Amherst, NY: Prometheus, 1998.

———. *Marx/Engels Gesamtausgabe*. Berlin: Dietz Verlag, 1975.

———. *Karl Marx and Frederick Engels: Selected Letters*. Moscow: Progress Publishers, 1975.

———. *The Communist Manifesto*. New York: Pocket Books, 2002.

———. *Karl Marx and Frederick Engels on Literature and Art*. A Selection of Writings Edited by Lee Baxandall and Stefan Morawski, with an Introduction by Stefan Morawski. Revised Edition with Supplementary Notes, Index and a new Introduction, "A Short History of Marxist Aesthetics," by Macdonald Daly. Nottingham, UK: Critical, Cultural and Communications Press, 2006.

———. *The Communist Manifesto*. Philadelphia: Brandywine Studio Press, 2008.

———. *The Communist Manifesto*. New York: Bloomsbury, 2015.

McCaffrey, Michael J. *Dante and Modern Culture*. Princeton, NJ: Princeton University Press, 2010.

McCool, Gerald A. *The Neo-Thomists*. Milwaukee: Marquette University Press, 1994.

McGrogan, Manus. *Who the Hell Is Karl Marx? And What Are His Theories All About?* La Vergne, TN: Bowden & Brazil Ltd, 2020.

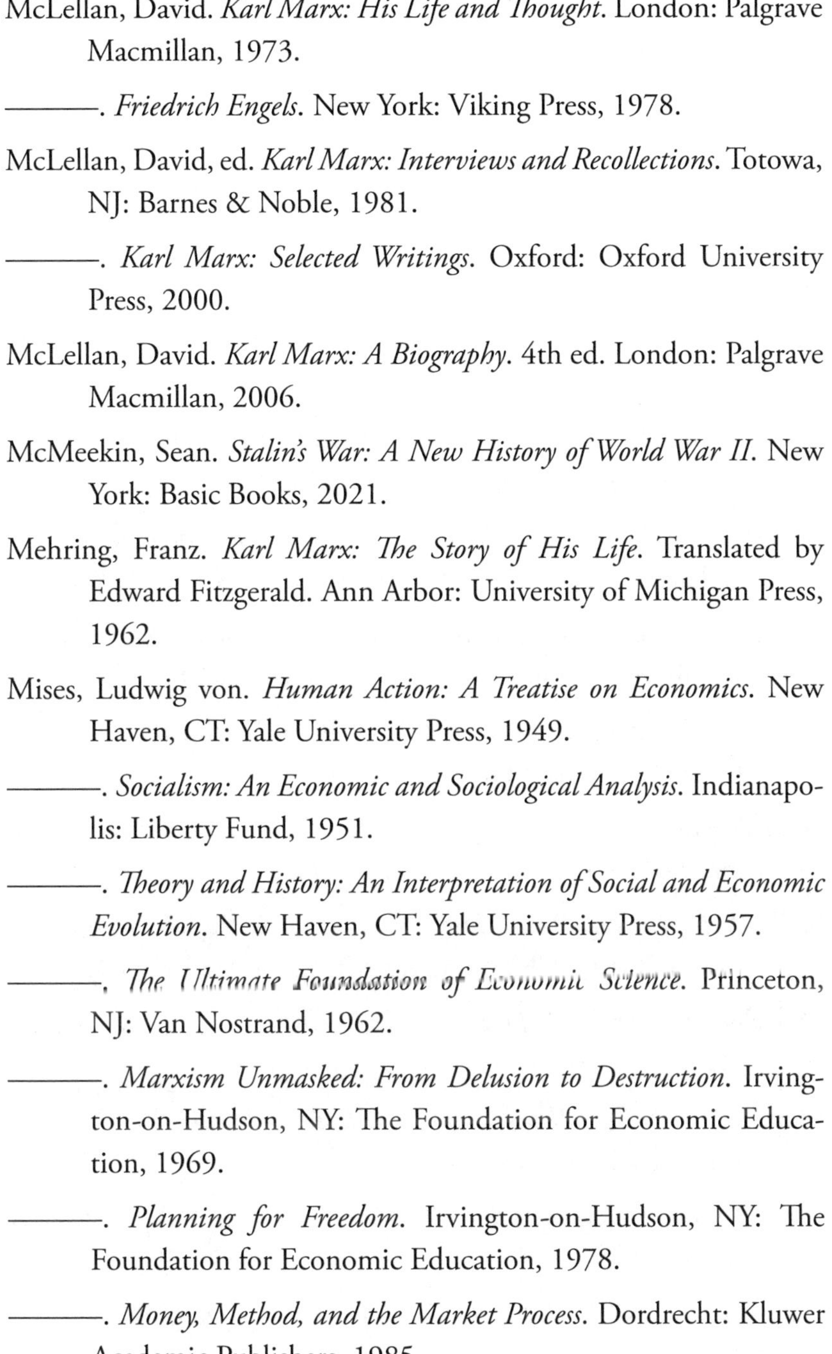

McLellan, David. *Karl Marx: His Life and Thought*. London: Palgrave Macmillan, 1973.

———. *Friedrich Engels*. New York: Viking Press, 1978.

McLellan, David, ed. *Karl Marx: Interviews and Recollections*. Totowa, NJ: Barnes & Noble, 1981.

———. *Karl Marx: Selected Writings*. Oxford: Oxford University Press, 2000.

McLellan, David. *Karl Marx: A Biography*. 4th ed. London: Palgrave Macmillan, 2006.

McMeekin, Sean. *Stalin's War: A New History of World War II*. New York: Basic Books, 2021.

Mehring, Franz. *Karl Marx: The Story of His Life*. Translated by Edward Fitzgerald. Ann Arbor: University of Michigan Press, 1962.

Mises, Ludwig von. *Human Action: A Treatise on Economics*. New Haven, CT: Yale University Press, 1949.

———. *Socialism: An Economic and Sociological Analysis*. Indianapolis: Liberty Fund, 1951.

———. *Theory and History: An Interpretation of Social and Economic Evolution*. New Haven, CT: Yale University Press, 1957.

———. *The Ultimate Foundation of Economic Science*. Princeton, NJ: Van Nostrand, 1962.

———. *Marxism Unmasked: From Delusion to Destruction*. Irvington-on-Hudson, NY: The Foundation for Economic Education, 1969.

———. *Planning for Freedom*. Irvington-on-Hudson, NY: The Foundation for Economic Education, 1978.

———. *Money, Method, and the Market Process*. Dordrecht: Kluwer Academic Publishers, 1985.

———. *Economic Policy: Thoughts for Today and Tomorrow*. Irvington-on-Hudson, NY: The Foundation for Economic Education, 1990.

———. *Interventionism: An Economic Analysis*. Irvington-on-Hudson, NY: Foundation for Economic Education, 1998.

Muller, Herbert J. *The Spirit of Tragedy*. New York: Alfred A. Knopf, 1956.

Musto, Marcello, ed. *Marx's Capital After 150 Years*. New York: Routledge, 2019.

Musto, Marcello. *The Last Years of Karl Marx: An Intellectual Biography*. Stanford, CA: Stanford University Press, 2020.

Musto, Marcello, ed. *Karl Marx's Writings on Alienation*. Cham, Switzerland: Palgrave Macmillan, 2021.

———. *The Marx Revival: Key Concepts and New Interpretations*. Cambridge: Cambridge University Press, 2020.

Newman, Michael. *Socialism: A Very Short Introduction*. Oxford: Oxford University Press, 2020.

Nicolaievsky, Boris, and Otto Maenchen-Helfen. *Karl Marx: Man and Fighter*. London: Routledge, 1936.

Noll, Mark. *Turning Points: Decisive Moments in the History of Christianity*. 3rd ed. Grand Rapids, MI: Baker Academic, 2012.

Oldridge, Darren. *The Devil: A Very Short Introduction*. Oxford: Oxford University Press, 2012.

Oliphint, K. Scott. *Thomas Aquinas: Great Thinkers*. Phillipsburg, NJ: P&R Publishing, 2017.

Orwell, George. *Nineteen Eighty-Four*. Cutchogue, NY: Buccaneer Books, 1949.

Padover, Saul K. *Karl Marx: An Intimate Biography*. New York: McGraw-Hill, 1978.

Padover, Saul K., ed. *The Letters of Karl Marx*. Englewood Cliffs, NJ: Prentice-Hall, 1979.

Parkes, Henry Bamford. *Marxism: An Autopsy*. Methuen, MA: The Riverside Press, 1939.

Payne, Robert. *Lenin: A Biography*. New York: Simon & Schuster, 1964.

———. *Marx: A Biography*. New York: Simon & Schuster, 1968.

Payne, Robert, ed. *The Unknown Karl Marx: Documents Concerning Karl Marx*. New York: New York University Press, 1971.

Pertile, Lino. *Dante's Plurilingualism: Authority, Knowledge, Subjectivity*. Toronto: University of Toronto Press, 2010.

Pesch, Heinrich. *Ethics and the National Economy*. Translated by Rupert J. Ederer. Bellingham, WA: Center for Economic Personalism, 2004.

Pieper, Josef. *The Silence of St. Thomas*. Translated by Daniel O'Connor. South Bend, IN: St. Augustine's Press.

Pipes, Richard. *The Russian Revolution*. New York: Knopf, 1990.

———. *Communism: A History*. New York: Modern Library, 2001.

Popper, Karl R. *The Open Society and Its Enemies*. London: Routledge, 1945.

———. *The Open Society and Its Enemies*. Princeton, NJ: Princeton University Press, 2013.

Pound, Ezra. *The Spirit of Romance*. London: J. M. Dent & Sons, 1910.

———. *The Cantos of Ezra Pound*. New York: New Directions Publishing, 1990.

Prawer, Siegbert S. *Karl Marx and World Literature*. London: Verso, 1976.

Proudhon, Pierre-Joseph. *De la Justice dans la Revolution et dans l'Eglise*. Paris: Librairie de Garnier Frères, Paris, 1858.

———. *The General Idea of the Revolution in the Nineteenth Century*. New York: Haskell House Publishers, 1969.

Ratzinger, Joseph Cardinal (Pope Benedict XVI). *Truth and Tolerance: Christian Belief and World Religions*. Translated by Henry Taylor. San Francisco: Ignatius Press, 2004.

Ricoeur, Paul. *Time and Narrative*, vol. 3. Translated by Kathleen Blamey and David Pellauer. Chicago: University of Chicago Press, 1984.

Roberts, William Clare. *Marx's Inferno: The Political Theory of Capital.* Princeton, NJ: Princeton University Press, 2018.

Rockmore, Tom. *Fichte, Marx and the German Philosophical Tradition*. Carbondale: Southern Illinois University Press, 1980.

Rosemann, Philipp W. *Understanding Scholastic Thought with Foucault*. New York: Palgrave Macmillan, 1999.

Rosenthal, Margaret F. *Dante and Modern Narrative*. New York: Palgrave Macmillan, 2007.

Rothbard, Murray. *Man, Economy, and State with Power and Market.* Auburn, AL: Ludwig von Mises Institute, 2009.

Rousseau, Jean-Jacques. *The Social Contract.* Translated by G. D. H. Cole. London: J. M. Dent & Sons, 1923.

———. *The Social Contract.* Translated by Maurice Cranston. London: Penguin Classics, 1968.

Royal, Robert. *Dante Alighieri: Divine Comedy and the Making of a World.* Washington, DC: Catholic University of America Press, 2014.

Russell, Bertrand. *A History of Western Philosophy*. New York: Touchstone, Simon & Schuster, 1972.

Russell, Jeffrey Burton. *Mephistopheles: The Devil in the Modern World*. Ithaca, NY: Cornell University Press, 1990.

———. *The Prince of Darkness: Radical Evil and the Power of Good in History*. Ithaca, NY: Cornell University Press, 1992.

Sandyford, Fergus. "What Thomism Has to Do with Marx." Review of *Ethics in the Conflict of Modernity: An Essay on Desire, Practical Reasoning, and Narrative* by Alasdair MacIntyre. *Tradistae*, May 1, 2020. https://tradistae.wordpress.com/2020/05/01/thomism-marxism/.

Schama, Simon. *Citizens: A Chronicle of the French Revolution*. New York: Vintage, 1989.

Schumpeter, Joseph A. *Capitalism, Socialism, and Democracy*. New York: Harper, 1942.

Scruton, Roger. *Fools, Frauds and Firebrands: Thinkers of the New Left*. London: Bloomsbury Continuum, 2015.

Seery, John Evan. *Political Returns: Irony in Politics and Theory from Plato to the Antinuclear Movement*. Boulder, CO: Westview Press, 1990.

Seigel, Jerrold. *Marx's Fate: The Shape of a Life*. Princeton, NJ: Princeton University Press, 1978.

Shakespeare, William. "Hamlet." In *The Complete Works of William Shakespeare*. Edited by W. J. Craig. London: Oxford University Press, 1914.

———. *Hamlet*. Edited by Harold Jenkins. London: Methuen, 1982.

———. *Hamlet, Prince of Denmark*. Edited by Philip Edwards. Cambridge: Cambridge University Press, 1985.

———. *Hamlet*. Edited by Ann Thompson and Neil Taylor. London: Bloomsbury, 2006.

Shattuck, Roger. *Forbidden Knowledge: From Prometheus to Pornography*. New York: St. Martin's Press, 1996.

Simon, Lawrence H., ed. *Karl Marx: Selected Writings*. Indianapolis: Hackett Publishing Company, Inc., 1994.

Simpson, James. *Who Was Karl Marx? The Men, the Motives and the Menace behind Today's Rampaging American Left*. Baltimore: Simpson Publishing, 2021.

Singer, Peter. *Marx: A Very Short Introduction*. Oxford: Oxford University Press, 1980.

Singleton, Charles. *Journey to Beatrice*. Cambridge, MA: Harvard University Press, 1958.

Skousen, Mark. *The Making of Modern Economics: The Lives and Ideas of the Great Thinkers*. 3rd ed. New York: M.E. Sharpe, 2015.

Skousen, Paul B. *The Naked Socialist*. Salt Lake City: Izzard Ink Publishing, 2016.

Skousen, W. Cleon. *The Naked Communist*. Salt Lake City: Izzard Ink Publishing, 2017.

Smith, Adam. *A Theory of Moral Sentiments*. 2 vols. London: W. Strahan and T. Cadell, 1790.

———. *An Inquiry into the Nature and Causes of the Wealth of Nations*. London: W. Strahan and T. Cadell, 1776.

———. *The Works of Adam Smith with an Account of His Life and Writings*. Edited by Dugald Stewart. London: Printed for T. Cadell and W. Davies, 1812.

Smith, Steven B. *Hegel's Critique of Liberalism: Rights in Context*. Chicago: University of Chicago Press, 1989.

Solomon, Robert C. *In the Spirit of Hegel*. New York: Oxford University Press, 1985.

Solzhenitsyn, Aleksandr. *The Gulag Archipelago*. London: Vintage, 2018.

———. *The Gulag Archipelago*. Translated by Thomas P. Whitney. New York: Harper & Row, 1974.

Spargo, John. *The Marx He Knew*. Chicago: C.H. Kerr & Co., 1909.

Spengler, Oswald. *The Decline of the West*, vol. 1. New York: Alfred A. Knopf, 1926.

Sperber, Jonathan. *Karl Marx: A Nineteenth-Century Life*. New York: Liveright, 2013.

Starnino, Rita. *Dante's Influence on Modern Existentialism*. Oxford: Oxford University Press, 2010.

Steiner, George. *The Death of Tragedy*. New Haven, CT: Yale University Press, 1996.

Strathern, Paul. *Spinoza in 90 Minutes*. Chicago: Ivan R. Dee, 1998.

Strauss, D. F. *Life of Jesus Critically Examined.* London: Swan Sonnenschein & Co., 1902.

Tawney, R. H. *Religion and the Rise of Capitalism*. New York: Harcourt, Brace & World, 1926.

Taylor, Charles. *Hegel.* Cambridge: Cambridge University Press, 1977.

Thayer, Joseph H. *Greek–English Lexicon of the New Testament*. New York: Harper & Brothers, 1889.

The Holy Bible. English Standard Version. Wheaton, IL: Crossway Bibles, 2001.

Thomas, Paul. *Karl Marx and the Anarchists*. London: Routledge & Kegan Paul, 1980.

Thompson, E. P. *The Making of the English Working Class*. New York: Vintage Books, 1966.

Torrance, Robert. *The Spiritual Quest*. Berkeley: University of California Press, 1997.

Treitschke, Heinrich von. *Deutsche Geschichte im Neunzehnten Jahrhundert*, vol. 5. Leipzig: S. Hirzel, 1905.

Trevelyan, George Macaulay. *British History in the Nineteenth Century (1782–1901)*. London: Longmans, Green, and Co., 1922.

Trueman, Carl R. *Histories and Fallacies: Problems Faced in the Writing of History*. Wheaton, IL: Crossway, 2010.

———. *Revelations: Stalin's War and the Legacy of Totalitarianism*. New York: Basic Books, 2019.

———. *The Rise and Triumph of the Modern Self: Cultural Amnesia, Expressive Individualism, and the Road to Sexual Revolution*. Wheaton, IL: Crossway, 2020.

Tucker, Robert. *Philosophy and Myth in Karl Marx*. Cambridge: Cambridge University Press. 1961.

———. *The Marxian Revolutionary Idea*. New York: Norton, 1972.

Turner, Alice K. *The History of Hell*. San Diego: Harcourt Brace & Company, 1995.

Unamuno, Miguel de. *The Tragic Sense of Life*. Translated by W. J. Payton. New York: Dover Publications, 2000.

Varoufakis, Yanis. *Talking to My Daughter About the Economy: A Brief History of Capitalism*. New York: Farrar, Straus and Giroux, 2017.

———. *Technofeudalism: What Killed Capitalism*. London: Verso, 2023.

Vidal, Matt, Tony Smith, Tomás Rotta, and Paul Pew, eds. *The Oxford Handbook of Karl Marx*. Oxford: Oxford University Press, 2018.

———. *The Oxford Handbook of Karl Marx*. New York: Oxford University Press, 2019.

Voegelin, Eric. *The New Science of Politics: An Introduction.* Chicago: University of Chicago Press, 1952.

———. *The Drama of Humanity and Other Miscellaneous Papers: 1939–1985*. Columbia: University of Missouri Press, 1996.

———. *The Collected Works of Eric Voegelin*, vol. 33: *The Drama of Humanity and Other Miscellaneous Papers: 1939–1985*. Edited by Gilbert Weiss and William Petropulos. Baton Rouge: Louisiana State University Press, 2004.

Walls, Jerry L., ed. *The Oxford Handbook of Eschatology*. Oxford: Oxford University Press, 2009.

Webb, Sidney, and Beatrice Webb. *The History of Trade Unionism*. London: Longmans, Green and Co., 1894.

Weber, Timothy. *Living in the Shadow of the Second Coming*. Chicago: University of Chicago Press, 1979.

Wessell, Leonard P. *Karl Marx, Romantic Irony, and the Proletariat: The Mythopoetic Origins of Marxism*. Baton Rouge: Louisiana State University Press, 1979.

Wheen, Francis. *Karl Marx: A Life*. New York: W.W. Norton & Company, 2000.

———. *Das Kapital: A Biography*. New York: Grove Press, 2007.

White, Hayden. *Metahistory: The Historical Imagination in Nineteenth-Century Europe*. Baltimore: Johns Hopkins University Press, 1975.

White, James D. *Karl Marx and the Intellectual Origins of Dialectical Materialism*. Basingstoke, UK: Macmillan, 1996.

Wilson, A. N. *The Victorians*. New York: W.W. Norton & Co., 2003.

———. *Dante in Love*. London: Atlantic Books, 2011.

———. *Goethe His Faustian Life*. London: Bloomsbury, 2024.

Wolff, Richard D. *Understanding Marxism*. New York: Democracy at Work, 2019.

Wolff, Robert Paul. *Moneybags Must Be So Lucky: On the Literary Structure of Capital*. Amherst, MA: University of Massachusetts Press, 1988.

Wurmbrand, Richard. *Marx and Satan*. Bartlesville, OK: Living Sacrifice Book Company, 1986.

———. *Was Karl Marx a Satanist? A Documented Study*. 3rd ed. Torrence, CA: The Richard Wurmbrand Foundation, 2022.

Zuboff, Shoshana. *The Age of Surveillance Capitalism: The Fight for a Human Future at the New Frontier of Power*. New York: PublicAffairs, 2019.

Articles and Chapters

Baldissone, Riccardo. "Materialism: A Caring Obituary." *Anthropocenes – Human, Inhuman, Posthuman* 2, no. 1 (2022). https://doi.org/10.16997/ahip.1056.

Bauer, Bruno. "Die eigenthümlichen Lehren des Christenthums rein biblisch dargestellt. Erster Band." *Jahrbücher für wissenschaftliche Kritik* (1834): 196–200.

Betancourt, Mauricio. "'To Struggle!' A Review of Marcello Musto's *The Last Years of Karl Marx*." *Monthly Review* (2024): 58–61.

Boyer, Eric. "Reviewed Work(s): *Karl Marx: An Intellectual Biography*, by Rolf Hosfeld." *The Historian* 77, no. 3 (2015): 611–12.

Brown, Theodore M., and Elizabeth Fee. "Friedrich Engels: Businessman and Revolutionary." *American Journal of Public Health* 94, no. 12 (2004). https://www.ncbi.nlm.nih.gov/pmc/articles/PMC1447947/.

Brown, Wendy. "Foreword." In Karl Marx, *Capital*, vol. 1. Translated by Paul Reitter. Edited by Paul North and Paul Reitter, xv–xxx. Princeton, NJ: Princeton University Press, 2024.

Camara, Helder. "What Would Saint Thomas Aquinas, the Aristotle Commentator, Do If Faced with Karl Marx?" *Journal of Religion* 58 (1978): S174–S182. https://doi.org/10.1086/jr.58.41575989.

Carver, Terrell. "Making Marx Marx." *Journal of Sociology* 17, no. 1 (2017):10–27.https://doi.org/10.1177/1468795X17691388.

Clark, Brett, John Bellamy Foster, and Stefano B. Longo. "Metabolic Rifts and the Ecological Crisis." In *The Oxford Handbook of Karl Marx*. Edited by Paul Prew, Tomas Rotta, Tony Smith, and Matt Vidal, 651–58. Oxford: Oxford University Press, 2019.

Cooper, Lane. "Reviewed Works: Dante and Aquinas by Philip H. Wicksteed." *The Philosophical Review* 23, no. 4 (1914): 443–51.

Critchley, Peter. "Dante and Marx." *Being and Place*, October 26, 2016. https://pcritchley2.wixsite.com/beingandplace/post/2016/10/26/dante-and-marx.

Daigle-Williamson, Marsha. "Dante: A New Pauline Apostle?" *Christian Scholar's Review* 40, no. 1 (2010): 39–58.

Eagleton, Terry. "Disappearing Acts." Review of *Thomas Aquinas: A Portrait* by Denys Turner. *London Review of Books* 35, no. 23 (2013). https://www.lrb.co.uk/the-paper/v35/n23/terry-eagleton/disappearing-acts.

Feaver, George. "Popper and Marxism." *Studies in Comparative Communism* 4, no. 3–4 (1971): 3–24.

Gabriel, Mary. "Love and Capital: Karl Marx's Marriage Was Decidedly Not Marxian." *The Daily Beast*, September 21,

2011. https://www.thedailybeast.com/love-and-capital-karl-marxs-marriage-was-decidedlynot-marxian.

Gatto, Alfredo. "The Life and Works of Joachim of Fiore—An Overview." In *A Companion to Joachim of Fiore*. Edited by Matthias Riedl, 13–34. Leiden: Brill, 2017.

Gattuso, Reina. "The Struggling Vineyards That Helped Inspire Karl Marx's Communism." *Atlas Obscura*, June 13, 2019. https://www.atlasobscura.com/articles/where-was-karl-marx-born.

Grosse, Sven. "Thomas Aquinas, Bonaventure, and the Critiques of Joachimist Topics from the Fourth Lateran Council to Dante." In *A Companion to Joachim of Fiore*. Edited by Matthias Riedl, 144–89. Leiden: Brill, 2018.

Hart, David Bentley. "Death, Final Judgment, and the Meaning of Life." In *The Oxford Handbook of Eschatology*. Edited by Jerry L. Walls. Oxford: Oxford University Press, 2009.

Harvey, David. "History versus Theory: A Commentary on Marx's Method in Capital." *Historical Materialism* 20, no. 2 (2012): 3–38. http://dx.doi.org/10.1163/1569206X-12341241.

Havenga, Marthinus J. "Sizwe Bansi Is Dead: On Politics, Performance and Identity." *Stellenbosch Theological Journal* 10, no. 1 (2024): 1–17. http://dx.doi.org/10.17570/stj.2024.v10n1.m2.

Heller, Henry. "Class and Class Struggle." In *The Oxford Handbook of Karl Marx*. Edited by Paul Prew, Tomas Rotta, Tony Smith, and Matt Vidal, 57–76. Oxford: Oxford University Press, 2019.

Hess, Moses. *Briefwechsel*. Amsterdam: Mouton & Co., 1959.

Himmelfarb, Gertrude. "Let Marx Be Marx." *The New Republic* 223, no. 4 (2000): 34–41.

Hobsbawm, Eric. "Marx and History." *Diogenes* 32, no. 125 (1984): 103–14. https://doi.org/10.1177/039219218403212507.

Huster, Sam. "The Nature and Consequence of Karl Marx's Skin Disease." *British Journal of Dermatology* 158, no. 1 (2008): 1–3. https://doi.org/10.1111/j.1365-2133.2007.08282.x.

Hwang, Haewon. "Introduction." In *London's Underground Spaces: Representing the Victorian City, 1840–1915*. Edinburgh: Edinburgh University Press, 2013.

Jiang, Hongsheng. "Frederick Engels on Socialist Literature." *International Critical Thought* 15, no. 1 (2025): 15–37.

Joseph, Smitha, and Bibin Thomas. "Marxist Aesthetics: Summary of 'Preface to Marx and Engels on Literature and Art'." *Critical Aesthetics 2015* (blog), July 15, 2015. https://criticalaesthetics2015.wordpress.com/2015/07/16/marxist-aesthetics-summary-of-preface-to-marx-and-engels-on-literature-and-art/.

Kamenka, Eugene, ed. "Introduction." In *The Portable Karl Marx*, xi–xlv. New York: Penguin, 1985.

King, Martin Luther, Jr. "Can a Christian Be a Communist?" Sermon delivered at Dexter Avenue Baptist Church, Montgomery, Alabama, September 1953. In *The Papers of Martin Luther King, Jr.*, vol. 6. Edited by Clayborne Carson. Berkeley: University of California Press, 2007.

Knight, Kelvin. "After Tradition? Heidegger or MacIntyre, Aristotle and Marx." *Analyse & Kritik* 30, no. 1 (2008): 33–52.

Levin, Michael. "From Marxism to Communism: A Review Article." *Europe-Asia Studies* 49, no. 8 (1997): 1519–25.

Linebaugh, Peter. "Thefts of Wood: The Manifestation of State and Class Exploitation." *Crime and Social Justice* 6 (1976): 5–16.

Liu, Xunqian. "A Comparative Study of Marx Biographies by Mehring and Riazanov." *Philosophy Study* 13, no. 12 (2023): 558–63.

Lobkowicz, N. "Karl Marx's Attitude Toward Religion." *The Review of Politics* 26, no. 3 (1964): 319–52. https://doi.org/10.1017/S0034670500005076.

Mahlburg, Kurt. "Karl Marx's Obsession with the Devil." *Intellectual Takeout*, July 10, 2024. https://intellectualtakeout.org/2024/07/karl-marxs-obsession-the-devil.

Marx, Karl. "A Contribution to the Critique of Hegel's *Philosophy of Right*." In *Karl Marx: Early Writings*. Edited and translated by T. B. Bottomore. New York: McGraw-Hill, 1964.

———. "Doctoral Thesis: Difference between the Democritean and Epicurean Philosophy of Nature." In *Karl Marx: Early Writings*. Edited and translated by T. B. Bottomore. New York: McGraw-Hill, 1964.

———. "On the Jewish Question." In *Karl Marx: Early Writings*. Edited and translated by T. B. Bottomore. New York: McGraw-Hill, 1964.

———. "Invocation of One in Despair." In *Karl Marx: Early Works*. Edited and translated by Dirk J. Struik. New York: International Publishers, 1975.

———. "On the Jewish Question." In *Early Political Writings*, edited and translated by Joseph O'Malley. Cambridge: Cambridge University Press, 1994.

———. "A Contribution to the Critique of Hegel's Philosophy of Right: Introduction." In *Marx: Early Political Writings*. Edited by Joseph J. O'Malley. Cambridge: Cambridge University Press, 1994.

McCallum, Pamela. "Questions of Haunting: Jacques Derrida's *Specters of Marx* and Raymond Williams's Questions of Haunting:

Jacques Derrida's *Specters of Marx* and Raymond William's *Modern Tragedy Modern Tragedy*." *Mosaic* 40, no. 2 (2007): 231–44.

McCarey, Peter, and Mariarosa Cardines. "The Harrowing of Hell and Resurrection: Dante's Inferno and Blok's Dvenadtsat." *The Slavonic and Eastern European Review* 63, no. 3 (1985): 337–48.

McCarthy, Anna. "Marx, Memory, Loss: Ways of Reading Capital." *Social Text* 34, no. 3 (2016): 105–25.

McGinn, Bernard. *Apocalyptic Spirituality*. New York: Paulist Press, 1979.

———. "Introduction: Joachim of Fiore in the History of Western Culture." In *A Companion to Joachim of Fiore*. Edited by Matthias Riedl, 1–19. Leiden: Brill, 2018.

Mearsheimer, John. "Why the Ukraine Crisis Is the West's Fault." *Foreign Affairs* 93, no. 5 (2014): 77–89.

Mohler, Albert. "Karl Marx Meets the Devil: A Conversation with Historian Paul Kengor." *Thinking in Public*, February 21, 2021. https://albertmohler.com/2021/02/10/paul-kengor/.

Morrissey, C. S. "Marxist Found Way to Faith via Aquinas' Arguments." *The B.C. Catholic. Voices*, July 18, 2018. https://bccatholic.ca/voices/c-s-morrissey/marxist-found-way-to-faith-via-aquinas-arguments.

O'Rahilly, Alfred. "Aquinas versus Marx. Part II: The So-Called Labour Theory of Value." *Studies: An Irish Quarterly Review* 31, no. 124 (1942): 493–503.

Paden, Roger. "Marx's Critique of Utopian Socialists." *Journal of Utopian Studies* 13, no. 2 (2002): 67–91. https://libcom.org/article/marxs-critique-utopian-socialists.

Peterson, G. Paul. "Karl Marx and His Vision of Salvation: The Natural Law and Private Property." *Review of Social Economy* 52, no. 3 (1994): 377–90. https://doi.org/10.1080/758539244.

Popowich, Sam. "Did Marx Base *Capital* on Dante's *Inferno*?" *International Socialism* 157 (2018). https://isj.org.uk/did-marx-base-capital-on-dantes-inferno/.

Prawer, S. S. "Karl Marx and Poetry." *Modern Language Review* 65, no. 1 (1970): 1–19.

Preda, Adrian Eugen. "The Dictatorship of the Proletariat Road to Totalitarianism and a New Class." *Annals of the Constantin Brancusi University of Targu Jiu-Letters & Social Sciences Series* 2 (2023): 147–53.

Prew, Paul, Tomas Rotta, Tony Smith, and Matt Vidal. "The Enduring Relevance of Karl Marx." In *The Oxford Handbook of Karl Marx*. Edited by Paul Prew, Tomas Rotta, Tony Smith, and Matt Vidal, 3–34. Oxford: Oxford University Press, 2019.

Prinz, Arthur M. "Background and Ulterior Motives of Marx's 'Preface' of 1859." *Journal of the History of Ideas* 30, no. 3 (1969): 437–50. https://doi.org/10.2307/2708568.

Rayman, John. "Review: Reading Marx, by Slavoj Zizek, Frank Ruda, and Agon Hamza." *Contemporary Political Theory* 19 (2020): 179–182.

Recht, Linus. "Understanding Karl Marx's Critique of Hegel's *Philosophy of Right*." *Science & Society* 85, no. 4 (2021): 474–500. https://doi.org/10.1521/siso.2021.85.4.474.

Rehman, Jan. "Ideology as Alienated Socialization." In *The Oxford Handbook of Karl Marx*. Edited by Paul Prew, Tomas Rotta, Tony Smith, and Matt Vidal, 111–28. Oxford: Oxford University Press, 2019.

Roberts, Deborah. "Family, Life, and Revolution." *International Socialist Review* 83. https://isreview.org/issue/83/family-life-and-revolution/index.html.

Roberts, William Clare. "Marx in Hell: The Critique of Political Economy as Katabasis." *Critical Sociology* 31, no. 1–2 (2005): 39–55.

Rothbard, Murray N. "Karl Marx: Communist as Religious Eschatologist." *The Review of Austrian Economics* 4, no. 1 (1990): 123–79. https://cdn.mises.org/rae4_1_5_2.pdf.

———. "Karl Marx as Religious Eschatologist." *Mises Daily*, October 9, 2009, 2. https://mises.org/mises-daily/karl-marx-religious-eschatologist.

Rubel, Maximilien. "Les Cahiers d'études de Karl Marx I (1840–1853)." *International Review of Social History* 2, no. 3 (1957): 392–420. https://www.jstor.org/stable/44581370.

———. "Les Cahiers d'études de Karl Marx II (1853–1856)." *International Review of Social History* 5, no. 1 (1860): 39–76. https://www.jstor.org/stable/44581427.

Ryan, Kiernan. "Hamlet and Marxism." *Shakespeare Quarterly* 39, no. 1 (1988): 27–48.

Sachs, Jeffrey D. "The West's False Narrative about Russia and China." *JDS*, August 22, 2022. https://www.jeffsachs.org/newspaper-articles/h29g9k7l7fymxp39yhzwxc5f72ancr.

Sayers, Sean. "What Is Marxism?" *International Critical Thought* 11, no. 3 (2021): 377–88. https://doi.org/10.1080/21598282.2021.1965493.

Schwarzwalder, Jr., Robert F. "Marx's New Religion." *Journal of the Evangelical Theological Society* 62, no. 4 (2019): 775–88.

Singh, Kaninika. "An Analysis of Shakespeare's Hamlet through Terry Eagleton's Conception of Tragedy." *International Journal of English Literature and Social Sciences* 8, no. 4 (2023): 207–13.

Steiner, George. "'Tragedy,' Reconsidered." *New Literary History* 35, no. 1 (2004): 1–15.

Stirner, Max. "Review of Bruno Bauer's *Trumpet of the Last Judgment*, 1842. *The Anarchist Library*." https://theanarchistlibrary.org/library/max-stirner-review-of-bruno-bauers-trumpet-of-the-last-judgment (accessed April 15, 2025).

Swain, Dan. "Alienation, or Why Capitalism Is Bad for Us." In *The Oxford Handbook of Karl Marx*. Edited by Paul Prew, Tomas Rotta, Tony Smith, and Matt Vidal, 361–68. Oxford: Oxford University Press, 2019.

Tabak, Mehmet. "Marx's Theory of Proletarian Dictatorship Revisited." *Science and Society* 64, no. 3 (2000): 333–56.

Triggiano, Tonia Bernardi. "Dante's Heavenly Lessons: Educative Economy in the Paradiso." *Essays in Medieval Studies* 26 (2010): 15–26.

Welsh, John. Review of David Harvey, *A Companion to Marx's Capital. Capital & Class* 38, no. 3 (2014): 648–50. http://dx.doi.org/10.1177/0309816814551268n.

Wendling, Amy E. "Technology and Science." In *The Marx Revival: Key Concepts and New Interpretations*. Edited by Marcello Musto, 363–75. Cambridge: Cambridge University Press; 2020.

Wetzel, James. "A Meditation on Hell: Lessons from Dante." *Modern Theology* 18, no. 3 (2002): 375–94.

Wheeler, Melissa A. "The Paradox of Virtue Signaling." *Psychology Today Canada*, September 6, 2021. https://www.psychologytoday.com/ca/blog/ethically-speaking/202109/the-paradox-of-virtue-signaling.

Zeldin, Mary-Barbara. "The Religious Nature of Russian Marxism." *Journal for the Scientific Study of Religion* 8, no. 1 (1969): 100–11.

Endnotes

1 "Marx to Engels, March 5, 1852," in *Karl Marx & Frederick Engels Collected Works* [henceforth, *MECW*], vol. 7 (London: Lawrence & Wishart, 1977). For a list of all fifty volumes, see https://www.marxists.org/archive/marx/works/cw/ (accessed April 16, 2025). All "marxists.org" references are to the Marxists Internet Archive (MIA).

2 Thomas Carlyle, *On Heroes* (N.P.: East India Publishing Company, 2023), 81.

3 *Hamartia* is the main Greek term used in the New Testament for "sin." Aristotle is famous for using the term in his *Poetics* to refer to a tragic character's flaw. Its original meaning was to "miss the mark" (as in archery). It later gained a strong moral dimension and was used to relay the later Judeo-Christian conception of sin in the New Testament. For a thorough treatment of *hamartia* and of sin, please see David Konstan, *The Origin of Sin: Greece and Rome, Early Judaism and Christianity* (New York: Bloomsbury Academic, 2022). See note 125.

4 Karl Marx, *The German Ideology*, trans. Joseph Fracchia and Gregor Benton (New York: International Publishers, 1970).

5 Carlyle, *On Heroes*, 83.

6 A. N. Wilson, *Dante in Love* (London: Atlantic Books, 2011), 227.

7 The protests following George Floyd's death in May 2020 led to widespread unrest across numerous US cities, resulting in extensive property damage, clashes with law enforcement, and the destruction of businesses and public buildings. While many demonstrations remained peaceful, significant portions devolved into violence and destruction. Demonstrations occurred in cities nationwide, including Minneapolis, New York, Los Angeles, Atlanta, and Chicago. In Minneapolis alone, approximately 1,500 properties were damaged, with nearly 100 completely destroyed; Jon Jackson, "More Than 1,500 Minnesota Businesses Damaged in George Floyd Protests, Expect to Take Years to Rebuild," Newsweek, June, 1, 2021, https://www.newsweek.com/businesses-year-after-floyd-1596610 (accessed April 15, 2025). The damage was unprecedented, with insured losses estimated between $1 billion and $2 billion, making it one of the most expensive civil disturbances in US history; Jennifer A. Kingson, "Exclusive: $1 billion-plus riot damage is most expensive in insurance history," *Axios*, September 16, 2020, https://www.axios.com/2020/09/16/riots-cost-property-damage (accessed April 15, 2025). Among the most infamous events of the unrest was the burning of the Minneapolis Police Department's Third Precinct on May 28, 2020.

Protesters stormed the building, forcing officers to evacuate before setting it ablaze. The flames engulfing the precinct became a defining image of the riots, symbolizing not only the anger but also the lawlessness that took hold; "George Floyd: Protesters set Minneapolis police station ablaze," BBC, May 29, 2020, https://www.bbc.com/news/world-us-canada-52844192 (accessed April 15, 2025). Throughout the protests, numerous police officers were injured in the clashes, though exact figures vary depending on the city and incident. In many areas, law enforcement was overwhelmed as rioters looted businesses, set fires, and caused chaos with little immediate consequence. Despite the scale of destruction, legal consequences were inconsistent. While some individuals faced prosecution, many incidents went largely unpunished. In Minneapolis, one man was sentenced to four years in prison and ordered to pay $12 million in restitution for his role in setting the Third Precinct ablaze. However, the widespread nature of the riots made it nearly impossible for authorities to pursue every case of property destruction, looting, or assault. Businesses were left devastated, with many small and minority-owned establishments destroyed beyond repair, further deepening the economic damage caused by the unrest. The events of 2020 were not simply about racial injustice or police reform but revealed something deeper—an eruption of frustration fueled by years of academic post-Marxist thought that reframed revolution through identity politics. This was not the class struggle Marx envisioned but rather an ideological movement driven by resentment, nihilism, and revisionism. The destruction left in the wake of these protests was unlike anything seen in modern American history, and despite the staggering damages, there was little reckoning for those responsible. Instead, the demonstrations continued to be framed as part of a righteous struggle, even as they left entire communities shattered. The specter of Karl Marx still lingers, shaping movements in distorted forms through modern media and academia, where the spirit of revolution remains detached from any coherent or constructive vision.

8 Manus McGrogan, *Who the Hell Is Karl Marx? And What Are His Theories All About?* (La Vergne, TN: Bowden & Brazil Ltd, 2020), 107: "Some 150 years after the publication of *Das Kapital*, most countries still live under capitalism, and continue to endure its gross inequality and rampant oppression." A more cynical interpretation would be more accurate. George Floyd was not murdered. He died of a fentanyl overdose. The trial was a sham. Black Lives Matter (BLM) is a grift. The riots were used by the Left to gain political power. Rioters used the opportunity to enrich themselves. Nothing changed except the further destruction of minority urban communities, but the Democrats gained the presidency, and the leaders of BLM bought new homes in multiple cities. All was rationalized using left-wing racial ideology. The postmodernist Left replaced Marxist class struggle with racial and gender struggle, but it retains the same paradigm of group conflict. By abandoning economic issues, the cultural Left is able to ally with wealthy elites

who can continue the status quo exploitation of the working class. Pushing cultural Marxism in this way has no effect on BlackRock's bottom line.

9 "The specter of communism haunts Europe; we must prepare for the coming storm with unshakable resolve." Marx to Engels, February 29, 1848, *MECW*, vol. 6. In *Specters of Marx*, Derrida positions Marx as a kind of Dante. According to Rachel Falconer, *Hell in Contemporary Literature: Western Descent Narratives since 1945* (Edinburgh: Edinburgh University Press, 2005), 38, "Derrida conjures a 'spirit of Marxism,' disembodied from the dogma of party and proletariat, that yet retains something of Marx's original project." She says: "Allowing this spectre to survive in us, Derrida suggests, we can continue to resist capitalism's most egregious injustices, particularly the prejudicial nature of current international law" (38). Finally, "for Derrida, then, the descent journey to 'speak with ghosts' becomes a form of active political dissent rather than a passive relinquishing of desire and voice to Dis" (38).

10 Karl Marx and Friedrich Engels, *The Communist Manifesto* (1848). For an English translation of the original German, see, for example, the version published in New York by Pocket Books in 2002; in Philadelphia by Brandywine Studio Press in 2008, and in New York by Bloomsbury in 2015. An online version is available from https://www.marxists.org/archive/marx/works/download/pdf/Manifesto.pdf (accessed April 15, 2025).

11 Sean Sayers, "What Is Marxism?" *International Critical Thought* 11, no. 3 (2021): 377–88, at 377, https://doi.org/10.1080/21598282.2021.196549.

12 The "narrow views" I refer to are precisely the kind of reductive economic determinism found in Marx's framework. Unlike the classical thinkers—Smith, Aristotle, Aquinas—who acknowledged inequality as a persistent reality of the human condition, Marx collapsed all social relations into class struggle and material exploitation. For him, economics became a zero-sum game: if one gains, another must lose. There is no room in his framework for creative expansion of wealth or the moral dimensions of work, generosity, or human dignity. This cynical flattening of economic and social life into pure antagonism is what I mean by a "narrow view." My book explores the irony—the tragedy—that while Marxism sets out to critique what it sees as narrow, exploitative worldviews, it ends up substituting its own form of reductionism: one that dismisses virtue, ignores spiritual meaning, and denies the possibility of shared prosperity. It trades theological hope for political fatalism. This point is central to my argument, because it contrasts Marx's inverted eschatology with the more expansive vision of classical and religious thought—where inequality is not erased, but human life retains dignity, meaning, and moral purpose despite it.

13 Terry Eagleton, *Tragedy* (New Haven, CT: Yale University Press, 2020), 3.

14 Wilson, *Dante in Love*, 305.

15 Eagleton, *Tragedy*, 180.

16 Ibid., 169.

17 "The great modern masters of suspicion, at any rate, tended to assume that any accurate etiology of religion would lead back ultimately to pathetic human longing for some sort of compensation beyond the grave, some final reward or release, and that the religious impulse in human culture is principally from a deeply felt social and psychological need to make the burdens of our existence more tolerable and the fear of death less agonizing." David Bentley Hart, "Death, Final Judgment, and the Meaning of Life," in *The Oxford Handbook of Eschatology*, ed. Jerry L. Walls (Oxford: Oxford University Press, 2009), 476–90, at 478.

18 "Consider your origins: you were not made to live as brutes, but to follow virtue and knowledge." Dante, *Inferno*, Canto XXVI, line 118. For a brief discussion of Marx and Dante, see Sam Popowich, "Did Marx base Capital on Dante's Inferno?" *International Socialism* 157, January 9, 2018, https://isj.org.uk/did-marx-base-capital-on-dantes-inferno/.

19 *Inferno*, Canto XXVI, lines 119–20. All translations, unless stated otherwise, are from the Digital Dante project at Columbia University available at https://digitaldante.columbia.edu/commento-baroliniano (accessed April 15, 2025).

20 Moses Hess, Letter to Karl Marx, November 19, 1844, in *Der Briefwechsel zwischen F. Engels und K. Marx*, vol. 1 (Stuttgart, 1913).

21 In defining tragedy, we usually think in terms of "the everyday sense of the word in mind. Grieving over the death of a child, a mining disaster or the gradual disintegration of a human mind is not confined to any particular culture. Sorrow and despair constitute a lingua franca. Yet tragedy in the artistic sense is a highly specific affair. There is no close equivalent of it, for example, in the traditional art of China, India or Japan." Eagleton, *Tragedy*, 1.

22 Karl Marx, *Economic and Philosophic Manuscripts of 1844*, trans. Martin Milligan (New York: International Publishers, 1964).

23 Dante himself was deeply influenced by the eschatological visions of Joachim of Fiore (c. 1135–1202), an Italian theologian and founder of the monastic order of San Giovanni in Fiore, who proposed a tripartite division of historical epochs, each corresponding to a person of the Holy Trinity: the Age of the Father (Old Testament), the Age of the Son (New Testament), and the forthcoming Age of the Holy Spirit—a future era characterized by spiritual enlightenment and ecclesiastical renewal. See Alfredo Gatto, "The Life and Works of Joachim of Fiore—An Overview," in *A Companion to Joachim of Fiore*, ed. Matthias Riedl (Leiden: Brill, 2017), 13–34.

24 "There is tragedy as a metaphor of revolution, given that in neither case can there be a glorious birth without a violent breaking; and there is the philosophical sense of the term, for which liberty assumes its highest form in a voluntary deference to authority. Freedom and necessity are shown to be identical, as they are in the very form of the work of art." Eagleton, *Tragedy*, 177.

25 Paul Ricoeur, *Time and Narrative*, vol. 3, trans. Kathleen Blamey and David Pellauer (Chicago: University of Chicago Press, 1984), 246.

26 Hans-Georg Gadamer, *Truth and Method*, trans. Joel Weinsheimer and Donald G. Marshall (London: Bloomsbury Academic, 2004), 278.

27 William Shakespeare, *Hamlet*, ed. Harold Jenkins (London: Methuen, 1982), Act 3, Scene 2, lines 20–24.

28 "One might well complain that if tragedy demands no more of human beings than to be human, then it demands too little of them, and we purchase our tragic stature on the cheap. Is tragedy really just some sentimental humanism, as eighteenth-century domestic tragedians like John Lillo seem to have believed? Are we all equal in the eyes of Zeus? To claim that anyone can be a tragic subject, however, is not to suggest that every tragedy is as poignant or momentous as every other. The loss of a child may be more catastrophic than the loss of a fortune, or even than the loss of one's mind. The point is just that there are now no distinctions in principle between potential candidates for such cataclysms. Tragedy returns as everyday experience at exactly the point when a democratic age has grown wary of it as ritual, mystery, heroism, fatalism and absolute truth." Terry Eagleton, *Sweet Violence: The Idea of the Tragic* (Oxford: Blackwell, 2003).

29 "According to my dictionary, tragedy is 'a dramatic composition of serious or somber character, with an unhappy ending.' Add that this ending is usually death, and the popular conception is complete. It is too simple a conception, of course. It is the complement of the naïve assumption that when a Hollywood beauty gets her man her success is a happy ending; whereas any mature person knows that this is actually a beginning, most likely of another mess. The tragic vision of life is the antithesis of the popular vision, or lack of vision, in its comprehension of complexity, incongruity, and paradox." Herbert J. Muller, *The Spirit of Tragedy* (New York: Alfred A. Knopf, 1956), 140.

30 "In the *Divine Comedy*, he embodied all the strains of medieval life, the contradictions of its spirituality and its worldliness, the extremities of its hopes and its fears. A devout believer, dedicated to the supreme business of salvation, he was also a patriotic Italian and fierce political partisan, engrossed in the business of this life. A humble believer, often quaking in fear, he was also a proud individualist who made himself the hero of his supernatural epic, elected himself to the company of the greatest poets of antiquity, and introduced himself into heaven, even into the presence of God." Muller, *The Spirit of Tragedy*, 140.

31 "From the nineteenth century to the present day, Marx's writings on the capitalist economy, reinforced by psychoanalytic accounts of subjectivity, have contributed to the valence of the idea that a descent into Hell can be the means of recovering—or discovering—selfhood. But these more recent frameworks have combined with earlier literary and religious models of katabatic narrative to produce the notion of a self made ethical by its encounter with the underworld." Falconer, *Hell in Contemporary Literature*, 304.

32 Stephen Greenblatt, *Hamlet in Purgatory* (Princeton, NJ: Princeton University Press, 2001), 50.

33 Eagleton, *Tragedy*, 83.

34 William Shakespeare, *The Tragedy of Hamlet, Prince of Denmark*, ed. George Richard Hibbard (Oxford: Oxford University Press, 1987), 3.1.30. All further references to Hamlet refer to this edition unless otherwise noted.

35 "Karl Marx is one of the most influential writers in history. Despite repeated obituaries proclaiming the death of Marxism . . . Since his death in 1883, Marx's lasting global impact has been greater and wider than of any other figure in the humanities or social sciences. His theoretical contributions have had profound impacts on politics, sociology, economics, political economy, history, philosophy, geography, anthropology, law, ecology, literary studies, media studies, and even management studies . . . In the realms of social theory and in politics, Marx's ideas have spread to virtually every corner of the planet." Paul Prew, Tomas Rotta, Tony Smith, and Matt Vidal, "The Enduring Relevance of Karl Marx," in *The Oxford Handbook of Karl Marx*, ed. Paul Prew, Tomas Rotta, Tony Smith, and Matt Vidal (Oxford: Oxford University Press, 2019), 3–34, at 3.

36 "Dante's purpose corresponds to Paul's self-described mission in Acts 26:18: 'To open [people's] eyes so that they may turn from darkness to light . . . so that they may receive forgiveness of sins and a place among those who are sanctified by faith.'" Marsha Daigle-Williamson, "Dante: A New Pauline Apostle?" *Christian Scholars Review* 40, no. 1 (2015): 39–58, at 40.

37 "The case has been advanced that like so many of the traditional modes of religious discourse, apocalypticism has not so much disappeared from the scene as it has adopted a variety of secular disguises. Over the past few decades there have been serious attempts to understand the theological significance of apocalypticism in Jewish and Christian thought. One could point first of all to the studies of the biblical and intertestamental origins of apocalypticism, which have enriched us with new and better editions of texts, a wealth of detailed investigations, and a number of broad treatments that attempt to define the essence of the genre 'apocalypse' and to determine the content of apocalypticism. . . . German theologians like Ernst Käsemann, Wolfhart Pannenberg, Karl Rahner, and Jürgen Moltmann have devoted much thought to the theological significance of apocalypticism. Swiss theologian H. Mottu has recently studied the implications for contemporary theology of Joachim of Fiore, the foremost medieval apocalyptic author. Without attempting to describe or evaluate these critical retrievals of apocalypticism, their very existence should be enough to make our point: Apocalypticism remains a serious concern for contemporary Christianity." Bernard McGinn, *Apocalyptic Spirituality* (New York: Paulist Press, 1979), 2–3.

38 Harold Bloom, ed. *Hamlet* (New York: Chelsea House Publishers, 1990), 109.

39 "He loved Dante and Goethe as much as Shakespeare, even though he knew enough of the Weltanschauung of the two former writers to be sure that in

important respects it conflicted with his own. Here the historical imagination had also to be called into play: Marx had nothing but scorn for those of his contemporaries who condemned Klopstock's poetry, for instance, because the attitudes to life implicit in it differed from neo-Hegelian attitudes." Siegbert Prawer, *Karl Marx and World Literature* (London: Verso, 1976), 419.

40 Dante, *Inferno*, Canto I. See David McClellan, *Karl Marx: His Life and Thought* (London: Palgrave Macmillan, 1973), 9, 15. For the meaning of "midway on our life's journey," see James Wetzel, "A Meditation on Hell: Lessons from Dante," *Modern Theology* 18, no. 3 (2002): 375–94, at 380.

41 To further illuminate the tragic psychology of Hamlet, one can trace a profound continuity between Dante's metaphysical imagination and Shakespeare's portrayal of paralyzing introspection. As one literary critic observes, Dante offers perhaps the most precise articulation of the very quality in Hamlet's mind that justifies the play's tragic trajectory. In *Inferno*, Canto II, lines 37–47, Dante writes: "And like the man who unwills what he willed, / And for new thoughts doth change his first intent, / So that he cannot anywhere begin, / Such became I upon that slope obscure, / Because with thinking I consumed resolve, / That was so ready at the setting out." Bloom, *Hamlet*, 33. Similarly, in Purgatorio Canto V, lines 16–18, Dante captures the self-thwarting nature of excessive reflection: "For always he in whom one thought buds forth / Out of another farther puts the goal, / For each has only force to mar the other." Bloom, *Hamlet*, 33. Dante, the metaphysician, defines not only the structure of such a mind but also its outcome: indecision and failure. The connection to Hamlet becomes especially striking when read alongside the soliloquy: "Thus conscience [i.e., consciousness] doth make cowards of us all: / And thus the native hue of resolution / Is sicklied o'er with the pale cast of thought, / And enterprises of great pith and moment / With this regard their currents turn awry / And lose the name of action." Shakespeare, *Hamlet*, Act 3, Scene 1. Such lines reflect what Dante so precisely intuited centuries before Shakespeare: the introspective mind, through endless rumination, becomes an obstacle to itself. Hamlet's self-awareness only deepens his paralysis. Like Dante's wanderer on the "slope obscure," he unwills what he once willed—turning action into abstraction, and conviction into hesitation.

42 Johann Wolfgang van Goethe, *Poetry and Truth*, vol. 1, trans. John Oxenford (London: H.G. Bohn, 1848), vii.

43 "The linking of Virgil with tragedy (*Inf.* XX, 113) and of Dante with comedy (*Inf.* XVI, 128; XXI, 2) not only associates Virgil with the lofty style and Dante with the low style intrinsic in his choice of the vernacular for his poem but, as few currently acknowledge, associates the Aeneid with a tragic plot, one that ends unhappily, and the Comedy with a 'comic.'" Eagleton, *Sweet Violence*, 119.

44 Aristotle defines tragedy as "an imitation of an action that is serious, complete, and of a certain magnitude; in language embellished with each kind of artistic ornament, the several kinds being found in separate parts of the play; in the form of action, not of narrative; through pity and fear effecting the proper purgation of these emotions." See Aristotle, *Poetics*, trans. S. H. Butcher (London: Macmillan & Co., 1902), 23.

45 For the etymology of *katabasis*, *Gehenna*, *inferna*, *Hohle* (German: cave), and *hell*, see Falconer, *Hell in Contemporary Literature*, 19.

46 On the role and authority of Virgil, see Wetzel, "A Meditation on Hell," 375–94.

47 William Clare Roberts, *Marx's Inferno: The Political Theory of Capital* (Princeton, NJ: Princeton University Press, 2018). Peter Critchley, "Dante and Marx," *Being and Place*, October 26, 2016, https://pcritchley2.wixsite.com/beingandplace/post/2016/10/26/dante-and-marx.

48 "Although, inserting throughout references ranging from Aeschylus to Herodotus, Homer to Aristotle, Plutarch to Lucretius, Shakespeare to Darwin, Cervantes to Dickens, and more, Marx displays an erudition and reading that vastly exceeds these primary sources. Nevertheless, because Engels bases his 1884 *The Origin of the Family, Private Property, and the State* on Marx's excerpts from Morgan's book, these are the best known of his ethnological notes." Eduardo Cadava and Sara Nadal-Melsio, *Politically Red* (Cambridge, MA: MIT Press, 2023), 318.

49 The word *katabasis* derives from the Greek *kata* ("down") and *basis* ("walking or stepping"), a downward journey, a descent. Its opposite, *anabasis*, refers to an ascent. However, *katabasis* has transcended its literal meaning, taking on profound metaphorical dimensions over the centuries, becoming a rich symbol for journeys into physical, emotional, moral, or spiritual depths. See note 46.

50 "Dante's Hell is an elaborate reworking of the Hades from Virgil's *Aeneid*, which, in turn, draws many of its central tropes from Homer's portrayal in the *Odyssey*. When one examines this direct citational lineage—Homer to Virgil to Dante—there emerges a tendential pattern that produces certain expectations of Marx's *katabasis*." William Clare, Roberts, "Marx in Hell: The Critique of Political Economy as Katabasis," *Critical Sociology* 31, no. 1–2 (2005): 39–55, at 43.

51 There are two schools of thought on Hell according to Falconer. The Katabatic school comprises "those who think something of value can be gained from the descent to Hell." Examples include classical tradition and Judeo-Christian tradition; Job and Jonah; Saul/Paul on the road to Damascus; and Augustine's Confessions. The Secular school comprises those "for whom the infernal journey is valueless . . . the secular fall-out from the Judeo-Christian belief in Hell; according to this view, Hell is a place of eternal torment but without orthodox religion's traditional rationale for the suffering." See Falconer, *Hell in Contemporary Literature*, 32.

52 "Our Virgil holds out to his readers this prospect of founding a fourth empire—to succeed the Roman, Catholic, and modern empires—the counter-empire of materiality, of revolution, of the multitude." Roberts, "Marx in Hell," 53.

53 "Respected visitors, we are ourselves authors of a tragedy, and that the finest and the best we know how to make. In fact, our whole polity has been constructed as a dramatization of a noble and perfect life; that is what we hold in truth to be the most real of tragedies." Plato, *Laws* 7.817b, cited in George Steiner, "'Tragedy,' Reconsidered," *New Literary History* 35, no. 1 (2004): 1–15, at 2.

54 Eagleton, *Tragedy*, 42.

55 For the text, see John A. MacCulloch, *The Harrowing of Hell: A Comparative Study of an Early Christian Doctrine* (Edinburgh: T&T Clark, 1930).

56 *Inferno*, Canto II, lines 28–30.

57 "The inferno is a historically determined timespace; its physical and moral topographies are constantly developing and changing. While the medieval idea of Hell as a region of punitive justice is still very much with us, modern usage of the name tends to focus on the suffering of the damned . . . Dante's Hell bears the famous inscription on its gateway: 'Justice made me'. In direct contrast, modern Hells are places of injustice where the innocent suffer." Falconer, *Hell in Contemporary Literature*, 18.

58 Alice K. Turner, *The History of Hell* (San Diego: Harcourt Brace & Company, 1995), 242. Modern writers have used the hell metaphor with great imagination in a number of ways. Ironic phantasmagoria is pervasive. Goethe's *Faust: Part Two* led to the "Night-town," or underworld brothel section of James Joyce's *Ulysses* (1922), and hence to Thomas Mann's *Doktor Faustus* (1947), William Gaddis's *The Recognitions* (1955), and Salman Rushdie's *The Satanic Verses* (1988), though this last one is more about devils than it is about hell. A straightforward journey into dangerous territory, frequently a jungle or a war zone, can also parallel an inner journey; Joseph Conrad's novel *Heart of Darkness* (1902) is a well-known example. But when Francis Ford Coppola updated it to the period and setting of the Vietnam War for his 1979 film, *Apocalypse Now*, he chose a phantasmagoric technique, which seems more natural to the post-World War II era. Joseph Heller used the same technique in *Catch-22* (1961), as did Günter Grass in *The Tin Drum* (1959), Jerz Kosinski in *The Painted Bird* (1965), and J. M. Coetzee in *The Life and Tim* (1983).

59 Eagleton, *Tragedy*, 172.

60 For more on how Dante was following the biblical use of allegory in Paul, see Wilson, *Dante in Love*, 83.

61 Paul Kengor, *The Devil and Karl Marx: Communism's Long March of Death, Deception, and Infiltration* (Gastonia, NC: TAN Books, 2020), 37.

62 See notes 4 and 136. On *hubris*, see Aristotle, *Rhetoric* II.5; on *hamartia,* see Aristotle, *Poetics* XIII; on *arete*, see Aristotle, *Nicomachean Ethics* II.6. See

also George Steiner, *The Death of Tragedy* (New Haven, CT, Yale University Press, 1996), 17–19; H. G. Liddell and R. Scott's *Greek-English Lexicon, Abridged: The Little Liddell* (Oxford: Clarendon Press, 2007).

63 Smitha Joseph and Bibin Thomas, "Marxist Aesthetics: Summary of 'Preface to Marx and Engels on Literature and Art'," *Critical Aesthetics 2015* (blog), July 15, 2015, https://criticalaesthetics2015.wordpress.com/2015/07/16/marxist-aesthetics-summary-of-preface-to-marx-and-engels-on-literature-and-art/. See also Boris Krylov, "Preface," in *Karl Marx and Friederich Engels on Literature and Art* (Moscow: Progress Publishers, 1976), 15–37.

64 Miguel de Unamuno, *The Tragic Sense of Life*, trans. W. J. Payton (New York: Dover Publications, 2000).

65 Eric Voegelin, *The Collected Works of Eric Voegelin*, vol. 33: *The Drama of Humanity and Other Miscellaneous Papers: 1939–1985*, ed. Gilbert Weiss and William Petropulos (Baton Rouge: Louisiana State University Press, 2004), 339–40, explains: "The Prometheus story to which one usually refers is that of Aeschylus. There one gets immediately the problem of deformation. The critical passage is the scene where Prometheus is being fettered to the rock. Hermes, the messenger of Zeus, is standing down there on the beach looking up, and Prometheus speaks the line 'In one word, I hate all the gods.' That is the line quoted by Marx in his doctoral thesis. But the scene goes on. After Prometheus has pronounced that line, Hermes, down on the beach, says, 'I think that is no small kind of madness'—it is like a disease. That second line was omitted by Marx. There you have the problem of disease and the magic. Berthollet in his *History of Chemistry* and then Festugière in *Hermes Trésmégiste* have presented very well the transformation of Prometheus into the light-bringer to mankind—the sense that Marx wants us to take. That is a gnostic transformation, and there are several such transformations of the Prometheus myth: from the revolt against the gods into human independence of the gods; or the story of the Fall transformed into that of the envious god against whom mankind will now, at last, sin and be perfectly happy. (What was prevented by God now can be produced by Marx. These gnostic transformations have been historically effective. It depends always which kind of Prometheus you take as an example. In the *Philebus* of Plato you find the light-bringer who brings philosophical wisdom to some select people who then transmit the wisdom. It's another Prometheus."

66 Shattuck, *Forbidden Knowledge*, 103, argues that "Faust's problem is that, as a learned doctor, in spite of his attempts to abandon that condition, he can never give himself over completely to resolute action. Thought, reflection, consciousness, scruple—they all interfere with action. At this point, it is almost impossible not to recognize that Faust stands closer to Hamlet than to Prometheus. The solvent power of thinking, of self-awareness, surfaces with Hamlet and comes increasingly to haunt literature and philosophy. The conscience-consciousness motif permeates Faust. Nietzsche had read both works attentively."

67 A further problem of definition springs from the fact that "tragedy" can have a triple meaning. Like comedy, it can refer at once to works of art, real-life events and worldviews or structures of feeling. You can be comic without being optimistic, or comic but not funny, like Dante's best-known work. As far as the art/life distinction goes, we do, after all, inherit the concept of tragedy from a social order which made less of a hard-and-fast distinction between the poetic and the historical than we do, and had no conception of the autonomously aesthetic. Indeed, it was a civilization which once based a territorial claim on a verse from the Iliad. The modern age, by contrast, distinguishes more sharply between art and life, as well as between artefacts and ways of seeing. Terry Eagleton, *Sweet Violence*, 9.

68 Contra Marx, Unamuno sees suffering as an inescapable part of being human, not something that can be eliminated: "Since life is tragedy and the tragedy is perpetual struggle, without victory or the hope of victory, life is contradiction." Miguel de Unamuno, *The Tragic Sense of Life in Men and Nations*, trans. J.E. Crawford Flitch (Mineola, NY: Dover, 1954 [1913]): 13–14.

69 Even for Hegel, the tragic sensibility is tempered by the recognition of one's finitude and particularity in the face of a higher universal—a movement toward freedom through self-negation. What grounds tragedy, for Hegel, is not only conflict, but the painful yet educative realization that our fixed identities must yield to the universal. As Charles Taylor, *Hegel* (Cambridge: Cambridge University Press, 1975), 149, explains, citing *Phenomenology of Spirit* §148: "For Hegel, a crucial factor in the education of men, in the transformation which brings them to the universal, is the fear of death. The prospect of death shakes them loose, as it were, from all the particularities of their life. Hegel uses the image here of a life which has hardened in a certain form. The menace of death then makes it that consciousness 'has been inwardly dissolved, has trembled to its depths, and everything fixed in it has quaked.' This tension recurs in Hegel's *Philosophy of Right*, where war is seen—controversially—as a force that disrupts narrow preoccupations and returns individuals to the universal embodied in the state. The tragic, in Hegel's schema, is not annihilation but a painful dialectic through which spirit rises, shaken into the truth of its impermanence."

70 "Tragedy argues an aristocracy of suffering, and excellence of pain. The point needs to be made accurately. It has nothing to do with social snobbery, with hazard, with fortuitous circumstances of priestly or regal or titled patronage, as pseudo-Marxist chatter would have it. The motives are of the essence." Steiner, "'Tragedy,' Reconsidered," 9.

71 In the final lines of *The Communist Manifesto*, Marx and Engels write that "the proletariat have nothing to lose but their chains." Here, as elsewhere, chains signify the bondage of capitalism. See Marx and Engels, *The Communist Manifesto*, 58.

72 *Paradiso*, Canto XXII, lines 55–57.

73 Daigle-Williamson, "Dante," 39: "Although in one sense, Dante's pilgrim sense represents the Everyman during this spiritual journey, Dante structures certain events, especially in the *Paradiso*, to link the pilgrim's journey experiences to Paul's life and mission. . . . Since the identity of Dante the poet overlaps with Dante the pilgrim, the link between the pilgrim and Paul necessarily implies an association between the poet and Paul. And in fact, Dante does believe he is engaged in apostolic activity as he writes his *Commedia*." She then quotes Dante's "Letter to Can Grande": "Although the literal subject of his poem is the state of souls after death, its allegorical subject is how 'man . . . in the exercise of his free will . . . is deserving of reward or punishment.' This of course is in line with Paul's teaching that at judgment 'everyone [will] receive the things done in his body, according to that he hath done, whether it be good or bad' (2 Cor 5:10)" (40).

74 Ludwig von Mises, *The Ultimate Foundation of Economic Science* (Princeton, NJ: Van Nostrand, 1962), 98.

75 Spinoza's work was placed on the Index of Forbidden Books (Index Librorum Prohibitorum) by the Catholic Church.

76 Eagleton, *Tragedy*, 106.

77 "Mainstream social science identifies capitalism as an economic system based in markets organized by free competition and spurred by the profit motive. But where is the power to make and destroy worlds in this formulation, to draw everything into its orbit, to permeate and transform every physical and psychic cell of earthly life?" (xv–xvi) "Indeed, what Marx's work forever challenged was not only capitalism's exploitative nature and commodifying effects, for which he is readily known, but the reduction of economics to markets and thus to a domain of knowledge and practice imagined to be independent of social relations, histories, laws, family forms, politics, policing, religion, language, representation, and psyche. In its place, Marx developed an understanding of political economy as the distinctive mode through which we build entire worlds through our singular cooperative powers—transforming nature, elaborating divisions of labor and organizations of ownership, producing wealth, creating ways of life, institutions, social forms, subjects, and subjectivities" (xvi). Wendy Brown, "Foreword," in Karl Marx, *Capital*, vol. 1, trans. Paul Reitter, ed. Paul North and Paul Reitter (Princeton, NJ: Princeton University Press, 2024), xv–xxx.

78 "Bart van Es sees *Hamlet* in such transitional terms, as a play 'divided between a feudal order (in which kingdoms are contested through single combat) and a modern world of Realpolitik, dominated by ambassadorial letters and secret deals. It has a ghost who suffers in medieval Catholic purgatory while his son returns from Wittenberg, the home of Luther and his new Protestant ideas. The philosopher Carl Schmitt writes of Shakespeare's hero as standing in the middle of the schism of Europe', at the crossroads between the old theology and the rise of the new nation-state." Eagleton, *Tragedy*, 70.

79 Richard D. Wolff, *Understanding Marxism* (New York: Democracy at Work, 2019), 9. Neither Marx nor Engels themselves used the term "Marxism" to describe their views; it was first employed by Marx's opponents. Indeed, as Engels reports, Marx responded to its use by some of his French would-be followers in the 1870s by saying: "Tout ce que je sais, c'est que je ne suis pas Marxiste" ("All I know is that I am not a Marxist"); Friedrich Engels, Letter to E. Bernstein, November 2, 1892, https://www.marxists.org/francais/engels/works/1882/11/fe18821102.htm (accessed April 15, 2025). Toward the end of Engels's life, however, the term began to be used by the followers as well as the opponents of Marx, and it rapidly gained wide acceptance; see Sayers, "What Is Marxism?", 377. Also, Louis Althusser, *For Marx* (New York: Pantheon Books, 1969), even went so far as to maintain that there is a sharp "epistemological break" in the development of Marx's thought, and that his early writings were not yet properly Marxist; but this claim is widely disputed; see McLellan, *His Life and Thought*, 379. However, it does raise the issue of which of the works that Marx himself wrote should be regarded as truly Marxist. According to Alasdair MacIntyre, *Marxism and Christianity* (South Bend, IN: University of Notre Dame Press, 1984), 6: "Stalinism becomes for them the paradigm of Marxism, which is as misleading as it would be to try to understand the nature of the New Testament by considering the attitudes and beliefs of the Emperor Constantine. But of course, religious or quasi- religious attitudes and modes of belief do appear in the course of the history of Marxism, and if the thesis that I wish to present is correct, it will have some relevance to the explanation of these phenomena."

80 Following a series of quotes from scholars who note the similarities between Marx and Christianity, Schwarzwalder summarizes: "Marx used a Christian framework to define human destiny or, as Halfin puts it, Marx used a Christian 'plot structure.'" Robert F. Schwarzwalder, Jr., "Marx's New Religion," *Journal of the Evangelical Theological Society* 62, no. 4 (2019): 775–88, at 785.

81 Nietzsche offers a similar case. While the Nazis invoked Nietzsche to justify their ideology, Nietzsche was lamenting the decay of true Christianity and condemning the "slave morality" of resentment, not advocating for the rise of fascism. Ironically, Marx shared a similar sentiment, railing against the inequalities of his time and lamenting a society that he saw as consumed by resentment and alienation. Nietzsche does not distinguish between "true" Christianity and slave morality. For him, the two are inherently intertwined. See *Genealogy of Morals*, Essay I, and *Beyond Good and Evil*, Part V.

82 Ludwig von Mises, *Socialism: An Economic and Sociological Analysis* (Indianapolis: Liberty Fund, 1951), 385.

83 Joseph A. Schumpeter, *Capitalism, Socialism, and Democracy* (New York: Harper, 1942), 5.

84 Robert Payne, *Marx: A Biography* (New York: Simon & Schuster, 1968), 11.

85 Ludwig von Mises, *Marxism Unmasked: From Delusion to Destruction* (Irvington-on-Hudson, NY: The Foundation for Economic Education, 1969), 134.

86 "Despite the many attempts to bury Marx and Marxism, the strength of his ideas is undeniable. His profound critique of capitalism and of the different modes of production in human history remain, to this day, unparalleled (on modes of production and Marx's materialist theory of history." Vidal et al., "Enduring Relevance," 4.

87 Alasdair MacIntyre, *Ethics and Politics Selected Essays*, vol. 2 (South Bend, IN: University of Notre Dame Press, 2006), 150.

88 Karl Marx, Letter to Arnold Ruge, March 13, 1843, *MECW*, vol. 3, 142.

89 As he prepares to depart Purgatory, Dante describes himself as "puro e disposto a salire a le stelle" ("pure and disposed to mount unto the stars"), the stars signifying Paradise (*Purgatorio*, 33.125). Many literary and cultural traditions reference the stars as an idiomatic way of speaking about the transcendent, something beyond material experience.

90 "The nineteenth century was very much animated by visions of human potential and perfectibility, inspired by the Enlightenment. One of the core sentiments of the Enlightenment is that humanity, released from the bondage of authority and tradition, is free to actualize possibilities hitherto thought beyond the reach of human achievement. The future is open and bursting with possibilities we have yet to discover, and by employing the resources of education, science, and social engineering, we have the power to perfect society on our own. Rather than look to God, we must take the initiative to accomplish this ourselves." Jerry L. Walls, "Introduction," in *The Oxford Handbook of Eschatology*, ed. Jerry L. Walls (Oxford: Oxford University Press), 3–19, at 8.

91 *Inferno*, Canto I, lines 1–3 (Longfellow). See note 70.

92 Jerrold Seigel has also illuminated Marx's dilemma. Seigel explains: "As the expected transformation of capitalist society receded into an indefinite future, Marx was caught between his philosophical vision and his materialist conviction." Seigel titles one of his sections "The Sickly Scholar" and sees Marx's "self-induced illnesses" as a means of avoiding the difficulties of completing the remaining volumes of Capital. Jerrold Seigel, *Marx's Fate: The Shape of a Life* (Princeton, NJ: Princeton University Press, 1978), 362, 382–87, 389.

93 In addition to his chronic smoking, Marx frequently took opium and arsenic to combat the boils that covered his body. His refusal to bathe regularly likely contributed to his declining health. Marx's health problems and refusal to bathe are recounted in Isaiah Berlin, *Karl Marx: His Life and Environment*, 4th ed. (Oxford: Oxford University Press, 1978), 154–55.

94 The young son of Karl Marx who died in their London apartment and did not receive an immediate burial due to the family's poverty was named Edgar Marx. Known affectionately as "Musch" by his family, Edgar was Karl Marx's

fourth child, born in 1847. He passed away in 1855 at the age of eight, a death that deeply affected both Karl and his wife, Jenny. Mary Gabriel, *Love and Capital: Karl and Jenny Marx and the Birth of a Revolution* (New York: Little, Brown and Company, 2011), 249.

95 Francis Wheen, *Karl Marx: A Life* (New York: W.W. Norton & Company, 2000), 322–24.

96 Letter from Marx to Weydemeyer, August 2, 1851; *Marx-Engels-Gesamtausgabe* [henceforth, MEGA], III/4 (Amsterdam: Internationale Marx-Engels-Stiftung, 1984), 164. The project is available at https://megadigital.bbaw.de/.

97 Marx's appreciation for wine extended beyond social customs; it was deeply rooted in his personal history. His family-owned vineyards in Trier, Germany, and even when he was residing far from his hometown, his father, Heinrich Marx, would send him cases of the family wine. This lifelong connection to wine is highlighted in the article "Karl Marx's Views on Wine," which states: "Marx was a lifelong wine connoisseur. Even though he resided a great distance from their Trier home, his father, Heinrich, would give him a case of the family wine." "Karl Marx's Views on Wine," *This Day in Wine History*, June 5, 2022, https://thisdayinwinehistory.com/karl-marxs-views-on-wine/?utm_source=chatgpt.com (accessed February 20, 2025).

98 McLellan, *Life and Thought*, 377–79.

99 British Blue Books were official government reports, often bound in blue covers, documenting parliamentary inquiries, colonial administration, and diplomatic correspondence. They played a significant role in shaping public discourse, particularly in the nineteenth and early twentieth centuries. Notable examples include reports on working conditions, colonial governance, and wartime diplomacy. See The National Archives, "Blue Books: A Window into British Colonial Rule," blog.nationalarchives.gov.uk (accessed February 15, 2024).

100 Paul Lafargue recalled that Marx believed that "books were tools for his mind, not articles of luxury." See *Reminiscences of Marx and Engels* (Moscow: Foreign Language Publishing House, 1957), 73. See also McLellan, *Life and Thought*, 354.

101 On Nietzsche's critique of Dante's inscription on the gate to hell "I too was created by eternal love," see Wetzel, "A Meditation on Hell," 376: "Dante has "tactlessly disclosed what is for Nietzsche the open secret about hell: that the place is the favorite fiction of resentful moralists."

102 Schumpeter, *Capitalism*, 5.

103 His one attempt at a job was as a train ticket collector or conductor, but he was not hired because he had poor handwriting. Gabriel, *Love and Capital*, 302.

104 Marx received financial support from various sources throughout his life, including inheritances from family members and friends. In March 1864, he inherited a combined 1,500 British pounds from his mother, Henriette

Marx, and his friend Wilhelm Wolff. This substantial sum allowed the Marx family to move to a more comfortable residence at 1 Modena Villas in Kentish Town, London. Additionally, Marx's uncle, Lion Philips, provided him with financial assistance. After Henriette Marx's death in 1863, Philips, as one of her executors, paid Marx the remaining inheritance, amounting to 7,000 Dutch guilders. This support was crucial for Marx, who often faced financial difficulties. See Matthew Plowright, "Karl Marx's London," Migration Museum, January 10, 2019, https://www.migrationmuseum.org/karl-marxs-london/ (accessed February 15, 2024). For context, during the mid-nineteenth century, the average annual income of a British worker was approximately 40 to 50 pounds. Therefore, an inheritance of 1,500 pounds would have been equivalent to about 30 to 37.5 years' worth of a worker's wages. Similarly, 7,000 guilders would have represented a substantial sum relative to the average worker's earnings in the Netherlands during that period; see https://en.wikipedia.org/wiki/Karl_Marx (accessed January 5, 2024). These inheritances provided Marx with significant financial resources, enabling him to focus on his intellectual and political work without the immediate pressure of securing a regular income. At the time of his death in 1883, Marx left a personal estate valued at 250 pounds. "Karl Marx," *Stanford Encyclopedia of Philosophy*, August 26, 2003, https://plato.stanford.edu/entries/marx/ (accessed February 20, 2025).

105 "It was evidently a staphylococcal infection, which could be treated before the invention of the sulfa drugs only in the most elementary way. The infection was able to spread because he was physically run down, smoked too much, had eaten highly spiced foods for many years, and was a prey to overwhelming nervous crises. He took almost no exercise except on Sundays, and rarely took baths. He was therefore in no state to resist the ever-present staphylococcal germs, and indeed it is surprising that he did not suffer from boils many years earlier." David McLellan, *Karl Marx: A Biography*, 4th ed. (London: Palgrave Macmillan, 2006), 347.

106 McLellan, *Karl Marx*, 388.

107 This theme is extensively discussed in Marx's *Economic and Philosophic Manuscripts of 1844*, particularly in the section "Estranged Labour." In this work, Marx examines how the worker's productive activity is externalized and becomes a means of survival rather than a fulfilling endeavor, resulting in a loss of autonomy and self-realization. For a precise reference, see Marx, *Economic and Philosophic Manuscripts of 1844*.

108 Peter Singer, *Marx: A Very Short Introduction* (Oxford: Oxford University Press, 1980), 35.

109 "Social and economic at the outset, in Rousseau and Marx the concept of alienation has acquired a specific gravity, an ontological weight illustrated by absolute or pure tragedy. A legacy of guilt, the paradoxical, unpardonable guilt of being alive, of attaching rights and aspirations to that condition,

condemns the human species to frustration and suffering, to being tied to 'a wheel of fire.'" Steiner, "'Tragedy,' Reconsidered," 4.

110 Dante Alighieri, *Inferno*, trans. Allen Mandelbaum (New York: Bantam Classics, 1982): 32:124–29, 33:56–73. For further discussion of Ugolino, see Wetzel, "A Meditation on Hell," 375–94.

111 McLellan, *Life and Thought*, ch. 5.

112 Johann Wolfgang von Goethe, *Faust*, trans. Walter Kaufmann (New York: Anchor, 1961), 161. Marx's ideology aimed to dismantle the structures of capitalism. See *MECW*, vol. 11, 108.

113 Concerning Marx's aspiration to have a bourgeois lifestyle, including the employment of maidservants and housekeepers, see Gabriel, *Love and Capital*. Gabriel's work explores the personal lives of Karl and Jenny Marx, shedding light on their household arrangements and Marx's complex relationship with bourgeois comforts.

114 Regarding Karl Marx's reliance on domestic servants and his failure to compensate them adequately, see Wheen, *Karl Marx: A Life*.

115 This is in reference to Marx's 1867 preface to *Das Kapital*, where he describes his work as an exploration of the rules of capitalism, saying: "It is the ultimate aim of this work to lay bare the economic law of motion of modern society" (my italics). See https://www.marxists.org/archive/marx/works/1867-c1/p1.htm?utm_source=chatgpt.com (accessed February 20, 2025). See also Karl Marx, *Capital: A Critique of Political Economy*, vol. 1: *The Process of Production of Capital*, trans. Samuel Moore and Edward Aveling (Moscow: Progress Publishers, 1887).

116 Dante's *Divine Comedy* serves as both a profound journey through the afterlife and an incisive investigation into the moral state of humanity. As Dante traverses hell, purgatory, and heaven, he encounters souls whose fates reflect their earthly virtues and sins, thereby commenting on the moral and ethical dilemmas of his time. This exploration is a moral allegory, demonstrating how the choices individuals make have eternal consequences. For instance, in *Inferno*, Dante encounters the gluttonous in the third circle, where he observes. "They were like the dogs that fight for scraps." This line illustrates the degradation that results from succumbing to base desires (Dante, *Inferno*, Canto VI). In *Purgatorio*, he observes the significance of repentance, as he hears the souls proclaim "In His will is our peace" (Dante, *Purgatorio*, Canto III), emphasizing the need for aligning one's life with divine purpose. Ultimately, Dante's journey highlights the importance of moral integrity and the transformative power of grace, as he concludes in *Paradiso*: "The love that moves the sun and the other stars" (Dante, *Paradiso*, Canto XXXIII), signifying the ultimate virtue of love as the guiding force in the universe. Alighieri, *Inferno*, trans. Allen Mandelbaum; Alighieri, *The Divine Comedy: Purgatorio*, trans. Allen Mandelbaum (New York: Bantam Classics, 1982); Dante Alighieri, *The Divine Comedy: Paradiso*, trans. Allen Mandelbaum (New York: Bantam Classics, 1982).

117 One example of a Marx citing Dante: "The final lines of the *Capital* preface contain a citation (slightly doctored by Marx) of *Purgatory*; 'Every opinion based on scientific criticism I welcome. As to the prejudices of so-called public opinion, to which I have never made concessions, now as before the maxim of the great Florentine is mine: 'Follow your own course, and let the people talk.'" Roberts, "Marx in Hell," 42.

118 "Dante's poetic imagination provides, then, a detailed depiction of the place that is purgatory. It is a place of intense suffering shot through with the joy of certainty in progress toward the vision of God. It is both heaven's antechamber and earthly He (embodied, time-bound, penitential) as it should be—earthly life without sin, though with sin's memory and effects, and also with an increasing sense of God and an unshakable certainty of eventually seeing and knowing God as he is. Dante wanted, as most painters of purgatory want, to encourage living Christians to make their earthly lives as much like the purgatorial life as possible. Heaven is beyond us here on earth, but purgatory is not; imaginations of it may, if allowed her proper force and value and if chastened by properly modest doctrinal formulations, begin to transfigure life on earth into their own image." Paul J. Griffiths, "Purgatory," *The Oxford Handbook of Eschatology*, ed. Jerry L. Walls (Oxford: Oxford University Press), 427–45, at 441.

119 The reference to Count Ugolino gnawing on skulls appears in *Inferno*, Canto XXXIII, lines 76–78. In this passage, Ugolino is found in the second ring of the ninth circle of hell (Antenora), reserved for traitors against their own country. He is eternally gnawing on the skull of Archbishop Ruggieri, who betrayed him and his sons, leading to their starvation: "His mouth raised up above the savage feast, that sinner wiped his lips upon the hair of the head he had stripped behind"; Alighieri, *Inferno*, trans. Allen Mandelbaum.

120 McLellan, *Karl Marx*, 33.

121 "Influences on Karl Marx," https://en.wikipedia.org/wiki/Influences_on_Karl_Marx (accessed July 12, 2025).

122 "We probably ought to mention the fact that Württemberg was a Protestant territory dominated by Catholics (cf. Ulster today), so that Hegel grew up in a state of religious tension (the young Marx comes to mind here too) and he had a pronounced prejudice against Catholicism." Robert C. Solomon, *In the Spirit of Hegel* (New York: Oxford University Press, 1985), 115.

123 Michael Heinrich, *Karl Marx and the Birth of Modern Society: The Life of Marx and the Development of His Work*, trans. Alexander Locascio (New York: Monthly Review Press, 2019), 265.

124 Paul Johnson, *Intellectuals* (New York: Harper & Row, 1988), ch. 4.

125 Marx's poem entitled "Feelings" depicts a sense of persistence; Heinrich, *Karl Marx*, 179–80. "The Fiddler," however, is a cry of defiance against God; *MECW*, vol. 1, 22.

126 Gabriel, *Love and Capital*, ch. 3.

127 Robert C. Tucker, *Philosophy and Myth in Karl Marx* (Cambridge: Cambridge University Press, 1961), 111.

128 "Estrangement, or alienation, became, as Bertell Ollman . . . puts it, 'the intellectual construct in which Marx displays the devastating effect of capitalist production on human beings, on their physical and mental states and on the social processes of which they are a part.' As a result, alienation is simultaneously one of the most contested and most enduring of Marx's concepts, having inspired generations to criticize and rebel against capitalism while also being subject to intense theoretical debate and scrutiny." Dan Swain, "Alienation, or Why Capitalism Is Bad for Us," in *The Oxford Handbook of Karl Marx*, ed. Paul Prew, Tomas Rotta, Tony Smith, and Matt Vidal (Oxford: Oxford University Press, 2019), 361–68, at 361.

129 MacIntyre notes: "In many premodern social orders, just because the poor provide products and services that the rich need, there is still something of a reciprocal relationship between rich and poor, governed by customary standards. And in such societies characteristically the poor will have, and be recognized as entitled to, their own resources: a share of the product of the land they work, customary rights over common land, and the like. But the relationship of capital to labor is such that it inescapably involves an entirely one-sided dependence, except insofar as labor rebels against its conditions of work. The more effective the employment of capital, the more labor becomes no more than an instrument of capital's purposes, and an instrument whose treatment is a function of the needs of long-term profit maximization and capital formation." MacIntyre, *Ethics and Politics*, 147.

130 "According to Engels, Marx in 1847 adopted the term 'communist' in preference to the term 'socialist,' because socialism had by that time acquired a flavor of bourgeois respectability. However that may have been and however we choose to explain this fact if it was a fact—more than once we have seen good reason for interpreting socialism as a product of the bourgeois mentality—there cannot be any doubt that Marx and Engels themselves were typical bourgeois intellectuals. Exiles of bourgeois extraction and tradition-this formula accounts for a lot both in Marx's thought and in the policies and political tactics he recommended. The astounding thing is the extent to which his ideas prevailed." Schumpeter, *Capitalism*, 312.

131 Karl Marx, "Part I: Feuerbach. Opposition of the Materialist and Idealist Outlook: A. Idealism and Materialism," in *The German Ideology*, https://www.marxists.org/archive/marx/works/1845/german-ideology/ch01a.htm (accessed February 20, 2025).

132 Eric Hobsbawm, *The Age of Revolution: 1789–1848* (London: Weidenfeld & Nicolson, 1962; repr. New York: Vintage Books, 1996), discusses the widespread political and social impacts of the 1848 revolutions. According to George Macaulay Trevelyan, *British History in the Nineteenth Century (1782–1901)* (London: Longmans, Green, and Co., 1922), ch. 19, "the year 1848 was the turning-point at which modern history failed to turn."

See https://archive.org/stream/dli.bengal.10689.1749/10689.1749_djvu.txt (accessed February 20, 2025). Trevelyan reflects the profound sense of missed opportunity and the subsequent disillusionment among revolutionaries like Marx.

133 Paul and Dante (the poet) are both exiled (Paul to prison, Dante from Florence), another similarity: "Dante and pre-modern readers accepted Pauline authorship of now-contested letters, believing he wrote them from prison, just as Dante wrote from exile." Daigle-Williamson, "Dante," 55.

134 Berlin, *Life and Environment,* ch. 4.

135 Biographer Robert Payne remarks: "There were times Marx seemed to be possessed by demons." See Payne, *Marx*, 315; Kengor, *The Devil and Karl Marx*, 57.

136 Prawer, *Karl Marx and World Literature*, ch. 1.

137 Eagleton, *Tragedy*, 5.

138 Goethe, *Prometheus*, line 3; St. Paul, 1 Corinthians 13:11 (KJV).

139 For more on the descent into hell as a narrative form, see above. See also Falconer, *Hell in Contemporary Literature*, 18–19; Roberts, "Marx in Hell," 43–49.

140 Karl Marx's father, Heinrich Marx, passed away on May 10, 1838. Notably, Karl did not attend his father's funeral. This absence is documented in several biographies: McLellan, *A Biography* (McLellan notes Marx's absence from the funeral and discusses the strained relationship between father and son leading up to Heinrich's death); Wheen, *Karl Marx: A Life* (Wheen provides an account of Marx's activities during this period, highlighting his preoccupation with his work and personal issues, which contributed to his absence); Gabriel, Love and Capital (reports that Marx had just made the 5-day journey home to see his father, departing four days before Heinrich's death. Gabriel also notes that Marx kept a daguerreotype of his father in his coat pocket for the rest of his life. When he died, Engels placed the image in his grave).

141 Karl Marx, Letter to Arnold Ruge, January 25, 1843, in *MECW*, vol. 27, 415. In this letter, Marx discusses his financial difficulties and mentions his mother's reluctance to provide further support. He writes: "I have fallen out with my family and, as long as my mother lives, I have no right to my inheritance."

142 Marx, *Theses on Feuerbach*, 1845, XI. A version of this work can be seen at https://www.marxists.org/archive/marx/works/1845/theses/theses.htm (accessed February 20, 2025).

143 Karl Marx and Friedrich Engels, *The German Ideology* (Amherst, NY: Prometheus, 1998), 37.

144 "Now might I do it pat, now he is praying; And now I'll do't. And so he goes to heaven; And so am I revenged. That would be scann'd"; *Hamlet*, Act 3, Scene 3. See William Shakespeare, *Hamlet*, ed. Ann Thompson and Neil Taylor (London: Bloomsbury, 2006).

145 Friedrich Engels, "The Condition of the Working Class in England. 1845," *American Journal of Public Health* 93, no. 8 (2003): 1246–49.

146 Ibid.

147 G. K. Chesterton, *The Outline of Sanity* (London: Methuen, 1926), ch. 3.

148 "Marx's critique of political economy, then, was a critique of then-prevailing political economic thought, a critique of the order it analyzed, and a critique of capital's self-representation. It was also a critique of the popular political ideologies built from and consolidating this self-representation, both bourgeois ideologies and those emanating from the left, such as utopian socialism. And it was a critique of extant epistemologies, ontologies, cosmologies, and historiographies. All of this was vital to discovering and explaining not just what capitalism is but what it does—to human lives, thinking, spirit, associational and institutional forms; to historical trajectories and constraints; and to the surface of the earth." Brown, "Foreword," xviii.

149 "The only people he respects are the aristocrats, the genuine ones who are well aware of it. In order to drive them from government, he needs a source of strength, which he can find only in the proletariat. Accordingly, he has tailored his system to them. In spite of all his assurances to the contrary, and perhaps because of them, I took away with me the impression that the acquisition of personal power was the aim of all his endeavours." Gustav Techow (August 1850), quoted in David McLellan, ed., *Karl Marx: Interviews and Recollections* (Totowa, NJ: Barnes & Noble, 1981), 18.

150 William Clare Roberts writes, "Marx borrowed key features of Dante's *Inferno* for his own critique of political economy, and that Marx thereby situated his critical journey through economics as the heir to the Western tradition of the *katabasis*, the formative descent into the underworld." See Roberts, "Marx in Hell," 39.

151 "Communism . . . is the genuine resolution of the antagonism between man and nature and between man and man; it is the true resolution of the conflict between existence and essence, objectification and self-affirmation, freedom and necessity, individual and species. It is the riddle of history solved and knows itself as the solution." Karl Marx, "Private Property and Communism," in *Economic and Philosophic Manuscripts of 1844*, 43.

152 The Greek word *hamartia*, translated as "sin" in the New Testament, literally means "to miss the mark," reflecting a failure to meet God's moral standard or intended purpose for humanity (see note 4). In biblical theology, *hamartia* is not merely an act of wrongdoing, it is a pervasive condition of separation from God, requiring redemption through divine intervention. As Paul writes, "For all have sinned and fall short of the glory of God" (Romans 3:23, NRSV), emphasizing humanity's universal need for reconciliation with God. Moreover, Paul describes sin as a dominating power leading to spiritual death, contrasting it with the gift of eternal life through Christ (Romans 6:23, NRSV). Outside biblical contexts, *hamartia* is used in Greek philosophy, such as in Aristotle's *Poetics*, to describe a "tragic flaw"

or error in judgment that leads to downfall—missing the ideal or higher purpose. This concept of sin diverges sharply from Marx's view of human nature. Marx rejected the idea of sin as a metaphysical condition, instead framing human flaws as products of historical and material conditions. Where Christianity sees sin as a spiritual estrangement from God, Marx viewed alienation as a socioeconomic phenomenon caused by exploitation under capitalism. For Christians, sin requires divine redemption through Christ's atoning sacrifice, but Marx placed his hope for human transformation in revolutionary action and the abolition of class structures. This difference reflects a fundamental divide: Christianity views the nature of man as fallen and dependent on God for restoration, while Marx sees human potential as inherently good but corrupted by external systems, which can be rectified through human agency. The Christian vision seeks spiritual reconciliation, while Marx's vision is rooted in material emancipation. See Joseph H. Thayer, *Greek–English Lexicon of the New Testament* (New York: Harper & Brothers, 1889); Romans 3:23; 6:23 (NRSV); Aristotle, *Poetics*, 13; Karl Marx, *Economic and Philosophic Manuscripts of 1844*.

153 Steiner, "'Tragedy,' Reconsidered," 2.

154 "Beyond any other genre outside of the philosophic dialogue itself, as we find it in Plato or Hume, tragedy has been the meeting point between the metaphysical and the poetic. Heidegger dramatizes this congruence when he asserts that western thought has turned on a choral ode in Sophocles' *Antigone*. What needs to be precisely understood are the connotations of the metaphysical and the theological in this context." Steiner, "'Tragedy,' Reconsidered," 4.

155 Karl Marx and Friedrich Engels, *The German Ideology*, ed. C. J. Arthur (New York: International Publishers, 1970), 59.

156 Johann Wolfgang von Goethe, *Faust*, Part One. The sentence is cited by Marx in chapter 1 of *The Eighteenth Brumaire of Louis Bonaparte*. See https://www.yorku.ca/comninel/courses/4090pdf/18Brumaire/ch01 (accessed 20 February 2025).

157 According to Boyer's review, Hosfeld's Marx "is neither hero nor villain, neither politician nor philosopher. Rather, Marx is revealed as something between a pragmatist and a prophet; a disciple of Hegel who 'was never quite able to decide between heaven and earth' . . . Hosfeld shows that in moments of political crisis and upheaval, Marx proved able to move quickly 'from philosophical speculation toward solid ground,' yet proved equally able to issue prophetic judgments that resounded with 'the violence of Old Testament prophets like Isaiah'." Eric Boyer, "Reviewed Work(s): *Karl Marx: An Intellectual Biography*, by Rolf Hosfeld," *The Historian* 77, no. 3 (2015): 611–12, at 611.

158 "In one important sense, Marxism is a religion. To the believer it presents, first, a system of ultimate ends that embody the meaning of life and are absolute standards by which to judge events and actions; and, secondly, a

guide to those ends which implies a plan of salvation and the indication of the evil from which mankind, or a chosen section of mankind, is to be saved. We may specify still further: Marxist socialism also belongs to that subgroup which promises paradise on this side of the grave." Schumpeter, *Capitalism*, 5.

159 Heinrich, *Karl Marx*, 68.

160 "Indeed phenomenology is a history of 'mind' or 'spirit' (Geist), designed to bring out the way in which man's estrangement results in the loss of his freedom. For man is dominated by forces of nature and society which he does not recognize as the creations of his own spirit." MacIntyre, *Marxism and Christianity*, 12.

161 The term "world spirit," or "Geist," originates in Hegelian philosophy and refers to the dynamic, universal consciousness or rational force guiding history toward greater freedom and self-realization. In Hegel's *Phenomenology of Spirit* (1807), *Geist* is both the collective spirit of humanity and the divine process through which history unfolds, progressively manifesting reason and freedom. Hegel's concept envisions history as a dialectical process where conflicting ideas (thesis and antithesis) resolve into a higher synthesis, culminating in absolute knowledge and the realization of human freedom. As Hegel states: "The history of the world is none other than the progress of the consciousness of freedom" (*Lectures on the Philosophy of History*, 1837). For Marx, however, the idea of *Geist* underwent a radical materialist transformation. Marx rejected Hegel's metaphysical interpretation, instead grounding historical development in material conditions and class struggle. In *The German Ideology* (1846), Marx critiques Hegel's idealism, asserting: "Life is not determined by consciousness, but consciousness by life." For Marx, history progresses not through the unfolding of a metaphysical spirit but through the concrete economic and social conditions that shape human relationships. Marx secularized *Geist*, replacing Hegel's divine or rational force with the dialectical movement of material forces, such as the conflict between bourgeoisie and proletariat. In comparison, the Christian view of history diverges from both Hegel and Marx by centering God's providence and the incarnation of Christ as the ultimate revelation and redemptive act. While Hegel's *Geist* aligns with a rational and immanent divine unfolding, Christianity emphasizes God's transcendent and personal nature, guiding humanity through grace rather than dialectical necessity. Marx, by contrast, removes any notion of the divine, positing that human agency alone drives historical progress. Thus, where Hegel's *Geist* represents the culmination of reason and Christianity looks to divine redemption, Marx sees history as the result of material forces and revolutionary praxis; see Georg Wilhelm Friderich Hegel, *Phenomenology of Spirit* (1807), trans. A. V. Miller (Oxford: Oxford University Press, 1977); Georg Wilhelm Friderich Hegel, *Lectures on the Philosophy of History* (1837), trans. John Sibree (New York: Dover Publications, 1956); Karl Marx, "The German Ideology," in *Karl Marx: Selected Writings*,

ed. David McLellan (Oxford: Oxford University Press, 2000). See Romans 8:28–30 for a Christian perspective on providence and redemption.

162 Gabriel, *Love and Capital*, 13.

163 Walls, "Introduction," 8, argues: "Kant's interpretation of 'religion within the bounds of reason alone,' with its rejection of historical revelation, had in effect reduced religion to morality. As Kant put it: 'For the final purpose even of reading these holy scriptures, or of investigating their content, is to make men better; the historical element, which contributes nothing to this end, is something which is in itself quite indifferent, and we can do with it what we like.' Eschatology in this scheme plays the innocuous role of providing images that inspire us to be morally earnest."

164 Bloom, *Hamlet*, 109.

165 Dante, *Inferno*, Canto I. See Dante Alighieri, *Inferno*, trans. Elio Zappulla (London: Vintage, 1999).

166 "That Marx mouths Virgil's reassurance to the pilgrim in the last instant before entering into the critique of political economy, suggests that the reader should expect to emerge similarly transformed and empowered, prepared even to found a new empire." Roberts, "Marx in Hell," 45.

167 Roberts, *Marx's Inferno*, 257.

168 Eugene Kamenka, "Introduction," in *The Portable Karl Marx*, ed. Eugene Kamenka (London: Penguin Books, 1983), xiv.

169 McLellan, *Life and Thought*, 1.

170 Letter from Heinrich Marx to Karl Marx, August 12, 1837; *MEGA*, I.1.1.2, 206.

171 Ibid., 55.

172 Institute of Marxism-Leninism, *Reminiscences of Marx and Engels* (Moscow: Foreign Language Publishing House, 1956), 130.

173 Franz Mehring, *Karl Marx: The Story of His Life*, trans. Edward Fitzgerald (Ann Arbor: University of Michigan Press, 1962), 2.

174 Heinrich, *Karl Marx*, 81; Jan Gielkens, *Karl Marx und seine niederländischen Verwandten: Eine kommentierte Quellenedition* (Trier: Karl-Marx-Haus, 1999), 32.

175 Gielkens, *Karl Marx*, 57.

176 Trier, originally known as Augusta Treverorum, was founded around 15 BC under Emperor Augustus and became a major administrative and economic center in the Roman Empire. As the capital of Gallia Belgica, and later an imperial residence, Trier played a crucial role in late antiquity. Its location along the Moselle River and at the crossroads of key Roman trade routes contributed to its prominence. Today, remnants of its Roman past, including the Porta Nigra, the Imperial Baths, and the Aula Palatina (Basilica of Constantine), reflect its historical significance; Jona Lendering, "Augusta Treverorum (Trier)," Livius.org, https://www.livius.org/articles/place/augusta-treverorum-trier (accessed February 25, 2024).

177 Gabriel, *Love and Capital*, 13.

178 "The Enlightenment and Human Rights," *Liberty, Equality, Fraternity: Exploring the French Revolution*, Roy Rosenzweig Center for History and New Media, George Mason University, https://revolution.chnm.org/exhibits/show/liberty--equality--fraternity/enlightenment-and-human-rights (accessed February 14, 2024).

179 The term "general will" originates from Jean-Jacques Rousseau's *The Social Contract* (1762) and refers to the collective will of the people aimed at the common good. Rousseau defined the general will as the expression of the common interest, distinct from individual or group interests, asserting that true freedom is achieved when individuals align their private will with the general will. As Rousseau states: "Each of us places in common his person and all his power under the supreme direction of the general will; and as a body, we receive each member as an indivisible part of the whole" (*The Social Contract*, book I, chapter 6). This concept became central to Enlightenment thought and the political philosophy that shaped revolutionary movements in Europe, including the French Revolution. In the context of its time, the general will was used both as a rallying cry for democratic ideals and as a justification for radical and often authoritarian actions during the Reign of Terror, (see note 150) where leaders like Robespierre invoked it to enforce conformity to revolutionary principles. The tension within Rousseau's concept—that the general will could both liberate and coerce—had a profound influence on later thinkers, including Karl Marx. Marx diverged from Rousseau by rejecting the abstraction of the general will in favor of a focus on material and class interests, seeing the proletariat's collective action as the true mechanism for achieving the common good; see Jean-Jacques Rousseau, *The Social Contract* (1762), trans. Maurice Cranston (London: Penguin Classics, 1968).

180 Marx would later write: "Religion, family, state, law, morality, science, art, etc., are only particular modes of production, and fall under its general law. The positive transcendence of private property as the appropriation of human life is, therefore, the positive transcendence of all estrangement that is to say, the return of man from religion, family, state, etc., to his human, i.e., social mode of existence. Religious estrangement as such occurs only in the realm of consciousness, of man's inner life, but economic estrangement is that of real life." *Karl Marx and Frederick Engels on Literature and Art.* A Selection of Writings Edited by Lee Baxandall and Stefan Morawski, with an Introduction by Stefan Morawski. Revised Edition with Supplementary Notes, Index and a new Introduction, "A Short History of Marxist Aesthetics," by Macdonald Daly (Nottingham, UK: Critical, Cultural and Communications Press, 2006), 55 (hereafter, *BM*).

181 "The aspiration to absolute freedom can be seen as an attempt to fill this lack in modern political theory, to find ground for identification with one's society which are fully in the spirit of modern subjectivity. We have grounds for identifying ourselves with our society and giving our full allegiance to

it when it is ours in the strong sense of being our creation, and moreover the creation of what is best in us and mostly truly ourselves: our moral will (Rousseau, Fichte), or our creative activity (Marx). From Rousseau through Marx and the anarchist thinkers to contemporary theories of participatory democracy, there have been recurrent demands to reconstruct society, so as to do away with heteronomy, or overcome alienation, or recover spontaneity. Only a society which was an emanation of free moral will could recover a claim on our allegiance comparable to that of traditional society." Taylor, *Hegel*, 411.

182 The Reign of Terror (1793–1794) was a period during the French Revolution characterized by mass executions, political purges, and authoritarian rule under the Jacobins, led by figures such as Maximilien Robespierre. The primary aim of the Reign of Terror was to protect the nascent French Republic from internal and external threats by enforcing revolutionary ideals through extreme measures. Robespierre famously justified the use of terror as a necessary tool to achieve virtue, declaring, "Terror is nothing other than swift, severe, inflexible justice; it is therefore an emanation of virtue" (*Speech on the Principles of Political Morality*, February 1794). During this time, the guillotine became a symbol of the revolution, and thousands, including King Louis XVI and Queen Marie Antoinette, were executed. The Reign of Terror reflected the tension between the ideals of liberty, equality, and fraternity and the practical demands of consolidating power in a deeply divided society. The revolutionary government invoked Rousseau's concept of the general will to justify suppressing dissent, framing their actions as necessary to safeguard the collective good. Marx viewed the Reign of Terror as a product of class conflict, seeing its excesses as the inevitable result of a bourgeois-led revolution that failed to address the deeper economic and social inequalities. See https://www.britannica.com/event/Reign-of-Terror (accessed February 13, 2023); Maximilien Robespierre, *Speech on the Principles of Political Morality*, February 5, 1794; Simon Schama, *Citizens: A Chronicle of the French Revolution* (New York: Vintage, 1989).

183 The dictatorship of the proletariat is a Marxist concept describing a transitional phase between capitalism and communism, during which the working class seizes state power to dismantle bourgeois structures and establish a classless society. Karl Marx defines it in *Critique of the Gotha Program/Programme* (1875), stating: "Between capitalist and communist society lies the period of the revolutionary transformation of the one into the other. Corresponding to this is also a political transition period in which the state can be nothing but the revolutionary dictatorship of the proletariat." Friedrich Engels further clarifies in his 1891 introduction to *The Civil War in France*, describing the Paris Commune of 1871 as "the dictatorship of the proletariat." See Karl Marx, *Critique of the Gotha Programme* (1875), in *MECW*, vol. 24, 531; Friedrich Engels, "Introduction to *The Civil War in France*," in *MECW*, vol. 27, 192.

184 Roger Paden, "Marx's Critique of Utopian Socialists," *Journal of Utopian Studies* 13, no. 2 (2002): 67–91, https://libcom.org/article/marxs-critique-utopian-socialists. See sources cited *ad loc.*

185 Acts of the Apostles (NRSV) (known as "Acts").

186 Acts 2:44–45 (NRSV)

187 Acts 4:32–35 (NRSV).

188 Micah Cobb, "The Christian Community in Acts 2:42–47," MicahCobb.com, https://www.micahcobb.com/p/the-christian-community-in-acts-242-47 (accessed January 5, 2024).

189 Friedrich Engels, "On the History of Early Christianity," Marxists Internet Archive, https://www.marxists.org/archive/marx/works/1894/early-christianity/ (accessed January 5, 2024).

190 Heinrich, *Karl Marx*, 7.

191 Ibid., 100.

192 *MECW*, vol. 1, 647.

193 Edgar von Westphalen, Karl Marx's future brother-in-law, described Marx's father, Heinrich Marx, as a "Protestant à la Lessing." This characterization highlights Heinrich's alignment with Enlightenment ideals, particularly those of Gotthold Ephraim Lessing, emphasizing reason, religious tolerance, and a deistic approach to faith.

194 Heinrich Marx, "Letter to Karl Marx," Trier, March 2, 1837, in *MECW*, vol. 1, 670–73.

195 Heinrich Heine, *Lutetia: Berichte über Politik, Kunst und Volksleben* (Hamburg: Hoffmann und Campe, 1855), 36.

196 McLellan, *Karl Marx*, 6.

197 Alasdair MacIntyre, *Marxism: An Interpretation* (London: SCM Press, 1953), 3, writes: "The true descendant of the doctrines of Aquinas is the labour theory of value. The last of the Schoolmen was Karl Marx."

198 *Summa Theologica*, I–II, Q. 87, Art. 4.

199 Payne, *Marx*, 22.

200 As we will see, "Marx wrote his dissertation on Epicurus, and he was familiar with Greek thought. Aristotle, as you will see, provides a frequent anchor for his arguments. Marx was also thoroughly trained in the way in which Greek thought came into the mainly German philosophical critical tradition— Spinoza, Leibniz and, of course, Hegel, as well as Kant and many others." Karl Marx, *Capital: A Critique of Political Economy*, Vol. 1., trans. Ben Fowkes (London: Penguin Classics, 1990), 7.

201 Gabriel, *Love and Capital*, 15; Payne, *Biography*, 23–24; Wilhelm Liebknecht, *Karl Marx: Biographical Memoirs* (New York: Greenwood Press, 1968), 65.

202 John Spargo, *The Marx He Knew*, available on Project Gutenberg. Accessed July 20, 2025. https://www.gutenberg.org/cache/epub/20743/pg20743-images.html.

203 See Wheen, *Karl Marx: A Life*; particularly chapter 2.

204 *MECW*, vol. 1. The letter was written from Trier. See https://libcom.org/library/letter-his-father. Accessed July 10, 2025.

205 Heinrich, *Karl Marx*, 101. "Since, therefore, the state appears to have been well ordered, the ruler desirous of happiness for the people and by his authority official positions occupied by the best men, since, moreover, the Augustan age appears to be not inferior to the best periods of Roman history, but different from the worst, and since parties and dissensions are seen to have ceased, whereas arts and letters flourished, the Augustan age deserves to be counted among the better epochs and the man held in high esteem who, although everything was permitted to him, nevertheless after his accession to power had only one aim, to ensure the safety of the state." Marx, *MECW*, vol. 1, 639.

206 Heinrich, *Karl Marx*, 102; *MEGA*, I.1.1212.

207 Ibid.

208 https://christiantreasury.org/content/karl-marx-union-faithful-christ (accessed February 25, 2025). Originally from Karl Marx, "On the Union of the Faithful with Christ According to John XV, 1–14, Described in Its Ground and Essence, in Its Unconditional Necessity and in its Effects," in *The Unknown Marx: Documents Concerning Karl Marx*, trans. ed. Robert Payne (New York: New York University Press, 1971).

209 Romans 11:17–24 (NRSV). Paul's vision of unity in the olive tree provides theological grounding for Marx's essay and adds layers to understanding his early thoughts. It suggests that, at this stage of his life, Marx was not only grappling with religious ideas but also with his own identity as a Jew in a Christian-dominated intellectual environment. By emphasizing the unity of Jews and Gentiles in Christ, Paul—and by extension Marx in this essay—offers a vision of inclusivity that transcends divisions, even as Marx would later abandon these theological roots. This passage from Paul, when seen through the lens of Marx's essay, reveals a rich intersection between theological reflection and Marx's later preoccupations with alienation, unity, and reconciliation. It sets the stage for exploring how these early ideas shaped Marx's philosophical trajectory, even as he moved away from explicitly religious frameworks.

210 "Virgil's promise of '*tanto ben*' (so much good) is a reminder of the restorative power of Beatrice's love and anticipates a happy ending to the imminent endeavor." Tonia Bernardi Triggiano, "Dante's Heavenly Lessons: Educative Economy in the Paradiso," *Essays in Medieval Studies* 26 (2010): 15–26, at 16.

211 Heinrich, *Karl Marx*, 122.

212 Marx was not an alcoholic, but he drank regularly, often heavily and sometimes engaged in serious drinking bouts. Part of his trouble was that from his mid-twenties, Marx was always an exile living almost exclusively in expatriate, mainly German, communities in foreign cities. He rarely sought

acquaintances outside them and never tried to integrate himself. Johnson, *Intellectuals*, 70.

213 Gabriel, *Love and Capital*, 22

214 McLellan, *Life and Thought*, 215: "He saw himself, at least symbolically, as a new Moses, a figure destined to lead his people, but one whose mission could not be realized until after he had undergone a personal metamorphosis. This is reflected not just in his intellectual transformation but in his personal appearance, as he gave up his customary appearance and sought to align himself with a new image—one that would better reflect his revolutionary ideals." See also Paul Kengor, *The Devil and Karl Marx: Communism's Long March of Death, Deception, and Infiltration* (Gastonia, NC: TAN Books, 2020), 89: "Marx's growing sense of self-importance was evident not only in his words but also in the way he presented himself. In his later years, particularly as his revolutionary ideals matured, he fashioned himself as a kind of new Moses—stripped of the trappings of bourgeois society, but claiming a mission to lead mankind toward a new social order."

215 Gabriel, *Love and Capital*, 35. For a Jewish prophet, the beard was not merely facial hair; it was a profound symbol of identity, authority, and divine connection. Rooted in the Torah, the beard signified consecration, a physical mark of being set apart for a higher purpose. The Torah explicitly forbids shaving the "edges of the beard" (Leviticus 19:27), a prohibition interpreted by scholars as a means to distinguish Jewish men from idolatrous practices and to uphold spiritual integrity. Kabbalistic teachings further elevate the beard's importance, viewing it as a conduit for divine mercy and spiritual energy. Isaac Luria, a prominent Kabbalist, was known to avoid even touching his beard to prevent any hairs from falling out, underscoring its sacredness. Marx's prophetic appearance—especially his iconic beard—evoked traditional religious symbolism, aligning him visually with figures like Moses. In Judaism, the beard is more than personal style; it is regarded as a sacred channel between intellect and action, rooted in both Torah law and Kabbalistic teaching. Marx himself acknowledged the symbolic weight of his beard, lamenting its removal as a kind of ritual sacrifice during his final days in Algiers. See Aron Moss, "The Beard," Chabad.org, https://www.chabad.org/library/article_cdo/aid/160973/jewish/The-Beard.htm (accessed July 20, 2025); "Beards, Sidelocks (Peot), and Shaving," *My Jewish Learning*, https://www.myjewishlearning.com/article/beards-sidelocks-peot-and-shaving/ (accessed July 20, 2025); and Tristram Hunt, "The Last Journey of Karl Marx," *Los Angeles Review of Books*, March 24, 2018, https://lareviewofbooks.org/article/the-last-journey-of-karl-marx/.

216 According to some of his biographers, though it is debated, Marx was wounded in the duel, sustaining a small injury above his left eye. McLellan, *Life and Thought*; Sperber, *A Nineteenth-Century Life*; Mehring, *Story of His Life*. Gertrude Himmelfarb, in her review of the Francis Wheen's biography, argues: "Even more bizarre were his challenges of duels. He himself never

actually fought a duel, but one of his admirers did on his behalf and was wounded, only to find himself, shortly afterwards when he displeased the master, reviled in the usual fashion." Gertrude Himmelfarb, "Let Marx Be Marx," *The New Republic* 223, no. 4 (2000): 34–41.

217 Gabriel, *Love and Capital*, 22.

218 Jonathan Sperber, *Karl Marx: A Nineteenth-Century Life* (New York: W. W. Norton, 2013), 45–46, 120.

219 "Marx's Record of Studies Issued by the University of Bonn (1836)," in *The Portable Karl Marx*, ed. Eugene Kamenka (London: Penguin Books, 1983), 9.

220 Jeffrey Burton Russell, *Mephistopheles: The Devil in the Modern World* (Ithaca, NY: Cornell University Press, 1990), 168.

221 Ibid., 123.

222 Ibid., 126. See *MECW*, vol. 1, 64, 6.

223 Triers in French.

224 John Spargo, *The Marx He Knew* (Chicago: C.H. Kerr & Co., 1909), 23.

225 Gabriel, *Love and Capital*, 25.

226 Ibid., 33.

227 *Candide* XXI.

228 *Social Contract* I.1.

229 "In recent times, there has been a remarkable upsurge in "rights talk,' and a lot of political energy has been invested in the idea that the pursuit of individual human rights is a way (if not the way) to shape a more humane capitalist system. What Marx is signaling here is that there is no way that many of the important questions posed in rights terms can be resolved without being reformulated in class-struggle terms. Amnesty International, for example, deals well enough with political and civil rights but has a hard time extending its concerns to economic rights because there is no way that these can be resolved without taking a side, either that of capital or that of labor. So you can see Marx's point. There is no way to adjudicate 'fairly' between equal rights (both bearing the seal of the law of exchange). All you can do is to fight for your side of the argument." Marx. *Capital*, trans. Fowkes (London), 139–40.

230 Will Durant and Ariel Durant, *The Age of Napoleon: A History of European Civilization from 1789 to 1815* (New York: Simon and Schuster, 1975), 71–72.

231 Ibid.

232 Durant and Durant, *Age of Napoleon*, 880.

233 Mehring, *Story of His Life*, ch. 2. Available at https://www.marxists.org/archive/mehring/1918/marx/ch02.htm (accessed April 24, 2024).

234 Wheen, *Karl Marx*, 25.

235 Karl Marx, *Critique of Hegel's Philosophy of Right* (1844). Available at https://www.marxists.org/archive/marx/works/download/Marx_Critique_of_Hegels_Philosophy_of_Right.pdf (accessed February 15, 2024).

236 Marx adopted Hegel's dialectical method but forcefully rejected its metaphysical core. Where Hegel saw history as the unfolding of Spirit, Marx saw a distortion—philosophy rooted in abstraction rather than material reality. Inverting the idealist model, Marx placed real individuals and their social conditions at the center of history. He transformed the dialectic into a materialist engine: not Spirit seeking self-realization, but class struggle driving change. Alienation, for Marx, was no longer a metaphysical condition but a social and economic one, grounded in property relations. In this framework, the bourgeoisie preserved the status quo, while the proletariat—cast as history's executioner—would bring about revolutionary synthesis. Marx's vision was less a system of logic than a declaration of intent: revolution not as theoretical necessity, but as moral imperative disguised in philosophical terms.

237 Though Hegel is widely regarded as Marx's primary philosophical mentor, particularly for his dialectical method, it is essential to recognize the influence of Johann Gottlieb Fichte and Giambattista Vico on Marx's thought. Hegel's dialectic, focused on the synthesis of opposites, was built on Fichte's earlier model of thesis-antithesis-synthesis, which itself emphasized the role of subjective freedom in shaping reality. Additionally, Vico's cyclical theory of history, with its recurring patterns of rise, fall, and renewal, laid the groundwork for Marx's understanding of historical progression and societal transformation. While Marx drew heavily from Hegel's concept of dialectical synthesis, these philosophical antecedents—Fichte's emphasis on human agency and Vico's historical cycles—played a significant role in the development of Marx's historical materialism. See Tom Rockmore, *Fichte, Marx and the German Philosophical Tradition* (Carbondale: Southern Illinois University Press, 1980).

238 "When we try to understand Marx's mistaken view of man, we are less helped by economic facts than we are by knowing Hegel, against whom Marx was revolting. A knowledge of Hegel helps us in two ways. First, because Hegel taught us to understand the history of ideas in terms of a dialectical development in which men react against the views held by their predecessors and correct any one-sidedness in these views by going to the opposite extreme that, alas, is equally one sided. Secondly, because it was against Hegel's one-sided emphasis on spiritual factors that Karl Marx rebelled with his materialism." Walter Kaufmann, *From Shakespeare to Existentialism: An Original Study* (Princeton, NJ: Princeton University Press, 1980), 152.

239 "Marx saw the fact that labor took this form as needing historical explanation. In particular, he refused to accept the ideas of earlier political economists that work was necessarily and always burdensome and that the condition of modern workers could be explained according to some natural laws or 'imaginary primordial condition,' which 'simply pushes the question into the grey and nebulous distance' . . . This is in part because of his belief that productive activity was fundamental to the formation of human identity.

Following Hegel, Marx saw labor as a process by which human beings *objectify* themselves in nature and thus come to make themselves at home within it. Through engaging with and transforming the natural world we make it an extension of ourselves and thus become better able to recognize ourselves within it . . . Labor was thus (potentially) an action of freedom, the means by which people realize their identity in the world. For Marx, however, labor is never pure, unmediated labor. Rather, our existence as social beings means that we also undertake labor in specific social relationships." Swain, "Alienation," 362.

240 MacIntyre observes that narratives which point beyond themselves towards the theories that we in fact need are to be found in many places: in some folktales, in Sophoclean and Shakespearean drama, and above all in Dante's *Commedia*, which directs us beyond itself towards the kind of theoretical understanding provided by Aquinas's commentaries on the *Ethics* and *Politics*: "One of the things that we most need to learn, first from narrative and then from theory, is that it is one of the marks of someone who develops bad character that, as it develops, she or he becomes progressively less and less able to understand what it is that she or he has mislearned and how it was that she or he fell into error. Part of the badness of bad character is intellectual blindness on moral questions. It is important therefore at an early stage to possess resources for right judgment and action, which include resources for explaining how we may come to fail and have come to fail and what we have to do to avoid failure." Alasdair MacIntyre, *The MacIntyre Reader*, ed. Kelvin Knight (South Bend, IN: University of Notre Dame Press, 1998), 142.

241 Mehring, *Story of His Life*, ch. 2. Online version at https://www.marxists.org/archive/mehring/1918/marx/ch02.htm (accessed April 24, 2024).

242 Prawer, *Karl Marx*, 80, 288, clearly notes Marx's contempt for the Romantic movement but also provides instances of a similar approach, as, for example, between Schiller and Marx in the vision of unalienated man whilst in the Grundrisse he finds a "continuity of Marx's aesthetics with those of the Goethezeit, with Weimar classicism and the German Romantics."

243 Both terms discussed in Albert Mohler, "Karl Marx Meets the Devil: A Conversation with Historian Paul Kengor," *Thinking in Public*, February 21, 2021, https://albertmohler.com/2021/02/10/paul-kengor/.

244 See Kengor, *The Devil and Karl Marx*, esp. chs 1 and 3, for discussions on Marx's religious posture and thematic parallels to rebellion.

245 Heinrich Marx to Karl Marx, March 1837, quoted in McLellan, *Karl Marx*, 202.

246 *MECW*, vol. 1, 22.

247 Heinrich, *Karl Marx*, 182.

248 Karl Marx, "The Player" (1841). For more on this poem, see Kengor's interview with Jordan Peterson at https://singjupost.com/the-devil-and-karl-marx-dr-paul-kengor-full-transcript/ (accessed July 14, 2025).

249 Eagleton, *Tragedy*, 84–85, adds: "Tragic art, then, stages a revolt against the Olympians, marking a shift from pagan ritual to the ethico-political, myth to truth, fate to freedom, Nature to history, the despotic sway of warring deities to a redeemed people. Yet in Benjamin's eyes the hero's insurgency is doomed to be premature. Unable to articulate a new form of communal existence, and powerless to escape the clutches of myth and destiny, he is condemned to an eloquent silence or moral speechlessness. If he is struck dumb, it is because he derives his identity from a social order yet to be born, which once it has sprung into being will learn its language from his muteness. As such, he has the elusive quality of all signifiers of utopia."

250 In his early poetic drama *Oulanem*, Karl Marx employs a title that is an anagram of "Manuelo," which is a variant of "Immanuel," a biblical name for Jesus Christ meaning "God is with us." This inversion of a holy name is notable, as such reversals are often associated with blasphemous or subversive themes. Marx's choice reflects his early engagement with dark and rebellious motifs, challenging religious conventions. See Robert Payne, *The Unknown Karl Marx: Documents Concerning Karl Marx* (New York: New York University Press, 1971), 81–83.

251 Karl Marx, "Des Verzweiflenden Gebet," MEGA I.1.2, 30.

252 Niccolò Paganini, born in Genoa, Italy, was one of the most celebrated violinists of the nineteenth century, renowned for his unparalleled technical mastery and flamboyant performances. His extraordinary skill earned him a reputation as a virtuoso, but his dramatic persona and the almost supernatural quality of his music led to rumors that he had made a pact with the devil. Paganini's compositions, including his *Caprices for Solo Violin*, showcased his ability to evoke a wide range of emotions, from eerie, haunting melodies to frenetic and fiery passages. His public image as a tormented genius perfectly embodied the Romantic era's fascination with the sublime and the diabolical, making him an enduring figure of intrigue in both music and literature. See Maddy Shaw Roberts, "Niccolo Paganini was such a gifted violinist, people thought he sold his soul to the devil," *Classic FM*, October 25, 2024, https://www.classicfm.com/composers/paganini/niccolo-gifted-violinist-deal-with-devil/ (accessed April 15, 2024).

253 Payne, *Biography*, 62.

254 "Karl Marx's early poems—later referred to as the 'Savage Songs'—were published in the Berlin literary magazine *Athenaeum* in January 1841, when he was just twenty-two—seven years before *The Communist Manifesto*. The title they were published under and their content—brimming with anger and defiance—reflect his youthful radicalism and foreshadow his later revolutionary fervor." Kurt Mahlburg, "Karl Marx's Obsession with the Devil." *Intellectual Takeout*, July 10, 2024, https://intellectualtakeout.org/2024/07/karl-marxs-obsession-the-devil.

255 Marx, "The Player" (also known as "The Fiddler"), from 1841, can be found at the MIA at https://www.marxists.org/archive/marx/works/1837-pre/verse/verse4.htm.

256 A. N. Wilson writes that Goethe, after meeting Beethoven, described him this way: "He wanted to belong to the clean, ordered, pre-revolutionary world of his youth, the world against which, as a Storm and Stress man, he had a different attitude. He had, as a young man, been instrumental in helping to blow that world to bits. But, knowing how delicate a thing is civilization, he was moved by it, cherished it. The music of the Easter choir comes to Faust's ears and saves him from the ultimate act of rebellion, suicide. Yet, 'I hear the message loud and clear; only I lack belief." A. N. Wilson, *Goethe: His Faustian Life* (London: Bloomsbury, 2024), 291.

257 In this passage, *Ode to Joy* is referenced as a contrast to Marx's rejection of divine transcendence. *Ode to Joy*, the choral finale of Beethoven's *Symphony No. 9*, sets to music Friedrich Schiller's poem celebrating universal brotherhood and divine grace. Beethoven's composition is often associated with an uplifting vision of humanity, where love and joy are raised to a sacred, almost heavenly ideal. Marx, however, in his early poetry and later philosophy, subverts this tradition of transcendence, replacing it with materialist determinism and the negation of divine knowledge. Instead of music being a vehicle for spiritual elevation, as seen in Beethoven's *Ode to Joy*, Marx's interpretation inverts this, reflecting a world devoid of divine presence or teleology. Marx himself saw Beethoven's music as culturally significant but dismissed such artistic expressions as mere reflections of material conditions rather than as vehicles of divine inspiration. As he and Engels wrote in *The German Ideology*: "The production of ideas, of conceptions, of consciousness, is at first directly interwoven with the material activity and the material intercourse of men, the language of real life." Marx and Engels, *The German Ideology*, 47 (ed. Arthur). This view starkly contrasts with the spiritual exaltation found in *Ode to Joy*, making its absence in Marx's thought all the more pronounced.

258 Payne, *Marx: A Biography*, 64.

259 Karl Marx, "Invocation of One in Despair" (1837), is on the MIA at https://www.marxists.org/archive/marx/works/1837-pre/verse/verse11.htm.

260 Heinrich, *Karl Marx*, 178; *MEGA* I.1.485.

261 Letter from Heinrich Marx to His Son, March 2, 1837, *MECW*, vol. 1, 670–73. See it on the MIA at https://marxists.architexturez.net/archive/marx/letters/papa/1837-fl2.htm.

262 "Invocation of One in Despair." See note 236.

263 Letter from Karl Marx to His Father, November 10, 1837. *MECW*, vol. 1, 17. It is online at https://libcom.org/library/letter-his-father.

264 The surname Feuerbach in German is composed of two parts: *Feuer* and *Bach*. *Feuer* means "fire." *Bach* means "stream" or "brook." So, Feuerbach literally translates to "fire stream" or "stream of fire."

265 Spargo, *The Marx He Knew*, Sec. I. See online at Project Gutenberg at https://www.gutenberg.org/cache/epub/20743/pg20743-images.html.

266 As John Milton writes in *Paradise Lost*: "The mind is its own place, and in itself / Can make a Heaven of Hell, a Hell of Heaven" (Book I, lines 254–55). This is a reminder that, once foundational anchors are removed, chaos often follows.

267 Heinrich, *Karl Marx*, 175; Mehring, *Story of His Life*, 26, 27.

268 McLellan, *Life and Thought*, 186.

269 Payne, *Marx: A Biography*, 78.

270 *Les Pensées* (1670).

271 Letter from Heinrich Marx to His Son, February 10, 1838, *MECW*, vol. 1, 691–94.

272 Ibid.

273 Letter from Heinrich Marx to His Son, November 19–29, 1835, *MECW*, vol. 1, 645–48.

274 Heinrich, *Karl Marx*, 110; *MECW*, vol. 1, 646.

275 Gabriel, *Love and Capital*, 32.

276 McGrogan, *Who the Hell Is Karl Marx?* 9.

277 Payne, *Biography*, 20.

278 Sperber, *A Nineteenth-Century Life*, 31; Heine, *Lutetia*, 57. Spargo, *Marx*, 26, said the following about Henriette: "She was a simple, good-natured soul of the domestic type with no particular intellectual gifts." Subsequently, this judgment was simply adopted by most biographers of Marx; see, for example, Auguste Cornu, *Karl Marx: L'Homme et l'Oeuvre. De l'Hégélianisme au Matérialisme Historique* (Paris: Alcan, 1934), 53; McLellan, *Life and Thought*, 4; Padover, *Karl Marx: An Intimate Biography*, 13.

279 Francis Wheen, *Das Kapital: A Biography* (New York: Grove Press, 2007), 8.

280 Karl Marx, *Writings of the Young Marx on Philosophy and Society*, trans. Lloyd D. Easton (Garden City, NY: Doubleday, 1967), 36. This passage reflects Marx's early emphasis on choosing a profession aligned with personal dignity and the betterment of humanity. For a comprehensive understanding, you can refer to the full text of *Reflections of a Young Man on the Choice of a Profession* available through the MIA, see https://www.marxists.org/archive/marx/works/download/Marx_Young_Marx.pdf?utm_source=chatgpt.com (accessed April 24, 2024).

281 "There is a familiar and well-trodden path that leads from Hegel via the Young Hegelians to the early Marx. The standard account derives its plausibility from Marx himself. This would be satisfactory if Marx were a reliable guide to his own intellectual development. However, Marx himself warned us not to judge individuals by their own self-estimation . . . Marx's self-presentation was part of the Young Hegelian tendency to emphasise rationality and Enlightenment as against mysticism and Romanticism." Michael Levin, "From Marxism to Communism: A Review Article," *Europe-Asia Studies* 49, no. 8 (1997): 1519–26, at 1522.

282 Gabriel, *Love and Capital*, 85.

283 Ibid., 86.

284 Heinrich, *Karl Marx*, 175.

285 Mehring, *Story of His Life*, 25.

286 Heinrich, *Karl Marx*, 121.

287 Letter from Jenny to Karl on June 24, 1838, *MEGA* III.1.332.

288 Sperber, *A Nineteenth-Century Life*, 75.

289 "Hegel should be read as a thinker of antagonism, rather than as a reductive universalist." John Rayman, "Review: Reading Marx, by Slavoj Zizek, Frank Ruda, and Agon Hamza," *Contemporary Political Theory* 19 (2020): 179–182, at 180.

290 Bruno Bauer, "Die eigenthümlichen Lehren des Christenthums rein biblisch dargestellt. Erster Band," *Jahrbücher für wissenschaftliche Kritik* (1834): 196–200 at 200.

291 Heinrich, *Karl Marx*, 274.

292 Hegel's *Lehre von der Religion und Kunst: von dem Standpuncte des Glaubens aus beurtheilt* (Leipzig: Otto Wigand, 1842).

293 The Young (or Left) Hegelians' criticism of religion was D. F. Strauss's *Life of Jesus*, the first volume of which was published in 1835, the second a year later. Strauss's starting point is the typically Hegelian one that the idea of God-manhood, of humanity as the essential content of the divine, does not depend for its perfection or reality on how far it was in fact realized in the person of Jesus: the perfection and reality of the idea are intrinsic to it as an idea: "The author is aware that the essence of the Christian faith is perfectly independent of his criticism. The supernatural birth of Christ, his miracles, his resurrection and ascension, remain eternal truths, whatever doubts may be cast on their reality as historical facts. Historically, Jesus was the first to introduce it to the minds of men: therein lies His glory. But the idea is independent of the person: herein lies the idealism of Strauss. The life of Jesus is mythical, and by myth is meant the clothing of religious ideas in historical form." D. F. Strauss, *Life of Jesus Critically Examined* (London: Swan Sonnenschein & Co., 1902), Preface. This work is also available on the Project Gutenberg site at https://www.gutenberg.org/files/64037/64037-h/64037-h.htm (accessed May 5, 2025).

294 Mehring, *Story of His Life*, 33.

295 G. W. F. Hegel, *Lectures on the History of Philosophy*, Section Three, E: "Final Result." See it on the MIA at https://www.marxists.org/reference/archive/hegel/works/hp/hpfinal.htm. See also G. W. F. Hegel, *Lectures on the History of Philosophy: The Lectures of 1825–1826*, ed. Robert Brown (Berkeley: University of California Press, 1990).

296 Wheen, *Das Kapital*, 11.

297 Mehring, *Story of His Life*, ch. 2 (online, MIA), writes: "The bourgeois enlightenment movement of the eighteenth century revived the Greek philosophies of self-consciousness: the doubts of the Sceptics, the hatred

the Epicureans bore towards religion, and the republican sentiments of the Stoics."

298 MacIntyre, *Marxism and Christianity*, 10, writes: "The question that Hegel puts in his early writings, the *Jugendschriften*, concerns the nature and significance of the transition from the Greek to the Christian world. The answer Hegel gives in these early writings is one that rests on his view of the relation of Jesus to Judaism. The Jewish nation are the people who have, more than any other, externalized the law: what is essentially written in the hearts of men is transmuted by them into the external observances of a written law."

299 Heinrich, *Karl Marx*, 91; *MECW*, vol. 1, 28.

300 Marx's assertion that "Greek philosophy seems to come to an end with Aristotle" reflects a pivotal perspective on the trajectory of classical thought. For Marx, Aristotle represented both the culmination and the limitation of Greek philosophy. As the last major philosopher of antiquity to synthesize and systematize the philosophical inquiries of his predecessors, Aristotle brought an unparalleled depth and coherence to metaphysics, ethics, and the natural sciences. However, this systematic rigor also marked a stopping point in the philosophical creativity of the Greek tradition. Unlike his teacher, Plato, who left space for speculation and transcendence, Aristotle's philosophy grounded knowledge in empirical observation and rational deduction, closing the door to further metaphysical innovation. In Marx's view, Aristotle's philosophy became the definitive framework of its era, leaving little room for philosophical evolution until external historical and material conditions necessitated new approaches. This "dull ending," as Marx provocatively characterizes it, speaks to a tension within classical philosophy: its intellectual achievements became, in a sense, its own limitation. As Hegel later argued in his *Lectures on the History of Philosophy*, Aristotle's work represented the "absolute maturity" of Greek philosophy, but one that also exhausted its capacity for further development without a fundamental historical shift. See Hegel, *Lectures on the History of Philosophy*, vol. 2, trans. E. S. Haldane and Frances Simson (London: Routledge and Kegan Paul, 1894), 114–115. Marx interprets this "end" not as a critique of Aristotle himself but as a recognition that philosophy, like all human endeavors, is shaped and constrained by the historical and material conditions of its time. Thus, the end of Greek philosophy with Aristotle sets the stage for the eventual rise of new paradigms in thought, such as medieval scholasticism and modern materialism.

301 "Greek philosophy's Alexander of Macedon. . . . Epicureans, Stoics and Sceptics are regarded as an almost improper addition bearing no relation to its powerful premises." Heinrich, *Karl Marx*, 302; *MECW*, vol. 1, 34.

302 McGrogan, *Who the Hell Is Karl Marx?* 28.

303 Epicureans are mentioned only once in the Bible—in *Acts 17:18*, where Paul debates both Epicurean and Stoic philosophers in Athens. While the biblical text does not directly label them as "dogs" or "street dwellers," later Christian interpretations, especially among Church Fathers and early moralists, often

characterized Epicureans as worldly, hedonistic, and materially indulgent. This reputation led to symbolic associations with lowly imagery—such as scavenging animals, including dogs—and even with the poor who live from scraps, metaphorically "eating from the garbage." Some modern scholars and commentators have described them as "early hippies" due to their emphasis on withdrawal from public life, living simply, and seeking pleasure in moderation away from political or religious ambition. See Acts 17:18 (NRSV); Everett Ferguson, *Backgrounds of Early Christianity*, 3rd ed. (Grand Rapids, MI: Eerdmans, 2003), 307–9; Peter Gay, *The Enlightenment: An Interpretation*, vol. 1, *The Rise of Modern Paganism* (New York: W.W. Norton, 1966), 31–35; Norman DeWitt, *Epicurus and His Philosophy* (Minneapolis: University of Minnesota Press, 1954), esp. ch. 15, "The Gospel of Relaxation."

304 His reputation as a "swine" began in Roman times. See https://www.britannica.com/topic/Western-philosophy/Epicureanism (accessed July 20, 2025).

305 "It has frequently been pointed out that Marx's dissertation is not just concerned with a comparison of the philosophies of Epicurus and Democritus, but also with the relation between the philosophy of Epicurus and that of Aristotle . . . but Schmidt goes a step further by determining that this comparison is not just background but is the original project of Marx's dissertation." Heinrich, *Karl Marx*, 297.

306 "In siding with Epicurus against Democritus, Marx wants to remain faithful to a thought of contingency, read as subjective openness to being otherwise, as itself internal to the system of causality itself. In doing so, Marx argues, we remain faithful to a strange thought of freedom in causal relations themselves. Indeed, by thinking in a more immanent mode of relationality, what Democritus wanted to imagine as an external or dualistic relation of causality, we hit upon the possibility of thinking, Marx writes, 'the chance of thought itself,' the eventalness we might say in which our contingent freedom participates." Ward Blanton, *A Materialism for the Masses: Saint Paul and the Philosophy of Undying Life* (New York: Columbia University Press, 2014), 60–61.

307 Doctoral dissertation: "The Difference between the Democritean and Epicurean Philosophy of Nature" (University of Jena, 1841). It is available in *MECW*, vol. 1, 25–73.

308 "Yet, none of these abstract concepts, aspects, or distinctions appears to the naked eye or within the discourse of capitalist societies. Rather, each captures something real about capital without having a direct referent in the object world. In this regard, Marx's infamous invitation to his readers to depart 'the noisy sphere of the market' for 'the hidden place of production' to discover the secret of capital itself oversimplifies this discovery. For even on the factory floor, nothing about where profit and capital come from is immediately self-revealing. What is needed instead is a critical theory that will crack the code of a multifaceted and complex, humanly produced order that is philosophical in nature." Brown, "Foreword," xxi.

309 His family and Jenny also appear to have grown impatient. Bauer's remark in a letter from March 31, 1841, hints at that: "If only I could be in Trier to present the matter to your people." *MEGA* III.1.354.

310 Gabriel, *Love and Capital*, 34.

311 Heinrich, *Karl Marx*, 319–20.

312 "Marx's thesis for his doctorate is part of his study of what happened to Greek philosophy after Aristotle. What happened to Greek philosophy is that it became practical. It turned from speculative metaphysics to ethics. This suggests the solution of Marx's problem. Hegel has in principle completed the task of speculative philosophy. But Hegel's philosophy remains in the realm of speculation, of the ideal. What has to be done is to realise the ideal in the world, not simply of thought, but of material reality. Hegel's theory must be converted into Marx's practice. This is Marx's problem." MacIntyre, *Marxism: An Interpretation*, 39.

313 Ibid., ch. 5.

314 Wheen, *Karl Marx*, 11.

315 Heinrich, *Karl Marx*, 283.

316 McLellan, *Karl Marx*, 1.

317 "Had Marx achieved the university teaching appointment that he had hoped for at Bonn in 1842, his first lectures would have been on Aristotle. In the years 1841–1845, while a radical journalist, he made dose study of Aristotle's *Politics*. And when he refers to Aristotle in his mature economic writings, it is always with a kind of respect that he showed few of his contemporaries. Indeed, he takes Aristotle to have described accurately the forms of economic exchange of the ancient Greek world and the history of their development. When he moves beyond Aristotle in order to understand the distinctive economic forms and development of the modern world, he still employs key concepts as Aristotle used them essence, potentiality, goal-directedness." Alasdair MacIntyre, *Ethics in the Conflicts of Modernity: An Essay on Desire, Practical Reasoning and Narrative* (Cambridge: Cambridge University Press, 2016), 94. See also Fergus Sandyford, "What Thomism Has to Do with Marx," Review of *Ethics in the Conflict of Modernity: An Essay on Desire, Practical Reasoning, and Narrative* by Alasdair MacIntyre. *Tradistae*, May 1, 2020. https://tradistae.wordpress.com/2020/05/01/thomism-marxism/.

318 Padover, *An Intimate Biography*, ch. 2.

319 For more on the Jungian "shadow," see https://www.thesap.org.uk/articles-on-jungian-psychology-2/about-analysis-and-therapy/the-shadow/ (accessed July 20, 2025).

320 Roberts NYDT 4 April 1853 – L 174–75.

321 Take this example at the end of the 1859 Preface to *A Contribution to the Critique of Political Economy*: "But at the entrance to science, as at the entrance to Hell, this demand must be registered: Here one must abandon every suspicion; every cowardice must here be slain." Roberts, "Marx in Hell," 42.

322 *The German Ideology* (1845).

323 Marx, *Contribution to the Critique of Hegel's Philosophy of Right* (1844).

324 *La Bohème* is based on the novel *Scènes de la vie de bohème* (1851) by Henri Murger. The opera is set in Paris during the 1830s and explores the lives of impoverished artists and students in the Latin Quarter, capturing themes of love, poverty, and artistic aspiration. Its depiction of the bohemian lifestyle resonated with the social and artistic revolutions of the time, including Marxist and Romantic ideals. Giacomo Puccini's *La Bohème* (opera) premiered on February 1, 1896, at the Teatro Regio in Turin, Italy.

325 "Second, the socialist thinkers of the nonage provided many a brick and many a tool that proved useful later on. After all, the very idea of a socialist society was their creation, and it was owing to their efforts that Marx and his contemporaries were able to discuss it as a thing familiar to everyone. But many of the utopians went much further than that. They worked out details of the socialist plan or of certain variants of it, thereby formulating problems—however inadequately and clearing much ground. Even their contribution to purely economic analysis cannot be neglected. It provided a much-needed leaven in an otherwise distressingly stodgy pudding." Schumpeter, *Capitalism*, 308.

326 Karl Marx and Friderich Engels, *The Holy Family or Critique of Critical Criticism* (1845), https://www.marxists.org/archive/marx/works/1845/holy-family/.

327 Karl Marx and Friedrich Engels, *The German Ideology*, in *The Marx-Engels Reader*, ed. Robert C. Tucker (New York: W.W. Norton & Company, 1978), 146–200; Marx and Engels, *The German Ideology*, 67; Karl Marx, *The Holy Family*, trans. C. P. Magill (New York: International Publishers, 1968), 35.

328 This text is available on the MIA at https://www.marxists.org/archive/marx/works/1844/jewish-question/.

329 This text is available on the MIA at https://www.marxists.org/archive/marx/works/1844/manuscripts/preface.htm.

330 Karl Marx, "Introduction," in *The German Ideology*, (1845).

331 Karl Marx's first article for the *Rheinische Zeitung*, titled "Comments on the Latest Prussian Censorship Instruction," was published on May 5, 1842. This piece was prompted by debates on press freedom in the Rhineland Diet. In it, Marx critiques Prussian press legislation, marking his initial foray into political journalism. See the article on MIA, https://www.marxists.org/archive/marx/works/download/Marx_Rheinishe_Zeitung.pdf?utm_source=chatgpt.com (accessed April 24, 2024).

332 Engels was sent to Manchester to work at Ermen & Engels, a textile firm partially owned by his father, Friedrich Engels, Sr., as part of his expected role in the family's industrial ventures. See W. O. Henderson, *The Life of Friedrich Engels* (London: Routledge, 1976), 45. During his time in Manchester, Engels documented the extreme poverty, exploitation, and harsh labor conditions of the working class, culminating in his influential work, *The Condition of the Working Class in England*; Engels, "The Condition of the Working Class in England. 1845," 12. Engels was already influenced by

Young Hegelian philosophy and socialism. His exposure to England's radical political movements, including the Chartists, strengthened his revolutionary convictions. See David McLellan, *Friedrich Engels* (New York: Viking Press, 1978), 64. On his way to England, Engels wrote articles for Marx and Arnold Ruge's radical journal, *Deutsch-Französische Jahrbücher*, laying the groundwork for his future collaboration with Marx. See Sperber, *A Nineteenth-Century Life*, 2013, 122.

333 Heinrich von Treitschke, *Deutsche Geschichte im Neunzehnten Jahrhundert*, vol. 5 (Leipzig: S. Hirzel, 1905), 201.

334 Wheen, *Das Kapital*, 11.

335 McLellan, *A Biography*, 113.

336 Alex Callinicos, *The Revolutionary Ideas of Karl Marx* (Chicago: Haymarket Books, 2011).

337 McGrogan, *Who the Hell Is Karl Marx?* 11.

338 "Capital's requirements of increased labor exploitation over time—exploiting more workers and exploiting them more intensively—and in space—ever-expanding markets for its commodities—constitute the life and death drives of capitalism, drives that are as insatiable as they are unsustainable. They reduce the masses to impoverishment, concentrate wealth among the few, and pile up crises that spell the system's eventual collapse, overthrow, or, as we have later learned, reinventions through the social state, the debt state, neoliberalism, financialization, and the asset-enhancing and de-risking state. Since growth is essential for what Marx called the 'realization of surplus-value' or profit, capitalist development becomes an almighty shredder of all life forms and practices, including its own recent ones." Brown, "Foreword," xviii–xix.

339 "Marxism is as relevant today as when Marx himself was alive. Reasons for that abound: appalling levels of wealth inequality and exploitation, workplace alienation, and social alienation; the instability of finance, financialization, globalization, and the political turmoil that threatens our fragile parliamentary democracies; gender and racial oppression; climate change and the looming environmental collapse; imperialism; fiscal austerity; immigration crises, unemployment, and job insecurity." Prew et al., "Enduring Relevance," 3–4.

340 "Critical Notes on the Article 'The King of Prussia and Social Reform. By a Prussian,'" *Vorwarts!* 63, August 7, 1844, https://www.marxists.org/archive/marx/works/1844/08/07.htm.

341 "Marxism is capitalism's most radical self-criticism. It critically analyzes the deep roots of our social system. It unveils the structures and the internal logic that organize our economies, cultures, and politics. Once these deeper structures are brought to the fore, Marxism then offers a path to overcome our challenges—both via critique of existing social structures and analysis of ideology and human agency, including a theory of the working class as the necessary agent for transcending capitalism." Prew et al., "Enduring Relevance," 4.

342 Their plight was echoed in the loss of jobs in the United States Rust Belt from 1991 to 2007. The loss of manufacturing jobs resulted in significant economic hardship for many communities. From 2001 to 2010, these states collectively lost about 1.5 million manufacturing jobs. recruitonomics.com For instance, Michigan's unemployment rate reached a peak of 15.5% in 1982, significantly higher than the national average of 10.8% at that time. amfg.ai Cities like Dayton, Ohio, experienced substantial population declines and increased poverty rates, with Dayton losing 50% of its population since 1960 and one-third of its current residents living in poverty. industryweek.com the loss of 1,000 trade-related jobs was associated with a 2.7% increase in opioid-related deaths. pmc.ncbi.nlm.nih.gov Counties with higher poverty and unemployment rates generally had higher rates of retail opioid sales and Medicare opioid prescriptions, as well as drug overdose deaths and opioid-related hospitalizations. Both the Moselle vintners and Rust Belt workers were adversely affected by policy decisions that exposed them to increased competition. In the Moselle case, the Prussian government's removal of protective tariffs led to an influx of foreign wines, undermining local producers. In the Rust Belt, trade liberalization policies facilitated the offshoring of manufacturing jobs to countries with cheaper labor, leading to deindustrialization. Marx's analysis of the Moselle crisis emphasized that the hardships faced by the vintners were not due to natural causes but were the result of deliberate policy choices that favored certain economic interests over others. This perspective aligns with critiques of modern trade policies that argue such decisions have prioritized corporate profits and consumer access to cheap goods over the livelihoods of domestic workers. This situation parallels the nineteenth-century crisis faced by the Moselle vintners in Prussia. Initially protected by tariffs, these winemakers thrived until the 1830s, when the Prussian government opened the market to foreign wines. This policy shift led to economic hardship for small producers. Karl Marx highlighted that this crisis was not a "natural phenomenon" but resulted from material conditions shaped by government policies. economics.ucr.edu

343 Reina Gattuso, "The Struggling Vineyards That Helped Inspire Karl Marx's Communism," *Atlas Obscura*, June 13, 2019, https://www.atlasobscura.com/articles/where-was-karl-marx-born. The quote is from *Rheinische Zeitung* 18, January 18, 1843.

344 Letter from Friedrich Engels to R. Fischer, February 2, 1895, *Marx-Engels Werke* [*MEW*], vol. XXXIX, 466. *MEW* is 44-volume set published by Dietz Verlag in Berlin. See https://de.wikipedia.org/wiki/Marx-Engels-Werke.

345 Karl Marx, *The German Ideology* (1845). See Peter Linebaugh, "Thefts of Wood: The Manifestation of State and Class Exploitation," *Crime and Social Justice* 6 (1976): 5–16.

346 In 1842, Karl Marx, as editor of the *Rheinische Zeitung*, authored a series of articles titled "Debates on the Law on Thefts of Wood," published between October 15 and November 3 of that year. These articles critically examined the proceedings of the Sixth Rhine Province Assembly concerning legislation

that criminalized the collection of fallen wood—a practice traditionally permitted for the impoverished. Marx argued that such laws transformed customary rights into criminal acts, thereby serving the interests of private property owners and institutionalizing class oppression. This analysis marked Marx's initial foray into economic critique, as he later reflected that this topic "provided the first occasion for occupying myself with economic questions." It is on the MIA at https://marxists.architexturez.net/archive/marx/works/1842/10/25.htm.

347 Please see the MIA at https://www.marxists.org/archive/marx/works/subject/newspapers/rheinische-zeitung.htm for these various articles.

348 Karl Marx, "Letters from the *Rheinische Zeitung*," in *Karl Marx: Selected Writings*, ed. David McLellan (Oxford: Oxford University Press, 1977), 119–123.

349 Hongsheng Jiang, "Frederick Engels on Socialist Literature," *International Critical Thought* 15, no. 1 (2025): 15–37. This article discusses Engels and his engagement with socialist literature in the 1840s.

350 Henderson, *Friedrich Engels*, 45.

351 This passage appears in chapter 2, "The Young Hegelians," where Mehring discusses Marx's early intellectual development and his interactions with contemporaries like Arnold Ruge and Bruno Bauer. Mehring emphasizes Marx's relentless pursuit of knowledge and his rigorous self-critique, which sometimes strained his relationships with collaborators and publishers. The full text of this chapter is available online on the MIA.

352 Heinrich, *Karl Marx*, 43.

353 Gabriel, *Love and Capital*, 44.

354 In his 1845 work, *The Condition of the Working Class in England* (*Die Lage der arbeitenden Klasse in England*), Engels vividly describes the brutal conditions workers faced in the factories and slums of industrial England. Engels wrote this work during his stay in Manchester, where he observed firsthand the harsh conditions during the Industrial Revolution. The book laid the groundwork for their joint development of Marxist theory. The book vividly describes the exploitation, poverty, and suffering experienced by the working class, and critiques the capitalist system that perpetuates these conditions. Marx later drew heavily on Engels's insights in his own works. Engels's portrayal of the suffering working class serves as both a searing critique of capitalism and a fervent call to action—a demand for revolution as the sole path to justice. Like Marx, he viewed revolution not only as a political necessity but as a moral imperative, a means of redeeming humanity from the dehumanizing effects of capitalism. Yet, this uncompromising commitment to revolution came at a cost to Marx and Engels. Their intense focus on overthrowing the existing order often led them to dismiss alternative approaches to social reform, leaving little room for dialogue or pragmatic adjustments to the capitalist system.

355 Eagleton, *Tragedy*, 93.

356 Friedrich Engels, *The Condition of the Working Class in England*, ed. W. O. Henderson and W. H. Chaloner (Oxford: Basil Blackwell, 1958), 10.

357 *MECW*, vol. 1, xiii.

358 Ibid.

359 Friedrich Engels, "Engels to Franz Mehring, London, July 14, 1893," in *Karl Marx and Frederick Engels: Selected Letters* (Moscow: Progress Publishers, 1975), 89–91, at 90.

360 *The German Ideology*, developing the principles of historical materialism and criticizing Ludwig Feuerbach, Bruno Bauer, and Max Stirner, as well as the theory of the "true socialists." The book's publication in Germany was made impossible due to the terms of the censorship. The book first appeared in the Soviet Union in 1932. Max Stirner, "Review of Bruno Bauer's *Trumpet of the Last Judgment*, 1842," *The Anarchist Library*, https://theanarchistlibrary.org/library/max-stirner-review-of-bruno-bauers-trumpet-of-the-last-judgment (accessed April 15, 2025).

361 *Purgatorio*, Canto XXX, 130–32 (trans. Mandelbaum).

362 Friedrich Engels, Sr. (1796–1860) was a prominent German industrialist and textile manufacturer. He owned a textile factory in Barmen and was a partner in a cotton-spinning factory in Manchester, England. His business interests provided his son, Friedrich Engels, with firsthand exposure to the conditions of industrial capitalism. Theodore M. Brown and Elizabeth Fee, "Friedrich Engels: Businessman and Revolutionary," *American Journal of Public Health* 94, no. 12 (2004), https://www.ncbi.nlm.nih.gov/pmc/articles/PMC1447947/.

363 Engels and Mary Burns's relationship exemplifies their shared critique of bourgeois institutions, including marriage. Their partnership, based on mutual respect and shared revolutionary ideals, reflects a commitment to personal and political freedom. This non-traditional arrangement underscores their dedication to challenging societal norms and advocating for a more equitable social order. John Green, *Friedrich Engels: A Biography* (New York: Macmillan, 1979); Tristram Hunt, *Engels: A Revolutionary Life* (New York: W.W. Norton, 2009).

364 *The Condition of the Working Class in England*, ch. 4.

365 Adam Smith, often referred to as the "Father of Economics," was a Scottish economist and philosopher best known for his seminal work *An Inquiry into the Nature and Causes of the Wealth of Nations* (1776). In this work, Smith introduced concepts such as the division of labor and the "invisible hand" of the market, arguing that individuals pursuing their self-interest can unintentionally promote the public good through a self-regulating market system. Wikipedia, "Adam Smith," https://en.wikipedia.org/wiki/Adam_Smith (accessed April 14, 2023). David Ricardo, an English political economist, further developed classical economic theory. His most notable contribution is the theory of comparative advantage, detailed in his work *On the Principles of Political Economy and Taxation* (1817). This theory posits that nations

should specialize in producing goods where they have a relative efficiency advantage, leading to increased overall economic welfare through trade. Britannica, "David Ricardo," https://www.britannica.com/money/David-Ricardo (accessed April 14, 2023).

366 For more on this leader, see his write-up on the University if Nottingham Manuscripts and Special Collections site: https://www.nottingham.ac.uk/manuscriptsandspecialcollections/learning/biographies/feargusoconnor(1796-1855).aspx (accessed July 10, 2025).

367 Ernest Jones (1879–1958) was a Welsh neurologist and psychoanalyst, renowned for being the first English-speaking practitioner of psychoanalysis and a close associate of Sigmund Freud. Born on January 1, 1879, in Gowerton, Wales, Jones pursued medical studies at University College London, specializing in neurology and psychiatry. His profound interest in Freud's theories led him to become a pivotal figure in introducing and establishing psychoanalysis in the English-speaking world. He founded both the British Psychoanalytical Society and the American Psychoanalytic Association, significantly contributing to the institutionalization of psychoanalytic practice. Jones is also noted for his comprehensive three-volume biography of Freud, which remains a seminal work in the field. He passed away on February 11, 1958, in London, England. Britannica, "Ernest Jones," https://www.britannica.com/biography/Ernest-Jones (accessed April 14, 2023).

368 Engels, *The Condition of the Working Class in England*, 10.

369 Charles Dickens, *Bleak House* (London: Bradbury and Evans, 1853), 502. In his novel *Hard Times* (1854), Dickens offers a scathing depiction of industrialization's dehumanizing effects. He describes Coketown, a fictional industrial city."Meanwhile, A. N. Wilson contends: "When Gustave Doré (1832–83) began to illustrate the Comedy in 1855—his first illustrations were published in Paris in 1861—no observer could fail to see the overlap in the artist's imagination between Dante's visionary Hell and the modern Hells of the slum-dwellers and the industrial waste-lands which were also Doré's eerie theme. It is noticeable as we read through the works of John Ruskin that the quotations from Dante increase as the art history of Italy is left behind and the comments on the condition of industrial England become Ruskin's chief concern. Horrified by the conditions of the urban poor, enraged by the indifference of the Victorian rich, Ruskin proclaimed, in his letters to the working classes, 'that one main purpose of the education I want you to seek is that you may see the sky, with the stars of it again, and be enabled, in their material light—riveder le stelle'. Dante for Ruskin became the visionary who could reclaim the essential humanity of a dehumanized industrial proletariat." Wilson, *Dante in Love*, 328.

370 Charles Dickens, *Great Expectations* (London: Chapman & Hall, 1861), 36.

371 Charles Dickens, *Oliver Twist* (London: Richard Bentley, 1839), 89.

372 Engels, *The Condition of the Working Class in England*, 108.

373 Ibid., 45–46.

374 Ibid., 50.

375 Ibid., 127.

376 Charlie Chaplin, *Modern Times*. Film. Directed by Charlie Chaplin, United Artists, 1936.

377 Karl Marx, *Economic and Philosophic Manuscripts of 1844*, trans. Martin Milligan (New York: International Publishers, 1964), 110–13.

378 Friedrich Engels, *Ludwig Feuerbach and the Outcome of Classical German Philosophy*, ed. I. B. Lasker (Moscow: Progress Publishers, 1946). This was originally published in 1888.

379 Marx, *Economic and Philosophical Mnucripts of 1844*, "Human Requirements and Division of Labour under the Rule of Private Property," https://www.marxists.org/archive/marx/works/1844/manuscripts/needs.htm(accessed April 20, 2024).

380 Marx, *Theses on Feuerbach*, Thesis XI (1845).

381 Karl Marx wrote *On the Jewish Question* (*Zur Judenfrage*) in 1843, and it was first published in 1844 in the *Deutsch-Französische Jahrbücher* (*German-French Yearbooks*). Karl Marx. "On the Jewish Question," in Karl Marx: *Early Writings*, ed. and trans. T. B. Bottomore (New York: McGraw-Hill, 1964), 1–26, at, 20.

382 "What is the worldly cult of the Jew?" asked Marx in *On the Jewish Question* in 1844. His answer: "Haggling. What is his worldly god? Money." He then adds: "The emancipation of the Jews is, in the last analysis, the emancipation of mankind from Judaism," which may be taken as a prescription not for the civil emancipation of Jews but for the "human emancipation" from the money-dominated culture represented by Judaism—that is, capitalism. Marx wrote *On the Jewish Question* as a notorious essay where he railed against both Jews and their perceived role in the capitalist system. He argued that Judaism was tied to the mercantile spirit, representing the bourgeoisie and capitalism. For Marx, to emancipate society from capitalism was to emancipate it from Judaism. Marx wrote that the problem of the status of Jews, which Bruno Bauer had seen as a problem in religious consciousness, would be abolished by reorganizing society so as to abolish bargaining: "As religion is the index of man's theoretical struggles, so is the political state that of his practical struggles." See *On The Jewish Question* on the MIA, https://www.marxists.org/archive/marx/works/1844/jewishquestion/ (accessed April 23, 2024).

383 "The state abolishes distinctions of birth, estate, rank, and education in a formal manner, when it declares birth, estate, rank, and education to be non-political distinctions, when it proclaims, without regard to these distinctions, that every member of the nation is an equal participant in national sovereignty, when it treats all elements of the actual life of the nation from the standpoint of the state." Karl Marx, "On the Jewish Question," in *Early*

Political Writings, ed. and trans. Joseph O'Malley (Cambridge: Cambridge University Press, 1994), 28–56, at 32.

384 Ibid., 40.

385 Marx, *Economic and Philosophic Manuscripts of 1844*, trans. Milligan, 113.

386 Marx, "Theses on Feuerbach," in *The German Ideology*, 571–574, at 572.

387 "Why was Prometheus so appealing to Marx? Because he led other Titans in an effort to dethrone the gods of Olympus. Marx, as a faithful disciple of Prometheus, spent his life seeking to dethrone the God of the Bible specifically and all gods in general." Schwarzwalder, "Marx's New Religion," 777.

388 In Isaiah 53, through Christian interpretation, the "Suffering Servant" is depicted as a figure who endures immense suffering to bring knowledge and empowerment to humanity. This portrayal parallels the myth of Prometheus, who defied the ruling powers to bring fire (symbolizing knowledge) to mankind, suffering as a consequence. While Prometheus's act is seen as a rebellion against divine authority, the Suffering Servant's suffering is viewed as a path to redemption. Both narratives highlight the theme of suffering for the benefit of humanity, though they emerge from different worldviews—one from Greek mythology and the other from Hebrew Scripture. See Karl Marx, "Doctoral Thesis: Difference between the Democritean and Epicurean Philosophy of Nature," in *Karl Marx: Early Writings*, ed. and trans. T. B. Bottomore (New York: McGraw-Hill, 1964), 33–110. For salvation in Christianity, see https://en.wikipedia.org/wiki/Salvation_in_Christianity (accessed April 3, 2024).

389 Ludwig von Mises, *Interventionism: An Economic Analysis: The Foundation for Economic Education* (Irvington-on-Hudson, NY: Foundation for Economic Education, 1998), 57.

390 *The German Ideology*, the work that laid out the foundation of Marxist theory, was written by Marx and Engels between late 1845 and early 1846. They completed the manuscript in mid-1846, though it was not published until much later, in 1932, due to political obstacles.

391 Marx and Engels, *The German Ideology*, 64.

392 Stedman Jones, *Greatness and Illusion*, 147.

393 *The German Ideology*, ch. 1; see the MIA version at https://www.marxists.org/archive/marx/works/1845/german-ideology/ch01a.htm (accessed April 15, 2024).

394 This quote is found in Marx's *Economic and Philosophic Manuscripts of 1844*, specifically in the "Estranged Labor" section. It illustrates Marx's idea that under communism individuals would not be constrained by the division of labor that limits them to a single profession. Instead, they would be able to freely pursue various forms of creative and productive activities according to their needs and desires. See Marx, *Economic and Philosophic Manuscripts of 1844*, trans. Milligan.

395 Singer 36.

396 Isaiah 11:6–9 (NRSV):
"The wolf shall live with the lamb,
the leopard shall lie down with the kid,
the calf and the lion and the fatling together,
and a little child shall lead them.
The cow and the bear shall graze,
their young shall lie down together;
and the lion shall eat straw like the ox.
The nursing child shall play over the hole of the asp,
and the weaned child shall put its hand on the adder's den.
They will not hurt or destroy on all my holy mountain;
for the earth will be full of the knowledge of the Lord
as the waters cover the sea."

397 Isaiah 2:4 (NRSV):
"He shall judge between the nations,
and shall arbitrate for many peoples;
they shall beat their swords into plowshares,
and their spears into pruning hooks;
nation shall not lift up sword against nation,
neither shall they learn war any more."

398 Singer, *Marx*, 36 (EPM 97).

399 Murray N. Rothbard, "Karl Marx: Communist as Religious Eschatologist," *The Review of Austrian Economics* 4, no. 1 (1990): 123–79, at 151, https://cdn.mises.org/rae4_1_5_2.pdf.

400 "In the same way as the return of the Messiah, in Christian theology, will put an end to history and establish a new heaven and a new earth, so the establishment of communism would put an end to human history." Murray N. Rothbard, "Karl Marx as Religious Eschatologist." *Mises Daily*, October 9, 2009. https://mises.org/mises-daily/karl-marx-religious-eschatologist.

401 "Man is born free, and everywhere he is in chains. One believes himself the master of others, and yet remains more of a slave than they" (*The Social Contract*, book 1, ch. 1); see Jean-Jacques Rousseau, *The Social Contract*, trans. G. D. H. Cole (London: J. M. Dent & Sons, 1923).

402 In 1850, in the *Rheinische Zeitung*, is where a series of articles called "The Class Struggles in France," appeared, and this is where Marx first used the term, See them on the MIA at https://www.marxists.org/archive/marx/works/1850/class-struggles-france/.

403 See endnote 421.

404 "Or as the Free Spirit adept from Erfurt, Johann Hartmann, put it, 'The truly free man is king and lord of all creatures. All things belong to him, and he has the right to use whatever pleases him. If anyone tries to prevent him, the free man may kill him and take his good.' As one of the favorite sayings of the Brethren of the Free Spirit phrased it, "Whatever the eye sees and covets, let the hand grasp it." Rothbard, "Karl Marx as Religious Eschatologist."

405 Himmelfarb, "Let Marx Be Marx," 41.

406 George Orwell, *Nineteen Eighty-Four* (Cutchogue, NY: Buccaneer Books, 1949), ch. 1.

407 Christopher Booker, *The Seven Basic Plots: Why we Tell Stories* (London: Continuum, 2004), 658.

408 Karl Marx, *Capital: A Critique of Political Economy*, vol. 1, trans. Ben Fowkes (Vintage Books, 1976), 128; Anti-Defamation League, "New Hate and Old: The Changing Face of American White Supremacy," https://www.adl.org/resources/report/new-hate-and-old-changing-face-american-white-supremacy (accessed February 20, 2025).

409 Karl Marx, "A Contribution to the Critique of Hegel's *Philosophy of Right*," in *Karl Marx: Early Writings*, trans. and ed. T. B. Bottomore (New York: McGraw-Hill, 1964), 43–44, at 43.

410 Karl Marx, "Letter to Arnold Ruge, May 1843," in *Karl Marx: Selected Writings*, ed. David McLellan (Oxford: Oxford University Press, 2000), 46.

411 The final issue of *Neue Rheinische Zeitung* (May 18, 1849), in *MEGA* VI.503; variant translation: "We are ruthless and ask no quarter from you. When our turn comes, we shall not disguise our terrorism. Revolutions are the locomotives of history."

412 "Terror is no longer used as a means to exterminate and frighten opponents, but as an instrument to rule masses of people who are perfectly obedient." Hannah Arendt, *The Origins of Totalitarianism* (New York: Harcourt, 1973), 6.

413 "All his resources of vituperation, innuendo, sarcasm, and spite were poured into a long polemical work." McGrogan, *Who the Hell Is Karl Marx?*, 322.

414 "The bourgeoisie, like Dante's damned, will not escape their judgment. For their actions, they will face the inferno of their own making, their systemic oppression reflected in the suffering of the workers they exploit." Karl Marx, *Letters to Engels* (1846–1878).

415 Marx, *Capital*, ch. 1.

416 Singer, *Marx*, 35. On page 32, Singer explains: "Capital is nothing else but accumulated labour. The worker's labour increases the employer's capital. This increased capital is used to build bigger factories and buy more machines. More sophisticated machinery increases the division of labour, thus putting more self-employed workers out of business. Now the formerly self-employed workers have no option but to sell their labour on the market. This intensifies the competition among workers trying to get work, and lowers wages." Richard Wolff, *Understanding Marxism*, 28, says: "In every society, he says, human beings survive by labor: transforming nature to meet their needs. They convert wool into clothing to keep warm, trees to build shelters from the rain and the storm, land into food, and so on. In laboring, humans use their brains and muscles to transform nature into useful consumable products upon which human societies depend." See also MacIntyre, *Marxism and Christianity*, 47.

417 In his *Economic and Philosophic Manuscripts of 1844*, Marx laid out his theory of alienation, and his vision of revolution was not merely a political program. Marx wrote: "Communism . . . is the genuine resolution of the antagonism between man and nature and between man and man. . . . It is the riddle of history solved." It was a utopian dream, a vision of a future in which all forms of alienation would be overcome, and humanity would be restored to its natural state and in a new eschaton, one that would first have to resolve the issue of the alienation from religion once and for all. For overview on development of the concept of alienation, see Marcelo Musto, *The Marx Revival: Key Concepts and New Interpretations* (Cambridge: Cambridge University Press, 2020), 3–24.

418 See Matthew 21:12–13; Mark 11:15–17; Luke 19:45–46; John 2:13–17.

419 The term "morphic" refers to the concept of structural or developmental transformation within a system, often implying a progression through distinct phases. In Marxist thought, this could be understood as the movement through historical stages—feudalism, capitalism, socialism—culminating in communism. This teleological framework, akin to a secularized eschatology, positions the working class as the agent of revolutionary change, replacing traditional messianic figures. Karl Marx, *A Contribution to the Critique of Political Economy* (Moscow: Progress Publishers, 1859), preface.

420 Marx's dissertation, "Differenz der demokritischen und epikureischen Naturphilosophie" ("The Difference Between the Democritean and Epicurean Philosophy of Nature"), written in 1841, focuses on the concept of the swerve (*clinamen*) in Epicurus's thought. This idea refers to the slight, unpredictable deviation of atoms from their determined paths, which allows for the possibility of free will within an otherwise mechanistic universe. Marx saw this as Epicurus's of preserving individual autonomy in a world ruled by material forces. However, as Marx moved toward historical materialism in the 1840s, particularly in *The German Ideology* (1845–1846) and *Theses on Feuerbach* (1845), his views changed dramatically. He abandoned the idea that individuals could exercise meaningful agency apart from the material conditions of their existence. Instead, he argued that the economic base—the structure of production and class relations—determined the ideological and cultural superstructure. His deterministic materialism came to mirror a kind of secular predestination, where individuals were seen as products of their historical and economic conditions rather than autonomous moral agents. This new perspective was fundamentally opposed to the Christian tradition. While Aquinas (*Summa Theologica*, I–II, q. 109, a. 2) and Dante (*Purgatorio*, Canto XVI, 76–79) saw free will as damaged but recoverable through grace, Marx denied its existence altogether, replacing it with class consciousness and historical necessity. In *The German Ideology*, he wrote: "Life is not determined by consciousness, but consciousness by life."

421 Karl R. Popper, *The Open Society and Its Enemies* (Princeton, NJ: Princeton University Press, 2013), 5.

422 Karl R. Popper, *The Open Society and Its Enemies* (London: Routledge, 1945), 268.

423 Eagleton, *Tragedy*, 56–57.

424 This tension between theoretical ideals and real-world execution results in a historical clash marked by violence, repression, and the betrayal of its own principles. The Apostle Paul, in his reflections on human alienation, articulates a similar struggle: "For I do not do the good I want, but the evil I do not want is what I do" (Romans 7:19, NRSV).

425 "It was St. Paul who, in a series of epistles, especially chapter 5 of Romans, recast human history and theology by linking Jesus Christ, over the heads of all other prophets, leaders, and lawgivers, to Adam. The original man's transgression is now redeemed by the obedience of another man, God's incarnate Son. Jesus becomes the second Adam in a symmetrical pattern known in biblical study as typology. Christian faith proposes, among other things, an all-encompassing narrative unity." Shattuck, *Forbidden Knowledge*, 50.

426 1 Corinthians 15:45–49 (NRSV): "Thus it is written, 'The first man, Adam, became a living being'; the last Adam became a life-giving spirit. But it is not the spiritual that is first, but the physical, and then the spiritual. The first man was from the earth, a man of dust; the second man is from heaven. As was the man of dust, so are those who are of the dust, and as is the man of heaven, so are those who are of heaven. Just as we have borne the image of the man of dust, we will also bear the image of the man of heaven." Paul contrasts Adam, the first human who brought sin and death, with Christ, who brings life and redemption, reinforcing the theme of spiritual renewal and transformation in Christian theology.

427 Romans 5:12–21; 1 Corinthians 15:45.

428 "Different faiths, different mythologies, different scenarios of secular anthropology and psychology, of political theory, provide programmatic narratives of, explanations of, the imperative of primordial guilt. They are as prevalent in modern positivism as they were in archaic hypotheses. The Judeo-Christian and Pauline fable of Adamic disobedience and inherited guilt has darkened the human prospect virtually to our day. It has modulated with intriguing ease into secular and profane models. Marx's 1844 manuscripts postulate a stage in human relations in which the primal exchange of trust for trust, of love for love, became fatally one of property and of money, dooming our species to the treadmill of labor and class conflict." Steiner, "'Tragedy,' Reconsidered," 3.

429 Ephesians 6:12 (NRSV): "For our struggle is not against enemies of blood and flesh, but against the rulers, against the authorities, against the cosmic powers of this present darkness, against the spiritual forces of evil in the heavenly places." Colossians 2:15 (NRSV): "He disarmed the rulers and authorities and made a public example of them, triumphing over them in it." Romans 8:38–39 (NRSV): "For I am convinced that neither death, nor life, nor angels, nor rulers, nor things present, nor things to come, nor powers,

nor height, nor depth, nor anything else in all creation, will be able to separate us from the love of God in Christ Jesus our Lord."

430 See previous note (Ephesians 6:12, NRSV).

431 See also Steiner, "'Tragedy' Reconsidered," 3: "The Judeo-Christian and Pauline fable of Adamic disobedience and inherited guilt has darkened the human prospect virtually to our day. It has modulated with intriguing ease into secular and profane models. Marx's 1844 manuscripts postulate a stage in human relations in which the primal exchange of trust for trust, of love for love, became fatally one of property and of money, dooming our species to the treadmill of labor and class conflict. Marx's prophetic rhetoric provides no account of how or when this fall from innocence came to pass."

432 Romans 5:12–21 (NRSV).

433 The term "dictatorship of the proletariat" refers to a Marxist concept describing a transitional state in which the working class (proletariat) seizes control of political and economic power from the bourgeoisie. It is a temporary phase meant to dismantle the structures of capitalism and establish the conditions for a classless, stateless society—ultimately leading to communism. The phrase was first used by Karl Marx in his writings, such as in his *Critique of the Gotha Program* (1875), and elaborated upon in *The Communist Manifesto* (1848). Unlike traditional notions of dictatorship, Marx and Engels envisioned this as the rule of the majority (the working class) over the minority (the capitalists), aiming to prevent the re-emergence of exploitation and inequality during the transition from capitalism to socialism. See *MESW*, vol. 3, 13-30.

434 1 Corinthians 15:22 (NRSV).

435 Here, the Apostle reflects on the source of his own alienation in Romans 7:24, lamenting: "Wretched man that I am! Who will deliver me from this body of death?" This shared recognition of alienation underscores their empathy for the human experience, but with a distinct and different understanding of the diagnosis. See notes 4 and 125.

436 The term "grand narrative" (also known as "metanarrative") was introduced by French philosopher Jean-François Lyotard in his 1979 work *The Postmodern Condition: A Report on Knowledge*. In this context, a grand narrative refers to an overarching story or ideology that attempts to explain various events in history and provides meaning by connecting disparate phenomena through universal truths or values. Examples include ideologies like Marxism, the Enlightenment belief in progress, and religious doctrines. Lyotard argued that in the postmodern era, there is an increasing skepticism toward these totalizing narratives. He suggested that such grand narratives have lost their credibility and that society is moving toward "little narratives" or localized representations that do not claim universal truth. Jean-François Lyotard, *The Postmodern Condition: A Report on Knowledge*, trans. Geoff Bennington and Brian Massumi (Minneapolis: University of Minnesota Press, 1984). See

the "Metanarrative" entry on Wikipedia at https://en.wikipedia.org/wiki/Metanarrative (accessed February 20, 2025).

437 In his epistles, the Apostle Paul frequently emphasizes the transformative experience of participating in a new life through union with Christ. For instance, in Romans 6:4, he writes: "Therefore we have been buried with him by baptism into death, so that, just as Christ was raised from the dead by the glory of the Father, so we too might walk in newness of life." Similarly, in 2 Corinthians 5:17, Paul states: "So if anyone is in Christ, there is a new creation: everything old has passed away; see, everything has become new!" These passages illustrate Paul's teaching that through faith and baptism believers undergo a profound transformation, leaving behind their old selves and embracing a renewed existence in Christ. This concept of dying and rising with Christ signifies a break from the past and the commencement of a new life characterized by righteousness and communion with God. Rothbard, "Communist as Religious Eschatologist," 150.

438 Eric Voegelin, *The New Science of Politics: An Introduction* (Chicago: University of Chicago Press, 1952), 120. His warning underscores the dangers of conflating transcendent salvation with earthly goals, a process Marx embraced by shifting the focus from divine restoration to revolutionary materialism. In examining the divergent prophetic messages of Marx and the Apostle Paul, it becomes evident that, despite their vastly different metaphysics, they share striking parallels in their concerns for the human condition and societal transformation, and the coming apocalypse.

439 Marx, *Theses on Feuerbach* (1845).

440 Heraclitus, Fragment 12 (DK B12), as recorded by Plato in *Cratylus* 402a.

441 1 Corinthians 15:22 (NRSV).

442 Galatians 3:28.

443 1 Timothy 6:10; Matthew 6:24

444 See Matthew 19:24; Mark 10:25; Luke 16:19; Luke 18:23; Luke 12:16–21; 1 Timothy 6:10; 1 Timothy 6:17; James 5:1; Revelation 3:17.

445 "Marxism: namely that there exists a social subject (the working class), which, on the basis of its particular position in bourgeois society, possesses a special ability to see through social relationships. Many representatives of traditional Marxism expressed the need to 'take the standpoint of the working class' in order to understand capitalism. But in doing so, they overlooked the fact that workers (just like capitalists) in their spontaneous consciousness are also subject to the delusions of the commodity fetish. . . . The capitalist mode of production brings forth other inversions and absurdities to which both workers and capitalists succumb. One cannot therefore speak of a privileged position of perception occupied by the working class—but one also cannot make the claim that fetishism is in principle impenetrable." Michael Heinrich, *An Introduction to the Three Volumes of Karl Marx's Capital*, trans. Alexander Locascio (New York: Monthly Review Press, 2004), 79.

446 Eagleton, *Tragedy*, 71.

447 Karl Marx, "The Class Struggles in France," in *Karl Marx: Selected Writings*, ed. David McLellan (Oxford: Oxford University Press, 2000), 350–75, at 374.

448 Romans 8:21 (NRSV). See also *The Holy Bible*, English Standard Version (Wheaton: Crossway Bibles, 2001), Romans 8:21 (ESV).

449 1 Corinthians 13:12.

450 For the Apostle Paul's acknowledgment of partial understanding, see, 1 Corinthians 13:12 (NRSV): "For now we see through a glass, darkly."

451 For Paul's mention of time, see Romans 5:6; 13:11; 1 Corinthians 4:5; 2 Corinthians 6:2; Galatians 4:4; Ephesians 1:10; Ephesians 5:16; Colossians 4:5; 1 Thessalonians 5:1; 2 Timothy 4:3, 4:6. See Karl Marx, "The Eighteenth Brumaire of Louis Bonaparte," in *Karl Marx: Selected Writings*, ed. David McLellan (Oxford: Oxford University Press, 2000), 300–325, at 300.

452 Karl Marx and Friedrich Engels, *The Communist Manifesto*, trans. Samuel Moore (London: Penguin Books, 1967), 1.

453 Romans 3:13 (ESV): "For rulers are not a terror to good conduct."

454 Matthew 22:21 (ESV).

455 Walter Kaufmann and James Hughes, *The Future of the Humanities: Teaching Art, Religion, Philosophy, Literature and History* (London: Routledge, 1995), 51.

456 Dante Alighieri, *The Divine Comedy: Purgatorio*, trans. Allen Mandelbaum (New York: Bantam Books, 1984); *Purgatorio*, Canto XIX, lines 115–17.

457 Carlyle, *On Heroes*, 79.

458 Wilson, *Dante in Love*, 85.

459 Turner, *History of Hell*, 133.

460 *Inferno*, Canto XXVIII, lines 34–36.

461 Peter Critchley, "Dante and Marx," *Being and Place*, October 26, 2016. https://pcritchley2.wixsite.com/beingandplace/post/2016/10/26/dante-and-marx.

462 Jenny Marx's letter to Joseph Weydemeyer, 1851. An excerpt is available in the *Chicago Daily Socialist* 3, no. 82, February 1, 1909. Also, see Gabriel's *Love and Capital*. Gabriel discusses the Marx family's financial difficulties and Jenny's unwavering support for Karl's work.

463 Karl Marx, "Marx to the Editorial Board," *Neue Rheinische Zeitung*, February 1849; reprinted in *Karl Marx: Selected Works in Two Volumes*, vol. 1 (Moscow: Foreign Languages Publishing House, 1951), 577.

464 Karl Marx, "Debates on the Law on Thefts of Wood," in *Karl Marx: Selected Writings*, ed. David McLellan (Oxford: Oxford University Press, 2000), 224–63, at 230–35.

465 Wheen, *Karl Marx*, 123–25.

466 McLellan, *His Life and Thought*, 189–90.

467 Gabriel, *Love and Capital*, 150; Shlomo Avineri, *Moses Hess: Prophet of Communism and Zionism* (New York: New York University Press, 1985), 45–47.

468 Liebknecht, *Biographical Memoirs*.

469 Payne, *Biography*, 121–22.

470 Gabriel, *Love and Capital*, 150.

471 Biographer Paul Kengor rightly points out that "Karl, champion of the proletariat, fulminator against low-paid workers, protester against wage exploitation, never paid Lenchen a penny." Kengor, *The Devil and Karl Marx*, 81.

472 Dante, *Inferno*, Canto II, line 32.

473 "Alluding to Marx's utopian phrasing in *The Critique of Hegel's Philosophy of Right,* he [Williams] comments that 'the idea of "the total redemption of humanity" [Marx] has the ultimate cast of resolution and order, but in the real world its perspective is inescapably tragic. It is born in pity and terror: in the perception of a radical disorder in which the humanity of some men is denied and by the fact that the idea of humanity itself is denied." Pamela McCallum, "Questions of Haunting: Jacques Derrida's *Specters of Marx* and Raymond Williams's *Modern Tragedy*," *Mosaic* 40, no. 2 (2007): 231–44, at 235.

474 Letter from Arnold Ruge to Karl Marx, 1843.

475 *MECW*, vol. 5, 469 (1859 Preface). Marx first published the Preface in the German newspaper *Das Volk* 5, June 4, 1859. See also Karl Marx, *A Contribution to the Critique of Political Economy*, trans. S. W. Ryazanskaya (Moscow: Progress Publishers, 1977), 21.

476 Wheen, *Karl Marx*, 123.

477 "There is much in Marx's early life which might have seemed to predestine him for a literary career. As his daughter Eleanor recalled in later years: He was a unique, an unrivalled story-teller. A taste for the eighteenth-century German classics was nourished by his father (who held up Schiller, in particular, for his son's admiration); while the Marx family's neighbour at Trier, Karl Marx's later father-in-law Ludwig von Westphalen, induced him to share his own admiration for Shakespeare. 'He never tired,' Eleanor told Wilhelm Liebknecht, 'of telling us.'" BM, 147.

478 Derrida, *Specters of Marx*, 176, cited in McCallum, "Questions of Haunting," 242.

479 Shakespeare, *Hamlet*, 1.5.188–189.

480 "From the moment when Hamlet cries: The time is out of joint; O cursed spite, That ever I was born to set it right! he becomes an example, unequalled in modern literature until Dostoevsky, of the Divided Man. 'God and the Devil are fighting there, and the battlefield is the heart of man.' That sentence of Dmitri Karamazov's expresses it, and because the infernal and celestial powers that are contending for the possession of Hamlet are so nearly in balance, the torture is prolonged and exquisite. He alternates between phases of anguished thought and feverish activity." Bloom, *Hamlet*, 109.

481 "In Hamlet, the play-within-the-play becomes not merely theatrical diversion but a scientific instrument of revelation. Just as Marx would seek to expose hidden structures beneath religious and capitalist appearances, Hamlet

deploys drama to 'catch the conscience' of his enemy. The dichotomy within Hamlet—between action and reflection—resolves momentarily in this strategy, as he transforms his art into an empirical tool to unveil truth, not through vengeance, but through exposure: 'The play's the thing / Wherein I'll catch the conscience of the King.' As one critic puts it, Hamlet's shift is 'an intimation straight from his own innermost genius. His evil spirit had told him to kill the King. His good angel tells him to show the King to himself by holding up the mirror of art before him.'" Bloom, *Hamlet*, 116.

482 "The Ghost in *Hamlet* alone can support several different versions of his belief; for Hamlet's thoughts about it reflect the contemporary Catholic view that ghosts came from purgatory, the orthodox Protestant view that they were evil spirits, and the skeptical view that they were hallucinations. But the endless disagreement among his religious interpreters itself reveals that Shakespeare did not plainly commit himself to any definite belief. Whatever Christian faith he may have had is certainly not so clear as that of Dante before him, of Calderón in contemporary Spain, or of Corneille and Milton after him." Muller, *The Spirit of Tragedy*, 147.

483 "Eagleton claimed that as passive suffering was not what constituted a real tragedy, it was of ultimate importance that the death of the tragic hero, of Hamlet, was central to the plot and made dramatically significant while being saved for the end." Kaninika Singh agrees with Eagleton, who compares tragedy to Aristotle's *katharsis*. Kaninika Singh, "An Analysis of Shakespeare's Hamlet through Terry Eagleton's Conception of Tragedy," *International Journal of English Literature and Social Sciences* 8, no. 4 (2023): 207–13, at 209.

484 Here, Kaufmann explains the unique role of tragedy; Walter Kaufmann, *Tragedy and Philosophy* (New York: Doubleday, 1968), 182.

485 "For MacIntyre aligns with Marx's instinct. What is to be resisted is injustice. Capitalism is to be understood as a society which is structured by institutional manipulation of people in pursuit of goods of effectiveness. Therefore, given the Aristotelian conception of justice as the virtue of treating people as they deserve, capitalism is to be understood as structurally unjust. MacIntyre's politics of resistance is one of collective action in defence of practices against institutional domination and corruption. The substantial control that capitalists, managers, politicians and bureaucrats exercise over practices does not preclude plain persons from resisting their institutionalized will to power." MacIntyre, *The MacIntyre Reader*, 23.

486 Karl Marx and Friedrich Engels, *The Communist Manifesto* (New York: Pocket Books, 2002): 1.

487 Marx, *The Communist Manifesto*.

488 "The Communist League (German: Bund der Kommunisten) was an international political party established on 1 June 1847 in London, England. The organisation was formed through the merger of the League of the Just, headed by Karl Schapper, and the Communist Correspondence Committee

of Brussels, Belgium, in which Karl Marx and Friedrich Engels were the dominant personalities." DBpedia, "Communist League," https://dbpedia.org/page/Communist_League (accessed April 5, 2024).

489 Marx and Engels, *The Communist Manifesto*, trans. Moore, 1.

490 McLellan, *His Life and Thought*, 189.

491 Marx to Engels, November 1847, *MECW*, vol. 6.

492 Eric Hobsbawm, "Marx and History," *Diogenes* 32, no. 125 (1984): 103–14, https://doi.org/10.1177/039219218403212507.

493 Shlomo Avineri, *Karl Marx: Philosophy and Revolution* (New Haven, CT: Yale University Press, 2019), ch. 4.

494 Marx and Engels, *The Communist Manifesto*, 36.

495 Ibid., 6. Marx and Engels articulate the dynamics of capitalist societies, famously stating "All that is solid melts into air" to describe the transient nature of modern life under capitalism. See also Avineri, *Philosophy and Revolution*, 12. Avineri provides a comprehensive analysis of Marx's works, highlighting the philosophical depth of *The Communist Manifesto* and its enduring impact on political thought.

496 Prawer, *World Literature*, ch. 3.

497 "All that is solid melts into air, all that is holy is profaned, and man is at last compelled to face with sober senses his real conditions of life, and his relations with his kind." Marx and Engels, *The Communist Manifesto* (1848).

498 William Shakespeare, *Hamlet*, act 1, scene 5.

499 Terry Eagleton, *Marx and Freedom* (New Haven: Yale University Press, 2007), 112.

500 Marx and Engels, *The Communist Manifesto*, 6.

501 Hamlet "exercises his agency actively, leading him to become a tragic hero. Even in the sense of procrastinating, Hamlet seems to practise his agency of neglecting social responsibilities temporarily. It becomes tragic for the audience—this is a shocking position since, despite the fact that extraneous circumstances attempt to hinder his path, it becomes the only accessible way for a man to affirm himself as genuine, to typify and realize himself in the world." Singh, "Analysis," 211.

502 By the 1860s, she had grown weary of their impoverished lifestyle, frequently remarking that their lives were "hardly worth living." In a letter from 1862, Jenny confided to a friend that she wished she and her children were safely in their graves: "She hated poverty because it removed from her the opportunity to be generous, and she hated squalor because it removed from her the opportunity to wear beautiful clothes. While she loved her husband passionately, she seems never to have been completely at ease in his presence: the seeds of distrust were sown very early. For her he was a stranger who had to be known afresh each day. In the end she became accustomed to him, as one becomes accustomed to strangers. Her real love was for her children." McLellan, *Life and Thought*, 387.

503 "The Communists disdain to conceal their views and aims. They openly declare that their ends can be attained only by the forcible overthrow of all existing social conditions." Marx and Engels, *The Communist Manifesto*, 67. Marx was influenced by Johann Wolfgang von Goethe's *Faust*, from which he often quoted: "Alles was entsteht, ist wert, dass es zugrunde geht." This translates to "All that exists deserves to perish." Goethe, *Faust*, Part One, lines 1339–40.

504 "The bourgeois sees in his wife a mere instrument of production. He hears that the instruments of production are to be exploited in common, and, naturally, can come to no other conclusion than that the lot of being common to all will likewise befall the women." Marx and Engels, *The Communist Manifesto*, 52. In terms of the family, "Engels argues that the nuclear family developed as a response to industrialisation and the growing trend to 'Own Private Property.' The Nuclear Family was set up so that capital (wealth) could legally be passed on to 'Heirs' (Children)—Money could stay within the Family. Monogamous Relationships were favoured so that men could be sure that their children really were their biological children. Monogamous Marriage ensured that women would be economically dependent on their male partners & as such would not stray & mother children by other men. Women become 'Glorified Prostitutes'—producers of heirs in exchange for economic security," https://thesociologyguy.com/wp-content/uploads/2019/03/marxism-and-family.pdf (accessed April 1, 2025).

505 "Communism abolishes eternal truths, it abolishes all religion, and all morality, instead of constituting them on a new basis; it therefore acts in contradiction to all past historical experience." Marx and Engels, *The Communist Manifesto*, 53.

506 "The theory of the Communists may be summed up in the single sentence: Abolition of private property." Marx and Engels, *The Communist Manifesto*, 49.

507 Marx and Engels, *The Communist Manifesto*, 33.

508 "The German soil chemist Justus von Liebig (1859) also helped generalize the concept of metabolism, using it to examine the exchange of nutrients between Earth and humans. In order to produce crops, soil must contain essential nutrients—such as (but not limited to) nitrogen, phosphorus, and potassium. As plants grow, they take up these nutrients. Liebig determined that the long-term productivity of the soil demanded following the 'law of compensation' or law of replacement, whereby the nutrients that are removed from the land must be restored . . . He pointed out that British high-farming techniques constituted a 'robbery system,' stealing nutrients from the soil, contributing to despoliation of the earth . . . Horrified by the scale of soil degradation, Liebig . . . exclaimed, 'Truly, if this soil could cry out like a cow or a horse which was tormented to give the maximum quantity of milk or work with the smallest expenditure of fodder, the earth would become to these agriculturalists more intolerable than Dante's infernal regions'. Drawing on this work, Marx developed a broader metabolic analysis, which he

demonstrated in his critique of capitalist agriculture. He recognized that soil fertility was influenced by the historical development of socioecological relations. For example, in many pre-capitalist societies, particularly in Europe, farm animals were directly incorporated into agricultural production. They were fed grains from farms, and the nutrients, in the form of manure, were actively reincorporated into the soil as fertilizer. Also, people who lived in the countryside or near production sources primarily consumed the food and beer, and local nutrient cycling was a regular practice." Brett Clark, John Bellamy Foster, and Stefano B. Longo. "Metabolic Rifts and the Ecological Crisis," in *The Oxford Handbook of Karl Marx*, ed. Paul Prew, Tomas Rotta, Tony Smith, and Matt Vidal (Oxford: Oxford University Press, 2019), 651–58, at 653.

509 Ibid., 38–39.

510 See note 376.

511 "Since the producers have no democratic control over what is being produced, how it is being produced, or how the surplus is being distributed, the products of their labor pile up on the other side of the divide—they become the wealth of the capitalist owners. Commodities turn into an alien power that is used against the workers by replacing them with new technologies and by ring them, impoverishing them, and making them 'superfluous.' This irrational system, that periodically destroys its own wealth by disastrous crises, is finally to be overcome by an 'association of free people' . . . What is this fetishism of African worshippers, compared to European fetishism, by which the entire regulation of societal production, which decides over the weal and woe of people, is handed over to the dynamics of the things produced!" Jan Rehman, "Ideology as Alienated Socialization," in *The Oxford Handbook of Karl Marx*, ed. Paul Prew, Tomas Rotta, Tony Smith, and Matt Vidal (Oxford: Oxford University Press, 2019), 111–28, at 117.

512 Marx and Engels, *The Communist Manifesto*, 6.

513 Ibid., 8.

514 Ibid., 8–9.

515 Ibid., 10.

516 Ibid., 12.

517 McGrogan, *Who the Hell Is Karl Marx?* 37.

518 Marx and Engels, *The Communist Manifesto* (1848).

519 Marx's aspirations were also marked by a deepening sense of alienation, both personal and intellectual. "In order to abolish the idea of private property, the idea of communism is completely sufficient. It takes actual communist action to abolish actual private property. History will come to it; and this movement, which in theory we already know to be a self-transcending movement, will constitute in actual fact a very severe and protracted process. But we must regard it as a real advance to have gained beforehand a consciousness of the limited character as well as of the goal of this historical movement—and a consciousness which reaches out beyond it." Karl Marx, "Economic

and Philosophic Manuscripts of 1844," in *The Marx-Engels Reader*, ed. Robert C. Tucker (New York: W.W. Norton & Company, 1978), 66–125, at 99.

520 Letter from Pierre-Joseph Proudhon to Marx, 1845.

521 "Awareness of complicity is suppressed in a promotion of a status quo in which war and revolution are seen as disturbances and upheavals to be avoided, if at all possible. To refuse to understand and be open to the situation of the other is, in Williams's words, 'to acquiesce in a disorder and call it order; to say peace where there is no peace,' and to expect people who are 'intolerably poor to rest and be patient in their misery'." McCallum, "Questions of Haunting," 236.

522 His reign was marked by efforts to modernize France, including significant infrastructure development, such as the expansion of railways and the transformation of Paris under Baron Haussmann. These projects aimed to position France as a modern industrial and cultural power. However, his regime was also characterized by authoritarianism and the suppression of political dissent, and would draw sharp criticism from contemporaries like Karl Marx.

523 In this work, Marx analyzes the 1851 *coup d'état* by Louis-Napoléon Bonaparte, contextualizing it within broader historical and social forces. He argues that while individuals and groups actively shape history, their actions are constrained by existing conditions and historical contexts. This perspective challenges the "great man" theory of history, which attributes historical events primarily to the actions of influential individuals. Instead, Marx emphasizes the significance of underlying social and economic structures in shaping historical outcomes.

524 Russell, *Mephistopheles*, 215.

525 MacIntyre, *Ethics and Politics*, 151.

526 Kamenka, "Introduction," xxiv.

527 Aeschylus, *Prometheus Bound*, trans. Vellacott, lines 435–40.

528 In *The Cooperative Commonwealth*, the concept of a "secular apocalypse" is discussed in relation to Marx's ideas. The text notes that "Marx himself expressed apocalyptic themes in the last book of Das Kapital." Joseph Blau, "The Cooperative Commonwealth as Secular Apocalypse," *Transactions of the Charles S. Peirce Society* 12, no. 3 (1976): 209–22, https://www.jstor.org/stable/40319774.

529 Payne, *Biography*, 13.

530 Johnson, *Intellectuals*, 56.

531 Pierre-Joseph Proudhon, *The General Idea of the Revolution in the Nineteenth Century* (New York: Haskell House Publishers, 1969), 251.

532 Pierre-Joseph Proudhon, *De la Justice dans la Revolution et dans l'Église* (Paris: Librairie de Garnier Frères, Paris, 1858), 540.

533 James Guillaume, *Bakunin on Anarchy* (George Allen & Unwin Ltd, 1971). Accessed via https://www.marxists.org/reference/archive/bakunin/works/various/mebio.htm#:~:text=On%20the%20other%20hand%2C%20Proudhon,head%20to%20foot%20an%20authoritarian.

534 Michel Bakounine, *Oeuvres*, vol. 2 (Paris: P.V. Stock, 1907), xiv.

535 Avineri, *Moses Hess*, 11.

536 Moses Hess, *Briefwechsel* (Amsterdam: Mouton & Co., 1959), 103.

537 Friedrich Engels, "Democratic Pan-Slavism," *Neue Rheinische Zeitung* 222, February 15, 1849.

538 Bakounine, *Oeuvres*, xii.

539 McLellan, *A Biography*, 82.

540 Johnson, *Intellectuals*, 56.

541 Ferdinand Lassalle to Karl Marx, 1848.

542 Hess to Marx, 1844.

543 Marx saw these upheavals as the dawn of the proletarian revolution he had envisioned. However, the initial euphoria was short-lived. The revolutionary movements lacked cohesion and a unified vision. In France, the newly formed Second Republic faced internal divisions. The closure of the National Workshops, which had provided employment to thousands, led to the June Days Uprising—a brutal and bloody confrontation between workers and the government. The uprising was suppressed with considerable loss of life, and the promise of the revolution began to wane. Across Europe, reactionary forces regrouped and regained control. In the Austrian Empire, the Habsburgs reasserted their dominance, quelling nationalist and liberal movements. In the German states, conservative monarchies reestablished their authority, dashing hopes for unification and liberal reforms.

544 Eagleton, *Tragedy*, 19.

545 Karl Marx, *Neue Rheinische Zeitung*, November 7, 1848, in *MECW*, vol. 8, 562.

546 Dante, *Paradiso*, Canto XVII.

547 "Dante's phrase 'the hope which begets true love' comes from Colossians 1 where Paul teaches that 'the hope which is laid up for you in heaven' (v.5) leads to 'the love which ye have for all the saints' (v.4). While the purpose of Paul's heavenly journey was the confirmation of faith (Inf 2.29), the purpose of [Dante's] journey is to strengthen the hope of believers." Daigle-Williamson, "Dante," 49.

548 Johnson, *Intellectuals*, 72.

549 Engels, *Marx und die Neue Rheinische Zeitung*, *MECW*, vol. 21, 19.

550 Karl Marx, *Das Kapital: Kritik der politischen Ökonomie* (Hamburg: Otto Meissner, 1867). In the preface to the first edition, Marx paraphrases Dante's *Purgatorio*, emphasizing his commitment to his path despite societal opposition.

551 Dante Alighieri, "Purgatorio," in *The Divine Comedy*, translated by Charles S. Singleton (Princeton, NJ: Princeton University Press, 1973). This work details the ascent through Purgatory, with terraces representing the seven deadly sins, illustrating the soul's journey toward purification; see Dante, *Purgatorio*, Canto V, line 13.

552 Mehring, *Story of His Life*, 213–15.

553 Wheen, *Karl Marx*, 206.

554 "The Victory of the Counter-Revolution in Vienna," *Neue Rheinische Zeitung*, November 7, 1848.

555 Pierre-Joseph Proudhon to Karl Marx, 1847.

556 Victor Considerant to Karl Marx, 1849.

557 Marx's Letter on Russian Revolution. In March 1877, Marx wrote to Russian revolutionary Vera Zasulich offering strategic advice on revolutionary tactics in Russia. This interaction reflected Marx's growing interest in revolutionary movements outside Western Europe. Stedman Jones, *Greatness and Illusion*, 417.

558 Boris Nicolaievsky and Otto Maenchen-Helfen, *Karl Marx: Man and Fighter* (London: Routledge, 1936), 281.

559 Migration Museum, "Karl Marx's London," https://www.migrationmuseum.org/karl-marxs-london/ (accessed April 1, 2024). This source details Marx's arrival in London in August 1849, the family's initial residence being in the Dean Street area of Soho, and the severe financial hardships they faced during their early years in the city. Deborah Roberts, "Family, Life, and Revolution," *International Socialist Review* 83, https://isreview.org/issue/83/family-life-and-revolution/index.html. This article discusses the Marx family's impoverished conditions, attributing their financial struggles to Marx's radical political activities and publications, which were not financially rewarding. It also highlights the crucial financial support provided by Friedrich Engels during these challenging times. Stedman Jones, *Greatness and Illusion*, 412–15, discusses the Marx family's time in London, highlighting their financial desperation and the impact of child mortality.

560 Institute of Marxism-Leninism, *Reminiscences*, 81.

561 Karl Marx's use of the nickname "Old Nick" reflects his engagement with themes of rebellion and defiance. "Old Nick" is a colloquial English term for the devil, a figure often associated with challenging authority. Marx's adoption of this moniker suggests a playful embrace of his role as a revolutionary thinker. The term has been used in English folklore as a colloquial name for the devil since at least the mid-seventeenth century. One theory suggests that it originates from "Old Iniquity," a character representing vice and evil in medieval morality plays. These plays often featured personifications of moral attributes, with "Old Iniquity" embodying sin and corruption. Over time, this character's name may have evolved into "Old Nick," becoming synonymous with the devil in English vernacular. However, the exact origin remains uncertain, and this derivation is one of several hypotheses. See *MECW*, vol. 46; this volume includes personal letters where Marx playfully signs as "Old Nick," reflecting his self-identification with the devilish moniker.

562 A term for the devil first used in the seventeenth century. It is possibly related to a German goblin called "Nickel." J. C. Cooper, ed., *Brewer's Book of Myth and Legend* (Oxford: Helicon Publishing Ltd., 1997). See also https://blog.oup.com/2013/06/old-nick-etymology-word-origin/?utm_source=chatgpt.com (accessed February 5, 2025).

563 Marcello Musto, *The Last Years of Karl Marx: An Intellectual Biography* (Stanford, CA: Stanford University Press, 2020). This work provides an in-depth analysis of Marx's final years, including his personal correspondences where he signed as "Old Nick," reflecting his self-identification with the devilish moniker. According to the Los Angeles Review of Books, Marx signed his letters to his daughters as "Old Nick," an English term for the Devil. Additionally, the MARX 200 project highlights that Marx used "Old Nick" as a signature in dedications to his grandchildren, such as writing: "To my little grandson Fouchtras. London, February 3rd, 1869. Old Nick." These sources suggest that "Old Nick" was a familial nickname used by Marx in correspondence with his family members; see https://libcom.org/article/demonology-working-class?utm_source=chatgpt.com (accessed April 14, 2023) and https://marx200.org/en/fotografien/index.html (accessed April 14, 2023).

564 Jenny von Westphalen to Karl Marx, 1849.

565 *MECW*, vol. 46. This volume includes correspondence detailing the family's eviction from their Chelsea residence in March 1850 due to unpaid rent, highlighting the seizure of their possessions by bailiffs. See McLellan, *A Biography*, 207: McLellan provides an account of the Marx family's financial struggles, noting the sale of their beds to pay debts owed to local tradespeople, including the butcher, milkman, chemist, and baker.

566 Karl Marx, Letter to Friedrich Engels, June 18, 1862, in *MECW*, vol. 41, 380 (see also MIA version).

567 Dante uses "biblical typology" to link the pilgrim and Paul; referred to in medieval exegesis as "*figura*" and "fulfillment": Daigle-Williamson explains: "A person or an event in the Old Testament, called the *figura*, can point to another person or event, called the 'fulfillment.' Moses, leading the Jews to the Promised Land, is a '*figura*' who foreshadows Christ, the fulfillment. In turn, the fulfillment can be reenacted later by another person or event [called a 'sub-fulfilment . . . Christ's death is reenacted by Stephen because similarly, he forgives those who are putting him to death as he commends his spirit to God (Acts 7:59–60)," Daigle-Williamson, "Dante," 42. She continues: "Dante's narration concerning his pilgrim and his experiences, especially in the Paradiso, is designed to reenact or 'recapitulate' the substance and the details of Paul's conversion experience, his heavenly visions, and his subsequent ministry, thereby establishing him as a 'sub-fulfillment' of the apostle Paul. However, because of the partial identification between the pilgrim and the poet, the poet is also presenting himself as a 'sub-fulfillment.' Dante's typological parallels, then, are intended to indicate the claim that Paul and his mission are being reenacted in another time and place."

568 Wheen, *Karl Marx*, covers Marx's financial troubles and how Engels frequently saved Marx's family from eviction.

569 Gabriel, *Love and Capital*, 310. This biography provides an in-depth look into the personal lives of Karl and Jenny Marx, detailing the financial struggles they endured and the impact of these hardships on their family, including the loss of their children.

570 McLellan, *A Biography*, 250. McLellan's work offers a comprehensive account of Marx's life, shedding light on the economic difficulties faced by the Marx family and the resulting personal tragedies, such as the deaths of their children.

571 *MECW*, vol. 38.

572 Letter from Marx to Engels, November 19, 1850. See *MECW*, vol. 38, 242.

573 "He lived a life of poverty, complicated, as Neil McInnes has put it, 'by his own notions of respectability, worsened by chronic illness, and saddened by the death of three children.'" Kamenka, "Introduction," xviii.

574 McLellan, *Life and Thought*, discusses the family's poverty and how their children suffered due to malnutrition and illness.

575 Karl Marx, Letter to Jenny Marx, 1850.

576 Karl Marx, "Letter to Friedrich Engels, July 30, 1862," in *The Letters of Karl Marx*, ed. Saul K. Padover (Englewood Cliffs, NJ: Prentice-Hall, 1979), 367.

577 Gabriel, *Love and Capital*, 327; this book details Marx's personal struggles, including his family's suffering, his procrastination, and his chronic health issues. McLellan, *A Biography*, 285; McLellan provides an in-depth examination of Marx's procrastination in completing *Das Kapital*, his poor health due to excessive smoking, and his tendency to blame external circumstances for his difficulties. Mehring, *Story of His Life*; 219; this biography discusses Marx's single-minded dedication to his ideological vision, often at the expense of his family's immediate needs.

578 Mary Gabriel, "Love and Capital: Karl Marx's Marriage Was Decidedly Not Marxian," *The Daily Beast*, September 21, 2011, https://www.thedailybeast.com/love-and-capital-karl-marxs-marriage-was-decidedlynot-marxian.

579 McLellan, *A Biography*, 297; Sperber, *A Nineteenth-Century Life*, examines Marx's struggles to support his family and the early deaths of his children.

580 Karl Marx, "Letter to Friedrich Engels, September 8, 1852." This letter details the illnesses within Marx's family and their inability to afford medical care, highlighting the severity of their financial distress. See https://marxists.architexturez.net/archive/marx/works/1851/letters/51_07_13.htm (accessed February 5, 2025).

581 Even with regular financial support from Engels, Marx's debts continued to accumulate. In a letter to Engels dated April 3, 1851, Engels remarked on the financial strain Marx was under, noting that Marx had to "keep quiet if we're not to be nabbed." https://www.marxists.org/archive/marx/works/1844/letters/44_10_01.htm (accessed April 14, 2024), Marx, Letter to Friedrich Engels, July 30, 1862: in this correspondence, Marx discusses his preoccupation with financial woes, including issues with his landlord, reflecting the ongoing economic pressures he faced.

582 Yanis Varoufakis, *Talking to My Daughter About the Economy: A Brief History of Capitalism* (New York: Farrar, Straus and Giroux, 2017).

583 Karl Marx, *The Eighteenth Brumaire of Louis Bonaparte*, trans. Samuel Moore and Edward Aveling (New York: International Publishers, 1964), 15. This work analyzes the 1851 coup in France, offering insights into historical repetition and class struggle.

584 Eagleton, *Tragedy*, 65.

585 Jenny Marx, "Short Sketch of an Eventful Life," in *Marx and Engels Through the Eyes of Their Contemporaries* (Moscow: Progress Publishers, 1972). In this autobiographical account, Jenny Marx reflects on the challenges faced by her family during their years of hardship.

586 J. Marx, "Short Sketch"; Louise Freyberger, "Letter to August Bebel, September 2 and 4, 1898." See https://www.intellectualhistory.net/thousand-manuscripts-blog/the-freyberger-letter (August 3, 2025). In this correspondence, Freyberger recounts Engels's disclosure regarding the paternity of Frederick Demuth, providing insight into the concealed aspects of the Marx household.

587 Mehring, *Story of His Life*, 312. Mehring provides an extensive biography of Marx, including personal anecdotes and his temperament in social settings.

588 Payne, *Biography*, 295. This biography provides a detailed account of Karl Marx's life, including the pivotal role Helene Demuth played in managing the household.

589 Gabriel, *Love and Capital*, 312. Gabriel's work delves into the personal lives of the Marx family, highlighting the sacrifices and challenges faced by those around Karl Marx.

590 Liebknecht, *Biographical Memoirs*, 45. Liebknecht offers personal recollections of Karl Marx, providing insights into the dynamics within the Marx household.

591 Payne, *Biography*, 258–60.

592 Johnson, *Intellectuals*; Gabriel, *Love and Capital*, 389. Gabriel provides a detailed account of the personal sacrifices Engels made to shield Marx's reputation, including claiming paternity of Demuth.

593 Gabriel, *Love and Capital*, 389.

594 Wilson, *His Faustian Life*, 154.

595 J. Marx, "Short Sketch."

596 Louise Freyberger, Letter to August Bebel, September 2 and 4, 1898. In this correspondence, Freyberger recounts Engels's disclosure regarding the paternity of Frederick Demuth, providing insight into the concealed aspects of the Marx household.

597 Karl Marx, "Letter to Friedrich Engels, December 15, 1856," in *MECW*, vol. 40, 207.

598 Karl Marx, "Letter to Joseph Weydemeyer, April 5, 1852," in *MECW*, vol. 39, 550.

599 Karl Marx, "Letter to Friedrich Engels, July 30, 1862," in *MECW*, vol. 41, 324.

600 Gabriel, *Love and Capital,* 412. Gabriel provides an in-depth exploration of Marx's personal struggles, his relationship with Jenny, and how their financial distress and public reputation crises were exacerbated by his own decisions.

601 Payne, *Biography*, 266.

602 J. Marx, "Short Sketch."

603 Payne, *Biography*, 268.

604 Freyberger, Letter to August Bebel, September 2 and 4, 1898.

605 Wheen, *Karl Marx,* 123. Wheen details Marx's dedication to his studies at the British Museum Reading Room, highlighting how this environment facilitated his intellectual development.

606 British Museum, "Reading Room," https://www.britishmuseum.org/about-us/british-museum-story/architecture/reading-room?utm_source=chatgpt.com (accessed February 20, 2025). This source provides historical context about the Reading Room's establishment and its significance as a center for scholarly research.

607 Karl Marx, "Letter to Paul Lafargue, August 28, 1866." in *MECW*, vol. 42, 304. This letter captures Marx's direct communication with Lafargue, emphasizing the standards he expected in the courtship of his daughter.

608 Karl Marx, "Letter to Paul Lafargue, August 13, 1866," in *MECW*, vol. 31, 518.

609 In Dante's *Divine Comedy*, the second circle of hell is reserved for those overcome by lust, where the "storm of hell" eternally buffets the souls who surrendered to their passions. As Dante describes in his encounter with the doomed lovers, Francesca and Paolo: "Love, that releases no beloved from loving, / seized me so strongly with delight in him / that, as you see, he never leaves my side." *Inferno*, Canto V, lines 103–5.

610 *Inferno*, Canto V, lines 103–5.

611 "The lower part of the mountain is a kind of preparation for purgatory ('ante-purgatory,' Dante calls it). It is for people whose earthly dilatoriness (in repentance, in charity) requires them to wait before purification can begin. When those who wait are ready to go on, they pass through an entrance gate to purgatory proper, and this part of the mountain is divided into seven terraces, each for one of the seven deadly sins or capital vices, which in Dante's order are pride, envy, wrath, sloth, avarice (and prodigality), gluttony, and lust. In each stage, satisfaction is made for sin by means of penance." Griffiths, "Purgatory," 439.

612 Dante, *Paradiso*. In Canto XVII, lines 55–60, Dante writes about the sorrow of leaving behind cherished things and the bitterness of eating others' bread and climbing their stairs.

613 Karl Marx, *The Eighteenth Brumaire of Louis Bonaparte*, 1852, in *MECW*, vol. 11, 103.

614 Though he would comment: "In a famous passage, the French Revolution took place only in the realm of ideas. What the French did in the streets and

on the barricades the Germans did in philosophy. In this comment we find the key to Marx's ability to fuse and not merely to 'combine' German philosophy, French politics, and English economics." Kamenka, "Introduction," xxv.

615 Marx, *The Eighteenth Brumaire of Louis Bonaparte.* In this seminal work, Marx examines the sociopolitical circumstances that enabled Louis Bonaparte's coup, emphasizing the oppressive influence of historical precedents on contemporary events.

616 Jenny Marx, Letter to Weydemeyer, March 1852.

617 Marx, *The Holy Family.* In this work, Marx and Engels critique the Young Hegelians and discuss the role of human agency in history.

618 Mehring, *Story of His Life*, ch. 6. See also Gabriel, *Love and Capital.* Gabriel provides a comprehensive account of the Marx family's struggles during their London exile, highlighting how these adversities influenced Marx's development as both an activist and a theoretician.

619 "Marx would have us descend through the spectrality of capitalism to retrieve the fundamental use value concealed at its base: a descent and return from Hell to 'true' selfhood." Meanwhile, "Derrida would concede the value of spectres to divorce us from ourselves; but Marx himself would be summoned as a spectre to haunt capitalist Europe, to remind us of our accountability to ideals of justice and human dignity." Falconer, *Hell in Contemporary Literature*, 36.

620 "Tied up with the question concerning the difference between Marx's value theory and classical value theory is the question of whether Marx had 'proven' the labor theory of value, that is, whether he had established beyond the shadow of a doubt that labor and nothing else underlies the value of a commodity. This question has been frequently discussed in the literature about Marx. But as we're about to see, Marx was not at all interested in such a 'proof.' Adam Smith had 'proven' the determination of a commodity's value through labor with the argument that labor entails effort and that we therefore estimate the value of something according to how much effort is involved in producing it. Here, value is ascribed directly to the rational considerations of isolated individuals. Modern neoclassical economic theory argues in a similar manner, taking utility-maximizing individuals as a point of departure and explaining exchange relationships on the basis of utility estimates. . . . Thus does Adam Smith define the 'propensity to truck, barter, and exchange' as the characteristic that distinguishes humans from animals, and from there it is of course no problem to derive the structures of an economy based upon commodity exchange from the rationality of this sort of person (the commodity owner) to declare these structures as universally human. For Marx, on the other hand, it was not the thought processes of individuals that are fundamental, but rather the social relations in which the behavior can—at least in principle—be changed. A society without commodities and money is conceivable." Heinrich, *An Introduction*, 45.

621 Adam Smith, *The Theory of Moral Sentiments* (1759), Part IV, Chapter I, 165, https://www.ibiblio.org/ml/libri/s/SmithA_MoralSentiments_p.pdf (accessed May 1, 2024).

622 Adam Smith, *The Wealth of Nations* (1776), Book IV, Chapter 2. The phrase "invisible hand" is most closely associated with Adam Smith, but it was not entirely original to him. The metaphor of an unseen force guiding human affairs can be found in earlier theological and philosophical writings. However, Smith was the first to use it explicitly in an economic context, shaping classical liberal economic thought. Adam Smith, *An Inquiry into the Nature and Causes of the Wealth of Nations* (London: W. Strahan and T. Cadell, 1776).

623 "And economic activity, above all in a free market context, cannot be conducted in an institutional, juridical or political vacuum. On the contrary, it presupposes sure guarantees of individual freedom and private property, as well as a stable currency and efficient public services. To fulfil this task, the State must adopt suitable legislation but at the same time it must direct economic and social policies in such a way that it does not become abusively involved in the various market activities, the carrying out of which is and must remain free of authoritarian, or worse, totalitarian superstructures and constraints." *Compendium of the Social Doctrine of the Church*, section 152, available at https://www.vatican.va/roman_curia/pontifical_councils/justpeace/documents/rc_pc_justpeace_doc_20060526_compendio-dott-soc_en.html (accessed May 3, 2025).

624 Smith, *The Wealth of Nations*.

625 R. H. Tawney, *Religion and the Rise of Capitalism* (New York: Harcourt, Brace & World, 1926), 36.

626 "The worker 'does not confirm himself in his work, but denies himself, feels miserable and not happy, does not develop free mental and physical energy, but mortifies his flesh and ruins his mind' . . . At worst, workers are reduced to mere appendages of a machine, with their bodies fundamentally marked by the kind of labor they perform. As John Berger vividly describes, 'The repetition by which gesture is laid upon gesture, precisely but inexorably, the pile of gestures being stacked minute by minute, hour by hour is exhausting. The rate of work allows no time to prepare for the gesture, to demand effort from the body. The body loses its mind in the gesture.'" Swain, "Alienation," 365.

627 Alejandro A. Chafuen, *Faith and Liberty: The Economic Thought of the Late Scholastics* (Lanham, MD: Lexington Books, 2003).

628 Tawney, *Religion and the Rise of Capitalism*, ch. 1.

629 Perry Anderson, *In the Tracks of Historical Materialism* (London: Verso Books, 1983).

630 Adam Smith: Panmure House, https://www.panmurehouse.org/adam-smith/smith-quotes-faqs/?utm_source=chatgpt.com (accessed May 1, 2025).

631 *The Theory of Moral Sentiments*, Part I, Section I, Chapter I.

632 Marx and Engels, *The Communist Manifesto*, trans. Moore, 57. Marx argues that capitalism, by its very nature, cannot be reformed but must be entirely dismantled through revolutionary means.

633 Marx, *Capital*, ch. 31, https://www.marxists.org/archive/marx/works/1867-c1/ch31.htm#n15 (accessed August 3, 2025).

634 "At its core was the rejection of all religious faith involving God . . . It simply replaces monotheism with monostatism—the final and complete authority of the state as the embodiment of, if not the will of the people, then of what those in power conceive as (or pretend to be) the people's best interests. This is used to justify the forced implementation of the Marxian political-economic agenda . . . 'Marx himself insisted that an atheistic state predicted in his philosophy would be a perfect realization of the essence of Christianity', writes Pavel Hanes." Schwarzwalder adds: "Yet this claim, made by Marx in 1844, was grounded in the belief that to achieve this 'perfect realization,' the faith it would replace must be eradicated." Schwarzwalder, "Marx's New Religion," 778.

635 Wilhelm Liebknecht, a close associate of Karl Marx's, provided personal recollections of their time together. He recounted that during their walks Marx would often recite long passages from Dante's *The Divine Comedy*, which he knew almost by heart, and perform scenes from Goethe's *Faust*, sometimes portraying Mephistopheles. Liebknecht noted Marx's astonishing memory and deep engagement with literature. These reminiscences are documented in McLellan, *Interviews and Recollections*, 62–63.

636 Dante, *Inferno*, Canto III, line 15.

637 Wilhelm Liebknecht, *Karl Marx: Biographical Memoirs* (London: Swan Sonnenschein, 1901), 175.

638 McLellan, *A Biography*, 271–75; Jenny Marx, "Letter to Friends, March 1852," in *MECW*, vol. 39, 510.

639 Gabriel, *Love and Capital*, 213–18.

640 McLellan, *A Biography*, 247.

641 Friederich Engels, *The Condition of the Working Class in England* (Oxford: Oxford University Press, 2009), 69.

642 Marx and Engels, *The Communist Manifesto*, trans. Moore, 67.

643 *Sturm und Drang*, meaning "Storm and Stress," was a German literary movement in the late eighteenth century that emphasized emotion and rebellion against Enlightenment rationality. See Maurice B. Benn, *The Drama of Revolt: A Critical Study of Georg Büchner* (Cambridge: Cambridge University Press, 1976), 15.

644 Karl Marx, *The Eighteenth Brumaire of Louis Bonaparte*, trans. Terrell Carver (Oxford: Oxford University Press, 1996), 3; Avineri, *Philosophy and Revolution*, ch. 6.

645 Letter from Marx to Weydemeyer, March 5, 1852, *MECW*, vol. 8; Karl Marx and Friedrich Engels, *The Communist Manifesto* (London: Penguin Classics, 2002), 219.

646 Karl Marx, *The Poverty of Philosophy* (1847); Marx, *The Eighteenth Brumaire of Louis Bonaparte*, 103. See *MECW*, vol. 6, 220.

647 Marx and Engels, *The German Ideology*; Marx, *The Eighteenth Brumaire of Louis Bonaparte*, 123.

648 Yanis Varoufakis, *Technofeudalism: What Killed Capitalism* (London: Verso, 2023).

649 Amazon is one of the most well-known tech firms that promotes charitable initiatives such as the Amazon Smile program, which donates to various causes. However, the company has faced criticism for its treatment of warehouse workers and its monopolistic practices. See Juliann Emmons Allison and Ellen Reese, *Unsustainable: Amazon, Warehousing, and the Politics of Exploitation* (Berkeley: University of California Press, 2023).

650 Google, now under its parent company Alphabet, is a corporate giant in both technology and philanthropy. While it has made significant donations to various causes, the company's practices, data privacy concerns, and its dominance in the digital advertising market have raised questions about its monopoly power. Christian Fuchs, *The Digital Economy: The Internet, The Information Society, and the Marxist Perspective* (London: Routledge, 2017), 88; Shoshana Zuboff, *The Age of Surveillance Capitalism: The Fight for a Human Future at the New Frontier of Power* (New York: PublicAffairs, 2019), 211. Amy Wendling states: "In the Grundrisse, Marx thus moved back and forth between negative and potentially positive aspects of technological development . . . For example, Marx wrote that 'all the sciences have been forced into the service of capital. . . . At this point, invention becomes a business, and the application of science to immediate production itself becomes a factor determining and soliciting science. This new motivation for science, however, contrasted with both the origins of science in the histories Marx had studied and with what Marx claimed should be its proper motivations, Mechanical science had studied, and then replaced, the detailed motions of the labourer, and so properly belonged to her rather than to the capitalist. In addition, the motivation for science ought not to be the norms of production, including profit extraction, but the dignifying of the human species. Marx showed that technologies were immersed in a system of values, and necessarily so. Were this system to have, as its goal, such dignity, technology would look very different." Amy E. Wendling, "Technology and Science," in The *Marx Revival: Key Concepts and New Interpretations*, ed. Marcello Musto (Cambridge: Cambridge University Press; 2020), 363–75, at 360.

651 Smith, *The Theory of Moral Sentiments*, Part I, Section I, Chapter I.

652 Marx, *The Communist Manifesto* (1848). See https://history.hanover.edu/courses/excerpts/165marx2.html (accessed August 3, 2025).

653 "What constitutes success in life becomes a matter of the successful acquisition of consumer goods, and thereby that acquisitiveness which is so often a character trait necessary for success in capital accumulation is further sanctioned. Unsurprisingly pleonexia, the drive to have more and more, becomes

treated as a central virtue. But Christian theologians in the Middle Ages had learned from Aristotle as well as from Scripture that pleonexia is the vice that is the counterpart to the virtue of justice. And they had understood, as later theologians have failed to do, the close connection between developing capitalism and the sin of usury. So it is not after all just general human sinfulness that generates particular individual acts of injustice over and above the institutional injustice of capitalism itself. Capitalism also provides systematic incentives to develop a type of character that has a propensity to injustice. Finally we do well to note that, although Christian indictments of capitalism have rightly focused attention upon the wrongs done to the poor and the exploited, Christianity has to view any social and economic order that treats being or becoming rich as highly desirable as doing wrong even to those who having accepted that goal succeed in achieving it. Riches are, from a biblical point of view, an affliction, an almost insuperable obstacle to entering the kingdom of heaven. Capitalism is bad for those who succeed by its standards as well as for those who fail by them, something that many preachers and theologians have failed to recognize. And those Christians who have recognized it have often enough been at odds with ecclesiastical as well as authorities, political and economic." MacIntyre, *Ethics and Politics*, 149.

654 Richard Wolff, *Understanding Marxism*, 23.

655 "A connected criticism focuses on the question of teleology. The idea of alienation appears embedded in a logic of separation and restoration, in which human beings objectify their powers, become separated from them, and then reappropriate them in a moment of final unity. Certainly, Marx's earlier works tended in this direction—representing Communism as a kind of final completion of the unity of humans and nature." Swain, "Alienation," 368.

656 Melissa A. Wheeler, "The Paradox of Virtue Signaling," *Psychology Today Canada*, September 6, 2021, https://www.psychologytoday.com/ca/blog/ethically-speaking/202109/the-paradox-of-virtue-signaling.

657 Harald Bauder, *Labor Movement: How Migration Regulates Labor Markets* (New York: Oxford University Press, 2006), 3.

658 Avineri, *Philosophy and Revolution*, 167.

659 The Crimean War, fought between the Russian Empire on one side and an alliance of the Ottoman Empire, France, Britain, and Sardinia on the other, was a conflict rooted in disputes over territorial control and religious authority in the declining Ottoman Empire. The war's primary theaters of operation included the Crimean Peninsula, the Balkans, and the Black Sea region, making it a pivotal moment in mid-nineteenth-century European politics. Marx's analysis of the war was rooted in his understanding of class struggle, as he examined the underlying economic and political forces driving the conflict. He viewed the war not simply as a struggle over land or religion but as a reflection of the broader dynamics of imperialist ambition and capitalist

competition. Marx saw the war as primarily a struggle for imperial control, rather than a noble cause of defending the rights of the oppressed. The war began when Russia occupied the Danubian Principalities and demanded the right to protect Orthodox Christians within Ottoman territory, provoking the Ottoman Empire into action. Marx argued that Britain and France, while presenting themselves as defenders of the Ottoman Empire, were motivated by their own imperial interests. He criticized Britain's fear that a strong Russia would threaten its imperial access to India and other colonies. France, under Napoleon III, also sought to assert influence in the region, particularly to protect Catholic interests and expand its own political power. Marx recognized that both nations, despite their claims of humanitarian concern, were deeply driven by imperialist interests, and the expansion of capitalism through war. See his articles from 1853 on the topic, available at https://www.marxists.org/archive/marx/works/subject/russia/crimean-war.htm. See Orlando Figes, *The Crimean War: A History* (New York: Picador, 2012): this comprehensive account delves into the causes, battles, and aftermath of the Crimean War, providing a detailed narrative that challenges traditional interpretations; Andrew Lambert, *The Crimean War: British Grand Strategy against Russia, 1853–56* (London: Routledge, 2011): this book offers an analysis of British strategic objectives during the war, shedding light on the political and military considerations that influenced the conflict's progression; Winfried Baumgart, *The Crimean War: 1853–1856* (London: Arnold, 1999): this work provides a concise overview of the war, examining its origins, major campaigns, and the diplomatic maneuvers that shaped its outcome.

660 Karl Marx, "The Belgian Massacres," in *MECW*, vol. 21, 123.

661 James Ledbetter, ed., *Dispatches for the New York Tribune: Selected Journalism of Karl Marx* (London: Penguin Classics, 2007), 30–45.

662 The war (1853–1856) was a major conflict involving Russia against an alliance of Britain, France, the Ottoman Empire, and Sardinia. See note 715.

663 Ledbetter, *Dispatches for the New York Tribune*, December 1853.

664 Ibid., January 1854. One wonders whether he is riffing here on Carl Von Clausewitz's saying: "War is diplomacy by other means."

665 Marx, *The Holy Family*.

666 Marx and Engels, *The German Ideology*.

667 Ledbetter, *Dispatches to the New York Tribune*, April 15, 1854.

668 Ibid., March 28, 1854.

669 Karl Marx, "The Crimean War," *New York Daily Tribune*, 1854; Anders Aslund, *Russia's War in Ukraine: The Return of the Russian Empire* (London: Yale University Press, 2023).

670 See John Mearsheimer, "Why the Ukraine Crisis Is the West's Fault," *Foreign Affairs* 93, no. 5 (2014): 77–89; Jeffrey D. Sachs, "The West's False Narrative about Russia and China," *JDS*, August 22, 2022, https://www.jeffsachs.org/newspaper-articles/h29g9k7l7fymxp39yhzwxc5f72ancr.

671 Marx also underscored how the Ottoman Empire itself was decaying, and that the powers involved were more interested in maintaining their imperial interests than genuinely protecting the Ottomans or their people. Marx's articles on the Crimean War provide an insightful critique of the conflict, emphasizing that the war was not about moral righteousness but rather a competition between capitalist nations for imperial control. Extracts form these articles from the New York Tribune are available on the MIA at https://www.marxists.org/archive/marx/works/subject/russia/crimean-war.htm. See note 715.

672 Ledbetter, *Dispatches to The New York Tribune*, November 22, 1855.

673 Johnson, *Intellectuals*, 56.

674 Ralph R. Fahrney, *Horace Greeley and the Tribune in the Civil War* (Cedar Rapids, IA Torch, 1936), 87–93.

675 In 1853, Marx published an article in *The New York Tribune* supporting British colonization of India, which he viewed as a necessary evil for modernizing the country. He saw British rule as both destructive and regenerative, a view that reflects the complexity of his opinions on imperialism. Lederman, *Dispatches to The New-York Tribune*, 1853.

676 Wheen, *Karl Marx*, 218.

677 Marx, *The Eighteenth Brumaire of Louis Bonaparte*, 15.

678 Ulysses delivers this line in *Inferno* 26.119-20.

679 Gareth Stedman Jones, *Karl Marx: Greatness and Illusion* (Cambridge, MA: The Belknap Press of Harvard University Press, 2016), 354–60.

680 Gabriel, *Love and Capital*, 265–72.

681 Marx, Letter to Engels, 1856.

682 The quote "I know that the first question I shall have to answer is: 'Is the God of the Bible the true God?'" is from a devotional commentary written by Karl Marx on August 17, 1835, titled "The Union of the Faithful with Christ," based on the fifteenth chapter of the Gospel of John. This work was part of Marx's graduation requirements at the Trier Gymnasium. The original manuscript is housed in the archives of the Friedrich Ebert Foundation in Bonn, Germany. The quote "Your exploration of capital must connect more explicitly to the struggles of the proletariat" is from a letter written by Friedrich Engels to Karl Marx on October 28, 1882. In this correspondence, Engels emphasizes the importance of linking theoretical analyses of capital to the practical struggles of the working class. This letter is included in *MECW*, vol. 46, 356.

683 Marx, Letter to Engels, 1856.

684 December 8, 1857; Engels, *The Condition of the Working Class in England*, 217.

685 Dante, *Inferno*, Canto III, line 9.

686 Smith, *The Theory of Moral Sentiments*, Part I, Section III, Chapter II.

687 Marx, *Capital*, trans. Fowkes, 91. There are a few relevant references where Marx alludes to an idealized future: *The German Ideology* (1846): Marx

describes communism as "the real movement which abolishes the present state of things" and suggests that a classless society would bring about true human freedom. *Economic and Philosophic Manuscripts of 1844*: Marx envisions communism as the restoration of "man's essence" and reconciliation between humanity and nature. *Critique of the Gotha Program* (1875): Marx outlines the idea of "from each according to his ability, to each according to his needs," a vision of a post-capitalist world that has echoes of utopian aspirations. *Capital* (1867): he frequently contrasts the horrors of capitalist exploitation with the potential for human liberation, though he never explicitly frames it as a return to Eden.

688 Rayman says that "there is much to say for this return to Plato's *Republic*, given its universal system of public education, abolition of private property among the ruling class, community of women and children, and critique of money and inequality, all of which are found in the Communist Manifesto as well." He adds that Karl Popper used this similarity to condemn both Marx and Plato. Rayman, "Review," 181.

689 "E quindi uscimmo a riveder le stelle" (*Inferno*, Canto XXXIV, line 139). This line signifies Dante and Virgil's emergence from hell, leaving behind the darkness and suffering of the inferno to gaze upon the stars once more—a powerful symbol of hope, renewal, and transcendence.

690 "Shakespeare, the Greeks, Faust, Balzac, Shelley, fairy tales, werewolves, vampires and poetry all turn up in its pages alongside innumerable political economists, philosophers, anthropologists, journalists and political theorists." Marx, *Capital*, trans. Fowkes, 4.

691 (Karl Marx and Friedrich Engels, *Selected Correspondence 1846–1895*, Moscow: Progress Publishers, 1975, p. 175)

692 Jenny Marx, *Letters and Correspondence*, ed. Saul Padover (New York: Liveright, 1979), 312.

693 Karl Marx to Jenny Marx, June 1864, *MECW*, vol. 8.

694 The text was not published until 1939–1941 in the Soviet Union and later became widely available in the West. Karl Marx, *Grundrisse: Foundations of the Critique of Political Economy*, trans. Martin Nicolaus (London: Penguin Books/New Left Review, 1973), 3–5.

695 *Rheinische Zeitung* (1842–1843): Marx began writing for this Cologne-based newspaper in 1842 and became its editor-in-chief later that year; *Deutsch-Französische Jahrbücher* (1844): in collaboration with Arnold Ruge, Marx published this journal in Paris, aiming to bridge German and French radical thought; https://en.wikipedia.org/wiki/Timeline_of_Karl_Marx (accessed February 24, 2024); *Vorwärts!* (1844): A Parisian newspaper that Marx contributed to, which was associated with the League of the Just; *Neue Rheinische Zeitung* (1848–1849): Marx founded and edited this revolutionary newspaper during the 1848 revolutions in Europe; *New York Daily Tribune* (1852–1862): Marx served as a correspondent for this American newspaper, writing numerous articles on European politics and society; *Die Presse*

(1861–1862): an Austrian newspaper for which Marx wrote articles, particularly during the American Civil War; *Der Sozialdemokrat* (1864): Marx contributed to this German socialist newspaper; *The Commonwealth* (1869): a London-based newspaper associated with the International Workingmen's Association, to which Marx contributed; *La Liberté* (1871): a French newspaper where Marx published writings, especially during the Paris Commune; *Der Volksstaat* (1871–1872): a German socialist newspaper that featured Marx's articles and correspondence; see Karl Marx, *Early Writings*, trans. Rodney Livingstone and Gregor Benton (London: Penguin Books, 1992), 202–7.

696 Marx, *A Contribution to the Critique of Political Economy* (1859), 55–57.

697 Giuseppe Garibaldi to Karl Marx, 1856, *MECW*, vol. 39, 202–7; Paolo Favilli, *The History of Italian Marxism: From Its Origins to the Great War* (Leiden: Brill, 2016), 45–50.

698 "But I also understood better than I had done earlier not only what had been right in official Catholic condemnations of Marxism, but also how much had been mistaken and rooted in obfuscating and reactionary social attitudes. Part of what Catholic theologians—and more generally Christian theologians—had failed to focus upon sufficiently was the insistence by both Marx and Marxists on the close relationships of theory to practice, on how all theory, including all theology, is the theory of some mode or modes of practice." MacIntyre, *Ethics and Politics*, 157.

699 Overall, Rayman argues that *Reading Marx* "sheds light on just why we should not expect a clear program of political emancipation. Theory cannot leap ahead of historical praxis in such a way as to set forth the precise means of liberation because its precise character depends upon and is justifiable solely on the basis of the historical situation, which we cannot anticipate, and the historical actors, whose voices we should not attempt to silence in advance." Rayman, "Review," 182.

700 Ferdinand Lassalle to Karl Marx, 1858.

701 Moses Hess to Karl Marx, 1857.

702 Marx, *Grundrisse*, 705. On commodity and use value: "Consider, then, the implications of this argument. You own a commodity called a house. Are you more interested in its use-value or its exchange value? You will likely be interested in both. But there is a potential opposition here. If you want to fully realize the exchange-value, you have to surrender its use-value to someone else. If you have the use-value of it, then it is difficult to get access to the exchange-value, unless you do a reverse mortgage or take out a home-equity loan. Does adding to the use-value of the house for oneself add to the potential exchange-value? (A new modern kitchen, probably yes; some special construction to facilitate a hobby, probably no.) And what happens to our social world when the house that was once conceptualized mainly in use-value terms as a home becomes reconceptualized as a way to build long-term savings (a capital asset) for a working-class family or even as a vehicle to be

'flipped' by anyone who has access to credit for short-term speculative gain? This use-value/exchange-value dichotomy is, well, useful!" David Harvey, *A Companion to Marx's Capital*, 2nd ed. (London: Verso Books, 2013), 25.

703 Marx, *A Contribution to the Critique of Political Economy*, trans. Ryazanskaya, 20.

704 The concept of "mystical materialism" arises from Marx's elevation of material conditions beyond mere economic realities, imbuing them with a quasi-transcendent force that actively shapes human history and consciousness. While traditional materialism—such as that seen in classical economic theory—focuses strictly on the tangible aspects of production, labor, and resources, Marx's approach transforms these elements into historical agents that shape and are shaped by ideology. This reflects a dialectical relationship where material conditions do not merely determine history but evolve through human agency. Marx critiques Feuerbach and other materialists for treating circumstances as fixed and deterministic without recognizing that "circumstances are changed by men"—a clear assertion that human consciousness plays a role in restructuring material conditions. Yet, even those shaping society must undergo transformation, as seen in Marx's assertion that "it is essential to educate the educator himself." This suggests that even revolutionaries remain products of the structures they seek to overturn, reinforcing the paradox of materialism as both a historically dynamic force and a quasi-mystical doctrine of historical inevitability. Despite rejecting spiritual mysticism, Marx reintroduces a form of secular eschatology, where material reality functions as a force of historical necessity that will inevitably lead to transformation. This aligns with critiques that Marx's materialism, despite its scientific pretensions, functions not merely as an economic theory but as a grand vision of history with apocalyptic overtones—a framework scholars have described as a form of mystical materialism. Karl Marx, *Theses on Feuerbach*, in *Marx/Engels Selected Works*, vol. 1 (Moscow: Progress Publishers, 1969), 13.

705 Ludwig Feuerbach, in *The Essence of Christianity*, argues that theology is essentially anthropology—meaning that religious beliefs are projections of human qualities onto the divine. He contends that God is not an external, independent being but rather a reflection of human nature itself—a construct shaped by human consciousness. Marx was deeply influenced by Feuerbach's critique, yet he sought to go further, arguing that not only is theology a human projection, but so too are all ideological structures, including morality, law, and politics, which are shaped by material conditions rather than pure human thought. This insight became fundamental to Marx's theory of historical materialism, which contended that ideas arise not from abstract contemplation but from real economic and social structures. Ludwig Feuerbach, *The Essence of Christianity*, trans. George Eliot (New York: Harper & Brothers, 1957), 12–15.

706 Marx credited Feuerbach with shifting the focus of philosophy from abstract metaphysics to tangible, material conditions, which deeply influenced his development of historical materialism. However, while Feuerbach rejected Hegel's idealism, he still maintained a form of humanist materialism that centered on individual consciousness. Marx would later critique Feuerbach for failing to recognize that human consciousness itself is shaped by material conditions and social relations—a key departure that led Marx to develop his own theory of dialectical materialism. Karl Marx, "Theses on Feuerbach," in *MESW*, vol. 1, 13–15.

707 Karl Marx, "Afterword to the Second German Edition of Capital, Volume 1," in *MECW*, vol. 35, 19.

708 Marx himself critiques Feuerbach for failing to see that changing material conditions transform not only social structures but human thought itself. See note 694.

709 "Marx, like the pre-mils (or 'millenarians'), went further to hold that the reign of evil on earth would reach a peak just before the apocalypse ('the darkness before the dawn')." Rothbard, "Karl Marx as Religious Eschatologist."

710 Marx's materialist dialectic draws from thinkers like Feuerbach, integrating the dialectical methodology of Hegel while also being deeply rooted in the millenarian movements of the nineteenth century, particularly those originating from Joachim of Fiore. While Hegel's dialectics emphasize the unfolding of "spirit" through history, Marx reorients this process, grounding it in the tangible realities of economic and social life. Marx's vision of historical materialism, then, retains an apocalyptic structure, replacing the spiritual eschatology of Joachim and Hegel with an economic one, where history is propelled toward an inevitable revolutionary climax. See Karl Löwith, *Meaning in History* (Chicago: University of Chicago Press, 1949), 49–58; Ernst Bloch, *The Principle of Hope*, vol. 1 (Cambridge, MA: MIT Press, 1986), 306–12.

711 Ludwig von Mises, *Money, Method, and the Market Process* (Dordrecht: Kluwer Academic Publishers, 1985), 89.

712 "First of all, if the socialist schemes of those centuries were dreams, most of them were rationalized dreams. And what individual thinkers more or less perfectly succeeded in rationalizing were not simply their individual dreams but the dreams of the non-ruling classes. Thus, those thinkers were not living completely in the clouds; they also helped to bring to the surface what slumbered below but was getting ready to wake up. In this respect even the anarchists, back to their medieval predecessors who flourished in many a convent and still more in the tertiary groups of the Franciscan Order, acquire a significance which Marxists usually do not accord to them. However contemptible their beliefs may seem to the orthodox socialist, much of the propelling force of socialism comes, even today, from those irrational longings of the hungry soul—not belly—which they voiced." Schumpeter, *Capitalism*, 308.

713 Karl Marx explores the paradoxical nature of money as both a universal connector and a force of alienation in human life. He argues that money serves as the "bond of all bonds," linking individuals to society and nature and yet simultaneously acts as the universal agent of separation, reducing all human relationships to mere economic transactions. This insight reflects Marx's broader critique of commodity fetishism and the alienation inherent in capitalist economies, where social bonds become subordinated to the logic of monetary exchange. Marx, *Economic and Philosophic Manuscripts of 1844*, in *MECW*, vol. 3, 324.

714 Leszek Kołakowski, *Main Currents of Marxism: The Founders, the Golden Age, the Breakdown*, trans. P. S. Falla (Oxford: Oxford University Press, 1978), 139.

715 Georg Lukács, *History and Class Consciousness: Studies in Marxist Dialectics* (Cambridge, MA: MIT Press, 1971), 149.

716 Ibid., 187.

717 Joachim of Fiore, *Liber Concordiae Novi ac Veteris Testamenti*, c. 1200.

718 Marx, *A Contribution to the Critique of Political Economy*, trans. Ryazanskaya, 20–21.

719 Friedrich Engels, *Anti-Dühring: Herr Eugen Dühring's Revolution in Science*, trans. Emile Burns (Moscow: Progress Publishers, 1947), 208–9.

720 Karl Marx and Friedrich Engels, *The German Ideology*, trans. Clemens Dutt, W. Lough, and C. P. Magill (Moscow: Progress Publishers, 1964), 14–15.

721 While figures like Kugelmann (1828–1902), Liebknecht, and Jones recognized the intellectual importance of Marx's ideas, they also reflected the broader need for a more accessible and hopeful revolutionary narrative. The critiques of 1859 anticipate the challenges that Marx would face in the coming years, as he grappled with translating his dense theoretical frameworks into a vision that could inspire and mobilize the masses. While outwardly railing against the ruling classes, Marx wrote to Engels in 1862 referring to fellow revolutionaries in derogatory terms. In one letter, he shockingly called Ferdinand Lassalle a "Jewish N-word," revealing not only the depth of his racial views but the hypocrisy in his supposed fight for equality. His use of racist slurs stands in stark contrast to the supposed values of a man who claimed to fight for the oppressed. In his writing for *The New York Tribune*, covering various topics, including international politics and economics, Marx also revealed his racial views on emigration: "Society is undergoing a silent revolution, which must be submitted to, and which takes no more notice of the human existences it breaks down than an earthquake regards the houses it subverts. The classes and the races, too weak to master the new conditions of life, must give way. But can there be anything more puerile, more short-sighted, than the views of those Economists who believe in all earnest that this woeful transitory state means nothing but adapting society to the acquisitive propensities of capitalists, both landlords and money-lords?" He also wrote: "Christ drove the Jewish moneychangers out of the temple, and

that the moneychangers of our age enlisted on the side of tyranny happen again chiefly to be Jews, is perhaps no more than a historical coincidence. The loan-mongering Jews of Europe do only on a larger and more obnoxious scale what many others do on one smaller and less significant. But it is only because the Jews are so strong that it is timely and expedient to expose and stigmatize their organization." His knowledge is a caricature of Jewish history even as witnesses through the light of Christian revelation miss the promise of the "covenant" as the Apostle Paul reminds us in his letter to the Romans: "And you show that you are a letter of Christ, prepared by us, written not with ink but with the Spirit of the living God, not on tablets of stone but on tablets of human hearts." 2 Cor 3:3.

722 Marx, *A Contribution to the Critique of Political Economy*, trans. Ryazanskaya, 21.

723 In the section "On the Implied Certainty of Marxist Doctrine," Marx says: "The claim to total explanation promises to reduce the infinite complexity of reality to the derivation of a single idea, and this releases men from the burden of thinking." Ibid., 470.

724 Ludwig von Mises, *Theory and History: An Interpretation of Social and Economic Evolution* (New Haven, CT: Yale University Press, 1957), 211.

725 "The crucial goal—communism—is an atheized version of a certain type of religious eschatology; that the alleged inevitable process of getting there—the dialectic—is an atheistic form of the same religious laws of history; and that the supposedly central problem of capitalism as perceived by 'humanist' Marxists, the problem of 'alienation,' is an atheistic version of the selfsame religion's metaphysical grievance at the entire created universe." Rothbard, "Karl Marx as Religious Eschatologist."

726 "So long as we read Marx as a social scientist of theorist, we are misdirected by the ironic surface of his discourse, and that we thereby remain blind to his operations and to the effects he has on us whether we notice them or not. Reading Marx simply as a scientist is, like seeing modern society simply as a monstrous accumulation of commodities, a paralyzing mystification. I have reached this conclusion by attending to Marx's reiteration of tropes from a Christian text, but this does not thereby pigeon-hole Marx as a religious thinker, as a prophet, or as a priest. He is, rather, a canny literary tactician, deploying and redeploying figures from multiple traditions in his campaign to change the world." Roberts, "Marx in Hell," 53.

727 Ludwig von Mises, *Economic Policy: Thoughts for Today and Tomorrow* (Irvington-on-Hudson, NY: The Foundation for Economic Education, 1990), 25.

728 The rich "divide with the poor the produce of all their improvements. They are led by an invisible hand to make nearly the same distribution of the necessaries of life, which would have been made, had the earth been divided into equal portions among all its inhabitants, and thus without intending it, without knowing it, advance the interest of the society, and afford means

to the multiplication of the species." Adam Smith, *A Theory of Moral Sentiments*, 2 vols. (London: W. Strahan and T. Cadell, 1790), vol. 1, 466.

729 "It was characteristic of Hegel that he tended to see his world-spirit in terms of military metaphors or gigantism, exerting ruthless power. Hegel's secularized version of Christian theology has many of the characteristics of a Christian heresy rather than of non-Christian unbelief. Marxism is in consequence a doctrine with the same metaphysical and moral scope as Christianity, and it is the only secular post-Enlightenment doctrine to have such a scope. It proposes a mode of understanding nature an account of the direction and meaning of history and of the standards by which right action is to be judged, and a nature and human explanation of error and of evil, each of these integrated into an overall worldview, a worldview that can only be made fully intelligible by understanding it as a transformation of Christianity." MacIntyre, *Ethics and Politics*, 146.

730 MacIntyre, *Marxism and Christianity*, 2.

731 Eagleton, *Tragedy*, 18.

732 Ludwig von Mises, *Planning for Freedom* (Irvington-on-Hudson, NY: The Foundation for Economic Education, 1978), 47.

733 Marx, Capital, vol. 1. See https://socialism.com/fs-article/karl-marx-on-the-struggle-for-a-shorter-workday/ (accessed August 3, 2025).

734 Payne, *Biography*, 497.

735 René Descartes, *Meditations on First Philosophy*, ed. John Cottingham (Cambridge: Cambridge University Press, 1996).

736 "Marxism has often been portrayed as Christian heresy. Rather, this article proposes that Marxism is an entirely different faith, one containing theological, anthropological, and eschatological arguments." Schwarzwalder, "Marx's New Religion," 775.

737 On *pharmakos* and tragedy: "Terry Eagleton goes on to criticize the ideas of the Left about the tragedy in his last chapter titled 'Thomas Mann's Hedgehog.' He comments that these Radicals view tragedy as one associating sacrifice through mythic, cultic, and religious notions. This would entail the idea that 'suffering is an energizing, revitalizing part of human existence' and what is created by the Gods ought to go back to them. For this, a sacrifice is deemed necessary which would be 'dismembered to be renewed' (SV 275). Thus, in a sense hinting at how we are earthly beings and will go back to being dirt, precisely conveyed in Adam's words: 'For dust you are, and to dust you shall return' (Gn 3:19)." Singh, "Analysis," 211.

738 "Hegel's conception of it as an essential dimension of modern society. Hegel goes on seeing the 'invisible hand' as an instrument of the cunning of reason even while grasping its appalling inadequacy to produce a just society, or even save society from dissolution. The division of labour, the refinement of taste, the economy of individual enterprise all were essential to the development of modern individuality and the specialization and differentiation which were inseparable from it, as we saw above. For Hegel there can be no

question of abolishing the bourgeois economy. Rather its inherent drive to dissolution must be contained through its subordination to the demands of the more ultimate community which is the state. This higher allegiance and the rules which flow from it must keep men from giving way to those extremes of the drive for self-enrichment which pull society into the slipstream of uncontrolled growth." Taylor, *Hegel*, 437.

739 "The four pillars of Christian questioned belief are scripture, tradition, reason, and experience. The first three had already been called into question by philosophy, history, and biblical criticism. Now the fourth personal experience was by psychoanalysis, which compared religious experience with neurotic experience. Until the late nineteenth century, psychology had been a branch of philosophy. With the growth of scientific medicine, psychology achieved its independence and moved in the direction of becoming a science, though its basic methods and epistemology are still unsettled." Russell, *Mephistopheles*, 226.

740 Marx's troubled relationships extended to his family. His mother, Henrietta, provided financial support throughout much of his early life, but their relationship became increasingly strained. In 1863, when she destroyed an IOU that Marx had written to her, Marx saw this not as a final act of generosity but as a necessary closing of a financial burden. He showed little gratitude, continuing to expect financial support from her until her death in the same year. It is telling that Marx expected his mother to continue supporting him, even though he offered little in return and showed no concern for her well-being. This estrangement from his family, including his sisters, underscores his inability to maintain meaningful personal relationships. See Berlin, *His Life and Environment*, 108.

741 Henriette Marx, quoted in McLellan, *A Biography*, 356. This remark by Marx's mother expressing frustration over her son's theoretical pursuits rather than financial success has been widely cited in biographical discussions. It highlights the contrast between Marx's intellectual ambitions and his family's economic struggles

742 Marx, *Collected Correspondence*, 1835, https://www.marxists.org/archive/marx/letters/ (accessed February 23, 2024).

743 *MECW*, vol. 41, 441; Gabriel, *Love and Capital*, 303.

744 *MECW*, vol. 41, 441; Gabriel, *Love and Capital*, 303–4.

745 Friedrich Engels to Karl Marx, January 26, 1863, in *MECW*, vol. 41, 537.

746 Gabriel, *Love and Capital*, 304; *MECW*, vol. 41, 443.

747 Gabriel, *Love and Capital*, 304; see *MECW*, vol. 41, 444–45. Wolff was a German revolutionary and close friend of Marx who was involved in revolutionary activities.

748 Ibid., 304–5; *MECW*, vol. 41, 446–48, 455.

749 Berlin, *His Life and Environment*, 238.

750 Payne, *Biography*, 12.

751 Marx attended the opera in Berlin in 1861 during his attempt to reapply for German citizenship: This is discussed in Avineri, *Philosophy and Revolution*, 172–73. Other biographers have not corroborated this specific incident. Sperber's *Karl Marx: A Nineteenth-Century Life* provides an extensive account of Marx's life during this period but does not mention the opera event or an attempt to regain Prussian citizenship. Similarly, Francis Wheen's *Karl Marx: A Life* (New York: W.W. Norton & Company, 1999) does not reference this occurrence. The absence of this anecdote in these comprehensive biographies suggests that the evidence for Marx's attendance at the opera with the king may be limited or not widely recognized among scholars.

752 Marx's confrontational approach often led to strained relationships with contemporaries who held differing views. Weitling, one of the earliest labor organizers and utopian socialists, grew disillusioned with Marx's intellectualism and lack of pragmatic action. "I see in Marx nothing else than a good encyclopedia but no genius." Pierre-Joseph Proudhon solidified their break, in particular after the publication of *The Poverty of Philosophy*, where he writes, "To be governed is to be watched, inspected, spied upon . . . all under the pretext of public utility," to illustrate his anarchist rejection of Marx's more structured vision of proletarian control. Lassalle, too, once considered himself a disciple of Marx but later diverged in his political advocacy, focusing on state-supported cooperative workshops. Marx dismissed this approach, arguing that Lassalle was "degenerating into a sect leader, not a revolutionary." Mehring, *Story of His Life*, 440.

753 Lane Cooper, "Reviewed Works: Dante and Aquinas by Philip H. Wicksteed," *The Philosophical Review* 23, no. 4 (1914): 443–51, at 448.

754 Letters to Engels, 1846–1878, ed. McLellan, 158.

755 *Marx and Engels Selected Works* [henceforth, *MESW*], vol. 1 (Moscow: Progress Publishers, 1975), 22–25. For a list of volumes in this series, see https://www.marxists.org/archive/marx/works/sw/index.htm (accessed April 20, 2025).

756 *Inferno*, Canto II, lines 13–30.

757 Payne, *Biography*, 12.

758 Wendy Lesser, *The Life Below Ground* (Boston: Faber and Faber, 1987), 3.

759 Peter Ackroyd, *London Under: The Secret History Beneath the Streets*, (London: Vintage 2011), 13.

760 Ibid., 14.

761 Dickens, *Bleak House*, 1. Dickens portrays London as a city enshrouded in fog and corruption, mirroring the inefficiency and decay of the British legal system. Dante Alighieri, *The Divine Comedy*: *Inferno*, trans. John Ciardi (New York: New American Library, 2003), Canto VI, line 47. Florence is intricately woven into Dante's *Inferno*, with many of its political figures placed in Hell, shaping the narrative's moral and political dimensions.

762 Karl Marx and Friedrich Engels, *The Communist Manifesto* (1848).

763 Fyodor Dostoevsky, *Notebooks for Notes from Underground* (1863). See also Haewon Hwang, "Introduction," in *London's Underground Spaces: Representing the Victorian City, 1840–1915* (Edinburgh: Edinburgh University Press, 2013).

764 "In Marx's writerly hands, the concept of 'original accumulation'—as he acknowledges, itself a translation and revision of Adam Smith's 'previous accumulation'—emerges simultaneously as a capitalist description and a colonial justification of what the noncapitalist world experiences as theft, expropriation, and relentless plunder. As he puts it in his 1853 essay on 'The Future Results of British Rule in India,' 'The profound hypocrisy and inherent barbarism of bourgeois civilization lies unveiled before our eyes, turning from its home, where it assumes respectable forms, to the colonies, where it goes naked.' For Marx, history is a history of destruction and, in this history, there can be no capitalism without colonialism. If colonialism is just one index of capitalism, it nevertheless reveals the violence of capital in all its nakedness. This is why "so-called primitive accumulation" is in fact the opposite of what it presents itself as—a mechanism for the accumulation of wealth; it is instead of a means of expropriation and impoverishment, of dispossession and death, with force and violence as its modus operandi. Scarcely an idyllic paradise, it is, in Marx's word, a Dantean 'inferno'." Cadava and Nadal-Melsio, *Politically Red*, 305–6.

765 Marx, *Das Kapital*, trans. Fowkes, 342.

766 Marx, *Das Kapital* (1867).

767 Marx to Paul Lafargue, August 13, 1866, *MECW*, vol. 42, 308.

768 Gabriel, *Love and Capital*, 7, 502–3, 585–86, 591–92.

769 Marx, *Das Kapital*, trans. Fowkes, 547.

770 Marx, *Das Kapital* (1867).

771 Marx criticized European elites for their lack of full support for the Union, attributing their hesitation to self-interest. These elites feared that a Union victory would disrupt their economic dependence on the South's slave-driven production of raw materials like cotton. For Marx, the Civil War represented more than a battle between North and South; it was a clash between two modes of production—one based on free labor and industrialization, the other on slave labor and agricultural exploitation. He argued that the Union's triumph would dismantle the economic and political power of the southern ruling class, fundamentally altering the relationships that underpinned global capitalism.

772 Karl Marx, "Letter to Friedrich Engels, January 23, 1862," in *MECW*, vol. 41, 262.

773 Marx's analysis placed the Civil War within a broader framework of class struggle, portraying the abolition of slavery as a crucial step in advancing the cause of labor worldwide. By breaking the Southern slave economy, he believed the Union victory would challenge entrenched systems of exploitation and pave the way for broader social and economic transformations. In "The

North and the South" (December 1861), Marx wrote: "The issue in America is not just the fate of slavery, but the triumph of the free labor system, which will inevitably create a new world economy and shift the balance of power in the modern capitalist system." He recognized that the conflict was more than a local American issue; it was a significant event with implications for the entire capitalist world. Marx's commentary on the Civil War also distinguished him from other European socialists and intellectuals who were more cautious or reserved in their support for the Union cause. In his articles for *The New York Tribune*, Marx's focus was less on the moral dimensions of slavery itself and more on how the destruction of slavery would contribute to a fundamental restructuring of the capitalist world. His historical materialism led him to believe that the war was an inevitable clash of class forces, one that would eventually lead to a new, more progressive society. See notes 756 and 757.

774 "Marx, who had a thorough classical education and who therefore inherited the special interest of Europeans for the Greeks and Romans, treated slavery in Ancient Greece and Rome as a distinct mode of production. According to him, direct forced labor was the foundation of the ancient world. In slavery wealth confronted forced labor not in the form of capital but rather as a relation of direct domination . . . Sainte-Croix saw ancient or chattel slavery as one form of unfree labor that also included serfs and debt bondsman. The great ages of slavery were the fifth and fourth centuries before Christ in Greece and the second and first centuries before Christ in Rome. The late Roman Empire saw a decline in slave labor and an increase in the use of serfs." Henry Heller, "Class and Class Struggle," in *The Oxford Handbook of Karl Marx*, ed. Paul Prew, Tomas Rotta, Tony Smith, and Matt Vidal (Oxford: Oxford University Press, 2019), 57–76, at 61.

775 Marx, *Das Kapital*, trans. Fowkes, 251.

776 Sidney Webb and Beatrice Webb, *The History of Trade Unionism* (London: Longmans, Green and Co., 1894), 232–47; John F. C. Harrison, *The Early Victorians, 1832–51* (London: Weidenfeld and Nicolson, 1971), 84–92.

777 E. P. Thompson, *The Making of the English Working Class* (New York: Vintage Books, 1966), 717–40; Asa Briggs, *The Age of Improvement, 1783–1867* (London: Longman, 1959), 357–72.

778 "Marx to Engels, June 18, 1867," in *MECW*, vol. 9.

779 Karl Marx, "Letter to Friedrich Engels, January 23, 1862," in *MECW*, vol. 41, 262; Marx, *Das Kapital*, 15 (Meisner).

780 "Marx to Kugelmann, July 11, 1868," in *MECW*, vol. 10; "Karl Marx, Letter to Friedrich Engels, April 30, 1868," in *MECW*, vol. 43, 32.

781 Gabriel, *Love and Capital*, 395–97; Wheen, *Karl Marx*, 282.

782 Eleanor began writing correspondence on behalf of her father when she was sixteen and spent her life working to aid the poor. While living in London with her husband Edward Aveling in 1884 and 1885, she took a formal leadership role in the Social Democratic Foundation, even as she taught reading

and writing to the working class. Eleanor's biographer Rachel Holmes writes, "Karl Marx was the theory; Eleanor Marx was the practice." See Holmes, *Eleanor Marx: A Life* (London: Bloomsbury, 2014), 229–32.

783 In a letter to Paul and Laura dated March 5, 1870, Marx discussed various personal and political matters, reflecting his ongoing involvement in their lives. Throughout their marriage, Laura and Paul faced significant personal challenges, including the loss of their three children in infancy. Despite these tragedies, they remained dedicated to their political work, translating Marx's writings into French and promoting socialist ideals in France and Spain. *MECW*, vol. 42, 537.

784 *MECW*, vol. 30, 305.

785 Mikhail Bakunin, *Statism and Anarchy* (Cambridge: Cambridge University Press, 1990), 170.

786 Paul Thomas, Karl *Marx and the Anarchists* (London: Routledge & Kegan Paul, 1980), 349–56.

787 *MECW*, vol. 30, 608.

788 Karl Marx, *Herr Vogt* (London: Lawrence & Wishart, 1982), 126.

789 Ibid.

790 Friedrich Engels to Marx, *MECW*, vol. 42, 352.

791 Ibid.

792 "For all the propaganda about 'building socialism,' the truth was that most of Stalin's great new industrial works were modeled on, and in many cases directly imported from, Western capital firms, especially American ones. The construction of Stalin's iron and steel combines, in theory planned by the State Institute for the Design of Metallurgical Factories (Gipromez) of Leningrad (as Petrograd was renamed in 1924), was overseen by the Frey Engineering Company of Chicago, Illinois, hired in May 1927. Magnitogorsk was designed from top to bottom by Arthur G. McKee and Company of Cleveland, Ohio, based on the prototype of a US Steel plant in Gary, Indiana. . . . The main copper smelting plant in the USSR, the Karabash Combinat in the Urals, employed eleven Yankee engineers. The Soviet bauxite-mining and aluminum-smelting industry, critical in the construction of tanks and warplanes, was designed from scratch by the American expert Frank E. Dickie, hired from the Alcoa corporation in 1930 (though French aluminum experts were later imported too). Small wonder a Soviet chronicle of the first Five Year Plan, *Za industrializatsii* was forced to admit in 1933 (in a passage later purged from office accounts of the period) that it was 'a combination of American business and science with Bolshevik wisdom' that had 'created these industrial giants in three or four years.' Stephen Kotkin, *Stalin Waiting for Hitler, 1929–1941* (New York: Penguin, 2017), 28–29.

793 Karl Marx, Letter to Arnold Ruge, September 1843, See https://www.marxists.org/archive/marx/works/1843/letters/43_09.htm (accessed August 3, 2025).

794 Hobsbawm, *The Age of Revolution*, 97.

795 In Dante's *Divine Comedy*, the influence of St. Thomas Aquinas serves as a counter to the Marx-Hegelian-Feuerbach project and is both subtle and pervasive, creating a theological and philosophical framework that structures the entire epic. Aquinas, the great scholastic theologian, sought to harmonize Christian doctrine with classical philosophy, particularly Aristotle's teachings, as did Dante. His *Summa Theologica* represents the pinnacle of this synthesis, offering a comprehensive view of the Christian cosmos, rooted in the existence of a rational, orderly, and purposeful universe. Dante's journey through hell, purgatory, and heaven is more than just an epic poem—it's a reflection of this medieval worldview, built on Aquinas's understanding of sin, redemption, and the ultimate destiny of the human soul. Aquinas believed that all of creation was oriented toward God, the *summum bonum* (the highest good), and that every soul, by its nature, sought unity with the divine. Sin, in this context, was the turning away from this ultimate end, a misalignment of the soul's desires from its proper object—God.

796 Marx, *Critique of Hegel's Philosophy of Right*, trans. Annette Jolin and Joseph O'Malley (Cambridge: Cambridge University Press, 1970).

797 Eagleton, *Tragedy*, 33.

798 Cooper, quoting Wicksteed again: "'When Dante speaks of love, it is generally this noble and specifically human love he has in mind, but he also frequently recognizes it in its widest meaning. Love in the wider sense is the sole motive power of the universe, and therefore no conscious or unconscious being can be actuated by any other principle'." Cooper, "Reviewed Works," 448.

799 Karl Marx, *Theories of Surplus Value*, trans. Terrell Carver (London: Lawrence & Wishart, 1951), 169.

800 Ibid. See also Adam Smith, *The Wealth of Nations*, vol. 2 (New York: Collier, 1902 [1776]); David Ricardo, *On the Principles of Political Economy and Taxation*, in *The Works and Correspondence of David Ricardo*, vol. 1, ed. Piero Sraffa (Cambridge: Cambridge University Press for the Royal Economic Society, 1951 [1817]).

801 Smith, *The Wealth of Nations*, 160.

802 Marx, *Das Kapital*, trans. Fowkes, 172. Marx laid out his critique of political economy, challenging the fundamental assumptions of classical economists like Adam Smith and David Ricardo in his book *Theories of Surplus Value*, for their "faulty architectonics." While Smith and Ricardo had argued that labor was the source of value, Marx took this idea further, developing his theory of surplus value: "Marx's labor theory of value posits that the value of a product is determined by the amount of socially necessary labor time invested in it. However, under capitalism, workers do not receive the full value of what they produce. Instead, capitalists pay workers only a fraction of the value, which Marx called 'necessary labor,' and keep the 'surplus value' for themselves. This surplus value forms the basis of profit in a capitalist system and

represents the exploitation of labor." Marx, *Theories of Surplus Value*, trans. Carver, 178.

803 "Smith argued that the needs of society—more and cheaper clothes, shelter, food; the stuff of prosperity—could not be met with moralisers or do-gooders. Only the capitalists' passion for profit could provide these. Why? Because to profit, it was not enough to squeeze the living daylights out of their workers. After all, their competitors did the same. No, to steal a march on the competition, capitalists had to invest—in new machines, for example, that could cut their costs and allow them to undercut their competitors' prices. It was in this manner, driven by the profit motive, that society would equip itself to manufacture sufficient quantities of life's essentials and at the lowest prices possible. According to Smith, it is because of the capitalists' cut-throat profit-hunger, not in spite of it, that capitalism begat wealth and progress." Varoufakis, *Technofeudalism*, 108.

804 Smith, *The Wealth of Nations*, 160.

805 Chapter 3, book II.

806 Skousen, 20

807 Marx, *Capital* (1867).

808 Marx, *A Contribution to the Critique of Political Economy* (1859); *Theses on Feuerbach* (1845).

809 Johnson, *Intellectuals*, 62–63.

810 Payne, *Biography*, 121.

811 Marx, *Das Kapital*, trans. Fowkes, 929.

812 *Das Kapital* (1867).

813 "Spengler's 'Faustian man' loses all overtones of Promethean heroism. The motif of striving has become deeply enmeshed in irresoluteness, overweening selfishness, and favorite-son treatment. But Spengler's coinage remains sound. We probably deserve no more heroic a figure on the prow of our ship than flamboyant, bumbling Faust. Both Faust and Frankenstein deliver us directly into the condition and the problem of excess." Shattuck, *Forbidden Knowledge*, 105.

814 Marx, *Das Kapital*, trans. Fowkes, 527.

815 Christopher Marlowe, *Doctor Faustus*, ed. David Bevington and Eric Rasmussen (Manchester: Manchester University Press, 1993), act 1, scene 1, line 20.

816 Padover, *An Intimate Biography*, ch. 9.

817 McLellan, *His Life and Thought*, 321.

818 Karl Marx to Friedrich Engels, April 30, 1867, in *MECW*, vol. 42, 358.

819 Marx, *Das Kapital*, trans. Fowkes, 638.

820 René Descartes famously asserted, "Cogito, ergo sum" ("I think, therefore I am"), emphasizing the primacy of reason as the foundation of knowledge. Later, Søren Kierkegaard countered with "Dubito, ergo sum" ("I doubt, therefore I am"), reflecting a more existential approach to self-awareness and truth. René Descartes, *Meditations on First Philosophy*, trans. John

Cottingham (Cambridge: Cambridge University Press, 1996), 18; Søren Kierkegaard, *Philosophical Fragments*, trans. David F. Swenson and Howard V. Hong (Princeton, NJ: Princeton University Press, 1985), 37.

821 MacIntyre, *Marxism and Christianity*, 82–83.

822 Steiner, "'Tragedy' Reconsidered," 5.

823 "Both Jacques Derrida's *Specters of Marx* and Raymond Williams's *Modern Tragedy* address the question of how the present is haunted by the persistence of past revolution." McCallum, "Questions of Haunting," 231.

824 Eric Hobsbawm, *How to Change the World: Tales of Marx and Marxism* (New Haven, CT: Yale University Press, 2011), 54–56, analyzes Marxism's near-religious faith in historical inevitability, comparing its utopian aspirations to messianic movements in religious history.

825 Rothbard, "Communist as Religious Eschatologist."

826 McLellan, *His Life and Thought*, 278–81. McLellan discusses Marx's use of Dantean imagery in *Das Kapital* and other writings, framing capitalist exploitation in terms of infernal punishment and historical inevitability.

827 Eugen von Böhm-Bawerk, *Karl Marx and the Close of His System*, trans. Alice M. Macdonald (New York: Augustus M. Kelley, 1949), 3–55.

828 Ludwig von Mises, *Human Action: A Treatise on Economics* (New Haven, CT: Yale University Press, 1949), 389–92.

829 Friedrich A. Hayek, *The Road to Serfdom* (Chicago: University of Chicago Press, 1944), 94–102.

830 "According to Austrians, capital accumulation is not inherently exploitative, as Marx argued. Instead, Austrians view the accumulation of capital as a necessary part of economic growth, which benefits all society by increasing productivity and living standards. The Austrian School also defends the role of interest as compensation for saving and delaying consumption, countering Marx's view that capitalists simply extract surplus value from workers." "We turn next to the distribution of capitalist surpluses. That distribution illustrates how capitalism's organization of the surplus deeply influences so many other aspects of societies where it exists (and especially where it prevails). "Capitalists distribute significant portions of the surplus they appropriate to themselves for their consumption. They do so both for personal satisfaction and to underscore their differences (in homes, dress, transport, etc.) from the wage-earners. The differences in consumption level results of the inequality produced and sustained by capitalism can then be transformed ideologically into signs of inherent attributes of individuals that make some surplus appropriators and others surplus producers." Murray Rothbard, *Man, Economy, and State with Power and Market* (Auburn, AL: Ludwig von Mises Institute, 2009), 379–82, explains the Austrian School's perspective on capital accumulation, productivity, and the role of interest in economic growth, countering Marx's labor theory of value; Von Mises, *Human Action*, 533–38, argues that capitalist accumulation leads to societal prosperity and defends profit as a mechanism for economic progress rather than exploitation. Mark

Skousen, *The Making of Modern Economics: The Lives and Ideas of the Great Thinkers* (Armonk, NY: M.E. Sharpe, 2009), 195–99, discusses how Austrian economists refuted Marx's exploitation theory, emphasizing that capital investment and innovation drive economic growth, raising living standards rather than oppressing workers.

831 Catholic social teaching affirms that "the free market cannot be judged apart from the ends that it seeks to accomplish and from the values that it transmits on a societal level." The Holy See, *Compendium of the Social Doctrine of the Church*, §348 (all quotes from the Holy See can be found on https://www.vatican.va/content/vatican/en.html). The market "cannot find in itself the principles for its legitimization" and must be oriented by individual conscience and public responsibility toward integral human development (*Compendium*, §348; cf. John Paul II, *Centesimus Annus*, §41). Likewise, "the action of the State must create situations favorable to the free exercise of economic activity" while being guided by solidarity and subsidiarity (*Compendium*, §351; cf. *Centesimus Annus*, §15). The Church rejects both the idolization of the market and the expansion of an all-encompassing welfare state, calling instead for a balance where economic freedom is placed at the service of the human person (*Compendium*, §353–354; cf. *Centesimus Annus*, §§48–49). Pius IX was the first pope to condemn socialism and communism soon after the publication of *The Communist Manifesto* in 1849 (*Nostis Et Nobiscum*). Pope Leo XIII, who began the Catholic Social Thought tradition, sought to counter the rise of socialism. Pius XI declared in *Quadragesimo Anno* (1931): "No one can be at the same time a good Catholic and a true socialist." Martin Luther King, Jr., was late to the party. Alasdair MacIntyre adds: "And in a society of small productive units, in which everyone has an opportunity to own (and not indirectly through shareholdings) the means of production the type of economy envisaged by Chesterton and other distributists free markets will be a necessary counterpart to freedom of ownership and freedom of labor. (This is a type of economy which does in fact give expression to the understanding of human freedom of the encyclical *Centesimus Annus*, an encyclical whose exaggerated optimism about the actualities of contemporary capitalism, both in Eastern Europe and in the United States, has led to unfortunate misconstruals of its doctrine.) But in the markets of modern capitalism prices are often imposed by factors external to a particular market: those, for example, whose livelihood has been made subject to international market forces by their having become exclusively producers for some product for which later on there is no longer sufficient demand, will find themselves compelled to accept imposed low prices or even the bankruptcy of their economy. Market relationships in contemporary capitalism are for the most part relations imposed both on labor and on small producers, rather than in any sense freely chosen." MacIntyre, 148–49. The enduring tension between Marxist materialism and Christian theology was addressed not only by early Church teachings but

deepened in modern Catholic social thought. As Pope John Paul II wrote in *Centesimus Annus*, Marxism fails fundamentally because it "reduces man to a series of social relationships" and denies the transcendent dignity of the human person, made in the image of God. Marxism, in its attempt to eradicate injustice, instead proposes a system that undermines human freedom and moral agency. This critique builds upon the economic personalism articulated in works like Heinrich Pesch's *Ethics and the National Economy* (esp. ch. 6), which emphasized the importance of ethical structures within economic life rather than the abolition of private property or class altogether. This theological and philosophical incompatibility was also echoed in the words of Martin Luther King, Jr. Together, these voices reveal a profound divergence: where Christianity seeks transformation through grace and love, Marxism calls for rupture through violence. Where Christian anthropology affirms the sacredness of the person, Marxist materialism sees only economic function and class identity. See Heinrich Pesch, *Ethics and the National Economy*, trans. Rupert J. Ederer (Bellingham, WA: Center for Economic Personalism, 2004); Martin Luther King, Jr., "Can a Christian Be a Communist?" Sermon delivered at Dexter Avenue Baptist Church, Montgomery, Alabama, September 1953, in *The Papers of Martin Luther King, Jr.*, vol. 6, ed. Clayborne Carson (Berkeley: University of California Press, 2007), 144–46.

832 "Communism's Challenge to Christianity," https://kinginstitute.stanford.edu/kingpapers/documents/communisms-challenge-christianity (accessed April 15, 2024); cf. Mary-Barbara Zeldin, "The Religious Nature of Russian Marxism," *Journal for the Scientific Study of Religion* 8, no. 1 (1969): 100–11, at 111: "The two sides (Christianity and Marxism) . . . can reach a higher synthesis not by both being transcended, aufgehoben, but only if one of them is willing entirely to give up its essential nature and thus its very existence."

833 "Engels regarded Marx's preoccupation with Russia to be an unnecessary diversion which only served to postpone the completion of *Capital* whereas actually the two areas of work were closely intertwined. The Russian studies were delaying the completion of *Capital* by providing evidence that made it unfinishable. . . . A year later Marx died and White asserts that Engels ignored his writings on Russia when putting together volumes 2 and 3 of *Capital*." Levin, "From Marxism to Communism,"

834 "Friedrich Engels to Marx," in *MECW*, vol. 42, 352.

835 Payne, *Biography*, 121.

836 Sayers, "What Is Marxism?" 382.

837 Hayden White, *Metahistory: The Historical Imagination in Nineteenth-Century Europe* (Baltimore: Johns Hopkins University Press, 1975), 363; Karl Marx, *The Ethnological Notebooks of Karl Marx*, ed. Lawrence Krader (Assen: Van Gorcum, 1972), 98–102, discusses Marx's later reflections on indigenous societies and how external state intervention, rather than purely economic forces, led to their destruction; Friedrich Engels, *The Origin of the Family, Private*

Property and the State (New York: International Publishers, 1972), 175–80, examines how state-imposed policies and colonial domination, rather than natural economic evolution, dismantled primitive communal systems; Kevin B. Anderson, *Marx at the Margins: On Nationalism, Ethnicity, and Non-Western Societies* (Chicago: University of Chicago Press, 2010), 154–58, argues that Marx's later writings increasingly acknowledged the role of state violence and imperialism in disrupting non-capitalist societies.

838 However, according to Hayden White (1928–2018), a prominent historian and theorist, Marx's awareness of the complexities of economic and social forces led to a significant shift in his thinking. White argues that Marx, beginning with the first volume of *Das Kapital* and increasingly so in the second German edition and the French translation, began "eliminating the philosophical structure which had been built up in earlier drafts." James D. White, *Karl Marx and the Intellectual Origins of Dialectical Materialism* (Basingstoke, UK: Macmillan, 1996), 209–10.

839 Gabriel, *Love and Capital*, ch. 10.

840 Von Mises, Socialism, 94.

841 His approach, often referred to as historical materialism or dialectical materialism, aimed to understand society, economics, and historical change in a materialist and historical context. "Here the materialist conception of history underpins the possibility of communism. According to Marx's view of history, as the economic basis of society is transformed, so is our consciousness, greed, egoism, and envy are not ingrained forever in the character of human beings. They would disappear in a society in which private property and private means of production were replaced with communal property and socially organized means of production. We would lose our preoccupation with our private interests. Citizens of the new society would find their own happiness in working for the good of all. Hence a communist society would have a new ethical basis." Marx - Singer, 82.

842 "Another biographer, Jerrold Siegel (*Marx's Fate: The Shape of a Life*) titles one of his sections 'The Sickly Scholar' and sees Marx's 'self-induced illnesses' as a means of avoiding the difficulties of completing the remaining volumes of *Capital*." Levin, "From Marxism to Communism," 15.

843 Karl Marx, "Letter to Friedrich Engels, April 8, 1881," Marx-Engels Correspondence, Volume 5.

844 *The Civil War in France* (1871). 57–60.

845 Karl Marx, "The Civil War in France," in *The Marx-Engels Reader*, ed. Robert C. Tucker (New York: W.W. Norton & Company, 1978), 618–53, at 618.

846 Levin mentions an 1868 letter from Marx to Engels describing a physical experience in a museum: "I suddenly became so very unwell that I had to close the very interesting book I was reading. There was something like a black veil before my eyes. In addition, a frightful headache and chest constriction. So I crept home . . . My state is such that I really should give up working for some time." Levin, "From Marxism to Communism," 15.

847 Karl Marx, "Critique of the Gotha Program," in *The Marx-Engels Reader*, ed. Robert C. Tucker (New York: W.W. Norton & Company, 1978), 525–41, at 532.

848 Karl Marx, Letter to Friedrich Engels, March 25, 1868, in Karl Marx and Friedrich Engels: Collected Works, Volume 43: 1868–70 (New York: International Publishers, 1988), 67. In this letter, Marx reflects on the challenges he faces in his work, acknowledging the formidable opposition of prevailing societal structures.

849 Karl Marx, Letter to Arnold Ruge, January 25, 1843, written after the Prussian government dissolved the newspaper *Neue Rheinische Zeitung*, of which Marx was the editor. *MECW*, vol. 1, 396–98.

850 "Alas, your conduct has consisted merely in disorder, meandering in all the fields of knowledge, musty traditions by sombre lamplight; degeneration in a learned dressing gown with uncombed hair has replaced degeneration with a beer glass. And a shirking unsociability and a refusal of all conventions and even all respect for your father. Your intercourse with the world is limited to your sordid room, where perhaps lie abandoned in the classical disorder the love letters of a Jenny [Karl's fiancée] and the tear-stained counsels of your father." Heinrich Marx quoted in McLellan, *A Biography*, 27. Also, see quotes in Gabriel, *Love and Capital*, for more context.

851 Spargo, *Marx*, 61.

852 Marx and Engels, *The German Ideology* (1881), 199–201.

853 Dermatologist Sam Shuster diagnoses Marx with hidradenitis suppurativa, a chronic skin disease that caused painful abscesses, particularly in areas such as the groin and armpits. Shuster argues that the pain and isolation from this condition contributed to Marx's personal feelings of alienation, which were reflected in his theoretical writings on social alienation. Sam Huster, "The Nature and Consequence of Karl Marx's Skin Disease," *British Journal of Dermatology* 158, no. 1 (2008): 1–3, https://doi.org/10.1111/j.1365-2133.2007.08282.x. See also Sperber, *A Nineteenth-Century Life*, 474. Sperber notes that Marx suffered from painful carbuncles, which not only affected his physical health but also contributed to his psychological distress and deepened his sense of alienation. He describes how the condition made it difficult for Marx to sit for long periods, exacerbating his frustration and isolation. McLellan explains how Marx's skin condition was aggravated by his poor living conditions and stress. He writes that the affliction added to Marx's already growing disillusionment, making him increasingly irritable and detached, further alienating him from those around him, including his family and political allies. McLellan, *A Biography*, 393.

854 Karl Marx, "Letter to Friedrich Engels, May 20, 1877," in *MECW*, vol. 45, 288. In this letter, Marx candidly discusses his persistent health issues, particularly the painful carbuncles that hindered his ability to work. His reluctance to take arsenic underscores his determination to maintain intellectual sharpness despite physical suffering.

855 Marx, *Writings of the Young Marx*, 36; Marx, "Reflections of a Young Man on the Choice of a Profession," *MEGA* I.1.1.2, 164–67.

856 Wheen, *Karl Marx*, 370. Both Sperber and Wheen provide detailed accounts of Marx's relentless focus on completing *Das Kapital*, even as his health and personal life deteriorated. They highlight the sacrifices made by both Marx and those closest to him, particularly Jenny, whose unwavering support was instrumental in his intellectual pursuits. These citations reinforce the paradox of Marx's life—his singular drive to complete his magnum opus at the cost of his personal well-being while also cementing his influence on history.

857 Sperber, *A Nineteenth-Century Life*, 429.

858 Ibid., 592. Sperber captures Marx's profound despair following Jenny's death, highlighting how central she was to his life and work. This statement, "Without her, I am nothing," reflects the depth of his emotional dependence on her, despite his often-dominant intellectual persona.

859 McLellan, *His Life and Thought*, 125.

860 Jenny Marx, "Letters from Jenny Marx to Karl Marx," in *The Marx-Engels Correspondence*, ed. Saul Padover (New York: McGraw-Hill, 1979), 78. These citations provide insight into Jenny Marx's role in Karl's life, not just as a wife but as a devoted intellectual partner who endured the weight of his ambitions. The quoted letter reveals the emotional strain she endured, illustrating the personal costs of Marx's ideological commitments.

861 Mauricio Betancourt quotes Marx's daughter Eleanor describing a scene shortly before Jenny died: "Our mother lay in the large front room, Moor in the little room behind . . . Never shall I forget the morning when he felt strong enough to go into my mother's room. When they were together they were young again—she a loving girl and he a loving youth, on the threshold of life, not an old man devastated by illness and an old dying woman parting from each other for life." Mauricio Betancourt, "'To Struggle!' A Review of Marcello Musto's *The Last Years of Karl Marx*," *Monthly Review* (2024): 58–61, at 60.

862 Musto, *The Last Years*, 98; McLellan, *His Life and Thought*, 127. McLellan's biography contextualizes their relationship within the broader narrative of Marx's life and struggles.

863 "At the beginning of 1863, Jenny gave the following description of her daughters to one of her friends: Even if the word 'beautiful' is not fitting for them, I must still say, even at the risk of being laughed at for my maternal pride, that all three of them look very neat and interesting. Jennychen is strikingly dark in hair, eyes and complexion and, with her childishly rosy cheeks and deep, sweet eyes, has a very attractive appearance. Laura, who is in everything a few degrees lighter and clearer, is in fact prettier than the eldest sister as her features are more regular and her green eyes under her dark brows and long lashes shine with a continual fire of joy. . . . We have made every effort we could towards their education. Unfortunately, we could not do so much for them in music as we would have hoped, and their musical

accomplishments are not distinguished, although they both have particularly pleasant voices and sing with a very pretty expressiveness. But Jenny's real strong point is elocution; and because the child has a very beautiful voice, low and sweet, and from childhood had studied Shakespeare with fanaticism, she would in fact long ago have been on the stage had not regard for the family etc. held her back. . . . Neither would we have placed any obstacle in her way if her health were sounder. . . . The third one, the baby, is a true bundle of sweetness, charm and childish frenzy. She is the light and life of the house." McLellan, *A Biography*, 307.

864 Sperber, *A Nineteenth-Century Life*, 586. Wheen and Sperber both provide extensive detail on the emotional devastation Marx experienced following Jenny's death. Their works depict how deeply Marx depended on her, not just emotionally but also in managing their household and supporting his intellectual pursuits. These citations reflect Marx's profound grief and the parallels between his loss and the tragic heroines of literature, reinforcing the classical allusions to figures like Beatrice, Gretchen, and Ophelia.

865 June 20, 1844.

866 March 15, 1848.

867 November 5, 1851.

868 February 2, 1855.

869 July 8, 1861.

870 June 1, 1864.

871 September 12, 1867. Also, *The Communist Manifesto* was a joint venture, not only intellectually but emotionally, with Jenny at Karl's side. Gabriel, *Love and Capital*, ch. 5.

872 October 14, 1870.

873 April 7, 1874.

874 December 2, 1881.

875 Karl Marx, *Letters to His Wife Jenny*, ed. and trans. Saul K. Padover (New York: Simon & Schuster, 1974), 76. Marx's letters to Jenny reveal the depth of his emotional dependence on her, depicting their relationship as one of intense devotion despite the hardships they endured. This passage underscores a different side of Marx—one not of the revolutionary theorist, but of a man whose personal life was shaped by love, longing, and loss.

876 The rosemary she gives represents remembrance, suggesting that even in the midst of despair there is a longing to be remembered, a longing that parallels Jenny's life and death (*Hamlet*, Act 4, Scene 7). See William Shakespeare, "Hamlet," in *The Complete Works of William Shakespeare*, ed. W. J. Craig (London: Oxford University Press, 1914), 574.

877 Gretchen speaks this line in despair as she comes to terms with the consequences of her actions and her suffering. It speaks to the tragic fate that overtakes her, echoing Jenny's own suffering and her emotional and intellectual isolation near the end of her life; Johann Wolfgang von Goethe, *Faust*, trans. Walter Kaufmann (New York: Anchor, 1961), 175.

878 Her character represents divine love and redemption. In the context of Jenny, this quote can symbolize a lost love, a lost chance for purity and spiritual salvation, one that Marx now mourns. Dante, *The Divine Comedy: Paradiso*, Canto 33, line 145.

879 TC 97 IPC 20203.

880 In *The Divine Tragedy*, Marx's life and legacy mirror key elements of Walter Benjamin's theory of *Trauerspiel*, or mourning play. First, Marx's end exemplifies "ruin without redemption": he dies isolated, betrayed by the very ideas he once championed. His vision of revolutionary transformation collapses into "power without substance," where he appears as a prophet ensnared in his own illusions. History, in this framework, becomes not a forward march of progress but "a pile of wreckage"—the legacy of communism revealing repression rather than salvation. Rather than a coherent mythos, Marx's life unfolds as allegory—a failed Christ-figure whose mission ends not in resurrection but reversal. Finally, there is "mourning, not catharsis": no resolution is offered, only alienation, tragedy, and collapse, leaving the audience not cleansed, but haunted.

881 Sperber, *A Nineteenth-Century Life*, 590.

882 "Marxist mythology, history is wholly the product of social and economic forces. . . . Such was the view of history which Marx derived from Hegel and Aeschylus, and his own remorseless studies. He was not however a historian, and there is no reason to believe that history follows the laws invented by Marx." McClellan, *A Biography*, 363.

883 Karl Marx, Letter to Friedrich Engels, 1882; Sperber, *A Nineteenth-Century Life*, 594. Sperber recounts this moment as an instance of Marx's declining health and his rare self-deprecating humor. The reference to his "prophet's beard" suggests both his iconic status and his awareness of his own image, while the act of shaving it off reflects a moment of resignation in his final years.

884 Musto, *The Last Years of Karl Marx*, 168. Musto highlights Marx's symbolic shedding of his identity, comparing it to an actor removing his mask. This moment suggests Marx's recognition of the end of his ideological struggle and the weariness that came with it.

885 Just as the Jewish prophets would often mourn the unrepentant sin of their people, Marx's gesture seemed to mourn a different kind of futility: the inability to reconcile his ideas with the complexities of the human condition. This act of shaving can be interpreted as a moment of profound vulnerability, an almost liturgical shedding of the role he had played for decades. The prophet of revolution, who had sought to cast off the chains of tradition and history, now symbolically cast off the external sign of his authority and defiance. Musto, *The Last Years of Karl Marx*, 169. Musto suggests that Marx's decision to shave his beard may symbolize an internal reckoning with his life's struggles. It reflects a subconscious acknowledgment of disillusionment—perhaps a silent recognition that his revolutionary aspirations had not materialized as he had hoped.

886 Friedrich Engels, "Speech at the Grave of Karl Marx, March 17, 1883," in *MECW*, vol. 24, 468. Engels delivered this eulogy at Marx's funeral, marking the end of an era. His words framed Marx as the foremost intellectual force of his time, emphasizing his impact on historical materialism and socialist thought.

887 Marx's death on March 14, 1883, is described in Wheen, *Karl Marx*, 452.

888 Sperber, *A Nineteenth-Century Life*, 548. Sperber also includes an illustration of the original gravesite as it was before the British Communist Party erected an enormous bust of Marx in 1956 (300).

889 Engels, "Speech at the Graveside of Karl Marx," 468. Engels's eulogy at Marx's funeral reflects the deep personal loss felt by those closest to him, particularly his daughter Eleanor and Engels himself. His words capture the gravity of Marx's passing and his enduring influence on the struggle for human liberty.

890 Spargo, *Marx*, 82–83.

891 See Stephane Courtois et al., *The Black Book of Communism* (Cambridge, MA: Harvard University Press, 1999), 4.

892 The current memorial was erected in 1956 by the British Communist Party to replace the original modest headstone from 1883. The inscription "Workers of all lands unite" was chosen to reflect the famous closing line of *The Communist Manifesto*. Marx's remains were also moved a few feet from their original resting place to a more prominent location in Highgate Cemetery. For more, see Wheen, *Karl Marx*, 384.

893 This statement, one of Marx's most famous, encapsulates his shift from philosophy to revolutionary praxis. It underscores his belief that intellectual work should not merely interpret reality but actively seek to transform it through political and social action. Karl Marx, "Theses on Feuerbach," in *MECW*, vol. 5, 5 (Thesis 11).

894 Dante, *Inferno*, trans. Ciardi, Canto XXXIV, lines 364–67: Dante's *Inferno* presents the soul's descent through hell as a moral and spiritual journey, culminating in redemption through purgation and ultimate ascension. John Freccero, *Dante: The Poetics of Conversion*, ed. Rachel Jacoff (Cambridge, MA: Harvard University Press, 1986), 95–102, explores Dante's *Divine Comedy* as a structured journey from sin to redemption, positioning hell as a necessary stage in the soul's transformation. Robert Hollander, *Dante: A Life* (New York: Farrar, Straus and Giroux, 2021), 221–26, discusses Dante's use of hell as a narrative tool to illustrate the consequences of sin and the eventual possibility of redemption.

895 "Christianity made total tragedy implausible. Whatever the sorrow or transient injustice, there is, as Milton put it, 'no time for lamentation now.' The fall of man, pivotal to absolute tragedy, is a *felix culpa*, a necessary prologue to salvation. Goethe's *Faustus II* ends by celebrating the Christian contract with hope, its investment in absolution. Goethe's is a reply to Marlowe's *Faustus*, one of the very few tragedies to defy Christological optimism. Mar-

lowe's tremendous intuition that a God capable of pardoning Faustus is not a God whom a free spirit can take seriously, let alone worship, leads to hell and everlasting torment. The reasoned blackness of Marlowe's dramaturgy, its philosophical dialectic, are profoundly non-Shakespearean. Shakespeare skates the abyss; Marlowe enters it. As does God-denying Shelley in *The Cenci*, an indictment of religious hypocrisy, a mapping of gratuitous horror the ironic paths of whose end—Beatrice's 'Well, 'tis very well'—comes near to being unbearable." Steiner, "'Tragedy,' Reconsidered," 13.

896 Eagleton, *Tragedy*, 31; Oswald Spengler, *The Decline of the West*, vol. 1 (New York: Alfred A. Knopf, 1926), 354. Spengler discusses the Faustian spirit as the driving force behind Western civilization—a boundless pursuit of power, knowledge, and control over nature. While Marx admired Goethe's Faust, he failed to recognize that the pact represents not just an external struggle but an internal one: the cost of relentless ambition and the unintended consequences of revolutionary fervor. Marx, in his pursuit of historical materialism, overlooked the existential and metaphysical warnings embedded in Faust, failing to see how his own ideological path mirrored the tragic overreach of Goethe's protagonist. Dante, *Inferno*, trans. Ciardi, Canto XXXIV, lines 139–40; Goethe, *Faust*, trans. Kaufmann, Part Two, lines 11581–92. William Shakespeare, *King Lear*, ed. Stephen Orgel (New York: Penguin Classics, 1999), Act 5, Scene 3, lines 305–10. Dante's *Inferno* presents the ultimate tragedy of ambition that leads to self-damnation—Satan himself is frozen in a prison of his own making. Marx, in his own way, sought to construct a new paradise but ended in exile and disillusionment, metaphorically trapped in his own ideological inferno. Goethe's Faust warns of the cost of unchecked ambition—Marx, like Faust, sacrificed personal well-being and relationships in his relentless pursuit of historical and economic truth, failing to see how his theories could be weaponized beyond his control. Finally, *King Lear* speaks to the folly of visionary arrogance: like Lear, Marx lost everything—his health, family, and peace—while clinging to a belief that ultimately consumed him. These works illuminate the deep irony of Marx's life, where the pursuit of liberation led to personal entrapment, making his story one of the great modern tragedies.

897 Goethe, *Faust*, Part One.

898 In Part Two of *Faust*, Faust he reflects on his actions, haunted by the knowledge that he has exchanged his soul for a false promise. The bargain Faust made, meant to grant him all he desired, instead condemns him to a life of perpetual yearning, never truly fulfilled. Faust's tragic realization comes too late—he has chased an ideal, sacrificing his moral compass for the fleeting satisfaction of his desires, and now he must face the dire consequences of his choices. For Karl Marx, the metaphorical pact with Mephistopheles is clear—though Marx's revolutionary ideals seemed to promise a better future, they, too, came with a hidden cost. Marx's impassioned rejection of capitalism and his quest for a just, classless society mirror Faust's desire for ultimate fulfillment.

899 McLellan, *A Biography*.

900 Spargo, *Marx*, 85–86; Karl Marx and Friedrich Engels, *The Communist Manifesto*, trans. Samuel Moore (London: Penguin Classics, 2002), 94.

901 Marx's life more closely resembles a Benjaminian *Trauerspiel* than a classical tragedy. There is no catharsis, no moment of self-recognition that leads to redemption. Like the sovereign in the Baroque mourning play, Marx performs the gestures of revolution while history slips into ruin behind him. If Dante's Comedy moves upward toward divine light, Marx's drama spirals downward into a mournful entanglement of false hopes and failed prophecies—an allegory without transcendence. See Walter Benjamin, *The Origin of German Tragic Drama* (London: Verso, 1998), esp. 57–158.

902 Betancourt argues that "Musto describes the difficulties of Marx's last years, including 'chronic cough, pleurisy, insomnia issues, and rheumatism,' as well as the death of Jenny from cancer 'sixty-three days before Marx's [death]. Naturally, this pained Marx profoundly, his only temporary and partial relief being a severe headache that distracted him from his emotional distress. As Marx himself put it: 'Physical pain is the only "stunner" of mental pain.' In fact these were Marx's last known written words." Betancourt, "'To Struggle!'" 61. Xunqian Liu says: "Mehring did not share the view of some [Riazanov and/or Lassalle—text is unclear] that Marx's last 10 years of life were a 'slow death.'" But Mehring believes that "in the last five years of his life, Marx's work on his major works was largely halted due to the recurrence of old illnesses. For the last 15 months of his life, Mehring even described it as a 'slow death.'" Discussion continue about what the end part of Marx's life was like according to biographers. Tragic tone." Xunqian Liu, "A Comparative Study of Marx Biographies by Mehring and Riazanov." *Philosophy Study* 13, no. 12 (2023): 558–63, at 562.

903 "Marx knew what the archives were and how to handle them. He knew how to look beneath and through the concepts that political economists deployed to discover their premises or predicates, how to artfully invert (or "evert," as North suggests) received formulations and antimonies, how to reveal the many- sidedness of seemingly simple or unified elements of political economy. And he knew how to discover relations and processes, histories, violence, and capacities in seemingly inert things, indeed how to make things 'speak' such that they could appear as agentic elements in a system." Brown, "Foreword," xvii.

904 "Williams's title [*Modern Tragedy*] situates tragedy within the historical experiences of modernity. His analysis of tragedy in the subsequent book sets out from 'the point where the roads cross' . . . , where the wider socio-cultural understanding of tragedy ('a mining disaster, a burned-out family, a broken career' are Williams's examples) intersects with the narrower literary tradition of 'tragic and tragic literature' . . . From his perspective, the rigid separation of the socio-cultural usage of tragedy from the literary genre represents an instance of ideological paralysis that blocks a recognition and

acknowledgment of the tragic affect circulating in and around human experience in modernity. Put in a somewhat different way, such an inflexible division denies the existence of tragedy lived out daily in 'the deferment and corrosion of hope and desire' . . . In other words, Williams's project attempts to recover tragic understanding and emotion repressed within the historical experiences of modernity and the narratives through which they are retold." McCallum, "Questions of Haunting," 232.

905 Karl Marx, "The Pale Maiden," in Karl Marx: *Early Works*, ed. and trans. Dirk J. Struik (New York: International Publishers, 1975), 22. In this early poem, Marx explores themes of spiritual turmoil and existential despair. The lines reflect a profound sense of inner conflict, revealing the young Marx's grappling with concepts of divinity and damnation. This work offers insight into the formative emotional and intellectual struggles that preceded his later revolutionary theories.

906 Cooper, "Reviewed Works," 449: "Wicksteed argues that Dante 'sees exactly what the sinner chose, and conceives of the Divine Justice as giving him that,' while Aquinas sees punishment as 'imposed upon the sinner by the sentence of a court simply on the ground that he deserves to be punished'." Cooper continues (about Wicksteed): "Dante's treatment illuminates the whole subject of evil choice, burning and freezing into our hearts the sense of the nature and meaning of sin itself; whereas Aquinas only insists on the awfulness of its consequences" (449). Then: "Possibly one may say that, on the whole, the writings of Aquinas serve better to illustrate the earlier parts of the *Divine Comedy*, except with reference to the division of sins, and the works of Bonaventura, especially the *Itinerarium Mentis ad Deum* throw more light upon the *Paradiso*. Yet the two philosophers constitute but a segment of the great orb of Dante's learning" (451).

907 (Sometimes the world is without words.)

908 Karl Marx, "Letter to Arnold Ruge, March 1843," in *Early Writings*, trans. Livingstone and Benton, 244.

909 Marx's and Engels's writings frequently invoked imagery of damnation and upheaval—particularly in *The Communist Manifesto*, *The Civil War in France*, and *The Eighteenth Brumaire of Louis Bonaparte*—but contain no substantive allusions to redemption, paradise, or eschatological harmony. For analysis of this rhetorical pattern, see McLellan, *A Biography*, 447–49; and Robert Tucker, *The Marxian Revolutionary Idea* (New York: Norton, 1972), 82–84.

910 Heinrich Marx would send him cases of the family wine. This lifelong connection to wine is highlighted in the article "Karl Marx's Views on Wine," which states: "Marx was a lifelong wine connoisseur. Even though he resided a great distance from their Trier home, his father, Heinrich, would give him a case of the family wine." "Karl Marx's Views on Wine," This Day in Wine History, June 5, 2022, https://thisdayinwinehistory.com/karl-marxs-views-on-wine (accessed April 15, 2204). See also Jens Baumeister, *How Wine*

Turned Karl Marx into a Communist (Trier: Trier Shop, 2018), 45. Baumeister's work explores the profound influence of the Mosel wine region on Marx's early life and thought. He details how Marx's father, Heinrich, would send cases of the family's wine to his son, fostering a lifelong appreciation. This connection to his roots not only influenced Marx's personal tastes but also his early economic perspectives, especially concerning the struggles of local vintners under oppressive economic policies.

911 Dante, *Inferno*, Canto XXXIII.

912 Shakespeare, *Hamlet*, act 1, scene 5.

913 Goethe, *Faust*, Part One.

914 MacIntyre acknowledges the substance of the critique: "Christians have far too often behaved badly—thereby confirming what Christianity teaches about sinfulness—in failing to recognize soon enough and to respond to the evils of such institutions. Long after the evils of North American and Latin American slavery and the possibility of abolishing it should have been plain to them, too many Christians remained blind to those evils. And when the wickedness of Fascism and that of National Socialism were all too apparent, too many Christians refused to acknowledge them, let alone to engage in resistance." MacIntyre, *Ethics and Politics*, 146.

915 Karl Löwith, *From Hegel to Nietzsche: The Revolution in Nineteenth-Century Thought*, trans. David E. Green (New York: Columbia University Press, 1964), 46. Löwith explores Marx's self-conception as a prophet-like figure, likening him to a modern Moses leading the proletariat toward liberation. This view aligns with Marx's revolutionary zeal and his role as a figure shaping the ideological destiny of the working class.

916 H. G. Wells, *Russia in the Shadows* (1920), available at https://libquotes.com/h-g-wells/quotes/human (accessed May 15, 2025).

917 He quotes Marx's "Union of the Faithful with Christ": "'Through our union with Christ, when we feel our total unworthiness and at the same time exult over our salvation, then only can we love God, who formerly appeared to us as an offended lord but is now a forgiving father and a benevolent teacher'." Schwarzwalder, "Marx's New Religion," 775.

918 Karl Marx, "Invocation of One in Despair," in *Karl Marx: Early Works*, ed. and trans. Dirk J. Struik (New York: International Publishers, 1975), 22. In this early poem, Marx delves into themes of profound despair and defiance. The lines reflect a tumultuous inner struggle, revealing his intense emotions and existential turmoil during his formative years. This work offers a glimpse into the personal and philosophical conflicts that influenced his later revolutionary ideas.

919 Gustav Techow, "Letter to Arnold Ruge, August 1850," quoted in McLellan, *Interviews and Recollections*, 18. In his letter, Techow reflects on Marx's complex character, acknowledging his intellectual brilliance while criticizing his perceived lack of moral integrity. Techow suggests that Marx's personal ambitions overshadowed his noble ideals, leading to a demeanor marked

by contempt for both allies and adversaries. This critique offers a nuanced perspective on Marx's personality and the interpersonal dynamics within revolutionary circles of the time.

920 Matthew 16:26 (NRSV): "For what will it profit them if they gain the whole world but forfeit their soul? Or what will they give in return for their soul?"

921 Dante, *Paradiso*, trans. Ciardi, Canto XXXIII, lines 142–45; Erich Auerbach, *Dante: Poet of the Secular World*, trans. Ralph Manheim (New York: New York Review Books, 2007), 112–15; Charles Singleton, *Journey to Beatrice* (Cambridge, MA: Harvard University Press, 1958), 1760–80. Dante's *Divine Comedy* ultimately leads toward transcendence and redemption, contrasting sharply with Marx's trajectory, which remains firmly grounded in materialism and historical determinism. Unlike Dante, who ultimately surrenders to divine mystery, Marx closes himself to the metaphysical, focusing instead on an earthly revolution. This distinction underscores the tragedy of Marx's life—his unyielding commitment to historical materialism left no room for the ascent Dante had envisioned.

922 Techow, "Letter to Arnold Ruge, August 1850," 18.

923 Spargo, *Marx*, 80–81. See also Sperber, *Nineteenth-Century Life*, 521; Liebknecht, *Biographical Memoirs*, 91–92.

924 Ibid.

925 Dante, *Inferno*, Canto XXIII, lines 21–30.

926 "The proletarians have nothing to lose but their chains. They have a world to win. WORKING MEN OF ALL COUNTRIES, UNITE!" Marx and Engels, *The Communist Manifesto*, trans. Brandywine, 57.

927 Shakespeare, *Hamlet*, Act 2, Scene 2.

928 Aeschylus, *Prometheus Bound*, lines 435–40.

929 *Faust*, Part Two, Act V ("Was ich besitze, seh' ich wie im Weiten, und was verschwand, wird mir zu Wirklichkeiten.").

930 Verses 1–3 and 9–12: *MECW*, vol. 1, 563–64.

931 Friedrich Engels, quoted in Berlin, *His Life and Environment*, 126.

932 Friedrich Engels, "Engels to F. Mehring, September 28, 1892," in *Marx Engels Selected Correspondence*, ed. I. Lasker and trans. S. W. Ryasanskaya (Moscow: Progress Publishers, 1975), 448.

933 Karl Marx, *Letters to His Daughters*, ed. and trans. Saul K. Padover (New York: Simon & Schuster, 1974), 112.

934 Ibid., 118.

935 Marx, *Writings of the Young Marx*, 39.

936 Drawing significantly on the Bible, as he will in *Monarchia*, Dante begins with the opening of Jeremiah's Lamentations, a text that has already resounded in *Vita nuova* (XXVIII, XXX) at the death of Beatrice. Now the city that sits solitary in her grief is Jerusalem, as the type not of Florence but of Rome, widowed by the Babylonian Captivity of Mother Church. These themes were fairly extensively visited in the final cantos of Purgatorio, with their ugly portraits of Clement and Philip the Fair, who were living at the

time, both of whom are castigated under pseudonyms in the epistle (XI, 8)." Robert Hollander, Dante: A Life in Works (New Haven, CT: Yale University Press, 2001), 148–49.

937 Dante's critique of the political and religious corruption in Italy echoed across centuries, a call for renewal that transcended his exile. Marx's critique was similarly focused on Europe's entrenched power structures, viewing capitalism as a modern empire poised to fall. For Dante, this "empire" was the political and religious institutions that had abandoned spiritual truths; for Marx, it was capitalism itself, an empire of industry that preyed upon the working class. Each man saw his society as deeply flawed and in need of salvation, though Dante sought redemption through faith and virtue while Marx sought it through revolution and redistribution.

938 Eagleton, *Tragedy*, 23.

939 Gertrude Himmelfarb, *The Idea of Poverty: England in the Early Industrial Age* (New York: Vintage Books, 1985), 304–25. Himmelfarb contends that while the Industrial Revolution introduced severe dislocations—especially in sanitation, housing, and working conditions—these were challenges of modernization rather than signs of systemic decay. See also Robert C. Allen, *The British Industrial Revolution in Global Perspective* (Cambridge: Cambridge University Press, 2009), 10–12, for evidence that industrial capitalism improved long-term living standards. For a Catholic perspective affirming reform over revolution, see Pope Leo XIII, *Rerum Novarum* (1891), §§15–19, which calls for the dignity of labor, just wages, and the mediation of social conflict through moral and institutional reform rather than violent upheaval.

940 "From Jean-Jacques Rousseau . . . to Karl Marx's modified yet substantially similar [to Rousseau] assertion in the *Eighteenth Brumaire* that people are agents of history, but not under the conditions of their own choosing, Enlightenment though resituated domination and oppression within societies as humanly constructed institutions that were open to transformation by human intervention." McCallum, "Questions of Haunting," 233.

941 The Fall of Lucifer (Isaiah 14:12–15, NRSV).

942 Joseph Cardinal Ratzinger (Pope Benedict XVI), *Truth and Tolerance: Christian Belief and World Religions*, trans. Henry Taylor (San Francisco: Ignatius Press, 2004), 66–69. Ratzinger emphasizes that Christianity does not reject reason, but instead deepens it through revelation, offering a vision of the human person grounded in both natural law and divine grace. Alasdair MacIntyre, *After Virtue: A Study in Moral Theory*, 3rd ed. (South Bend, IN: University of Notre Dame Press, 2007), 54–58. MacIntyre critiques Enlightenment moral theories for detaching ethical reasoning from its classical and religious foundations, particularly in their abandonment of teleological views of human nature.

943 Spargo, *Marx*, 61.

944 Gabriel, *Love and Capital*, 475.

945 Marx, *Writings of the Young Marx*, 36.

946 Johann Wolfgang von Goethe, *Faust*, Part II, trans. Bayard Taylor (Boston: Houghton Mifflin, 1883), 287; Terry Eagleton, *Marx and Freedom* (London: Blackwell, 1990), 62; Leszek Kołakowski, *Main Currents of Marxism*, vol. 1 (Oxford: Clarendon Press, 1978), 321.

947 Karl Marx, "Preface to A Contribution to the Critique of Political Economy," in *Marx: Early Political Writings*, ed. Joseph J. O'Malley (Cambridge: Cambridge University Press, 1994), 57–58.

948 V. I. Lenin, "What Is to Be Done?", in *Lenin: Selected Works*, vol. 1 (Moscow: Progress Publishers, 1963), 119–220.

949 Richard Pipes, *The Russian Revolution* (New York: Knopf, 1990), 493–504.

950 Robert Conquest, *The Great Terror: A Reassessment* (New York: Oxford University Press, 1990), 15–20, 311–29.

951 "When Popper attacks historicism, it is essentially this doctrine that historical development is governed by laws and that its future course is therefore predictable which he is concerned to undermine. Equally this is what Stalin defends. But in the definition of what is at issue Stalin and Popper shake hands. The Marxism that Stalin presents is recognisably the Marxism that Popper also presents. And it is this same conception of theory which is evident throughout the contemporary anti-theoretical empiricism that is fashionable in the West both in academic and in political circles. Its relevance to the present topic is solely that it provides the straitjacket within which it is possible to confine and misrepresent the Marxist alternative to liberal morality. If it were the case that Marxism was a system in which the clockwork of society was laid bare, then it would be true that 'the essence of the Marxist ethic is its futurism.' . . . For it would be true that the only effective way of remedying the evils of class-society would be to manipulate into existence the classless society; the blueprint of a mechanical system will tell us which levers we must pull to transform the system. And we pull the levers to contrive some new state of the system. The counterpart to a mechanical theory of society is a means–ends morality." MacIntyre, *The MacIntyre Reader*, 36.

952 Martin Malia, *The Soviet Tragedy: A History of Socialism in Russia, 1917–1991* (New York: Free Press, 1994), 21.

953 Aleksandr Solzhenitsyn, *The Gulag Archipelago*, trans. Thomas P. Whitney (New York: Harper & Row, 1974), 168.

954 Marx, *Contribution to the Critique of Hegel's Philosophy of Right*, trans. Jolin and O'Malley, 131.

955 Ibid.

956 Charles Dickens, *American Notes for General Circulation* (London: Chapman & Hall, 1842), 164, writes the following about American evangelicalism: "Wherever religion is resorted to, as a strong drink, and as an escape from the dull monotonous round of home, those of its ministers who pepper the highest will be surest to please."

957 For more on this subject, see MacIntyre, *Ethics and Politics*, 148.

958 Marx, *Critique of Hegel's Philosophy of Right*, trans. Jolin and O'Malley, 244.

959 Ibid.

960 Marx, *Economic and Philosophic Manuscripts of 1844*, trans. Milligan, 116.

961 Marx, *Critique of Hegel's Philosophy of Right*, trans. Jolin and O'Malley, 244.

962 Marx, *The German Ideology*, trans. McLellan, 42.

963 Marx, *The Communism of the Rheinische Beobachter*, 6.

964 Marx, *Economic and Philosophic Manuscripts of 1844*, trans. Milligan, 54.

965 Marx, *The Communist Manifesto*, 25.

966 "Marx's life was a complex and often painful exploration of the human condition, filled with moments of despair but also glimpses of hope. In his comments on the complexity of the human condition, Marx would expose his intentions. In Capital, Marx discusses the interplay of personal and societal forces." Marx, *Critique of Political Economy*, trans. Ryazanskaya, 94–96.

967 "When Williams seeks to recognize and understand the actual suffering in any revolutionary project, he retrieves the performative outlines of classical tragedy and its interaction with the audience. Shifting the focus from the final outcome or *catastrophe* of the play to the interactions of recognition (*anagnorisis*) and reversal in fortune (*peripeteia*), he underlines the emotions that circulate around these moments." McCallum, "Questions of Haunting," 239.

968 Ibid., 338.

969 Carlyle, *On Heroes*, 90.

970 Eagleton, *Tragedy*, 12.

971 "'The poverty has claimed the lives of our children,' Marx admitted in a letter to a friend." Padover, *Intimate Biography*, 349.

972 "Gramsci drew on the published work of Marx, Engels, and Lenin, the histories of the French and Bolshevik Revolutions, and his experience of fascism in Italy and the wider economic, political, and societal crises affecting interwar Europe and the United States. In a comment that could provide a good summary of Marx's own analyses of the modern state, Gramsci suggested that the state is 'the entire complex of practical and theoretical activities with which the ruling class not me best example is the German 'state derivation debate." Musto, *Revival*, 280. For some key contributions, see John Holloway and Sol Picciotto, eds., *State and Capital: A Marxist Debate* (London: E. Arnold, 1978). For an extended critique, see Bob Jessop, *The Capitalist State: Marxist Theories and Methods* (New York: NYU Press, 1982), 78–141.

973 Antonio Gramsci, *Selections from the Prison Notebooks*, eds. Quintin Hoare and Geoffrey Nowell Smith (New York: International Publishers, 1971). See especially his essays on intellectuals and hegemony for the foundation of his theory of cultural power.

974 Jacques Derrida, *Writing and Difference*, trans. Alan Bass (Chicago: University of Chicago Press, 1978); Terry Eagleton, *The Illusions of Postmodernism* (Oxford: Blackwell, 1996); John M. Ellis, *Literature Lost: Social Agendas and the Corruption of the Humanities* (New Haven, CT: Yale University Press,

1997); Michel Foucault, *Discipline and Punish: The Birth of the Prison*, trans. Alan Sheridan (New York: Vintage Books, 1995); Gramsci, *Selections from the Prison Notebooks*; Stephen R. C. Hicks, *Explaining Postmodernism: Skepticism and Socialism from Rousseau to Foucault. Expanded* (Tempe, AZ: Scholargy Publishing, 2004); Fredric Jameson, *Postmodernism, or, The Cultural Logic of Late Capitalism* (Durham, NC: Duke University Press, 1991); Lyotard, *The Postmodern Condition*; Roger Scruton, *Fools, Frauds and Firebrands: Thinkers of the New Left* (London: Bloomsbury Continuum, 2015).

975 Eagleton, *Tragedy*, 178.

976 Cooper, quoting Wicksteed: "'Dante not only knows where to stop himself, but he knows where science stops'." Cooper, "Reviewed Works," 447.

977 Eagleton, *Tragedy*, 179.

978 Levin describes two Marxes, one who "assumed there was empirical verification for a theory of universal history," and a second who "showed awareness of contrary evidence and confined his theory to western European development." He says: "World history, then, could not be packaged as neatly as Marx's philosophical tradition had led him to expect. In today's philosophical language, Marx lost faith in his grand narrative." Levin, "From Marxism to Communism," 15.

979 William Shakespeare, *Hamlet, Prince of Denmark*, ed. Philip Edwards (Cambridge: Cambridge University Press, 1985).

980 Eagleton, *Tragedy*, 17–18.

981 Sir Niall Ferguson, *The Essence of Marxism, Hoover Institution* (March 2, 2020), via the Hoover Institution website. While the exact phrase is a paraphrase of his broader critique of Marx, this summary captures his key assessment—that despite Marx's failed prophecies, his analysis of inequality remains relevant.

982 Eric Hobsbawm, *The Age of Revolution: 1789–1848* (New York: Vintage Books, 1996), 44–50; Paul Johnson, *Modern Times: The World from the Twenties to the Nineties* (New York: Harper & Row, 1983), 53–59; Niall Ferguson, *The War of the World: Twentieth-Century Conflict and the Descent of the West* (New York: Penguin Press, 2006), 77–83.

983 Courtois et al., *The Black Book of Communism*, 4–5. This work estimates that communist regimes were responsible for approximately 94 million deaths worldwide, including 65 million in China and 20 million in the Soviet Union. It presents these outcomes as direct consequences of Marxist ideological structures implemented at scale. Eric Hobsbawm, *How to Change the World: Tales of Marx and Marxism* (New Haven: Yale University Press, 2011), 340–42. Hobsbawm acknowledges the tragedies committed in Marx's name but argues that Marx's foundational insights into inequality and capitalist exploitation remain historically indispensable. He contends that later regimes often misapplied Marxist doctrine in ways inconsistent with Marx's nuanced historical materialism.

984 MacIntyre, *Ethics and Politics*, 155.

985 Falconer, *Hell in Contemporary Literature*, gives the example of 9/11 as a katabatic narrative: "When another novelist, Jay McInerney, described New York as a Dantean 'city of the dead,' he was referring not only to those who died in the attack but also to those who descended into its horror and survived" (225). Original military operation in 2001 was named "'Operation Infinite Justice' (later changed to Operation Enduring Freedom), recalling the famous inscription over Dante's gates of Hell ('JUSTICE MOVED MY HIGH MAKER' (Inf. 3.4) . . . Saddam's regime collapsed with unexpected swiftness and Western TV audiences had the satisfaction of seeing an American soldier clambering up a colossal statue of Saddam, like Dante climbing out of Hell on Satan's torso, to drape and American flag over the fallen dictator's face (hastily replaced by an Iraqi one, after shouted instructions from below" (228).

986 McGrogan, *Who the Hell Is Karl Marx?* 3: "Time after time, authorities and ruling parties have declared Marx's ideas dead and defunct, and yet they continue to inform public debate. In the aftermath of the 2008 economic crisis, sales of *The Communist Manifesto* and *Capital* soared." Greece has been devastated by the debt crisis: it suffered a massive economic downturn in the years after 2008. In the following ten years, there were vast spending cuts accompanied by huge tax increases. Unemployment reached 28 percent in 2013–2014. According to the Organization for Economic Cooperation and Development, around a third of the population of 10 million languished in poverty in 2018; household income had fallen by 30 percent, and people were unable to pay the bills. Even Britain, the fifth- or sixth-largest economy in the world, was adversely affected; in 2018, close to 14 million people were living below the official poverty line. See McGrogan, *Who the Hell Is Karl Marx?*, 80.

987 "Following the events of 2008, the Global North's central banks fell into the trap of pumping unending quantities of poisoned monies into the financial markets. Then, for the first time since capitalism had stirred two and a half centuries earlier, profit ceased to be the fuel that fired the global economy's engine, driving investment and innovation. That role, of fueling the economy, was taken over by central bank money." Varoufakis, *Technofeudalism*, 109, but see also 107–11.

988 Alasdair MacIntyre unmasks the truth that "liberalism is the politics of a set of elites, whose members through their control of party machines and of the media, predetermine for the most part the range of political choices open to the vast mass ordinary voters. Of those voters, apart from the making of elector choices, passivity is required. Politics and its cultural ambiance has become areas of professionalized life, and among the most important the relevant professionals are the professional manipulators of mass opinion. Moreover entry into and success in the arenas of liberal politics increasingly required financial resources that only corporate capital can supply, resources

that secure in return privileged access to those able to influence political decisions. Liberalism thus ensures the exclusion most people from any possibility of active and rational participation determining the form of community in which they live. Thirdly, the moral individualism of liberalism is itself a solvent participatory community." MacIntyre, *Ethics and Politics*, 153.

989 Payne, *Marx*, 11. The editors of *The Oxford Handbook of Karl Marx* claim that "Marxism is as relevant today as when Marx himself was alive," because of its influence on social theory and politics and because inequality under capitalism persists. See Paul Prew, Tomas Rotta, Tony Smith, and Matt Vidal, "The Enduring Relevance of Karl Marx," in *The Oxford Handbook of Karl Marx*, 3. Current communist nation-states include China, North Korea, Cuba, Laos, and Vietnam, and many other countries, including those in Western Europe, continue to be influenced by Marxist principles in the form of socialism. See David Lane, ed., *The Legacy of State Socialism and the Future of Transformation* (Oxford: Rowan & Littlefield, 2002).

990 With a larger population, India is not governed by Marxist principles, and global adherence to Marxist theory today is more symbolic than systematic. Nonetheless, the political rhetoric and institutional structures in a number of countries—including some authoritarian regimes—continue to invoke elements of Marx's legacy, not necessarily as a rigorous model, but as a symbolic narrative of anti-capitalist resistance. While these invocations often diverge radically from Marx's original writings, they underscore the lingering global influence of his thought—if not in practice, then as a rhetorical and ideological reference point.

991 For more on this idea see, MacIntyre, *Ethics and Politics*, 156.

992 David Leopold, *The Young Karl Marx: German Philosophy, Modern Politics, and Human Flourishing* (Cambridge: Cambridge University Press, 2007), esp. 82–110. See also Erich Fromm, *Marx's Concept of Man* (New York: Frederick Ungar Publishing Co., 1970).

993 Alasdair MacIntyre, *Marxism and Christianity* (Notre Dame: University of Notre Dame Press, 1968), 108.

994 1083 "Rumors that Stalin attended church services in the 1930s have never been substantiated. In Stalin's marginalia in works by Dostoevsky and Anatole France, he continued to be drawn to issues of God, the church, religion, and immortality, but the depth and nature of that interest remain difficult to fathom. Be that as it may, he had long ago ceased to adhere to Christian notions of good and evil. His moral universe was that of Marxism-Leninism." Kotkin, *Stalin*, 3.

995 Arendt, *The Origins of Totalitarianism*, 468.

996 Richard Pipes, *Communism: A History* (New York: Modern Library, 2001), 37.

997 Eric Voegelin speaks in an interview speaks of an event he attended in Vienna, which was "one of the famous dialogues between representatives of the Soviet government and Catholic theologians there (I was only an observer).

In the course of one evening—three or four hours—I jotted down the conditions that the Soviet representatives made for conducting such a dialogue with the Westerners. Certain premises must stay beyond discussion, must be accepted as true by everybody, including the Catholic theologians. First: Karl Marx's surplus theory of value; then: all workers are exploited by capitalists; philosophy is abolished and replaced by dialectical materialism; religion is out—everybody has to be an atheist; and, in case of war, the Soviet Union has the exclusive right to use the atom bomb because it represents the truth of history." Voegelin, *Collected Works*, vol. 33, 324.

998 What Marx had imagined as a revolution for justice and equality became a justification for a new form of tyranny. The tragic irony is that Marx's call for the violent overthrow of oppressive systems created a template that, in the hands of revolutionary or authoritarian leaders, was wielded as a moral justification for totalitarian rule, widespread suffering, and mass murder. Marxism, especially in its most extreme forms, advanced a vision of the future cloaked in the language of science but ultimately lacking its substance. Marx claimed to discover the "laws of motion" of history, presenting his theory as a scientific inevitability: capitalism would collapse under its contradictions and give rise to a utopian communist society. Yet, these so-called "scientific" predictions were rooted not in empirical validation but in a deterministic philosophical framework that misunderstood history and human nature. In rejecting the accumulated wisdom of the Western tradition—religious, intellectual, and moral—Marx constructed an abstract model of human progress severed from lived experience and spiritual insight. The tragic consequence of this pseudoscientific vision was its capacity to justify violence on an unimaginable scale. Under the guise of historical necessity, millions of lives were sacrificed for a future that never arrived. The more profound irony is that Marx, who sought to liberate humanity through reason and critique, helped unleash ideologies that rationalized repression in the name of reason itself. His descent into what I earlier called "a cold, deep pseudo-scientific moralism" was not simply a failure of foresight but a foundational error built into the system he created. In the twentieth century, communism brought unparalleled catastrophe, with the promise of a cleansed world leading to devastation. *The Black Book of Communism* estimates that Marxist regimes were responsible for the deaths of at least 100 million people.

999 "Marx erred, according to MacIntyre, in failing to complete his critique of the presuppositions of capitalism by scrutinizing his own and by elaborating a coherent alternative. Without any first principles of their own, later Marxists opposed but were also unable to escape the ethos of the modern world. Their failure to solve this dilemma was to have disastrous consequences." MacIntyre, *The MacIntyre Reader*, 23.

1000 "There is no doubt that utopian perspectives are 'a classical form of invigoration and hopeful protest' and 'a necessary mode of one area of social thought, but [Williams] is cautious about a prescription that moves too quickly from the tragic to the utopian." McCallum, "Questions of Haunting," 242.

1001 "Marxism is not merely a critique of capitalism but a historical vision of man's destiny." Fromm, *Marx's Concept of Man*, 48.

1002 "Our era is not only without a heavenly companion, Divine Wisdom, but it lacks also the earthly wisdom of the pagan Virgil who accompanied Dante through Hell and handed him over to Beatrice at the gates of Paradise (*Inferno* I.112–14)." Peter McCarey and Mariarosa Cardines, "The Harrowing of Hell and Resurrection: Dante's Inferno and Blok's Dvenadtsat," *The Slavonic and Eastern European Review* 63, no. 3 (1985): 337–48, at 339.

1003 Virgil, *Eclogues* X, line 69.

1004 Galatians 6:5.

Index